Partners for Peace

edited by George J. Lankevich

1. *The United Nations under Trygve Lie, 1945–1953* by Anthony Gaglione, 2001.
2. *The United Nations under Dag Hammarskjöld, 1953–1961* by Peter B. Heller, 2001.
3. *The United Nations under U Thant, 1961–1971* by Bernard J. Firestone, 2001.
4. *The United Nations under Kurt Waldheim, 1972–1981* by James Daniel Ryan, 2001.
5. *The United Nations under Javier Pérez de Cuéllar, 1982–1991* by George J. Lankevich, 2001.
6. *The United Nations under Boutros Boutros-Ghali, 1992–1997* by Stephen F. Burgess, 2001.

Source: United Nations.

The United Nations under Dag Hammarskjöld, 1953–1961

Peter B. Heller

Partners for Peace, No. 2

The Scarecrow Press, Inc.
Lanham, Maryland, and London
2001

SCARECROW PRESS, INC.

Published in the United States of America
by Scarecrow Press, Inc.
4720 Boston Way, Lanham, Maryland 20706
www.scarecrowpress.com

4 Pleydell Gardens, Folkestone
Kent CT20 2DN, England

British Library Cataloguing-in-Publication Information Available

Library of Congress Cataloging-in-Publication Data

Heller, Peter B.,
   The United Nations under Dag Hammarskjöld, 1953–1961 / Peter B. Heller.
     p. cm.—(Partners for peace ; no. 2)
   Includes bibliographical references and index.
   ISBN 0-8108-3699-8 (alk. paper)
     1. Hammarskjèld, Dag, 1906–1961. 2. United Nations—Biography.
   3. World politics—1955–1965. I. Title. II. Partners for peace ; v. 2.
   D839.7.H3 H37 2001
   341.23′09′045—dc21   2001020652

Contents

Preface   vii

Introduction: Dag Hammarskjöld's United Nations   ix

1   Hammarskjöld: A New-Style Secretary-General   1

2   Hammarskjöld and the Constitutional Framework   17

3   The Events: Extension of Hammarskjöld's Authority   37

4   The Events: Limits on Hammarskjöld's Authority   59

5   Breaking New Ground   91

6   Hammarskjöld's Last Hurrah: The Congo   115

7   Conclusion: Hammarskjöld—Flash in the Pan or Prophet of a New World Order?   147

Chronology of Dag Hammarskjöld's Life, 1905–1961   153

Chronology of Events, 1953–1961   155

Appendix A   Members of the United Nations   275

Appendix B   Excerpt from Chapter XV of the Charter of the United Nations   277

Appendix C   Hammarskjöld's Press Statement before Assuming Secretary-General Position   279

Appendix D   National Clearance Procedures   281

Appendix E   "Old Creeds in a New World"   283

Appendix F   *Tenth Annual Report*   285

Appendix G   Principal Members of the
              United Nations Secretariat as of
              December 31, 1960   289

Appendix H   ONUC Civilian and Military
              Representatives in the Congo, 1960–1961   293

Appendix I   Victims of DC–6 Aircraft Crash   294

Appendix J   *The New York Times* Editorial on
              Hammarskjöld's Death   295

Appendix K   Biographical Profiles   297
              Ralph J. Bunche   297
              Lester B. Pearson   298
              Patrice Lumumba   299
              Joseph Kasavubu   300
              Moise Tshombe   300
              Joseph-Désiré Mobutu   301

Bibliography   303

Index   319

About the Author   329

Preface

Why another book on Dag Hammarskjöld? The existing literature about or referring to the second Secretary-General of the United Nations, directly or tangentially, is already voluminous. But there are at least three reasons that justify this addition to an already crowded field. First, Hammarskjöld's untimely and to this day inconclusively explained death continues to cause speculation, as is the case with other persons of renown. Second, Hammarskjöld's cryptic autobiographical *Markings* still elicits only tentative interpretations. Third, many of those focusing on Hammarskjöld tend to be biased in one way or another about the man and his enterprise. This work attempts to provide a balanced picture about an individual who has been elevated to heroic fame perhaps more than most—witness his Nobel Peace Prize, his funeral attended by royalty, the streets and libraries named after him, and other symbols of recognition and respect. But it is also about a man who has been defamed as few others for good, for bad, and for no reason.

The present contribution to the literature, but not the mythology or the legend, thus tries to bring out various dimensions of what after all and even now is a very enigmatic individual. After establishing the international political context of the 1950s and thus of the United Nations, which faithfully reflected the world around it, the book takes stock of Hammarskjöld first as a person and then as an international functionary. Much of the story, so to speak, is told with reference to the major events that marked Hammarskjöld's eight and a half years in office. The latter are roughly dichotomized as those happenings in which the secretary-general's endeavors could be considered relatively successful—at least in the short run—and others in which he seemed to experience setbacks—again, at least in the short term. For that reason, the presentation is not strictly chronological or even divided between his first and second terms in office.

A separate chapter emphasizes the newer issues which, beyond the Cold War, came to occupy an increasingly important niche in the UN agenda and to which Hammarskjöld gave a growing amount of his attention and time on the way to the final denouement. Perhaps paradoxically, the latter involved one of these very issues—decolonization. The conclusion attempts to assess to what extent Hammarskjöld changed the world.

The case studies interspersed in the chapters were selected with an eye to diversity and topicality. Admittedly, different ones could have been picked. The same goes for the documents following the chronology. Some of the short biographical profiles suggest that even in Hammarskjöld's time, other statesmen, both in and out of the United Nations, also played an important role, no matter how much adumbrated by the secretary-general's long shadow.

Readers who plan to peruse the other volumes in this UN series, Partners for Peace, produced by Scarecrow Press, may find it challenging to make mental comparisons between and among the various UN secretaries-general and then to measure Dag Hammarskjöld in terms of both his human and professional qualities. If the author of the present text were to allow himself the luxury of being momentarily judgmental, he would assign a higher grade to the latter than to the former, to Hammarskjöld as a statesman than to Hammarskjöld as an individual. But then, who can penetrate a pane of glass?

Introduction:
Dag Hammarskjöld's
United Nations

In its obituary editorial on September 19, 1961, *The New York Times* wrote, "But for the patient, indefatigable leadership of Dag Hammarskjöld, the United Nations might not exist today. Quietly, shrewdly, persistently he labored to maintain it against heavy odds and to enhance its effectiveness in a world that teeters on the brink of catastrophe." This book argues that, even discounting Hammarskjöld's death in the cause of peace in the Congo and the consequent glorification of his virtues, the editorial judgment made was essentially appropriate. During Hammarskjöld's tenure, the UN secretary-general was identified with his institution to an extent that has never been equaled. To the public in many lands, "the Organization" was Dag Hammarskjöld. And, in a sense, the opposite was also true: he seemed as much a machine as a man.

Despite the voluminous literature already extant in the field of UN studies, this work hopes to demonstrate that a confluence of factors explains the evolution of the United Nations during his eight and a half turbulent years. Among them were the state of international and therefore UN affairs that held sway at the time of Hammarskjöld's inauguration in April 1953, the various crises that occurred during his tenure, his previous experience in the Swedish civil service, and his earlier work in international organizations. The secretary-general's unique persona and strong beliefs were vital assets that "mark his career as one of the great forces for a better world," as the *Times* editorial further asserted.

Indeed, Hammarskjöld was a man whose faith, as noted in his posthumous *Markings*, the near equivalent of a diary, was centered in the persuasion that "in our era, the road to holiness necessarily passes through the world of action." It was not surprising, then, that he sought to fill every smidgen of space left vacant by vague descriptions of the secretary-general's authority and duties in the UN Charter. Regarding the organization's purposes and mission, maximal interpretations of even specific instructions by the organization's political organs marked the secretary-general's tenure much of the time. The frequent stalemates in the Cold War-ridden world body and the repeated indecisiveness of its organs' members in tackling complex international issues provided Hammarskjöld with the coveted opportunity to lead. His activism was further compounded by the emergence of newly independent, developing nations—the Third World—with all their political, economic, social, administrative, and technological needs, and above all their need to survive.

Thus Hammarskjöld sought a better world in a period that saw the last gasp of colonialism. Some former imperialist powers—the French in Indochina and North Africa, the British at Suez, the Belgians in the Congo—and newcomers like the Soviets in Hungary had not yet read the handwriting on the wall about the end of empire. The 1950s were also a time when the world, engulfed in the protracted Cold War between the democratic-capitalist West and the totalitarian-Communist East, occasionally witnessed hot wars through the major adversaries' surrogates. It was a period, too, when the Arab–Israeli question kept manifesting itself in diverse forms and when the consequent Palestinian refugee problem assumed a permanent dimension. The latter issue alone overwhelmed the meager resources that the United Nations could devote to this purpose.

At any rate, when the 47-year-old Dag Hammarskjöld took the oath of office as the second UN secretary-general on April 10, 1953, few could have guessed the consequences. He assumed power at a time of great turmoil in the United Nations because his Norwegian predecessor, Trygve Lie, had become politically and administratively ineffective. The Soviet Union had ignored Lie since the start of the Korean War for "siding" with the United States. Soviet hostility was reinforced by Lie's seemingly enthusiastic cooperation with U.S. law enforcement agencies in hunting down alleged American Communists and fellow travelers working in the UN secretariat. In fact, Lie himself posed a problem for Hammarskjöld. The first secretary-general was very disappointed not to have had his tenure extended by the UN Security Council despite his earlier resignation. He had hoped to the end that the great powers would be unable to agree on any other candidate so that he could remain in his job by default. His frustration led to many "uncharitable references" by Lie about his successor, comments that Hammarskjöld, a consummate diplomat, allowed to pass without riposte.

At least on the face of it, relations between the two men improved somewhat when much later, on November 21, 1960, Lie returned to UN headquarters in New York to attend the unveiling of his portrait presented to the world organization by the Norwegian government. In his comments for the occasion, Hammarskjöld rescinded his earlier rejection, at times critical, of Lie's characterization of the secretary-general's task as being "the most impossible job in the world," which Lie had offered to his successor when Hammarskjöld arrived to take up his post in April 1953. The events of the seven and a half intervening years may have had a lot to do with Hammarskjöld's change of view.

How to cope with the problems bedeviling the world organization? "Ours is a work of reconciliation and realistic construction," Hammarskjöld told the UN General Assembly on his inauguration, and during his tenure he tried to do both. He rationalized that nations would adopt habits of cooperation as they increasingly came to need one another. He hoped to develop a new international mentality in which the United Nations could act distinctly from the member states that composed it, in synergistic manner.

Hammarskjöld was the first secretary-general to engage in such innovations as peacekeeping. The Charter sanctioned the use of force to check threats to the peace or aggression, but this secretary-general interposed a UN presence between antagonists to prevent violence. He also used other forms of UN "presence"—a term that became commonplace in the UN lexicon during his time—to challenge states too taken with their own sovereignty and nationalism and national interest. He offered them instead a vision of the cooperative existence essential in an increasingly interdependent world haunted by the specter of nuclear holocaust.

Through his diplomatic skills, his commitment to peace endeavors, his personal integrity, his extensive cultural polish, his tactics of private and preventive action, and his boundless energy and love of his job, Hammarskjöld delivered on the promise he made when he accepted the position—that he would be "active as an instrument, a catalyst, an inspirer." Whether with all this he managed to change the contours of international relations remains a puzzling question. For one thing, not all of Hammarskjöld's accomplishments proved long-lasting or concluded a final political settlement. For another, in the over 40 years since his untimely death on September 18, 1961, much in the world has changed.

But the fact remains that except for Hammarskjöld's conviction, determination, and perhaps even his monopolization of power, the arms race might have been even more feverish, the world an even more violent place, and the betterment of the lives of Third World peoples through economic, social, and other programs even more modest. But as global problems persist in their old or newer forms and as additional issues make their way to the world body's agenda, estimates of Dag Hammarskjöld's outsized aura and the future he bequeathed must necessarily be nuanced. It is to this task that the succeeding pages are devoted.

THE WORLD ON APRIL 7, 1953

On the day when Dag Hammarskjöld was elected the second UN secretary-general, the world was a curious mix of hopeful and frightening developments. The East–West conflict had been simmering since former British Prime Minister Winston Churchill, in his celebrated Fulton, Missouri, speech of March 5, 1946, described how an "iron curtain" had descended and divided Europe. His prophetic declaration foreshadowed a protracted conflict between the Eastern and Western blocs known as the Cold War, which was to last for some 45 years. But Soviet dictator Joseph Stalin had died on March 5, 1953, and it would have been difficult for his successor, Georgi M. Malenkov, to match his predecessor's tyranny and brutality. Thus many believed that the time was ripe for great power accommodation.

In the fall of 1952, the American presidential candidate, General Dwight D. Eisenhower, had campaigned by promising to bring peace to the Korean peninsula, engulfed in a UN-sanctioned war since June 1950. Still, in April 1953, the American-led United Nations Command was charging North Korea with war atrocities while the latter was accusing the U.S. forces of germ warfare.

In February 1953, soon after President Eisenhower took office, the United States had given assurances that it did not mean to sponsor an attack on mainland Communist China in order to establish the dominance of the American ally, Nationalist China, or Taiwan. The

Soviet Union and Communist China were still on friendly terms, observing that same month the third anniversary of their Treaty of Friendship and Mutual Aid. On its part, the U.S.-led Western alliance epitomized by the North Atlantic Treaty Organization (NATO) celebrated its fourth anniversary in early April 1953. The two atomic superpowers—the United States and the Soviet Union—displayed their mutual hostility in this bipolar world with frequently alleged, and invariably denied, incursions of American reconnaissance aircraft into Soviet airspace leading to the loss of some U.S. planes when they were shot down.

There were other trends as well. In dependent areas of the underdeveloped world, decolonization had begun but not without labor pains, partly because the colonizing powers were not always willing to depart gracefully. Moreover, the newly independent states faced a slew of ethnic and tribal, political, social, economic, and technological problems with which they were often unprepared to deal. Several governments of the growing Third World were exhibiting authoritarian features in their systems.

There were racial problems too. In South Africa, the National Party regime continued a policy of apartheid while refusing to relinquish its League of Nations mandate over South-West Africa. And in the Middle East, where Britain had voluntarily given up its mandate over Palestine in 1948, a seemingly endless Arab–Israeli conflict and its numerous sequels demanded constant UN involvement.

Neither were things all hunky-dory at the newly occupied UN complex along the East River in New York City. How could they be? After all, the world organization reflected to a large extent the political climate of the globe itself. It should be recalled that early in the world body's existence, Soviet representatives developed the practice of walking out of sessions or casting their Security Council vetoes against the Western-led majority in the United Nations of those years. In January 1950, the Soviet Union had temporarily withdrawn from all UN organs in which Nationalist China was represented, after unsuccessfully attempting to have Taiwan's representatives replaced by those of Communist China. Such Soviet obstructionism was countered by U.S. Secretary of State Dean Acheson's "Uniting for Peace" resolution in October 1950. This resolution, adopted by an overwhelming General Assembly majority in the teeth of Soviet bloc opposition, made it possible for the world body to transfer to the Assembly important but vetoed Security Council issues concerning

international peace. Acting under that measure, in February 1951 the
General Assembly formally accused Communist China of aggression
in Korea, hardly a promising augury for peaceful settlement there.
Only on July 27, 1953, was a Korean armistice signed at Panmunjom,
which was still in effect at the turn of the millennium.

Meanwhile, in the world at large, other dire omens gathered. In the
field of armaments, Britain produced its first atomic bomb in February 1952 while the United States exploded its first hydrogen weapon
in November. Shortly before that blast, in June, the United States
started to build its first atomic submarine, and in September 1952, it
used guided missiles in combat off the North Korean coast for the
first time. The Soviet Union would not lag far behind in such technological progress. More fruitfully, the United States signed a peace
treaty with Japan in April 1952, and soon thereafter the latter began
its reintegration into the global economic community. But much of
the world remained tense.

Nothing epitomized this better than Palestine, where clashes
involving land had been the rule since 1948. UN mediators—Count
Folke Bernadotte and then Ralph Bunche—had managed to engineer
various armistice agreements in 1949, but time made it increasingly
evident that peace would not follow soon. The best that the United
Nations could do to make up for its earlier failure to enforce its partition plan of November 29, 1947, was to organize a group of
observers—the United Nations Truce Supervision Organization
(UNTSO)—to oversee the cease-fires. The UN mediators and UNTSO
would also act as go-betweens, for the Arab and Israeli adversaries
would not negotiate face-to-face.

Elsewhere in the problems of decolonization, the United Nations
had already played a more successful mediatory role in the Indian
subcontinent, Indonesia, and the former Italian colonies. But the
intensifying Cold War, which increasingly interjected itself in these
colonial problems, had already had several important consequences
bearing on the United Nations. The Charter had assumed that the Military Staff Committee advising the Security Council would be the
linchpin of the peace enforcement system because this group of senior
officers representing the "Big Five" permanent members was
designed to function as the Security Council's general staff. But the
failure of the superpowers to agree on the type and quota of forces to
be supplied by each had reduced the role of this Military Staff Com-

mittee to mostly periodic but perfunctory meetings. Clearly, this reality, like most others, would command Hammarskjöld's attention.

There were also organizational problems for the new secretary-general to face. For instance, the existing UN system provided little coordination between the secretariat and the affiliated but autonomous agencies comprising the extended UN family. Boasting their own constitutions, administrators, constituencies, and independent budgets, these specialized agencies and other subsidiary bodies resisted coordination by the secretary-general despite the consequent gaps in service, overlaps, and financial waste. Indeed, the budget—that is, budgets of the United Nations proper and of the other units as well—was often unable to meet the demand for services compared to the funds available. Delegate pressure on the secretary-general to make secretariat appointments on a political rather than merit basis had already begun and would escalate during Hammarskjöld's tenure. Such, in brief, was the situation as the second secretary-general took over Trygve Lie's self-described "most impossible job in the world."

From 1946 to 1953, the political influence of the United Nations had been slight. The world organization was widely perceived as primarily an impotent debating society in which boring, repetitive, and endless speeches were made and mountains of documents in five official languages were churned out and just as quickly forgotten. Certainly, during its first eight years of existence, the world body had not shown the promise of actualizing the lofty principles of peace and cooperation, human rights, and individual and collective well-being emphasized in the UN Charter. Rather, the political life of the organization relied on rhetorical fog and legal improvisation needed to get around Cold War stalemates and the states' continuing devotion to the long-established principle of national sovereignty, sanctified by the Charter's exclusion of matters of "domestic jurisdiction" from the scope of its authority. In this vacuum, a new secretary-general might become the key to useful political action. Dag Hammarskjöld could not have arrived at a more opportune time.

Areas of Interest during Dag Hammarskjöld's Term

1

Hammarskjöld:
A New-Style
Secretary-General

HAMMARSKJÖLD'S PERSONA

As Dag Hammarskjöld took office on April 10, 1953, he declared that he would not advocate a "passive role" for the secretary-general but rather act as "an instrument, a catalyst, an inspirer."[1] In his inaugural speech, he added, "Ours is a work of reconciliation and realistic construction. This work must be based on respect for the laws by which human civilization has been built." Such a theme, combined with that of the international civil servant's obligation for mandatory neutrality, recurred constantly in Hammarskjöld's public addresses and could still be heard in his "valedictory" speech on Staff Day, September 8, 1961.

The initial impressions that Hammarskjöld created were mixed. He evidenced his democratic tendencies and his feel for public relations by shaking hands with each of the secretariat's 3,500 or so employees soon after his initial appointment, by eating in the staff cafeteria after standing in line with his tray and waiting for his turn to be served like everybody else, and by taking the public elevator to his 38th floor office. But later—some say because of work pressure— he got into the habit of having lunch with his immediate aides in the executive dining room next to his office. He even flew tourist class rather than first class on commercial airlines, at least for the first few months of his tenure. Subsequent evidence of authoritarian, even arrogant, behavior tended to dilute this initial impression.

In his person, Hammarskjöld displayed remarkable as well as difficult qualities. He had a shy, noncommittal elusiveness. His extreme

1

sensitivity, reserve, isolation, moodiness, and frostiness, as well as his mastery of avoidance techniques, were accompanied occasionally by a certain degree of ego-centeredness and condescension, which did not sit well with everyone. For instance, his restructuring of the top echelons of the secretariat focusing around himself and a few chosen men (but no women) of his inner circle did not command universal approval. However, the men he did select—the likes of Andrew Cordier, Ralph Bunche, Heinz Wieschhoff, Philippe de Seynes, and C. V. Narasimhan—met Hammarskjöld's exacting standards of inexhaustible work and perfection in performance as well as unlimited time devoted to duty. Hammarskjöld seems to have viewed his job as a quasi-religious responsibility.

He would often baffle the media and nearly everyone else by his hairsplitting to prove consistency or by his working around an issue in order to seem not to make a concession. Admittedly, the media had gotten used to the kind of hot news and controversial opinions voiced by the colorful Trygve Lie. A man who seemed humorless and took himself as seriously as Hammarskjöld appeared to do was not likely to make as good copy as his fellow Scandinavian predecessor. One day, in a fit of anger at the temporary UN offices in Lake Success, New York, Lie brought down the "walls of Jericho"—the makeshift partitions in his room. Hammarskjöld, while able to become very angry, always seemed to control his temper. But his remarkable self-control concealed the resentment he felt toward criticism. No matter how obviously motivated by partisan or national interest considerations his interlocutors may have been, Hammarskjöld viewed censure as a reflection on his personal integrity. Despite his long career in public life and therefore public debate, he never developed the tough hide of the traditional politician. His occasionally testy ripostes to negative comments seem to evidence this streak in his makeup.

Generally speaking, Hammarskjöld's dedication to his work, his good breeding, and his customary impartiality blunted the annoyance that many had harbored about him initially. He may have been a workaholic putting in 12 or 14 hours a day on the job and resenting those who did not follow suit, but there was more to Dag Hammarskjöld than just drudgery. He had a strong predilection for aesthetic things—nature, art, culture. He was an avid photographer of attractive landscapes and never went on a trip—private or official—without his camera. Whether overflying the Himalaya Mountains in

Nepal or enjoying his country residence in Brewster, New York, he was constantly marveling at nature's wonders, a carryover from childhood.

His literary tastes included the verses of the German Hermann Hesse and the American Emily Dickinson. Hammarskjöld was especially impressed by the Frenchman Alexis Saint-Léger, writing under the pen name of Saint-John Perse, a onetime diplomat who eventually won the Nobel Prize for literature. Hammarskjöld's tastes in prose and music were just as sweeping as his literary interests. In fact, he took his father's seat in the Swedish Academy, which awarded the Nobel Prize for literature. He even hoped to become the academy's secretary once his UN tenure was over.

Even when he was busy, Hammarskjöld would arrange small private dinner parties at his apartment on East 73rd Street in Manhattan for the likes of conductor Leonard Bernstein, violinist Fritz Kreisler, cellist Pablo Casals, author James Michener, and their wives. His fellow Swede, the reclusive movie actress Greta Garbo, was also a frequent guest. Some of his close aides, for example, Ralph Bunche, Andrew Cordier, and George Ivan Smith as well as others, would also be invited. Hammarskjöld took pride in the cuisine of his Swedish housekeeper and appears to have been a gourmet himself. At times he would prepare his own meals, especially at his weekend retreat in Brewster or at his summer farmhouse in southern Sweden during the brief interludes that his busy schedule allowed.

Hammarskjöld loved the theater but felt an aversion to being recognized by the audience—even the theater was secondary to his fanatical love of privacy. As an intellectual with a highly cultivated sense of aesthetics, Hammarskjöld was also knowledgeable in the visual arts. He was a connoisseur of painting and took great interest in the placement of art works donated by individuals and governments to the United Nations. It took all of his diplomatic skills to place works that he considered to have lesser artistic merit in less prominent locations in a way that did not offend the source. During his tenure he himself commissioned works such as Marc Chagall's stained glass windows in the UN Meditation Room. And in 1954, he borrowed paintings by the likes of Juan Gris, Henri Matisse, Pablo Picasso, and Georges Braque from the Museum of Modern Art in New York to display in his 38th floor office.

Perhaps above all, Hammarskjöld was an avid reader. Apart from his work on the Nobel Prize Committee for Literature, he tried to steal time to peruse sources as diverse as the Bible, Shakespeare, Cervantes, Goethe, Joseph Conrad, Thomas Mann, T. S. Eliot, and Marcel Proust. He explained his catholic tastes soon after taking up his duties: "My literary interests appear to invite misinterpretations. It's true I do like Thomas Wolfe very much. . . . but I don't like being pinned down to any one phase of literature, or anything else. I would prefer, for example, to be known as an admirer of both Thomas Wolfe and Virginia Woolf."

But for all this intellectual curiosity, Hammarskjöld also relished physical activities. He was an enthusiastic mountain climber and bicyclist and pursued these avocations in Sweden and abroad whenever he could. Such interests were reflected by his election to the board of directors of the Swedish Tourist Association in 1940 and to its vice presidency in 1950. He served as president of the Swedish Alpinist Club for many years, and his unremitting love of the outdoors was evidenced by his co-editorship of an anthology published in 1943 titled *Svensk Natur* (Nature in Sweden). Even on the surface, Hammarskjöld exhibited many interesting features. The inner man, however, was perhaps more fascinating.

THE INNER MAN

Even in the 1950s, there was much speculation about Dag Hammarskjöld's sexual orientation since, in his time, it was unusual for a public man—especially one so well-born, affluent, and cultured—to be unmarried and to seemingly shun the company of women. Except for absences mandated by his work, Dag Hammarskjöld had never been physically or emotionally far from his mother, Agnes Almquist Hammarskjöld, who was 40 when Dag was born. Perhaps because she had hoped to produce a daughter (which she never did), by all accounts she tended to treat the youngest of her four sons like a girl. This relationship may have had something to do with stunting Dag's emotional development when it came to the opposite sex. On the very few occasions when his married friends prevailed upon him to have a date, he invariably found some trivial excuse to discontinue the relationship.

Clearly, the future chief executive officer of the world organization did not feel comfortable with half of the human race. It is true that Hammarskjöld's workaholic tendencies conveniently crowded out the time for romance and provided a rationalization for a solitary existence. He sometimes expressed impatience with the benign tyranny of family life. Once, when the queen mother of Sweden asked him why, being such an eligible bachelor, he was still unmarried, Hammarskjöld replied that he could not ask any woman to share his hectic public life. However, his being single was only part of the story.

While he was still a senior official in one of the ministries in Stockholm, Hammarskjöld came home one day and found an unknown but completely undressed woman in his bed. Apparently she had gained entrance into the apartment by convincing the doorman that she was a chambermaid about to clean the bachelor's apartment. It turned out that she had applied for a job in Hammarskjöld's office and had thought up the scheme to impress him with her "credentials." Hammarskjöld summoned the police. They removed the woman, who was then reportedly institutionalized. For his part, Hammarskjöld promptly moved out of the apartment.

Does it follow from all this that Hammarskjöld was a homosexual? Manifestly his political detractors helped spread such a rumor—or at least failed to blunt its sting. On the very day his nomination as secretary-general was announced at a UN press conference, somebody characterized him as a "fairy." Unending gossip continued to swirl during his tenure, not because of any solid proof but because he seemingly lacked interest in or had any tender attachments to women.

However, the best evidence seems to indicate that Hammarskjöld was sexually neutral or undersexed and not gay at all. Admittedly, he felt most comfortable in the company of men, and the few female UN employees who made overtures to him were politely rebuffed. As a consummate diplomat, Hammarskjöld managed to control any feelings of embarrassment or annoyance he may have felt at being baited.

For instance, at a UN function, a female employee, more brazen than others, is supposed to have asked Hammarskjöld how come he was not dancing. Not losing his cool, his response was reportedly: "I was hoping you would ask me."

But in his autobiographical *Markings*, he noted with some bitterness, "Because it did not find a mate / They called / The unicorn perverted." Evidently the gossip had hurt. During his career, the few women to whom he gave more than a passing glance were artists, writers, or actresses. The seeming attachment was of the intellectual—and certainly platonic—variety. For instance, the British sculptress Barbara Hepworth, whose work Hammarskjöld admired greatly, was described as "his friend" by Hammarskjöld's aide Brian Urquhart. Her work *Single Form,* an abstract sculpture, was placed at the entrance of the secretariat building at UN headquarters in New York after the secretary-general's death. In May 1961, Hammarskjöld had visited a Hepworth exhibit in London and bought one of her wooden abstract sculptures for his office in New York. On his return, he wrote to her in his abstruse style that the art work was "a strong and exacting companion, but at the same time one of deep quiet and timeless perspective in inner space." He often talked of "inner space." In the same vein, Hammarskjöld greatly admired Djuna Barnes, the American author of *Nightwood.* By helping translate her verse play *Antiphon,* he introduced her opus to the Swedish public.

Hammarskjöld had a reasonable number of male friends, but it is unclear what close friendship meant to the sensitive, introverted Swede. At the United Nations, he seemed to find his top aides Ralph Bunche and Andrew Cordier congenial, and Hammarskjöld undertook a hiking tour in New Zealand with George Ivan Smith, the Australian UN public information officer. But most of all, he felt comfortable with Bill Ranallo, the U.S. Army private who had been Trygve Lie's personal chauffeur and then became Hammarskjöld's driver, bodyguard, valet, and occasional cook, especially at Hammarskjöld's weekend home in Brewster, where he often shared the KP with Hammarskjöld himself.

As Hammarskjöld's "man Friday," Ranallo seemed to sense his boss's moods better than most and knew when to be expansive or informal. In Ranallo's obituary of September 19, 1961, the day following the crash that killed Hammarskjöld, Ranallo, and everyone else on board, *The New York Times* described the Italian-American native of Pittsburgh only as a "friend of the Secretary-General." The army veteran and former New York policeman left a wife, a son from his former spouse, and two stepsons from his second marriage.

Hammarskjöld also maintained close contact with his friends in Sweden—those who had worked with him in the Swedish Foreign Ministry such as Leif Belfrage; Sture Petren, a judge; Karl Ragner Gierow, the poet and director of the Swedish Royal Dramatic Theater; and the painter Bo Beskow, whose luminous mural decorates the Meditation Room in the public lobby at UN headquarters. Most of these men had families. But even with close friends, Hammarskjöld seems to have maintained a cordon sanitaire so profound that many believed he was incapable of unbending even with his intimates. Never chummy, he was in the last analysis a very solitary man. As he put it, "When we come to our deepest feelings and urgings we have to be alone, we have to feel the sky and the earth and hear the voice that speaks from within us."

Perhaps most suggestive of Hammarskjöld, the inner man, was his creation of the aforementioned UN Meditation Room, a place where those of many faiths may sit and reflect inside a house of great controversy and argumentation. There is a plaque engraved with Hammarskjöld's words: "This is a room of quiet where only thoughts should speak." It is Hammarskjöld who planned the design, ordered the art work, and wrote the leaflet placed in the anteroom for visitors. The pamphlet, which refers to "those who come here to fill the void with what they find in their center of stillness" bespeaks the secretary-general's brooding and introspective nature.

MARKINGS

For the public, Hammarskjöld's spirituality becomes especially evident from his autobiographical diary, *Markings*, which, combined with a number of his actions, provides further insight into this dimension of his character. As Hammarskjöld explained in *Markings*, he tried to find peace with himself and his God, even though "we live in a rather insane world" where "nobody is bad and nobody is good." Its publication in 1964 revealed a profoundly mystical and religious inner man.

It seems that Hammarskjöld had great doubts about the meaning of life and the worthwhileness of it all. He was given to bouts of depression, and some believe he contemplated suicide as late as 1952, the year before his UN appointment. But after becoming secretary-general, when more than half of the entries in *Markings* were written (if one can go by their dates), his introspection became less agonizing. "At some moment I did answer Yes to Someone or Something— and from that hour I was certain that existence is meaningful and that, therefore my life, in self-surrender, had a goal." He put this concept even more succinctly when he wrote, "For all that has been, thanks. For all that will be, yes."

There are messianic overtones in *Markings*. In it, Hammarskjöld suggests he is destined to sacrifice his own ambitions and plea-

sures—reciprocated passion, a happy marriage, or even life itself—
for the sake of redeeming humanity from the sufferings of international strife. "The only value of life is its content—for others. . . .
Therefore, how incredibly great is what I have been given, and how
meaningless what I have to 'sacrifice.' " Gustaf Aulen, a Swedish contemporary, commented, "Hammarskjöld did not say that God
appointed him to be the Secretary-General of the United Nations, but
he nevertheless received the charge entrusted to him . . . as a divine
vocation." His Lutheran upbringing may have had something to do
with all this.

Hammarskjöld's mysticism and penchant for contemplation were
tempered because he was also a man of deeds. He himself stated that
"the road to holiness necessarily passes through the world of action."
Unlike other mystics, he embraced the affairs of this world. Several
entries in *Markings* dated 1956 and 1961 suggest that he viewed the
UN position as his personal salvation.

Perhaps most significantly, *Markings* contains no direct references
to individuals he knew, contemporary events, or milestones in his
life. Even when writing about himself, Hammarskjöld was detached,
using the second or third person singular rather than the first person.
His constant use of "it," "he," or "you" rather than "I" or "me," gives
Markings a dreamlike, remote quality.

Having suffered great spiritual distress for years until he discovered that self-sacrifice made his life meaningful, was Hammarskjöld
also narcissistic, excessively concerned with himself? Hammarskjöld
admits to that possibility but then explains it away by noting that he
was responding to his sense of unworthiness with defiance rather
than a sense of being the victim of vanity. But once he found his calling, his earlier agonizing self-appraisal seemed to fade and he came
to focus on greater verities. By now he was using the poetic form of
expression. (*Markings* is also a literary work.) The final stanza of one
of his last poems, dated July 19, 1961, reads: "Thou / Whom I do not
know / But whose I am. / Thou / Whom I do not comprehend / But
Who hast dedicated me / To my fate. / Thou—."[2] His entire work is
marked by this kind of brooding lyricism.

Hammarskjöld was the only one on the plane who was not burned
severely following the crash. Indeed, despite his fatal internal
injuries, he had managed to prop himself up against a rock, where
his body was found many hours later. His briefcase was intact
nearby. It contained a copy of the UN Charter, an English-language

edition of the New Testament and the Psalms that he always carried with him on trips, and the new edition of Israeli philosopher Martin Buber's *Ich und Du* (I and Thou), which Hammarskjöld had started to translate from German into Swedish for a Stockholm publisher.

Back in Leopoldville, his belongings included an article that he had just written for the prospective 1962 yearbook of the Swedish Tourist Association. The piece consisted of recollections from his student days at Uppsala when his father was lord lieutenant (or governor) of Uppland Province. Uppsala city, 40 miles northwest of Stockholm, seat of the Lutheran primate of Sweden and of one of the world's great universities, had special significance for Dag Hammarskjöld. The family lived in the lord lieutenant's official residence in the town's ancient castle. That is where Dag Hammarskjöld earned his law degree before the family moved back to Stockholm in 1930. Uppsala is also where the Hammarskjölds, including Dag, are buried.

A PRIVATE FACE IN A PUBLIC PLACE

In the end, it remains difficult to define Dag Hammarskjöld. One admiring aide (though not one of the "inner circle"), Brian Urquhart, the prolific undersecretary-general for special political affairs who had worked with Hammarskjöld through much of his tenure, wrote, "In life Hammarskjöld's personality was elusive and impossible to label or pin down, and it seems likely that it will remain so." Urquhart felt that no one could fully know such a complex, fanatically private, reticent, and diffident man, who bristled at any form of what he considered unwarranted intrusion by others, and who spoke "as through a pane of glass." Few, if any, penetrated his personal defenses. And it is not because Hammarskjöld had not had adequate exposure. In his eight and a half years, he visited 80 countries on 76 missions, and many international leaders became personally acquainted with him. He received honorary doctorates from 10 American colleges and universities, two Canadian ones, and Oxford University in England. But still the world did not really know him. He remained a private face in a public place.

Since his death, Hammarskjöld has come to be viewed as something of a martyr. His posthumous award of the Nobel Peace Prize completed his canonization. Yet a more balanced and dispassionate view must recognize not only his dedication to his work and his high standards of performance, but also his impatience with those who gave priority to their own private and family lives. While he was shy and soft-spoken, Hammarskjöld could also be arrogant and even gratuitously rude—for instance, to nosy newsmen—his anger manifesting itself only through a change of color behind the impassive facial expression. And even though he shunned most close personal contacts—especially with women—he could evidence touches of humaneness.

A close reading of *Markings* reveals additional chinks in his inner self. After this somber, personal, religious, and mystical autobiography was finally translated into English and published in 1964, it became evident that there was another Dag Hammarskjöld besides the refined Swedish diplomat. Inside the nature lover and mountain climber, the avid hiker and enthusiastic photographer, there was an inner man, a mystic with a messiah complex, who, in his characteristically remote style, compiled "a sort of white book concerning my negotiations with myself—and with God."

In his later book reminiscing about his own long career from the beginnings of the United Nations, Urquhart modified slightly his adulatory evaluation of the secretary-general made 15 years earlier.[3] He now wrote:

> Hammarskjöld was not an easy man. His relentlessly high intellectual and ethical standards made him intolerant of incompetence and impatient with slow or confused performance. He was at the same time shy but demanding, modest but arrogant, quiet but with a formidable capacity for anger and indignation. I do not think he was accustomed to dealing with people at close quarters, and he did not encourage intimacy or familiarity. Indeed those who attempted it usually suffered painful rebuffs. However, because his other qualities were so impressive, his aloofness seemed entirely natural.[4]

Since Hammarskjöld frequently made references to his own demise, some believe that he had a strong premonition about his death. Not long before it happened, he wrote a letter to his painter friend in Sweden, Bo Beskow, that he had "only the feeling of responsibility I always have in an existence of the uttermost uncertainty." He added that "it is a kind of protection to know that all things which may be of practical importance are well in hand independently of what may happen to me." Beskow was the same friend to whom Hammarskjöld had confided back in 1953, in response to the painter's suggestion that Dag would make a good secretary-general, "Nobody is crazy enough to propose me—and I would be crazy to accept."

CASE STUDY 1:
EARLY CAREER OF DAG HAMMARSKJÖLD

Dag (meaning "day") Hjalmar Agne Karl Hammarskjöld (literally "hammer and shield") was born on July 29, 1905, in the south central Swedish town of Jönköping in Smaaland Province. He was the youngest of four sons of Hjalmar Hammarskjöld and Agnes Almquist Hammarskjöld.

His parentage was significant. As Dag Hammarskjöld eventually mentioned, he inherited from his father—the descendant of generations of soldiers and public officials and the holder of several important positions—a strong belief that public service to country and humanity was the most worthwhile endeavor one could wish, even though it might require great personal sacrifice. From his mother's side, with its long line of scholars and clergymen, Dag acknowledged inheriting an acute sense of the equality of all human beings and a strong democratic inclination.

This was just as well, for Dag's father had a generally dour, authoritarian personality used to making pronouncements from high places. In fact, when Dag was born, the elder Hammarskjöld was president of the Court of Appeals in Göteborg. He always gave his duty to country precedence over that to family. In contrast, Dag's mother was a gentle woman, self-effacing, giving advice from the heart, warm, and gushing, dulling some of her husband's bluntness and making up for his frequent absences from home on official business as an international mediator, negotiator, ambassador abroad, and eventually Sweden's prime minister.

In fact, by all accounts, Agnes Hammarskjöld had a special relationship with her youngest son. It is true that she had wished for a girl after bearing three boys. But this was not to be. Perhaps for that reason, Dag became a "mama's boy." He was often dressed up as a girl and possibly was treated as one. Agnes Hammarskjöld liked to have her youngest son around as much as possible and at one point is reported to have said, "Dag has been much like a daughter to me."

Dag grew up to be the equivalent of the family's stay-at-home daughter. Even though his mother died in 1940, when Dag was 35 years old, he continued to live with his widowed father at the parental home till 1945. Only then, at age 40, did Dag acquire his own apartment in Stockholm. His father died in 1953, the year Dag Hammarskjöld assumed his UN position.

His earliest recollections were of living in Uppsala Castle, the residence of the governor of Uppland Province. His father had been appointed governor in 1907 following his stint as Swedish minister to Denmark, where the family had eventually followed him. The old, historic castle with its many nooks and crannies located in Sweden's oldest university town came to be cherished by young Dag. Perhaps that is where he developed his lifelong love of nature and the outdoors, for he would roam in the surrounding countryside and take great interest in the fauna and flora he discovered there.

One of his earliest friends was Jon Olof Soderblom, the son of Sweden's newly appointed Lutheran archbishop. Dag came to depend on Jon to offset his own natural shyness and lack of an outgoing personality. Indeed, Dag developed this don't-touch-me attitude at an early age—a paradoxical trait in an individual who was destined to interface with the world.

While young Dag was collecting butterflies, beetles, and other creatures of all kinds, his mother was predicting that her youngest would be a scientist, which Dag at 15 decided to be. But at home he would hear discussions of two Balkan wars, a world war, and scores of revolutions. He witnessed the first general mobilization in his own country in August 1914, following the outbreak of World War I. Such talk became quite commonplace in the Hammarskjöld household, especially since Hjalmar Hammarskjöld had been appointed Sweden's prime minister and minister of defense a few months earlier. However, the elder Hammarskjöld eventually fell out of favor, supposedly for being too conservative and pro-German during the conflict. He was forced to relinquish his post in March 1917. This made a deep impression on his son Dag, who brooded over how a talented man so dedicated to public service and principle could be derided. Perhaps Dag, because of his own introverted personality, failed to understand his father's inability to make direct, let alone warm, contact with other people, a tendency the boy himself may have inherited.

Dag stood out at school, not only because of his top performance but also by virtue of the breadth of his interests. He was especially keen on history and literature and philosophy, and came to know several foreign languages well, including English, French, and German. Both in high school and at Uppsala University, his academic career was a protracted success.

His graduate degrees were in economics and then law, notwithstanding his initial flirtation with science and literature. He also took to politics. Surprisingly or not, Hammarskjöld's Ph.D. dissertation at the University of Stockholm, entitled "The Spread of Boom and Depression: A Theoretical and Historical Survey of Market Trends" (1934), left his professors unimpressed. He did not earn the highest classification, *laudatur*, because his mentors did not feel that Dag's research had broken new ground. Even during his year at Cambridge University in England, one of his teachers, the world-renowned economist John Maynard Keynes, opined that Hammarskjöld's thoughts were unexceptional, a judgment in which the distinguished Swedish economist Gunnar Myrdal concurred.

As a colleague once remarked, Dag Hammarskjöld was "not a man of simple statements." Perhaps his use of tactful obfuscation and studied ambiguity, of the nuanced comment and calculated imprecision that became his trademarks at the United Nations, was already mystifying those who knew him in his early years. As a diplomat was later to observe, Hammarskjöld was "the only man alive who can be totally incomprehensible with complete fluency in four languages." Years later, Hammarskjöld himself confessed that on rereading certain passages from his doctoral dissertation, he could no longer explain portions of the abstruse, dreary, lengthy, and vastly intricate study. Perhaps because of this fact, more than his heavy Swedish accent, his public speaking remained unimpressive.

At any rate, Dag Hammarskjöld's early positions were in the fields of economics and finance. He entered government service as secretary of the Unemployment Commission in 1930, the year his father retired as governor of Uppland Province and the family moved to Stockholm. In 1935, Hammarskjöld was appointed secretary and in 1936 permanent secretary of the Bank of Sweden, the youngest person ever to hold that position. From 1941 to 1948, he was chairman of the bank's board of directors, a post that for a while overlapped his position as undersecretary at the Ministry of Finance from 1936 to 1945. In 1948, Hammarskjöld got his first "international" position as member and in 1950 as chairman of the Executive Committee of the Organization for European Economic Cooperation (OEEC). There he acquired a reputation for his ability to work out compromises, remembered when he was selected for his UN position in 1953. In

1951, he became Swedish deputy foreign minister following a stint as financial adviser in that ministry beginning in 1946. In that capacity he became a nonparty minister without portfolio in the Swedish cabinet. Hammarskjöld's initial contact with the United Nations was in 1949, when he became a member and then, in 1952, the vice chairman of the Swedish delegation at the seventh session of the General Assembly.

Clearly, Hammarskjöld's spectacular ascent to high places must have had something to do with his intellectual brilliance, passion for hard work, and possibly also the fact that he was connected with one of the best-known families in Sweden. This opened many doors for him, and at the very least did not hinder his uninterrupted success. On the face of it, Hammarskjöld led a charmed life. He enjoyed excellent health and had never known poverty. His citizenship in a neutral country had spared him the tribulations of deprivation, fear, and exile that his Norwegian predecessor, Trygve Lie, had experienced during World War II. His neutral-country citizenship also made Hammarskjöld acceptable to both the Western and Soviet blocs during the haggling over an acceptable successor to Trygve Lie.

Whatever his road to fame, by the time Hammarskjöld became secretary-general, he had gained a reputation for his participation in bilateral Swedish–British talks on postwar European economic reconstruction, for mediating a Swedish–U.S. dispute on an earlier trade agreement between the two countries, and for serving as Swedish delegate to the organizational meeting of the Marshall Plan, as well as for his work in the OEEC.

Apparently, all of Hammarskjöld's activities prior to 1953 had been considered uncontroversial by the UN Security Council, which recommended him to the $40,000-a-year, tax-free position of secretary-general after two years of disagreement over a successor to Trygve Lie. Even though Hammarskjöld was considered "the darkest of dark horses," the great powers believed that he would be an efficient administrator and went along with France's and Britain's recommendation of the Swedish diplomat. The Soviet delegate, Valerian Zorin, considered him "harmless" and did not veto his nomination. Those who knew Hammarskjöld better described him as a "realist who pricks balloons," while his own characterization of himself was that he was a "technician." One of the few negative voices was that of Trygve Lie, who likened Hammarskjöld to a "clerk."

Hammarskjöld's selection followed the great powers' failure to agree on the nomination of Lester B. Pearson, Canada's foreign minister and then president of the General Assembly, because of Soviet objection to his citizenship in a country allied with the West. After the West in turn rejected the candidacy of Mrs. V. J. Pandit, Indian Prime Minister Nehru's sister, the name of Hammarskjöld was submitted for a vote on March 31, 1953. His candidacy was a surprise to the other Security Council members who had not been apprised of the secret negotiations on the subject by the United States, Britain, France, and the Soviet Union. The vote was 10–0–1, with Nationalist China abstaining because Sweden had recognized the rival Communist People's Republic of China. It was even more of a surprise to Hammarskjöld when he was informed of the council's choice by cable. After consulting his father and the Swedish cabinet, he responded in the positive. The Security Council's recommendation was approved by 57 votes out of 59 in the General Assembly on April 7. He was sworn in on April 10, 1953. As secretary-general, Dag Hammarskjöld found a calling that gave full meaning to his life.

NOTES

1. Most direct quotations from Hammarskjöld are taken from Wilder Foote, ed., *Servant of Peace: A Selection of the Speeches and Statements of Dag Hammarskjöld* (New York: Harper & Row, 1962).

2. Dag Hammarskjöld, *Markings,* trans. Leif Sjöberg and W. H. Auden (New York: Alfred A. Knopf, 1965), pp. 214–215.

3. Brian Urquhart, *Hammarskjöld* (New York: Alfred A. Knopf, 1972).

4. Brian Urquhart, *A Life in Peace and War* (New York: Harper & Row, 1987), p. 126.

2

Hammarskjöld and the Constitutional Framework

A charter, like a constitution, basic law, or fundamental law, provides the ground rules under which an organization functions. Such a blueprint of governance may prescribe as well as proscribe some of the things that the organization or its members may or may not do. This was the case with the earlier Covenant of the League of Nations. It is now the case with its successor and similar document, the UN Charter.

However, few of these constitutions are codified. Few provide a comprehensive list of the powers, responsibilities, and rights of, as well as restraints on, the organizations or their members, leaving the relationship between the two often unclear. This is certainly true of the UN Charter. Its brief 19 chapters divided into 111 articles do not spell out these matters comprehensively, clearly, or at all. In short, the document, like many others, is often vague, contradictory, or even silent on important issues, including the most important one relating to conflict and its management. Dag Hammarskjöld turned out to be a past master at playing on the Charter's ambiguities, oxymorons, and silences to try to achieve his goals.

HAMMARSKJÖLD AND THE UN CHARTER

As Hammarskjöld put it, "it is in keeping with the philosophy of the Charter that the secretary-general should be expected to act . . . in order to help in filling any vacuum that may appear in the system which the Charter and traditional diplomacy provide for the safekeeping of peace and security." This thought encapsulates Hammarskjöld's attempts to make up for spaces left by the UN Charter, the resolutions of the UN political organs, and the body of UN precedent that he had to work with after 1953.

Hammarskjöld did not regard the Charter as a perfect instrument but thought that its rich potential for achieving international peace, world security, and human progress had not been fully utilized. For instance, in an address at the University of Chicago Law School on May 1, 1960, he noted, "The fact that important sections of the Charter—I think especially of Chapter VII which lays down the rules for intervention of the UN with military forces—so far have not been implemented does not mean that on these points we are facing a dead letter." He firmly believed that innovative use rather than revision of the Charter would lead to progress. In fact, he felt that internationalism because of the United Nations was more advanced at this stage of world history than the sense of global community. Therefore, it was essential that the United Nations improve its effectiveness in dealing with major international issues.

Dag Hammarskjöld held a positive and dynamic concept of what the United Nations might become as an instrument acting independently for the general good. Governments had to be guided to accept the world body as a source of creative capacity, able to take initiative in the service of peace, security, and progress. It was wrong to represent the organization as an institution that was rigid and unadaptable, as merely the lowest common denominator of what member states could agree on. According to Hammarskjöld, the Charter, both in its specific provisions such as article 99 and as a whole, empowered its chief executive officer to work against destructive national pressures and so benefit the international community. A secretary-general might even, if he had to, act without guidance from the major organs. Hammarskjöld had great distaste for the inaction epitomized by the time-honored excuse of "no government put it on the agenda." Often his willingness to raise issues encouraged member states to act in like manner. While he generally preferred to quote chapter and verse as the basis of his authority for decision making, when he was unable to do so Hammarskjöld would vaguely refer to "the authority of the secretary-general under the Charter."

Even though the legal sources of the secretary-general's authority were often ambiguous, in many cases the voids that Hammarskjöld filled were tolerated by the great powers. They recognized political necessities and Hammarskjöld's personal influence. Thus the frequent deadlocks in the Security Council and the changing majorities in the General Assembly, which shifted with nearly every issue, enabled the secretary-general to become the focus of action. For the only way that the world body could preserve its operational effectiveness was to permit its secretary-general to seize greater responsibilities. Since the two political organs—the General Assembly and the Security Council—were often unable to devise specific instructions for the implementation of their resolutions, Hammarskjöld's "moral magistracy," combined with his boundless energy, intellectual drive, and ability to project himself, enabled him to fill in the breach.

In May 1954, after only a year in office, Hammarskjöld wrote:

> Basically, the secretary-general's responsibility, as I see it, is to use whatever right he may be given and may be acknowledged to have, with the utmost flexibility and a very quick reaction, because time means so very much in these matters . . . The secretary-general's initiative . . . is, in principle, a supplementary one. When governments reach a deadlock, he may be the person to help them—and help them with their complete acceptance—out of the deadlock. . . . If governments are seized of a matter, if there is no deadlock, if discussions are going on and if contacts have been established . . . the secretary-general—no matter how concerned he may be—should keep back. . . . He has no reason to jump on the stage and take over the part of any responsible government.

HAMMARSKJÖLD AND
HIS POLITICAL ROLE

When the UN Charter was drafted, the secretariat was expected to be modeled on that of the League of Nations. In addition to being the only body in permanent session, the secretariat had developed great expertise in specific subject areas—for example, in economic, social, and scientific issues—and served member governments through support services such as documentation and publications. The only matters that were initially unclear at the founding San Francisco conference in 1945 were the political role of the secretary-general and the control to which he would be subjected.

The approved Charter clarified some of these issues. Chapter III (7) makes the secretariat one of the six principal organs of the "core" United Nations, side by side with the General Assembly, Security Council, Economic and Social Council, Trusteeship Council, and the

International Court of Justice (or World Court). However, more important details about the secretary-general and his staff are spelled out in Chapter XV (97–101). These stress the international and politically neutral character of the secretariat. But the articles also give the secretary-general a potentially more important political role than the League had done. As before, he was to be the chief administrative officer of the organization (art. 97) and was to act as such at all meetings of the other principal organs making up the "core" United Nations, except for the International Court of Justice. It was implied that as chief administrative officer, a secretary-general would coordinate the work of the subsidiary bodies and specialized agencies which, together with the "core" United Nations, compose the UN system, network, or family.

But the Charter also notes that the secretary-general "shall perform such other functions as are entrusted to him by these organs" (art. 98). Admittedly, these "other functions" can cover a lot of constitutional territory. Because they were delineated only vestigially by the General Assembly or the Security Council, an activist secretary-general such as Hammarskjöld had room for maneuver. Especially important from a political viewpoint was the fact that under article 99, "The secretary-general may bring to the attention of the Security Council any matter which in his opinion may threaten the maintenance of international peace and security." This provision has given the secretary-general freedom to take the initiative in cases where members may be too self-serving or inhibited to bring a serious dispute or situation to the attention of the world organization. The mere possibility that the secretary-general can invoke article 99, when warranted "in his opinion," may put members on notice. Hammarskjöld was not averse to using that threat much more than article 99 itself, which he only called upon once during his tenure. In short, the UN Charter—like the U.S. Constitution—provided opportunities for broad (as well as narrow) interpretations and for action (as well as inaction). A lot depended on the official doing the interpreting, that is, the one filling in the spaces.

Hammarskjöld made frequent and skillful use of press conferences, not only to inform the media about the significance of the world body but also to enlist their support for his diplomatic efforts. He also made extensive use of the *Annual Report of the Secretary-General to the General Assembly on the Work of the Organization*—nine of them on his watch—mandated by article 98. He used his introduction to those reports to express wide-ranging philosophical perspectives on the role of the secretary-general and that of the world organization. He also employed public forums for the purpose. In one of his most celebrated (and as it turned out final) speeches delivered at Oxford University in England on May 30, 1961, he epitomized much of what he had posited earlier. He stressed the secretary-general's duty to implement controversial political decisions. Especially, he stressed the need for the neutrality of international civil servants.[1]

After his unanimous reelection to a second term of office on September 26, 1957, with effect from April 10, 1958, Hammarskjöld, like some of the more activist American presidents, did not hesitate to add to his constitutionally delegated powers some undefined yet implied powers as well. He noted at the time that while he saw it as his duty to use his office to the utmost limit "and to the full extent permitted at each stage by practical circumstances . . . I believe that it is in keeping with the philosophy of the Charter that the secretary-general should be expected to act also without such guidance."

In 1960, when his activism came under heavy attack from countries such as the Soviet Union in connection with the Congo and from France in connection with its North African possessions, Hammarskjöld used a typical approach by delineating the alternatives of the world body's future:

1. a debating society robbed of its possibilities of action to preserve the peace, reverting to the passive and ineffective pattern of the League of Nations or
2. the active peace-maintaining organization that had been emerging since 1954 (i.e., soon after he took office)

As usual, Hammarskjöld gave his critics no alternatives but his own preferred solution. Among others, Soviet Premier Nikita Khrushchev realized that by broadly interpreting the directives of the Security Council or the General Assembly and by doing what he thought best when no guidance was forthcoming from these bodies, the secretary-general was in a way circumventing the Soviet veto; his decisiveness could unilaterally make up for the lack of appropriate majorities in these organs.

In his final *Annual Report* of August 1961, Hammarskjöld reiterated the dichotomy between a passive United Nations modeled on the League and the dynamic organization that he had been promoting for several years. He argued that the Charter itself went beyond the static concept of an international organization acting as a conference machine to resolve conflicts of interest and ideologies. The most conservative interpretation of the Charter contrasted with his own view that the United Nations was an evolving, dynamic instrument of executive action undertaken on behalf of all members. Its aims were to forestall crises by preventive diplomacy or resolve enduring conflicts by corrective diplomacy. Hammarskjöld kept repeating that where an international organ does not speak clearly, the secretary-general alone can implement policy and should do so.

In sum, Hammarskjöld came to believe that an individual, using powers granted to him in the UN Charter, UN resolutions, and common law precedent, and combining them with his own prestige and charisma, can stand up for principle even against the great powers. By doing so, he may at times influence important events. Hammarskjöld had discovered the path to circumvent stalemate, watered-down resolutions, and meaningless platitudes. As secretary-general, he would act when others did not. The position was about to evolve beyond the expectations of the world body's founders—or so Hammarskjöld may have thought, even though by now he should have known better.

Already during his first term, he was to learn the political weakness of the secretary-general's position when confronted by a determined major power. This happened in the case of Guatemala in 1954 and Hungary in 1956, when he was forced to comply against his better judgment with the wishes of the United States in the first case and the Soviet Union in the second.

Nevertheless, during his second term, Hammarskjöld continued to try to define his position in as broad a manner as possible—witness the Congo in 1960–1961. But he also showed that when it suited his purpose, he could adopt a minimalist stance, as he did in Lebanon in 1958. Still, he was at his best when he could use his initiative, as he did in Peking in 1955 when American fliers were held captive in Communist China.

HAMMARSKJÖLD AND
HIS ADMINISTRATIVE ROLE

What does the secretary-general, assisted by his staff, do? As the chief administrator, he is responsible for providing secretarial and support services (research, translation and simultaneous interpreting, organizing conferences, and other chores) to the other principal organs (except the World Court) as well as the affiliated bodies. He is also responsible for all personnel administration such as appointments, promotions, and disciplinary actions, including dismissals, as well as for budgeting and financial administration. The coordinating functions of the secretary-general are much more ambivalent because centralization is not clearly defined in the UN Charter and especially because the various subsidiary bodies have generally resisted it.

Administrative overlap becomes especially evident with reference to specialized agencies because the constitutional relationship between the principal organs (especially the Economic and Social Council [ECOSOC]) and these agencies (e.g., the World Health Organization) defies rational coordination. Each agency has its own charter, legislative and executive bodies, membership, and budget. Neither ECOSOC, which is supposed to coordinate the work of these organizations with the United Nations in general as well as with other specialized agencies, nor the secretary-general has any power of decision over their programs or budgets. Although Hammarskjöld took an active part in ECOSOC meetings, contributing his expertise in international economic matters, the record does not indicate that he had any substantial influence over specialized agencies, whose natural instinct is to guard their independence of action jealously.

It should also be recalled that even in Hammarskjöld's time, the several thousand secretariat employees located in New York, at UN European headquarters in Geneva, in most member countries, in field operations, and elsewhere dwarfed the League of Nations' 700 or so employees and made coordination that much more difficult. Linguistic, communications, attitudinal, and perspective problems compounded the complexity.

From the administrative viewpoint Hammarskjöld was primarily concerned with article 100 (1), which mandates the impartiality and independence of secretariat personnel, and with article 101 (3), which calls for their efficiency, competence, and integrity. Throughout his tenure, Hammarskjöld stressed fealty to the United Nations above everything else. On October 18, 1960, he told the General Assembly's Fifth Committee (the Committee on Administrative and Budgetary Questions) that "integrity means that officials should have only one loyalty in the performance of their duties, and that is the one to the UN." He disagreed completely with the view expressed by Soviet Premier Khrushchev that "while there are neutral countries, there are no neutral men." Hammarskjöld refuted Khrushchev's idea that an impartial international civil servant cannot exist in a deeply divided world.

HAMMARSKJÖLD AND
HIS ADMINISTRATIVE REFORM

Beginning with the administration of Trygve Lie and running down to this very day, many intergovernmental committees and groups of experts have examined UN work methods, personnel policies, compensation, planning, budgets and finances, decentralization, coordination, structure of the secretariat, functioning of the overall UN "system," and other administrative matters. Recommendations have sometimes been followed and occasionally implemented. Evaluations of the results have been produced.

During the Hammarskjöld era, initiatives for reform came mainly from the secretary-general himself. Upon his proposal, the General Assembly approved the creation of the Group of Three Experts in 1954, the Salaries Survey Committee in 1957, and the Committee of Eight Experts in 1960. It will be recalled that when Hammarskjöld assumed office, he had the reputation of being primarily an efficient administrator, and on his arrival in New York in April 1953, he pledged a commitment to his "overwhelming job as chief administrator of the United Nations Secretariat. To me it seems a challenging task to try and develop the United Nations administrative organ into the most efficient instrument possible." Halfway into his tenure, he had commented extemporaneously that "the first duty of the secretary-general must be to give to the staff and to staff problems their proper priority in the efforts. How can you possibly go into the field of political activity . . . if you have a feeling that the very basis on which these efforts have to be developed is a weak one?" Thus he constantly strived to streamline the administrative apparatus—in his own way.

The Charter does not specify how the top levels of the secretariat are to be organized. From the start, however, both the General Assembly and the "Big Five" created ground rules that had placed constraints on Trygve Lie in matters of organization and appointments. Lie did not find the arrangements that emerged totally satisfactory and had admitted to boredom with administrative details. In practice, lines of authority became increasingly blurred as senior secretariat officials (there were eight assistant secretaries-general) ended up being both heads of functional departments and top-level advisers to the secretary-general. Shortly before he left office, Trygve Lie recommended reforms for greater administrative efficiency that his successor ignored.

Rather, Hammarskjöld developed his own initiatives to bring personnel, finance, and legal affairs under his more immediate and personal direction. His plan took several years to implement, and by the end of his tenure the top echelons included the following:

> four heads of office—an undersecretary for General Assembly and related affairs, the legal counsel, the controller, and the director of personnel
>
> two undersecretaries for special political affairs (Hammarskjöld's additions) without portfolios, one of these also being the secretary-general's "chef de cabinet"
>
> three undersecretaries for political and security affairs, economic and social affairs, and trusteeship and information for nonselfgoverning territories
>
> one undersecretary for technical assistance (within the Department of Economic and Social Affairs)
>
> three undersecretaries for public information, conference services, and general services

In 1954, the second highest level had been upgraded from assistant secretary-general to undersecretary-general.

In his administrative as in his political functions, Hammarskjöld sought responsibility while giving himself maximum space for maneuver. For instance, he was always reluctant to commit himself to any permanent arrangements in case he was absent from UN headquarters or disabled. On this subject he reported to the General Assembly on November 7, 1957:

> It is only on those occasions when, due to unsatisfactory communications, the secretary-general is both absent and unavailable . . . that an arrangement should be made whereby a group or "panel," consisting of the under-secretary confronted with an urgent and important policy decision, not covered by existing policy lines, associated with two other

under-secretaries selected on the basis of geographical distribution, should make the decision.

His attitude was inconsistent with a General Assembly resolution of 1946 against excessive concentration of administrative power in the secretary-general's hands. Hammarskjöld noted that conditions had changed since then and that the secretary-general now had greater political responsibilities to shoulder. In one of his exchanges with the Advisory Committee on Administrative and Budgetary Questions he argued that "five years have passed since the adoption of new arrangements. . . . My personal experience does not lead me to share the misgivings of the Advisory Committee. Indeed, I should like to register the view that the present arrangements have proved entirely sound. . . . I do not myself see the slightest justification for proposing any changes."

There was continuing uneasiness that so much authority was being consolidated in his hands. In 1954, the Group of Three (dubbed "The Three Wise Men"), consisting of Lester B. Pearson of Canada, Victor A. Belaunde of Peru, and Prince Wan Waithayakon of Thailand, and in 1960 the Group (or Committee) of Eight Experts from Colombia, France, Ghana, India, the UAR, the United States, Britain, and the USSR again warned against concentrating excessive administrative authority in the secretary-general.

Occasionally, there were isolated expressions of dissent, even among senior staff. Conor Cruise O'Brien compared the relationship between Hammarskjöld and the latter to that "between a youngish headmaster and a bright sixth form." One of the best-known criticisms came from Guillaume Georges-Picot, a French senior secretariat official who publicly protested the great concentration of administrative power in Hammarskjöld's hands. Also, fault was found with his autocratic bureaucratic style, which regarded any significant disagreement with the secretary-general's views as "symptoms of a tendency to put other interests before those of the United Nations and—in some cases—of what I must call personal disloyalty." Georges-Picot resigned at the close of 1954, but the world was to hear from him again.

On June 14, 1961, the Group (Committee) of Eight Experts headed by Georges-Picot issued a divided report. Four members suggested reducing to no more than eight the number of officials reporting immediately to the secretary-general. Three other members of the committee proposed replacing the two existing undersecretaries for special political affairs with three new deputy secretaries-general serving one term and reflecting "the main political trends in the world order today." This would, in fact, have been a "subtroika" paralleling the Soviet Union's repeated preference for a troika of equal rank at the secretary-general's level. On June 30, 1961, Hammarskjöld, rejecting all three plans, issued a 40-point document including his own recommendations. In it he proposed two new categories of top aides: assistant secretaries-general for "political" duties and undersecretaries-general for "administrative" responsibilities. These plans were never put into effect.

Policy disagreements on the structure and workings of the secretariat were evidenced by some other high-profile separations from the service in the upper echelons under Hammarskjöld, terminations labeled "resignations" or "by mutual consent." Among the more notable ones, in addition to Georges-Picot, was the departure of Byron Price, assistant secretary-general for administrative and financial services, the top American at the United Nations at the time of his departure on January 29, 1954. Price was one of those who refused to accept the view, instituted by Trygve Lie, that unconditional loyalty to the secretary-general's prescriptions should be equated with loyalty to the United Nations. Hammarskjöld made such an autocratic attitude very evident when, in his letter of dismissal of a senior Danish secretariat official, Povl Bang-Jensen, of July 3, 1958, the secretary-general wrote the following, among others things:

> It is further my view that any moral reservations which might have prevented you from obeying my instructions do not ameliorate the impropriety of your conduct as a member of the Secretariat in refusing an order by the secretary-general relative to official papers. It is my view that if you considered your clear official duty to acknowledge my authority in Secretariat matters to be in conflict with your private moral convictions arising from an unauthorized assumption of authority, it was your duty to resign from the service.[2]

During Hammarskjöld's tenure, objections to the high compensation paid to secretariat personnel first became public. The secretary-general justified the pay scales on the grounds that UN salaries and fringe benefits at the senior level were far below corresponding diplomatic emoluments. He also stressed that a reduction in compensation would send a message to the world that UN jobs were unimportant and that the organization was not performing a useful function. Still, Hammarskjöld had to fight energetically to pay his undersecretaries a basic salary of $18,000 a year plus a representation allowance of $3,500 plus a special allowance, at the secretary-general's discretion, of $6,000 a year. Hammarskjöld's own base pay at the time was $40,000 a year. When first appointed, he had expressed a willingness to forgo all his emoluments but was dissuaded when others pointed out that such a precedent would not be fair to his successors, who might lack his independent means.

PERSONNEL PROBLEMS

By the end of Hammarskjöld's tenure, emphasis was already shifting to paragraph 3 of Charter article 101: "Due regard shall be paid to the importance of recruiting the staff on as wide a geographical basis as possible." Indeed, then as now, budget and personnel schedules were drawn up to satisfy the Fifth Committee of the General Assembly, responsible for allocating funds. Accordingly, on August 31, 1961, a total of 1,193 secretariat positions were subject to "geographic" distribution, and well over a third of these were held by personnel from developing countries, as indicated in table 2.1. These professional positions have always been the most important for secretariat personnel in terms of compensation, perquisites, prestige, and responsibility.

Historically, the developing countries have made two arguments to justify their insistence on, and even entitlement to, "equitable" geo-

Table 2.1   Origins of UN Professional Secretariat Staff Subject to Geographic Distribution on August 31, 1961

Western Europe	363
North America and Caribbean	294
Eastern Europe	107
Total developed regions	764
Asia	214
Latin America	112
Africa	61
Middle East	42
Total developing regions	429
Grand total	1,193

graphic distribution. First, they have proposed that efficiency necessarily involves adequate representation of all cultures and national perspectives. Second, even recruitment for the most top-level UN administrative posts has been politicized from the start. After the organization's founding, the permanent members in the Security Council came to an informal understanding about the division of the "spoils." Accordingly, the various assistant and later undersecretary positions have always gone to citizens of the "perms," so that there is, in fact, an operative "quota" system right at the top. Indeed, even Hammarskjöld's affiliation with a neutral country in a world divided into two major power blocs was an important consideration in his selection as secretary-general.

The increasing emphasis on geographic distribution at the expense of "merit" was paralleled by stress on short, fixed-term contracts as opposed to permanent career appointments. Hammarskjöld insisted that the proportion between the two forms of employment should also be determined by the secretary-general, and he favored a ratio of 75 percent permanent appointments and the balance fixed-term contracts. While he and his successor, U Thant, managed to uphold this distribution of positions, pressure was already building up to modify it. The new members' preference for fixed-term contracts stemmed from the fact that they had few eligible candidates whom they could spare for long to work at the United Nations instead of in their own hard-pressed national administrations. To them, rotation after anything from one to five years' UN employment made it possible for their representation in the higher echelons of the international civil service to be a basis of experience for use after the officials' repatriation.

The Soviet bloc countries also demanded fixed-term appointments for their nationals, but for a completely different reason. Despite Hammarskjöld's insistence on the neutrality of international civil servants, the Eastern bloc expected their personnel to retain primary loyalty to their home governments rather than to the international organization. Also, they were to stay in closer touch with their homeland, ties that the Communist states considered to be mitigated by long service abroad.

At the lower echelons of the secretariat, especially among staffers in the general services (in contrast to professional) category consisting mostly of secretaries, typists, clerks, and the like, it is not clear whether the sense of purpose and dedication—a major theme in Hammarskjöld's comments about the international civil service—

was very evident. Even the admiring Brian Urquhart conceded that "there were many staff members who felt neglected or insufficiently appreciated." After his initial "democratic" gestures mentioned earlier, Hammarskjöld did not have much involvement with those working below the 38th, executive, floor of the secretariat building. Staffers disagree about whether Hammarskjöld again made the rounds to shake hands with every employee in the complex after he was reelected for a second term. As Urquhart explained, "Under the pressures of political crises his [Hammarskjöld's] regular contacts with the various departments became increasingly spasmodic."[3]

Overall, by the end of the Hammarskjöld era, total secretariat personnel across the world had risen from 5,700 when he took office to some 7,000 by 1961, representing a 20 percent increase. This was consequent on the admission of new members and their demands for secretariat positions, the novel functions undertaken by the organization especially in economic and social development, and Parkinson's law of bureaucratic expansion and empire building. And this despite Hammarskjöld's constant efforts to save through tighter, more efficient, administration.

THE LOYALTY QUESTION

When Hammarskjöld assumed office in 1953, he found a new twist to the problem of loyalty. As the UN's host country witnessed an era of hysterically anti-Communist McCarthyism, there arose the question of the UN staffers' obligations to the state of their citizenship. American members of the UN secretariat were being asked if they had ever belonged to or were current members of the Communist Party or its fellow travelers or whether they had ever engaged in activities subversive to the U.S. government. This meant that it was now Hammarskjöld's turn to try to reconcile a member state's demand for a certain standard of national loyalty from its citizens on the one hand with UN requirements for employment demanding first and exclusive devotion to the world body and a pledge to act without political bias on the other.

Hammarskjöld had inherited a hot potato from his predecessor. Trygve Lie had dismissed 21 American secretariat members because they had invoked the Fifth Amendment of the U.S. Constitution protecting citizens against self-incrimination in their refusal to answer questions by federal investigative authorities. Secretary-General Lie refused to hire or retain any temporary or permanent secretariat employees who, as U.S. citizens, were even suspected of disloyal or subversive conduct against their own government. In this, he acquiesced to President Harry Truman's Executive Order 10422 of January 9, 1953, under which "full field clearance" was mandated for all American candidates seeking UN secretariat appointments. With minor procedural modifications, Hammarskjöld accepted the arrangements that he found in place. However, after taking office in April, he convinced the General Assembly that he should be the ultimate judge of the facts warranting dismissal or otherwise of employees whose conduct was alleged to violate the Charter and the UN *Staff Regulations*—the handbook of secretariat personnel behavior. He insisted that he should be the final arbiter of the validity of the evidence presented by governments about the disloyalty of their own citizens and that he would refuse to act on unsubstantiated charges against a staff member as long as the latter met the Charter's standard of integrity, independence, and impartiality. In short, he wished to ensure that the secretary-general's authority to appoint or dismiss personnel, which he enjoyed under the Charter and the *Staff Regulations*, were not invaded.

Theoretically, he could do this even vis-à-vis the United States. Under Truman's executive order, an International Organization Employees Loyalty Board was mandated to transmit confidentially to the secretary-general through the U.S. secretary of state its findings and reasons for regarding individual American secretariat employees as disloyal to their own country. It was then up to the UN secretary-general to assess the information and take any action (or none) on that basis. Since the loyalty findings represented opinions of the U.S. government, not directives to the secretary-general, Hammarskjöld theoretically had freedom to evaluate the latter on the basis of UN, not U.S. federal, standards.

But of course there was always the potential for political pressure, especially by a permanent member/leader of the non-Communist world, which hosted the world body and was also the largest contributor to UN assessments and voluntary outlays of all kinds. Conor Cruise O'Brien, the Irish scholar, delegate, and later UN representative in Katanga Province, Congo, observed years later: "On what might be called the McCarthy issue, Hammarskjöld bowed more gracefully and inconspicuously than Trygve Lie, but bowed none the less, to prevailing American opinion."[4]

CASE STUDY 2:
HIGH-PROFILE LOYALTY PROBLEMS

The following case is illustrative. On August 23, 1953, in Hammarskjöld's inaugural year, the UN Administrative Tribunal upheld the appeals of 11 of the Americans dismissed by Lie from the secretariat. Seven of these staffers had requested compensation instead of reinstatement and four the latter. But on September 2, Hammarskjöld notified the Administrative Tribunal that in the interest of the service, reinstatement for the foursome would be inadvisable and that therefore the tribunal should determine the indemnity due to them. The tribunal set the total at about $180,000.

The U.S. government objected to paying the staffers' compensation out of American taxpayers' money, asserting the General Assembly's right to reverse the Administrative Tribunal's awards. The General Assembly in turn requested an advisory opinion from the International Court of Justice at The Hague.

On July 13, 1954, by a vote of 9–3, the World Court determined that the General Assembly had no right on any grounds to refuse to give effect to a compensation award by the Administrative Tribunal. But on August 20, both houses of the U.S. Congress resolved that no funds paid by Washington to the United Nations could be applied to any of the awards. Thereupon Hammarskjöld proposed—and the U.S. government accepted—that a special indemnity fund of $250,000 financed from assessments on staff salaries—the UN's internal income tax—be used to cover these and future awards. The 11 Americans, represented by distinguished jurists such as Telford Taylor, Frank Donner, and Leonard Boudin, were finally paid in 1955. In effect, the American share of their compensation was still borne by the U.S. Treasury. But at least Hammarskjöld's face-saving compromise proved acceptable to all.

Hammarskjöld also worked out a clearer definition of the extraterritorial rights of the United Nations at its headquarters in New York vis-à-vis the host government. At that time, this matter also touched on the loyalty issue. Thus, in November 1953, he rescinded the permission that Trygve Lie had granted to the U.S. federal authorities to conduct surveillance, fingerprinting, and loyalty investigations "in the field" on UN premises. However, the security clearance requirements for American secretariat personnel, agreed to first by Lie and then by Hammarskjöld, continued until President Gerald Ford's

Executive Order 11890 of December 10, 1975, requiring a less onerous national security check.

But Hammarskjöld's problems with the host government were not limited to the loyalty of American UN personnel or UN extraterritorial privileges. There was also the issue of the U.S. State Department's denying passports to some American staff members ordered to travel abroad on UN business paralleling the State Department's refusal to issue visas to some foreigners bound for UN headquarters on official business. The 1947 Headquarters Agreement between the United Nations and the U.S. government specified free access for all individuals entering the country on legitimate UN business. Despite this, cases had occurred in which Washington either denied entry or placed restrictions on visitors' movements in the United States when they were considered "pinkos."

The cause célèbre in this respect involved Mrs. Alva Myrdal, a well-known Swedish sociologist who was the director of UNESCO's (United Nations Educational, Scientific, and Cultural Organization) Department of Social Sciences and the wife of Gunnar Myrdal, the executive secretary of the UN Economic Commission for Europe. In early 1953, just before Hammarskjöld took office, Mrs. Myrdal arrived in New York to attend a meeting of the UN Commission on the Status of Women. Because of her allegedly leftist leanings, the U.S. Immigration and Naturalization Service placed severe limitations on Mrs. Myrdal's movements in the United States after first refusing to honor her visa.

Hammarskjöld asked Henry Cabot Lodge Jr., the U.S. ambassador to the United Nations, to intervene with the federal authorities to define the access to UN headquarters of individuals found objectionable by the U.S. government, since the UN Headquarters Agreement between Washington and the international body does not spell out fully all privileges and immunities accruing to UN personnel. Recognizing the right of the host government to protect itself against genuine security threats, the two sides finally worked out a compromise. If any serious problem arose with respect to the access of a legitimate foreign visitor to UN headquarters or elsewhere, the federal authorities would consult with the secretary-general. Thus, by July of that year, Hammarskjöld was able to report that Mrs. Myrdal's visa would be valid outside of UN headquarters itself without impediments. There were no similar problems after that.

Hammarskjöld's contemporaries in the secretariat made widely different assessments as to whether the secretary-general managed to restore staff morale after the McCarthy episode. Brian Urquhart, the top Hammarskjöld aide who was undersecretary-general for special political affairs, remembered a definite improvement. Shirley Hazzard, later a well-known novelist but also a former secretariat employee holding at the time a relatively unimportant position, saw it differently. Commenting on President Truman's Executive Order 10422 permitting a full field investigation of Americans at the United Nations, she wrote of the "pervasive and repressive atmosphere created by such a condition, and in the debilitating conformity it implies and imposes among the majority of the approved."[5]

Obviously, not everyone was satisfied with the results. But the fact remains that UN staffers' loyalties to their own governments had particular relevance to secretariat employees who were U.S. citizens. Due to the hasty personnel recruitment in the early years of the organization, the number of Americans with experience from the Charter-writing San Francisco conference in 1945, the location of UN headquarters in New York, and the U.S. share of the UN budget, there was originally a disproportionately large ratio of American personnel. Such narrow geographic representation was greatly reduced following the admission of some 48 new members between 1955 and 1960 in Hammarskjöld's time. The newcomers, many from the underdeveloped world of Africa and Asia, demanded more equitable representation in the number of their nationals in the secretariat. And the record shows few cases of Hammarskjöld's challenging a member government when it lobbied for the appointment of ill-prepared senior staff.

This should be viewed in the context of his aforementioned Oxford University speech when he warned against attempts to politicize the international civil service. He explained that compromise with its necessary neutrality "might well prove to be the Munich of international cooperation," one "no less dangerous than to compromise with principles regarding the rights of a nation."

ADMINISTRATIVE PARADOX

Observers believe that at Hammarskjöld's death, some important issues in the secretariat relating to geographic distribution of positions, language requirements, permanent career possibilities as against fixed-term appointments, appointments by governments to particular posts, and working conditions—especially for female personnel—

remained unresolved. Hammarskjöld's record as the UN's chief administrative officer was a mixed bag. It is certainly not in that capacity that he won his legendary reputation. There is some irony in this inasmuch as *The New York Times* obituary of September 19, 1961, noted that "the big powers had selected Mr. Hammarskjöld . . . because they believed he would be content to be the efficient administrator and avoid a politically controversial role."[6] In fact, the truth turned out to be quite the opposite. The following chapter will show why.

NOTES

1. Hammarskjöld's Oxford University lecture is reproduced as "The International Civil Servant in Law and in Fact" in Wilder Foote, ed., *Servant of Peace: A Selection of the Speeches and Statements of Dag Hammarskjöld* (New York: Harper & Row, 1962), pp. 329–349.

2. UN press release SG/700, July 3, 1958.

3. Brian Urquhart, *A Life in Peace and War* (New York: Harper & Row, 1987), pp. 521–522.

4. Conor Cruise O'Brien, *Writers and Politics* (New York: Vintage, 1967), p. 211.

5. Shirley Hazzard, *The Defeat of an Ideal: A Study of the Self-Destruction of the United Nations* (Boston: Little, Brown, 1973), p. 58.

6. "Dag Hammarskjöld," *The New York Times*, September 19, 1961, sec. 1, p. 35.

3

The Events: Extension of Hammarskjöld's Authority

The previous chapter described how Hammarskjöld coped with the blueprint of governance—or lack of it—provided in the UN Charter. In order to do so, he used a number of techniques that gave him the flexibility he needed to project the world body into international affairs or at least to do his own bidding. After identifying these techniques, the chapter will discuss some of their more successful applications.

HAMMARSKJÖLD'S TECHNIQUES

Dag Hammarskjöld built a body of theory and practice that expanded the secretary-general's role—and with it that of the United Nations—to an unprecedented degree. More than any other person holding his position, he was committed to enhancing its authority to the maximum degree. Admittedly, the Charter's article 98 mandates the secretary-general to perform such nonadministrative duties as seem fit to the other principal organs (with the exception of the International Court of Justice), and no one was more willing to give these mandates the broadest interpretation than Hammarskjöld. But since he was reluctant to use article 99 to bring to the attention of the Security Council any peace-threatening dispute, Hammarskjöld began to devise techniques outside of specific Charter provisions to implement his activism. In this purpose, he was helped indirectly by the often vague or nonexistent guidelines that the Security Council and General Assembly provided to the secretary-general, being content to use "the means most appropriate in his judgment" to implement their directives. In short, there was ample opportunity to fill political space.

The techniques that Hammarskjöld used extensively emphasized his preference for quiet, behind-the-scenes maneuvering rather than open pressure. He always preferred preventive to remedial diplomacy and other methods. They all reflected his bias favoring solutions of the least intensity since, as he noted, "you can see how much more effective and smooth-working such a technique is than the regular one, which involves all the meetings and debates, and so on." Possibly, in using these quiet, behind-the-scenes techniques, Hammarskjöld had recalled the manner of operating of Sir Eric Drummond, first secretary-general of the League of Nations. The tradition of neutrality and non-partisanship that Drummond had brought over from the British civil service may also have impressed Hammarskjöld.

First, he used anticipatory diplomacy which, while vague and often overlapping with other techniques, was premised on his belief that prevention was better than cure. One of the better-known forms of this technique became peacekeeping, which Hammarskjöld did not invent but did help develop to its highest point as in the case of the United Nations Emergency Force (UNEF) at Suez in 1956 and especially of the United Nations Operation in the Congo, or ONUC (its French acronym) in 1960. Hammarskjöld identified preventive diplomacy as UN intervention in conflict outside of, or marginal to, Cold War struggles. UN action was designed to forestall the competitive intrusion of the rival power blocs. Hammarskjöld recognized most of the time that the United Nations could not enter the eye of the Cold War storm, the central arena of world conflict. When he failed to do so, he experienced setbacks, as the next chapter will evidence.

There were other manifestations of the UN "presence," whether by his personal representatives or special appointed groups. Hammarskjöld figured that when disputing member states became aware of such a UN presence, they would modify their political behavior from rigid to more tolerant. Such presence could also yield impartial information from UN personnel on the scene. Too, representatives of contending member governments might find release in sharing their concerns with UN intermediaries they could normally trust, especially secretariat personnel with an understanding of their positions. Hammarskjöld's representatives could intermediate with tact, impartiality, persistence, and with as little fanfare or "on the record" comment as possible. In short, he tried to avoid having an international dispute become a "federal case," so to speak, by its submission to the Security Council or the General Assembly. Rather, as in, say, the case of Cambodia and Thailand making mutual charges against each other in 1958 about aggression and border violations, Hammarskjöld managed to have them accept his good offices. Accordingly, a UN presence was at times tantamount to quiet diplomacy.

Indeed, as early as July 1955, in his introduction to the *Annual Report of the Secretary-General to the General Assembly on the Work of the Organization, 1954–1955,* Hammarskjöld pleaded for "more quiet diplomacy within the United Nations, whether directly between representatives of Member-Governments or in contacts between the Secretary-General and Governments."

He developed something akin to the U.S. constitutional principle of inherent powers. These powers flowed, he believed, from his position as secretary-general and its political and other duties, regardless of whether they were specifically provided for in the Charter or even authorized by the political organs of the United Nations. As the China case study will indicate, he came to call these inherent powers the "Peking formula." Most significantly, these techniques came into play in the Congo, a muddled internal and external situation in which the confident secretary-general did not hesitate to use his own judgment, with or without any kind of specific authorization, to do what he thought the intricate events called for. As he repeatedly explained in his Oxford University speech of May 30, 1961, in his final annual report for 1960–1961, and on other occasions, there were two possible views of the world organization. First, that it was a "static conference machinery" whose members could debate endlessly and fruitlessly. Or, second, that it was a "dynamic instrument" of evolution toward more effective forms of international cooperation. There was no question where the quiet secretary-general stood on this issue.

CASE STUDY 3: CHINA

On December 4, 1954, the United States, on behalf of the UN Forces in Korea, brought the question of 11 downed American airmen serving under that command before the ninth session of the General Assembly. The aircraft in which they had flown had been shot down on January 12, 1953, near the Yalu River marking the North Korean–Communist Chinese border. The crew was taken prisoner and eventually tried by a Chinese Communist military tribunal. On November 24, 1954, Radio Peking reported that they had been sentenced to long-term imprisonment as spies. On December 10, the General Assembly resolved that their detention as well as that of other captured UN personnel was a violation of the Korean Armistice Agreement of July 27, 1953, which called for the repatriation of all those who wished to go home.

The Assembly now requested the secretary-general to seek their release, perhaps with the hope that the United Nations, through its chief executive officer, would communicate with the People's Republic of China (PRC) better than the United States. The latter was the leading belligerent in the Korean War and active enemy of Communist China. Hammarskjöld, unlike Trygve Lie, had "clean" hands in regard to Korea, since he had long urged a negotiated settlement between the American-led United Nations Command and the North Korean–Chinese coalition. Hammarskjöld had also often supported the admission of Red China into the world body. For, as he explained, "if you want to negotiate with somebody, it is rather useful to have them at the table." Furthermore, Hammarskjöld's country, Sweden, had recognized the People's Republic of China and entertained diplomatic relations with it.

In deciding to contact the prime minister and foreign minister of the PRC, Chou En-lai, directly rather than through intermediaries, Hammarskjöld risked a rebuff that would have destroyed the possibility of getting the U.S. prisoners of war released. The secretary-general was also putting his own prestige on the line, since everything depended on Peking's interest in having any contact with a United Nations that, under U.S. leadership, had consistently denied Communist China a seat in the world body.

The members of the United Nations Command proceeded to instruct the secretary-general that he should attempt "by the means most appropriate in his judgment, continuing and unremitting efforts to this end," that is, to obtain the release of the airmen. But the tone of the resolution was judgmental and condemnatory, reflecting American hostility to the People's Republic.

By this time the United States, through the United Nations Command, had made five separate demands between September 9, 1953, and August 17, 1954, to get various POWs back from China, but without any concrete response. Still, Hammarskjöld stressed that in his capacity as secretary-general, his obligation was to try to reduce international tension anywhere in the world and that he did not work for any single power. It was thus the UN Charter, he explained, and not the General Assembly's action of December 10, that motivated his visit: "I go to Peking because I believe in personal talks—I can only say I will do my best." In short, he distanced himself from the Assembly's resolution and asserted instead his independent ability to intermediate with "authority under the Charter."

Hammarskjöld left New York on December 30, 1954, and was in Peking January 5–11, 1955. In his talks there, he treated the Assembly resolution offensive to the Chinese not as his orders, which had to be filled in every detail, but as a point of departure. He talked past it, stressing the personal nature of his visit and the secretary-general's own "special responsibility." He implied that he had come, not as an agent of the General Assembly but as the head of a coordinate principal UN organ, the secretariat. Rhetoric and diplomatic subterfuges aside, the bottom line was that China's Premier Chou En-lai agreed to meet with Hammarskjöld and that he was willing to accept the secretary-general's "Peking formula."

The latter was not based on Charter article 99 or any other, least of all on the Assembly's 47–5–7 resolution of December 10, 1954, but rather on Hammarskjöld's nebulous "authority under the Charter." In short, the Peking formula was one of Hammarskjöld's innumerable ambiguities used to fill in a constitutional or precedential space where he believed independent action was needed. His accomplishment not only improved his standing with the Eisenhower administration (especially as four other downed American airmen were released on May 29, 1955) but also established a precedent for the secretary-general's diplomatic initiatives in subsequent crises.

At first it seemed that Hammarskjöld had come back empty-handed from Peking. However, he made a point of continuing his personal contacts with Chou En-lai. But little more was heard about the airmen until, when celebrating his 50th birthday in Sweden on July 29, 1955, Hammarskjöld was advised that the 11 B–29 U.S. crewmen were about to be released. While the Chinese never acknowledged it, the world concluded that Hammarskjöld's ingenious and devious modus operandi had a lot to do with the gesture, as well as with their earlier release of the foursome who had been held captive in China since 1952 and 1953. Whatever the case, Hammarskjöld's mission to China became one of the major turning points in his UN career. His action in Peking demonstrated for the first time the effectiveness of his "quiet diplomacy" instead of the "bully pulpit." His success on that occasion and in the following year at Suez helped transform the secretary-general's office into one of key international importance. The "leave-it-to-Dag" syndrome began to take hold among the delegates from around that time.

SUEZ

During Hammarskjöld's tenure, the so-called Suez crisis had at least two dimensions. The first had to do with the Anglo–French–Israeli attack on Egypt, beginning on October 29, 1956, and its consequences. The second was related to Egypt's continuing refusal to allow Israel to use the Suez Canal running entirely through Egyptian territory. Although Egypt's denial of rights to Israel preceded the 1956 attack by several years, it will be shown that in fact there was some connection between the two and even linkages with the broader settlement of the entire Palestinian issue. It is in the first two cases that Hammarskjöld assumed a prominent role.

In a Security Council resolution of April 4, 1956, the secretary-general was requested to investigate the deteriorating situation in the Middle East and to report back within a month. Accordingly, Hammarskjöld left for the area on April 6 and issued his report on May 9, 1956, after visiting the countries concerned and consulting with their governments.

In the background of his trip were the armistice agreements of 1949 between Israel and its Arab enemies. These agreements had been repeatedly violated, especially during 1955 and 1956, when Israeli targets were attacked by so-called Palestinian fedayeen—suicide commandos operating primarily from the Egyptian-administered Gaza Strip and the Egyptian Sinai. Israel carried out reprisals and tension mounted. There were incidents along the Israeli–Syrian and Israeli–Jordanian cease-fire lines as well.

In his report of May 9 following up a progress report a week earlier, Hammarskjöld noted that the existing state of noncompliance with the four general armistice agreements was caused by political and practical circumstances as well as uncertainty regarding the agreements, not by an unwillingness of the governments to carry out their obligations. He went on to report that he had asked the governments concerned for assurances—which he received in every case—

that they would unconditionally observe their obligations under the cease-fire clauses provided the other party complied. In doing so, they merely reserved their right to self-defense under article 51 of the Charter. But Hammarskjöld also observed that "I have left aside those fundamental issues which so deeply influence the present situation," specifically, Egyptian interference with Israeli shipping through the Suez Canal and Israel's scheme for the diversion of the River Jordan. In his view, the reestablishment of full compliance with the armistice agreements represented a stage that had to be cleared to make progress possible on the main substantive issues, which he considered to be outside his mandate. He felt that if there was a general will to peace, it should be fostered and encouraged by the governments concerned. The world community, "as represented by the United Nations," should also support the establishment of peace.

However, new trouble was soon in the offing. On July 26, 1956, Egyptian President Gamal Abdel Nasser nationalized the Universal Suez Canal Company, after the United States, Britain, and the World Bank withdrew loans intended to help build the Aswan High Dam on the Nile. This move led to heavy protests by the British and French governments, whose national interests were most closely affected by the nationalization of the shareholder-owned company. Several public debates were held in the Security Council after the parties involved failed to reach agreement in the aftermath of the nationalization.

But it was in Hammarskjöld's office that the diplomatic work was really being done. On his own initiative, the secretary-general was meeting privately with the foreign ministers of Britain, France, and Egypt—the countries with the largest interest in the ownership, control, and operation of the waterway—with the hope of finding some basis for negotiations. Hammarskjöld synthesized what he heard and set down the following points of possible agreement:

1. free and open transit through the Suez Canal without discrimination
2. respect for Egypt's sovereignty
3. the operation of the canal to be insulated from the policies of any country
4. Egypt and canal users should agree on the level of transit tolls and charges
5. a fair proportion of these revenues to be allocated to the waterway's maintenance and improvement

6. disputes between the Universal Suez Canal Company (head-
   quartered in Paris), the owner and operator prior to nationalization, and the Egyptian government to be settled by arbitration

For a few weeks, it looked as if the three powers working discreetly
with Hammarskjöld would reach an agreement. A meeting to continue these discussions had been scheduled for October 29, 1956. That
was the day when Israel, with the fedayeen bases as their declared target, crossed the Egyptian border and invaded the Sinai Peninsula. The
next day, following a joint ultimatum to both Egypt and Israel to withdraw to within 10 miles of both sides of the canal (which in the case of
Israel meant a further advance of 100 miles into Egyptian territory), the
British and French began an air attack against Egypt. Their stated purpose was to secure unimpeded navigation of the canal for all nations.

But at the same time an Anglo–French invasion force was
approaching the area by sea from Cyprus. To observers, it seemed
apparent that the "invasion" and its "defense" had been prearranged.
Yet the Anglo–French charade continued when the two governments
"appealed" to the Egyptians and Israelis to halt all warlike operations
within 12 hours. Failing that, British and French troops would intervene to ensure that the canal remained open. Israel accepted the ultimatum, but Egypt promptly rejected it. (Subsequent memoirs by
British and French officials revealed that they had colluded first and
that Israel, through France, was brought in later to develop the script
of the tripartite attack.)

At the Security Council meeting of October 30, 1956, the British and
French vetoes blocked two draft resolutions by the American and
Soviet representatives for a cease-fire and the withdrawal of all foreign troops from Egyptian territory. Hammarskjöld was angered by
the fact that while he was negotiating with all parties, Britain, France,
and Israel were pursuing their own, different, agenda. He made it
very clear that he would have used article 99 of the Charter, empowering the secretary-general to bring peace-threatening situations to
the council's attention, had members not preempted him. He also
made it very evident that in a crisis such as this one, his views as secretary-general were necessarily activist. As he was to do several
times subsequently, he offered to resign if the members disagreed
with his broad interpretation of his duties. But in the meantime,
unaccustomed force and bluntness were evident in his verbal attacks
against Britain, France, and Israel for their invasion of Egypt. Many

delegations were surprised, but he received wide expressions of support in and out of the United Nations.

Because of the Security Council impasse, the Yugoslav representative called for transferring the issue to the General Assembly under the "Uniting for Peace" resolution of 1950, a procedural move to which the veto would not apply. This U.S.-sponsored resolution had provided for precisely such a procedure in case of Council deadlock in a peace-threatening situation. Yet this was the first time that "Uniting for Peace" was used. The motion to transfer the issue, which Hammarskjöld helped draft, passed 7–2–2, with Britain and France casting the negative votes. On November 2, the General Assembly adopted by 64–5–6 a U.S. draft resolution that followed the lines of the substantive Security Council version previously vetoed. It called for a cease-fire and the withdrawal of all foreign troops from Egyptian territory, and requested that the secretary-general report on compliance with the above. This time, the British and the French acquiesced, more because of American pressure than out of respect for the Assembly's resolution. Too, by now, the Soviets were threatening unilateral retaliation against the three invading powers, talking about the possible use of hydrogen weapons and recruiting "volunteers" to fight in Egypt.

During the Assembly debate, Lester B. Pearson, the Canadian delegate and foreign minister, first proposed the establishment of a UN police force, later known as a "peacekeeping force," "large enough to keep these borders at peace while a political settlement is being worked out." The Canadian resolution passed by 57–0–19. Despite Hammarskjöld's initial reservations about the concept and the practicability of such a force, he recognized that "my personal lack of optimism is of course no excuse for not exploring the field," an attitude he did not always evidence. But he drew up a plan for the United Nations Emergency Force (UNEF), unanimously approved by the General Assembly on November 5.

Using Lester Pearson's proposal for a "truly international peace and police force," the essential elements of Hammarskjöld's interpretations of the Canadian plan for a body "more than an observer corps but in no way a military [occupation] force" incorporated the following essentials:

1. The force would be temporary.
2. It would be strictly neutral; it could not be used to change the

military balance between the disputants; it would have the task of maintaining order, supervising compliance with the cease-fire, patrolling the truce lines, and observing the execution of the UN resolutions.

3. Troops for UNEF would not be accepted from the permanent members of the Security Council.

4. The force commander would be appointed by the United Nations and would be responsible to the Security Council or the General Assembly and be under the immediate supervision of the secretary-general.

5. An agreement of the parties on whose territory UNEF troops were to be deployed would be necessary.

Since the actual organization of UNEF became Hammarskjöld's responsibility and he had indeed asked the Assembly for "a margin of confidence" enthusiastically granted to him, he now negotiated with member governments over their specific troop and other contributions to the force and the conditions under which these would be used. He appointed Canadian Maj. Gen. E. M. L. Burns, until then chief of staff of the UN Truce Supervision Organization (UNTSO) overseeing compliance with the 1949 Arab–Israeli armistice agreements, to head the United Nations Emergency Force and worked out the rules of engagement with the general. Hammarskjöld also set up a UNEF Advisory Committee composed mostly of representatives from member states contributing troops to the force.

The first UNEF contingent landed in Egypt on November 14, 1956, and deployed along the Suez Canal zone. It consisted of some 500 men each from Brazil, Canada, Colombia, Denmark, Finland, India, Indonesia, Norway, Sweden, and Yugoslavia led by their own officers. The force eventually reached a full strength of over 6,000 men.

Designed for preventive rather than corrective action, UNEF's role was to interpose between two adversaries the presence of a third, neutral, party in the dispute. Accordingly, none of the troops came from a country even closely connected with the crisis. A peacekeeping force such as this may find itself compelled to engage in combat, as was to happen to ONUC in the Congo four years later, but such encounters remain a peripheral element of its mission. Unlike the United Nations Command in Korea under U.S. leadership, a peacekeeping force must always avoid intensified hostility. Its role is to prevent a dangerous interface from occurring in the first place or

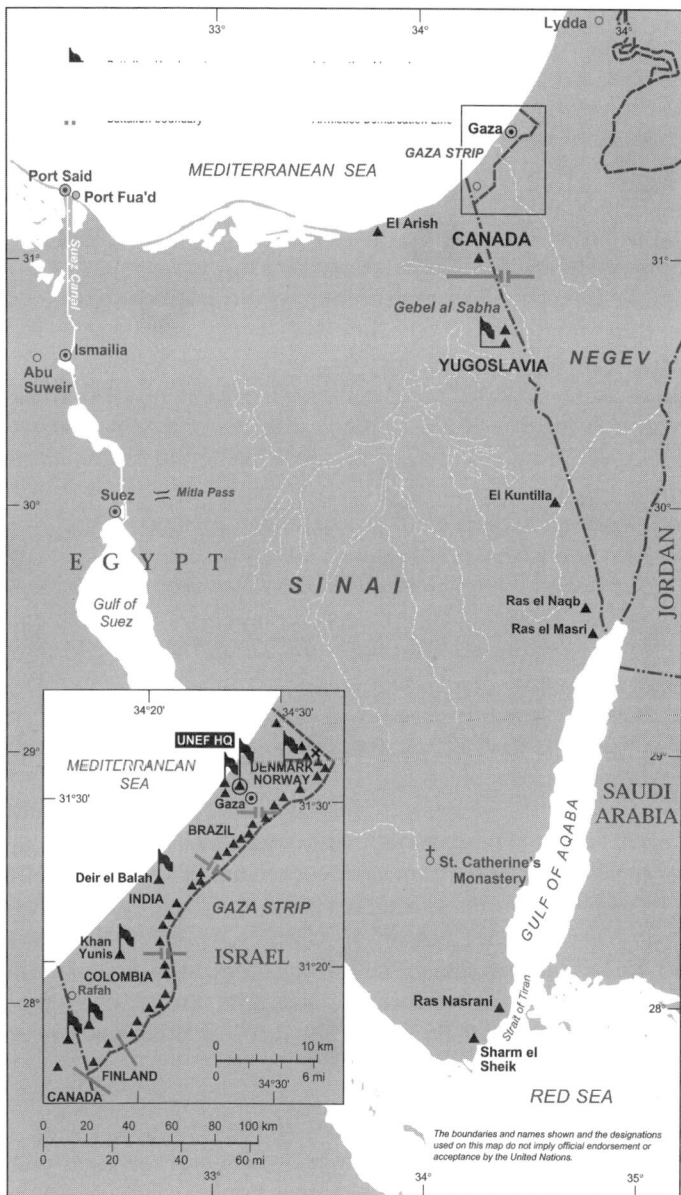

Map 3.1   UNEF I Deployment as of August 1957

Source: UN Cartographic Section.

from getting worse rather than to defeat an identified aggressor, as in the case of collective security under Chapter VII of the Charter.

Thus the UNEF mission at Suez consisted of two parts. First, it was to create a buffer zone between the Egyptian and Anglo–French forces and supervise the maintenance of the cease-fire under the General Assembly resolution of November 5. Second, it was later "to assure the scrupulous maintenance of the armistice agreements" between Israel and Egypt under the General Assembly resolution of February 2, 1957. The implied advantages of UNEF were even more important. The vacuum to be created by the withdrawal of British, French, and eventually Israeli troops would not be filled by superpower intervention. Too, the invaders were able to save face by claiming that they could now remove themselves because UNEF would assume responsibility for the security of unimpeded navigation through the Suez Canal. Finally, the arrangement obviated the need for even greater American opposition to the actions of its tripartite allies—Britain, France, and Israel. Of course, none of this would have been possible but for the fluke that the United States and the Soviet Union were on the same side of the issue.

The British and French forces withdrew by December 22, 1956, and the Egyptians reestablished their sovereignty over the Suez Canal zone. But negotiations were more difficult and drawn out between Hammarskjöld and Israel. Only after several General Assembly resolutions and especially increased American pressure did Israel finally remove its troops, first from the Sinai by January 22, 1957, and then from the Gaza Strip and the Sharm al-Sheikh enclave commanding the Straits of Tiran by March 7 and March 8, respectively. However, before Hammarskjöld could discuss the long-term UNEF role in the Gaza Strip—a narrow sliver of land 28 by 5 miles jammed with Palestinian refugees—the Egyptian administrators and police arrived and preempted several of UNEF's possible roles there. At any rate, the UN force began patrolling the entire 150 or so miles of the Egyptian–Israeli demarcation lines agreed on in 1949, but only on the Egyptian side. Israel had not granted UNEF permission to be stationed on its territory.

Before the force arrived in Egypt in November 1956, Hammarskjöld and his aides had ironed out with the host government questions relating to the size and makeup of the UNEF, its positioning in the country, and the rules of discipline applicable to its members. Except for the inclusion of troops from Canada—a British Commonwealth country and ally—there were few problems. The Canadian hitch was resolved by substituting logistical personnel in place of Canadian infantrymen from the Queen's Own Rifles regiment objectionable to Egypt. But this was not true regarding the terms of UNEF withdrawal from Egypt.

Under the gun, Hammarskjöld had gotten President Nasser to reluctantly limit Egypt's sovereign right to demand withdrawal before "its task is completed," a condition that Egypt would have to honor. As Hammarskjöld later explained:

> To push the text through, in spite of Nasser's determination to avoid this [condition], and his strong suspicion of the legal construction— especially of the possible consequences of differences of views regarding the task—I felt obliged, in the course of the discussion, to threaten three times that, unless an agreement of this type was made, I would have to propose the immediate withdrawal of the [UNEF] troops. If any proof would be necessary for how the text of the agreement was judged by President Nasser, this last-mentioned fact tells the story.[1]

But the conditions of such possible withdrawal continued to be ambivalent. Who was to determine when UNEF's task was "completed?" To wit, in an aide-mémoire that Hammarskjöld at one point characterized as a gentleman's agreement with Nasser, the secretary-general and the Egyptian president pledged to act in reciprocal good faith in any withdrawal of UNEF from Egypt. Under the terms of this "good faith" agreement that emerged after a seven-hour marathon meeting between Hammarskjöld and Nasser on November 17, 1956, when exercising its "sovereign rights," which included withdrawing its consent to the stationing of UNEF in Egypt, the latter would "be guided by good faith in the interpretation of the purposes of the force established in the General Assembly resolution of November 5" (creating UNEF "to secure and supervise the cessation of hostilities"). But as it subsequently transpired, there was more to this "good faith" interlock.

On June 18, 1967, Ernest A. Gross, a former U.S. deputy representative at the United Nations whom Hammarskjöld had consulted on occasion, revealed the existence of a memorandum written by Hammarskjöld on August 5, 1957, nine months after the creation of UNEF, insisting that all interpretations of the agreement had to be governed by his aide-mémoire. In the memorandum, reproduced in *The New York Times* on June 19, 1967, but whose distribution when written remains uncertain, Hammarskjöld noted that Egypt's acceptance of UNEF on its soil inferred that it also recognized the conditions of its withdrawal. To Hammarskjöld this meant prior approval by the General Assembly that the force's task had indeed been accomplished if the UNEF Advisory Committee first decided that such a step was necessary.

In defense of his highly criticized "hurried" action of removing UNEF from Egypt at Nasser's request at the end of May 1967 and the consequent Six Day War, Secretary-General U Thant was in turn critical of Hammarskjöld's actions. Reporting to the fifth emergency special session of the General Assembly on June 26, 1967, Thant said:

> It is understood that Mr. Hammarskjöld often prepared private notes concerning significant events under the heading aide-mémoire. This memorandum is not in any official record of the United Nations nor is it in any of the official files. The General Assembly, the Advisory Committee on UNEF, and the Government of Egypt were not informed of its contents or existence. It is not an official paper and has no standing beyond being a purely private memorandum, of unknown purpose or value, in which Secretary-General Hammarskjöld seems to record his own impressions and interpretations of his discussions with President Nasser. This paper, therefore, cannot affect in any way the basis for the presence of UNEF on the soil of the United Arab Republic as set out in the official documents, much less supersede those documents. . . . Israel, in the exercise of its sovereign right, did not give its consent to the stationing of the UNEF on its territory, and Egypt did not forgo its sovereign right to withdraw its consent at any time.

Thant further noted in regard to Hammarskjöld's statement that the final decision on UNEF withdrawal might have to be taken by the General Assembly: "This position is not only incorrect, but also unrealistic." It is hard to see what else the General Assembly could have decided "once United Arab Republic consent for the continued presence of the UNEF was withdrawn."[2]

Despite the controversy, the creation of a United Nations Emergency Force was a tour de force comparable to Hammarskjöld's triumph of personal diplomacy the previous year in Peking. In effect, soldiers who had been trained to fight and to kill were now asked to perform exclusively nonviolent tasks in a police-type force, obeying a top command structure that had little to do with their own leaders. The peacekeepers had to learn on the job to exercise a kind of self-restraint that was out of the ordinary in military preparedness. As U.S. ambassador to the UN, Adlai E. Stevenson, later told a Princeton University audience on March 23, 1964: "A United Nations soldier . . . is like no other soldier in the world—he has no mission but peace and no enemy but war." The establishment of UNEF meant that international order was no longer necessarily to be ensured by collective security action dependent on the consensus of all the permanent powers in the Security Council to use force in the interest of conflict management. It could also be provided by a peacekeeping force. Because UNEF had been approved by the General Assembly following the earlier stalemate in the Security Council, the conditions for its possible withdrawal were easier than if all five "perms" in the Security Council would have had to agree to its termination.

As far as Hammarskjöld was concerned, he had taken charge of an army, delegating great discretionary powers to himself in terms of operationalizing and administering the new international force. He even worked out the financing issue by getting the General Assembly to approve, on November 26, 1956, a special account of $10 million to be apportioned among all the member states on the same basis as their regular assessments. Hammarskjöld opined that these were "expenses of the Organization" within the meaning of article 17, paragraph 2 of the Charter.

But the members of the Communist bloc refused to contribute, claiming that all UN forces fell under the exclusive authority of the Security Council, which should also thus approve their funding. The aggressors should have been made to pay for peacekeeping consequent on their actions. Other states also eventually found the UN assessments inequitable and burdensome and either delayed payment or refused to contribute their share. It was only on July 20, 1962, because of the much more onerous funding of the United Nations Operation in the Congo, that the International Court of Justice at the request of the General Assembly issued an advisory opinion, in effect vindicating Hammarskjöld's view that peacekeeping expenses were also "expenses of the Organization" under the meaning of article 17 (2) of the Charter. During Hammarskjöld's tenure, UNEF expenses borne by the UN budget totaled some $115 million. The aggregate UN outlays for the force through its termination in May 1967 were some $200 million. These costs were exclusive of the regular pay of personnel and equipment, borne by the governments supplying the UNEF contingents.

The important bottom line of this novel venture was that it added up to a much more activist role for the secretary-general in maintaining the peace—at least in the short run. It went further than the specific provisions of Charter article 99, which merely allowed the secretary-general to place threats or breaches of the peace before the Security Council. While enhancing Hammarskjöld's image in President Eisenhower's administration in Washington as a skillful diplomat, the enterprise was also creditable to the world body itself. At that time, the peacekeeping innovation became the most conspicuous manifestation of the organization's role in the world, as well as of the secretary-general's.

LEBANON

The Lebanese crisis of 1958 was a domestic (intra-Lebanese) and regional (Lebanon versus the United Arab Republic of Egypt and Syria) conflict complicated by deep, mutual superpower suspicions. The Lebanese were divided among themselves because of President Camille Chamoun's plan to amend the Lebanese constitution to enable him to run for a second term. Chamoun, a Maronite Christian, also charged the United Arab Republic (UAR) with aiding and abetting the infiltration of Arab nationalists across the Syrian–Lebanese border to help Lebanon join the UAR. Accordingly, on May 22, 1958, Lebanon submitted a complaint to the Security Council charging intervention by the UAR in its domestic affairs. Lebanon alleged that the UAR had infiltrated armed bands from Syria into the country; that its nationals had participated in acts of terrorism and rebellion against the established authority in Lebanon and had supplied weapons to these; and that it had engaged in a violent radio and press campaign inciting the overthrow of the Lebanese government. The UAR rejected the charges, stating that the disturbances in Lebanon were purely internal and were mainly directed at the Lebanese president, who wished to amend the Lebanese constitution for his own purposes.

On June 10, 1958, a Swedish resolution recommended the dispatch of an observer group, approved by the Security Council, to determine whether there were illegal infiltrations of men or weapons across the Lebanese border. Hammarskjöld formed a three-member consultative body to become the Advisory Groups of the United Nations Observation Group in Lebanon (UNOGIL). It consisted of Galo Lasso Plaza, former president of Ecuador, as chairman; Maj. Gen. Odd Bull, commander of the Norwegian air force, as executive member and chief of staff in charge of military observers; and Rajeshwar Dayal, an Indian diplomat, assisted by a staff of observers. The three-member group was to evaluate the reports of these UN military observers and those from the United Nations Truce Supervision Organization (UNTSO) regarding possible infiltrations of personnel and equipment into Lebanon. In the meantime, Hammarskjöld shuttled back and forth between Cairo and Beirut, striving to secure pledges of noninterference by the UAR in Lebanon's internal affairs. The Lebanese government, along with the U.S. and British governments, distrusted Egypt's President Nasser as an Arab extremist and a willing tool of the Soviet Union.

When UNOGIL, in several reports, failed to confirm the alleged "mass infiltrations" charged by Lebanon, that country's foreign minister, Charles Malik, condemned its "inconclusive, misleading or unwarranted" findings. Thereupon, the Lebanese government increased its pressure on Washington to intervene. Although such pressure was supported by an array of Nasser's enemies, especially Iraq, Iran, Turkey, and Israel, it took a completely unrelated outside event to move the United States into action.

On July 14, 1958, a coup in Iraq eliminated the monarchic regime and replaced it with a government led by Brig. Gen. Abdel Karim Kassem. The U.S. Central Intelligence Agency (CIA) wrongly construed Kassem's coup as a Moscow-inspired, Nasser-led takeover threatening the Middle East. On July 15, the United States informed the Security Council that in response to a request by Lebanon for the help of friendly governments to preserve the country's integrity and independence, it had dispatched forces to Beirut. These were not to engage in hostilities, Washington explained, but only to assist Lebanon in its efforts to stabilize the situation. The U.S. forces, which had been instructed to cooperate with UNOGIL, would be withdrawn as soon as the United Nations could take over.

Accordingly, on July 16, some 10,000 U.S. Marines landed on a Beirut beach, shortly before British paratroopers started arriving in Amman, Jordan, of which fact the latter apprised the Council on July 17. The U.S. government justified its action, which Hammarskjöld had failed to deter, by using article 51 of the Charter, which states: "Nothing . . . shall impair the inherent right of individual or collective self-defense if an armed attack occurs against a Member of the United Nations, until the Security Council has taken measures necessary to maintain international peace and security."

On July 21, the Soviets vetoed a motion to expand UNOGIL to replace the U.S. force. And as was by now all too customary, no specific guidance or directives were forthcoming from either the Security Council or the General Assembly. But Hammarskjöld again filled the vacuum. After consultations with the UNOGIL Advisory Group, he created an expanded, better-equipped UNOGIL from a score of member states in order to provide an excuse for the U.S. Marines to withdraw while saving face for Washington.

In order to justify his initiative in expanding UNOGIL to comprise 636 men, 10 aircraft, and four helicopters on July 22, Hammarskjöld issued a quasi-ultimatum to the council: "Were you to disapprove of the way in which these [i.e., the council's] intentions are translated by me into practical steps, I would, of course, accept the consequences of your judgment." These words reechoed those he had used at Suez two years earlier and prefigured those he would use two years later in the Congo to justify his initiatives in filling space. In other words, he arrogated to himself the power to initiate or expand peacekeeping when the Security Council, frozen by veto, could not. Since the latter did not object to his act, this broadening of the secretary-general's authority became "constitutional" by default. Hammarskjöld repeated his initiatory role in Laos in 1959—and again got away with it. For no one had any better (or any) solutions and besides, nothing succeeds like success.

On July 31, with the election of General Fouad Chehab as Lebanese president and realizing that Iraq's coup had not in fact been part of a Soviet–Egyptian takeover plan, Washington accepted Brigadier Kassem's regime. On August 21, on the basis of an Arab draft resolution passed by the General Assembly, the secretary-general was requested to try to bring the affair to an end. By late September Hammarskjöld reported satisfactory compliance with the Assembly's resolution that he facilitate the withdrawal of U.S. forces from Lebanon (and British troops from Jordan). Withdrawal of the U.S. Marines was completed on October 25. On November 17, Lebanon notified the Security Council that cordial relations between Beirut and the UAR had been restored. The UNOGIL was terminated on December 9, 1958.

At one point, Hammarskjöld reportedly observed to aide Ralph

Bunche: "Of all Middle Eastern conflicts into which I have run, this is the one in which it would shock me most if it were to develop into a wide international clash." And it did not.

JORDAN

President Gamal Abdel Nasser's Arab nationalist profile cast its long shadow on Jordan as well as Lebanon. The Egyptian head of state had emerged larger than life after the Suez crisis in 1956–1957. He had won stature despite the tripartite invasion of his country and Egypt's swift and complete military defeat.

The rise in Nasser's stature in Jordan, especially among its large Palestinian population, as well as a hostile barrage by the Egyptian mass media against Jordan's King Hussein, threatened the survival of the Hashemite regime. The merger of Egypt and Syria as the United Arab Republic in February 1958 increased the perceived threat to Jordanian stability. As mentioned, in July 1958, the overthrow of a pro-Western government in Iraq and the assassination of King Feisal II—King Hussein's cousin—seemed to be the last straw precipitating the landing of British paratroopers in Jordan on July 17 and of U.S. Marines in Lebanon the previous day. Yet in the debates that occurred during the third emergency special General Assembly session of August 8–21, 1958, called by the veto-deadlocked Security Council, Hammarskjöld suggested that "some kind of radio truce" and even possibly "radio disarmament" between the feuding Arab "sister" nations could be arranged. The General Assembly resolution of August 21, applying to both Lebanon and Jordan, requested the secretary-general to make such practical arrangements as would adequately help to uphold the Charter principles and purposes in relation to Lebanon and Jordan, thus facilitating the early withdrawal of foreign forces from the two countries.

When Hammarskjöld arrived in Amman on August 27, his work was cut out for him. He had to achieve the withdrawal of British troops there, ease tensions between Jordan and the United Arab Republic (Egypt and Syria), and involve the United Nations in effective peacekeeping. However, the Jordanian government wanted neither a United Nations Emergency Force (as in Egypt) nor a border observation group (as in Lebanon). So, the ever inventive Hammarskjöld set up a "representative office"—without direct authorization by the Security Council or General Assembly—which was neither. When his plan was finally announced publicly on September 29, the secretary-general apprised the General Assembly that he had implemented its resolution of August 21 "to uphold the principles of the Charter in . . . Jordan." His purpose was to promote a good-neighbor policy among Arab states and to create an atmosphere favorable for the restoration of normal relations between Jordan and the UAR. The UN office in Amman was to watch local developments, keep headquarters fully informed, give well-considered advice where needed, and, if necessary, carefully mediate disputes.

Hammarskjöld appointed Pier Pasquale Spinelli, the undersecretary in charge of the UN European office in Geneva, as special representative of the secretary-general to assist in the implementation of the Assembly's August 21 resolution. Spinelli was to be in constant touch with Hammarskjöld and the Jordanian government. In addition to monitoring the Arab countries' radio broadcasts, he was to try to restore normal communications and transportation links between Jordan and other Arab countries, especially the UAR. The mission also eased at least one crisis. On November 10, 1958, eight days after the withdrawal of the last British paratroopers, a plane carrying King Hussein over Syrian territory was chased back into Jordan by two UAR fighter aircraft. After defusing that tinderbox, the mission acted as a catalyst among potentially hostile governments and as an outlet for their protests.

This technique of appointing special representatives was a favorite form of Hammarskjöld's "private diplomacy." Such UN presence allowed for face-saving arrangements to be worked out in private with a UN representative intermediating so that governments concerned could adjust their policies on controversial problems without public embarrassment. Admittedly, Hammarskjöld improved the odds of success by using the technique when chances of settlement were fairly good. He appointed skillful individuals for the task. Spinelli also performed ably in Togo in April 1960, when neighboring Ghana was rumored to have designs on the former French colony.

CAMBODIA/THAILAND

Late in 1958, several border incidents occurred between Cambodia and Thailand. Cambodia's historic fears of perceived Thai aggressiveness were indeed justified by past incursions into Cambodian territory by its more powerful neighbor. After Cambodia's complete independence from France in 1953–1954, pro-Western Thailand became concerned over Cambodia's cozy relations with the People's Republic of China. Charges and countercharges were exchanged in the fall of 1958, after negotiations between Cambodia and Thailand on a number of issues, including ownership of the inaccessible but symbolically important temple of Preah Vihear, had broken down. An abusive mass media campaign followed, and the world feared military escalation.

On November 29, 1958, Cambodia informed the secretary-general that Thailand was threatening international peace by concentrating troops and military equipment on the border and that Thailand had occupied the temple of Preah Vihear, which Cambodia considered to lie in its territory. The Thai response denied every Cambodian allegation. Thailand stated specifically that although it had increased police reinforcements along the border to prevent armed raids and infiltration by elements from Cambodia, it had not concentrated troops or military equipment. Finally, the Thais expressed a readiness to welcome a UN representative "to inspect our border area." Cambodia concurred.

Hammarskjöld's initiative was to appoint Baron Johan Beck-Friis of Sweden as his personal representative on December 22, 1958, to assist Cambodia and Thailand to find a way out of their difficulties, preferring that alternative to bringing the dispute to the attention of one or the other political organ of the United Nations. The Beck-Friis mission visited the two Asian countries from January 20 to February 23, 1959. On February 6, it was announced that the two governments had decided to restore normal diplomatic relations. The ambassadors from both returned to their respective posts two weeks later. Cambodia released all Thai prisoners it had captured, and the border was soon reopened.

Hammarskjöld was pleased at the rapid resolution of the dispute. He lauded the technique of sending missions as much more effective than the regular procedure of meetings and debates in public. He elaborated in his periphrastic style: "pragmatically we can find better ways to do the job, without at all departing from the Charter but, so to speak, adjusting the procedures so as to meet a concrete situation as conveniently and efficiently as possible." The fact that both sides had genuinely sought a settlement and were anxious to resume normal relations helped the process, which Hammarskjöld had described as "effective and smooth-working."

Still, the issue of sovereignty over the temple of Preah Vihear remained unresolved. On October 6, 1959, Cambodia began proceedings against Thailand at the International Court of Justice, complaining that the latter had persisted in the occupation of a piece of Cambodian territory where the ruins of the holy monastery stood. This was a sacred place of pilgrimage and worship for Cambodian Buddhists. Cambodia asked the World Court to declare Cambodia's territorial sovereignty in the area and to rule that Thailand must withdraw the detachments of armed forces it had stationed there since 1954. On May 23, 1960, Thailand filed preliminary objections to the Court's jurisdiction, and the proceedings on the merits were suspended pending resolution of the jurisdictional challenge.

On May 26, 1961, the Court delivered a judgment in which it rejected the two preliminary procedural objections raised by Thailand and upheld its jurisdiction. In its judgment on the merits rendered on June 15, 1962, the Court found that the temple of Preah Vihear was indeed located on Cambodian territory. It also held that Thailand was under an obligation to withdraw any military or police forces stationed in the temple or its vicinity.

PROLOGUE TO THE BAD NEWS

This chapter has included a diversity of cases straddling both terms of Hammarskjöld's tenure. In each case, the perceived national interests of the two superpowers were not diametrically opposed; often they were merely peripheral. Such political space made it possible for the secretary-general to actively enter the fray. Accordingly, fortunate circumstance and his diplomatic skills added up to his ability to achieve results—to manage international conflict. That these fortuitous factors would not always coincide—and their consequences—will become evident in the next chapter.

NOTES

1. Quoted from "The Hammarskjöld Memorandum," in Emery Kelen, ed., *Hammarskjöld: The Political Man* (New York: Funk & Wagnalls, 1968), p. 175.

2. Kelen, *Hammarskjöld*, pp. 175–177.

4

The Events: Limits on Hammarskjöld's Authority

Despite his many successes, Dag Hammarskjöld was not infallible at using or consolidating his powers or in projecting his influence to achieve the desired outcomes in trying to fill political space. The very terms "successful" and "unsuccessful," when applied to UN involvement, normally demand a distinction between tactical, short-term successes—such as securing a cease-fire or arranging for a peacekeeping force to stand between two adversaries and thereby defuse conflict—and strategic long-range results such as bringing about a lasting political settlement. Obviously, the application of different criteria can make a big difference in evaluating events.

For instance, Hammarskjöld's most innovative action—the deployment of the United Nations Emergency Force in Egypt in 1956—has proven in hindsight to have been merely a temporary stopgap measure, neither producing a permanent settlement of borders, solving the issue of navigation in the Suez Canal, nor answering the Palestinian refugee question. Only after two more wars between Egypt and Israel in 1967 and 1973, and President Jimmy Carter's personal mediation at Camp David was an agreement between the two former belligerents signed in 1979, long after Hammarskjöld's day. And it was not brokered by the United Nations at all. Even the Washington "handshake agreement" of 1993 between Israel and the Palestine Liberation Organization (PLO) barely mentioned the Palestinian refugee problem.

In the case of Hungary, where the Soviets proved less "persuadable" than the British and the French had been at Suez, it took the collapse of Communism and of the Eastern European bloc beginning in 1989 for the case to be "settled." Even with Western powers,

Hammarskjöld did not always prevail in the short run—say, with the Americans over Guatemala in 1954 or the French over Algeria or Bizerte in 1961—because specific circumstances and personalities were not propitious for the application of Hammarskjöld's political skills. His mediation in Laos in 1959 was equally unsuccessful if one considers that peace there was effectively restored only at the conclusion of the Vietnam War in 1975 on terms acceptable to a victorious North Vietnam.

The case of Povl Bang-Jensen illustrates that in Hammarskjöld's own bailiwick, at the UN secretariat, his dismissal of a subordinate may have proved to be a pyrrhic victory given the controversy that followed and the possible blemish on Hammarskjöld's administrative skills.

NAVIGATION RIGHTS
IN THE SUEZ CANAL

After his easy reelection in 1957, Hammarskjöld again momentarily forgot the limitations on his power. He declared that the secretary-general, though lacking both a territory of his own or a legislative body to back him up, "can talk with much greater freedom, much greater frankness and much greater simplicity in approaching Governments than any Government representative can do. . . . I do not know the exact capacity of this machine. It did take the very steep hill of Suez; it may take other and even steeper hills." Hammarskjöld's quote displays the pride he felt in the UN response to the tripartite invasion of 1956. But reversing the outcome of that invasion still left unsettled, among others, the vital issue of Egypt's continued prohibition of the use of the Suez Canal by Israeli ships or cargo in other vessels bound to and from Israel. Yet a confident secretary-general continued to believe that such a matter could be settled far more easily than through war. Clearing of the Suez Canal from the obstructions sunk in it by the Egyptians during the Suez War was begun on December 29, 1956. The waterway was reopened to international traffic on April 28, 1957.

Egypt adopted the legal position that under the Constantinople Convention of 1888 (signed by the Ottoman Empire—Egypt's overlord at the time—and the world's major maritime powers), it retained the right to take effective defensive measures against all its enemies.

Although the convention guaranteed freedom of navigation to all civilian and naval vessels, this guarantee was not meant to interfere with the right of Egypt—a sovereign state since 1922—to engage in all measures "necessary to take for securing by their own forces the defense of Egypt."

Since Egypt had never signed a peace treaty with Israel, merely the 1949 armistice following the first Arab–Israeli war, it claimed that its legal state of belligerency with Israel continued. Hence, that it could legally bar its enemy from its territory and waterway. In contrast, the Israeli position was that the armistice, while not establishing peace, was supposed to terminate "acts of belligerency." Since closing the canal to Israeli shipping was such an act, Egypt should discontinue it.

The controversy regarding Israel's freedom of navigation through the Suez Canal had started long before its nationalization by President Nasser in July 1956. On September 1, 1951, the Security Council had denied Egypt's claim that a state of war or defense necessities justified closing the waterway to Israeli shipping. The council called on Egypt to "terminate the restrictions on the passage of international commercial shipping and goods through the Suez Canal wherever bound." But the British forces stationed along the canal and thus in physical control of the waterway did not compel the Egyptians to open it for Israeli use. In 1954, the Israelis tried to force the issue by running one of their vessels, the *Bat Galim*, through the waterway. The attempt failed.

When the 80,000 British troops and airmen defending the canal finally withdrew in June 1956, thus implementing the Anglo–Egyptian agreement of October 19, 1954, the issue of Israeli navigation rights was still unresolved. But now, for the first time since the British invasion of 1882 and the defeat of an Egyptian army, the Egyptians took physical control of the "ditch built on the skulls of 100,000 Egyptians" (as President Nasser had put it in his nationalization speech). Financially, too, Egypt assumed control following nationalization when the Egyptian government decreed that the Egyptian Suez Canal Authority would take over title to the Universal Suez Canal Company and collect transit tolls.

On October 13, 1956, the Security Council reaffirmed its position. The council declared that "there should be free and open transit through the Canal without discrimination overt or covert," reechoing its 1951 resolution. In January and February 1957, while bargaining about their evacuation from occupied Egyptian territories, the

Israelis again raised the question of their freedom to use the waterway. Prime Minister David Ben-Gurion demanded that the United Nations guarantee the latter as a condition for Israeli withdrawal. President Eisenhower, while putting pressure on Israel to do so, said, "We should not assume that, if Israel withdraws (from the Sharm al-Sheikh area on the Straits of Tiran), Egypt will prevent Israel's shipping from using the Suez Canal or the Gulf of Aqaba. If unhappily, Egypt does hereafter violate the Armistice Agreement or other international obligations, then they should be dealt with firmly by the society of nations."

A few days earlier, U.S. Secretary of State John Foster Dulles injected a new dimension for settlement. In a memorandum of February 11, 1957, to the Israeli ambassador in Washington, he suggested, "In the absence of some overriding decision to the contrary, as by the International Court of Justice, the United States, on behalf of vessels of United States registry, is prepared to exercise the right of free and innocent passage and to join with others to secure general recognition of this right." In two letters by the Egyptian foreign minister to Hammarskjöld dated April 24 and July 18, 1957, Egypt accepted the compulsory jurisdiction of the International Court of Justice in all legal disputes arising from the application of the Constantinople Convention of 1888 and therefore relating to the Suez Canal. But Israel did not do likewise, possibly because it did not wish to raise the issue of the applicability of the 1888 convention to nonsigners like itself. Scholars of international law themselves are sharply divided over the respective merits of the Egyptian and Israeli positions regarding the closure of the canal to Israel, now merely of historical interest. Also of historical interest may be the fact that a later UN secretary-general, Boutros Boutros-Ghali, supported Egypt's legal stance at the time.

At any rate, while insisting that the continued state of belligerency between Egypt and Israel justified his closing the waterway to his enemy, President Nasser also noted that other Middle Eastern problems should have priority in solution. Israel's failure to internationalize Jerusalem as called for in the General Assembly's partition resolution of November 29, 1947, and its denial of the rights of Palestinian refugees also demanded international attention. Nasser wondered aloud why Egypt should reward what he called Israeli aggression by opening the canal so soon after its October 1956 attack. In the meantime, he indicated that he was satisfied with "peaceful conditions without a settlement."

While standing firm on their interpretation of principle, the Egyptian authorities temporarily closed their eyes to the passage of Israeli cargoes in non-Israeli bottoms transiting the canal. But on February 26, 1959, the Egyptian Suez Canal Authority impounded the cargo of a Liberian freighter carrying goods from Israel to Asian ports. On March 13, 1959, the incident was repeated with a West German ship. These events brought a firm protest from Hammarskjöld. In his view, Egypt's impoundments contravened its guarantee of freedom of navigation for all according to the Constantinople Convention. This was one of the few instances in which Hammarskjöld clearly voiced public criticism of a sovereign nation's policy. His censure echoed his public condemnation of the three countries that had attacked Egypt in 1956 and of the Soviet Union's aggression against Hungary. Egypt's legalistic reply to Hammarskjöld was that the cargo would be released if title to the freight had already passed to legitimate non-Israeli purchasers of the goods.

On July 2, 1959, Hammarskjöld met with President Nasser and Foreign Minister Mahmoud Fawzi in Cairo. The secretary-general had earlier characterized as "utter nonsense" a formula that Foreign Minister Fawzi first mentioned to Ralph Bunche on April 20. Hammarskjöld now borrowed and enshrined that "nonsense" into an "effective stand" benchmark. Goods shipped from Israel f.o.b. (free on board), that is, already belonging to a foreign destinee, and goods shipped to Israel c.i.f. (carriage, insurance, freight), title to which was still held by a foreign shipper until fully paid for in exchange for clearing documents, would not rate as Israeli cargo and thus qualify for Suez Canal transit. While the freight was passing in either direction through the waterway, some non-Israeli would hold title to it and thus Egypt would not lose face by letting the commodities through. Hammarskjöld urged secrecy about this particular tool of "quiet" diplomacy. Yet by July 6, the "effective stand" arrangement had been disclosed by at least one New York newspaper. The secretary-general still hoped that Egypt and Israel would make concessions and that it would be possible for all to go back to the situation that had existed between April 1957 and February 1959, when Egypt tacitly accepted the passage of Israeli cargoes through the waterway in non-Israeli vessels.

In December 1959, the Israelis tried to make another test run through the canal when a Greek freighter was carrying cement from Haifa to Djibouti. Despite Hammarskjöld's urging to let it through, the Egyptians held that prior publicity had already informed the world about the attempt. When the vessel finally arrived in Port Said, at the canal's northern entrance, on December 17, the authorities detained it. Israel now pressured the World Bank to withhold a proposed loan to Egypt for improving the waterway until the latter changed its policy regarding Israeli navigation through the canal. However, Egypt's loan was unanimously approved by the World Bank's board of directors, which refused to consider anything but the technical and development plans on which the loan was based. Israeli Prime Minister Golda Meir lambasted both the "helpless" secretary-general and the "Egyptian dictator" for this outcome.

Hammarskjöld and Ralph Bunche visited Nasser and Fawzi in January 1960. They were told that the entire incident involving the Greek vessel was a gimmick to break the Suez Canal blockade or freeze the World Bank loan. Hammarskjöld's reply that the Greek vessel had met Egypt's "effective stand" formula was ignored, and the two sides parted in frustration. Hammarskjöld received much criticism for his "disgraceful failure" from many sources, including the United States. From then on the Egyptians, after impounding the cargoes, would release the detained vessels, but Hammarskjöld recognized that it would be "time lost for me to argue the Suez case." He realized that Middle Eastern enmities were a matter of an irresistible force meeting an immovable object. If the issue was not complicated enough, the field of contention became even more chaotic when the superpowers began to arm the disputing parties. The Cold War joined with regional strife to prevent solution of the canal navigation issue.

At the end, the question of navigation rights for Israel through the Suez Canal was solved by political rather than legal or other means. Thanks to the intermediation of U.S. Secretary of State Henry Kissinger, the Egyptians allowed the Israelis to ship their cargoes through the waterway in foreign-flagged vessels as part of a Sinai disengagement agreement in 1975. But Israeli vessels flying their own flag did not transit the 100-mile "ditch" until the Egyptian–Israeli peace treaty of March 1979.

CASE STUDY 4: PALESTINIAN REFUGEES

Until the Palestinian refugee problem became evident between 1947 and 1949, it had always been assumed that any given refugee situation would only be a temporary one. The refugees would return to their homes or, alternatively, start new lives elsewhere. This perspective changed with the Palestinian situation.

The problem started on November 29, 1947, when the UN General Assembly, in response to Britain's formal notification that it would relinquish its post-World War I mandate over Palestine on May 14, 1948, proposed its partition plan. The latter called for dividing the area into a Jewish and an Arab state and for the internationalization of Jerusalem, a holy city for Jews, Christians, and Muslims. Even though the Jewish community leaders accepted the partition plan on the grounds that half a loaf was better than none, the Arab governments and Palestinian community heads rejected partition. With the Palestinian Arabs being the majority population in the British mandate, they expected to control the entire Holy Land and certainly not 43 percent of the area that the General Assembly had assigned to them by a 33–13 vote. As both sides had been feverishly arming for the anticipated military confrontation, the Palestinian exodus began, not only from sections with a Jewish majority but also from predominantly Arab towns. Whether out of fear, out of Jewish pressure, or in response to their own leadership, hundreds of thousands of Palestinian Arabs fled their homes in 1948 and 1949.

So unique was this flight that the Palestinians, unlike other refugees, never became the responsibility of the United Nations High Commissioner for Refugees (UNHCR) but temporarily remained the concern of a separate agency, the United Nations Relief for Palestine Refugees (UNRPR). When it started to appear that there would be no short-term Middle Eastern solution, the United Nations Relief and Works Agency for Palestine Refugees (UNRWA) was established on December 8, 1949. The UNRWA was to be financed by voluntary contributions and to act as a semiautonomous body. Its functions would provide emergency assistance and draft plans to integrate the Palestinians into the economies of their host countries. Indeed, such relief and works programs were to be carried out in collaboration with local governments. In February 1954, Hammarskjöld appointed Henri Labouisse, a Frenchman whom the secretary-general had met when both were involved with the Marshall Plan in Paris, to be the director-general (later commissioner-general) of the Beirut-based agency. Since then, the question of the Palestinian refugees has been considered at every General Assembly session, which yearly pledges amounts to meet the UNRWA budget. In Hammarskjöld's time, the agency provided a daily outlay of some U.S. $.10 per refugee to ensure a diet of 1,500 to 1,600 calories, shelter in huts or tents, and social and welfare services.

By the end of Hammarskjöld's tenure, living conditions for Palestinian refugees had generally improved. The UNRWA delivered to those on the refugee rolls (by now about a million) food and health care, but especially schooling and vocational training. Still a number of the younger men were becoming "fedayeen" (literally, those who sacrifice themselves), later known as terrorists by their detractors. And for most refugees, camp life to this day has meant boredom, poverty, insecurity, frustration, bitterness, and potential violence. From the start, most have been reluctant to resettle in host countries and insist on repatriation.

Palestinian refugees are also a problem because they have often been unwelcome in their Arab host countries, which, with the exception of Jordan, have refused to grant them citizenship. These stateless people are rarely integrated into the national life of the host countries for a number of political, social, and economic reasons. Clashes between these Palestinians and local authorities have been frequent, and some of these eventually resulted in further exile or even massacre.

Accordingly, by the time the various Arab–Israeli armistice agreements were signed in 1949, there were some 280,000 Palestine refugees in the West Bank (under Jordanian rule between 1948 and 1967), 70,000 in the East Bank in Jordan proper, 190,000 in the Gaza Strip (under Egyptian military control from 1948 to 1967), 100,000 in Lebanon, 75,000 in Syria, 7,000 in Egypt, and 4,000 in Iraq. In several of these countries the Palestinians were at best tolerated.

Palestinians at first hoped to return to the half dozen cities and some 370 villages from which they had come. Nearly all their property had been left behind. But the Israelis soon made it clear that the Palestinians' repatriation would be difficult if not impossible. According to the Israelis, the Palestinians had left voluntarily and their return to a Jewish state would cause a major security problem. Moreover, Jewish immigrants had in the meantime settled where the Palestinians had lived and assumed property rights. Thus Israeli policy has been that the return of any Palestinians—in minute numbers at best—would only occur in the context of an overall Arab–Israeli peace settlement. The same went for compensating Palestinians who had left property behind. In this regard Israel had counterclaims in respect to property left behind by Jews migrating—voluntarily or otherwise—from Arab lands to Israel.

In short, the General Assembly resolution of December 11, 1948, calling for either repatriation or compensation of the Palestine refugees has remained unimplemented. Hammarskjöld believed that the parties in the dispute should accept responsibility for the refugees and hoped that the General Assembly's resolution would be applied. He also worked on an alternative plan to help host countries develop sufficiently to enable them to integrate the refugees if there was such an inclination. However, the secretary-general sought a proviso that such de facto integration would not prejudice any of the refugees' rights under the 1948 resolution. To this end the United Nations and the World Bank were to fund an Arab development board that would assist host governments willing to resettle the Palestinian refugees in their countries. Nothing happened because of inter-Arab rivalry and because of the Arab host countries' suspicions that the plan was in fact a gimmick for permanent absorption of the Palestinians.

Even though the movement toward peace between Israel and the holdout Arab states and the Palestinians has intermittently looked more promising, the Palestinian refugee problem still awaits a political and financial solution. The problem has grown in scope since Hammarskjöld's time because of the Israeli occupation of the West Bank and Gaza Strip consequent to the 1967 Six Day War. Too, the poorer and more illiterate Palestinians have a high birthrate. Tragically, the end of the Jewish diaspora after two millennia and the beginning of the Palestinian diaspora have left in their wake dilemmas that have bedeviled Arab–Israeli and UN peace efforts well into the twenty-first century. Hammarskjöld realized that his best efforts could only nibble at the margins of the problem, and he proved to be right.

GUATEMALA

The Guatemalan case is noteworthy. It was the first time that a regional organization could have become involved in an issue discussed at the Security Council. It represents an unsuccessful effort by Hammarskjöld to score a point over a determined member government—the United States. To be sure, there had been a minor skirmish between Hammarskjöld and Washington sometime earlier. The secretary-general had questioned the prevalence of U.S. decision making in the supposedly unified United Nations Command in the

Korean War and had insisted on "peace without vengeance." However, in that "UN action," as in the Persian Gulf War of 1991, the role of the United Nations in truth was secondary to that of the powers directly concerned.

The disagreement between Hammarskjöld and the U.S. delegation to the UN in the Guatemalan situation flowed from Hammarskjöld's insistence that the case remain on the Security Council's agenda even though the adamant American position made the outcome nearly predictable. But first, the facts.

Late in 1953, the Eisenhower administration decided that the regime of President Jacobo Arbenz Guzman, having held office in Guatemala since March 1951 and known for its leftist tendencies, had to be replaced. The Arbenz government had earned the enmity of the United States by expropriating land belonging to the U.S.-based United Fruit Company under its Agrarian Reform Law of June 1952. A dispute ensued regarding the amount of fair compensation owed to United Fruit. Supported by the U.S. State Department, it demanded over $15 million, whereas the Guatemalan government was offering $627,572. But much more than money was involved. Guatemala had by now imported weapons from Communist Eastern Europe and instituted social reforms that were redolent of Communism in the eyes of the U.S. government. Accordingly, the American military and intelligence communities sponsored an invasion of Guatemala from neighboring Honduras led by another Guatemalan officer, Col. Carlos Castillo Armas, and a small band of rebel followers. As early as January 1954, the Arbenz regime had charged that a plot was being hatched between Washington and Colonel Castillo Armas. At that time, the U.S. government denied its involvement in any coup attempt. But President Dwight Eisenhower later admitted in his memoirs about the event that "we had a very desperate situation . . . and we had to get rid of a Communist government."

It was finally on June 17, 1954, that Colonel Armas with 150 supporters invaded Guatemalan territory from Honduras. On June 19, aircraft coming from the direction of Honduras and Nicaragua bombed Guatemala City, San Jose, and other towns. The ensuing fighting involved great incompetence on both sides, as the Arbenz regime had difficulty mobilizing its own army. Two U.S. planes shot down over Guatemala City were replaced by three more U.S. aircraft. The Arbenz administration capitulated on June 27 and a military junta headed by Col. Castillo Armas took over. Armas became

Guatemala's president about two weeks later, reversed all the social-istic measures of the Arbenz regime, returned the nationalized land to the United Fruit Company, and initiated a Communist witch hunt.

Back at the United Nations, the Guatemalan government had on June 19 requested an urgent meeting of the Security Council. It hoped for measures to halt hostile overflights of Guatemalan territory and "a stop to aggression in progress" at the bidding of "foreign monop-olies" supported by the United States. At that Security Council meet-ing, the Guatemalan minister of external relations charged that the invaders had already advanced nearly 10 miles inside his country, but both Honduras and Nicaragua denied it. They asked that the issue be transferred to the Organization of American States (OAS) from the Security Council. Together with Brazil and Colombia, they referred to Charter article 52, which provides that "nothing in the present Charter precludes . . . regional arrangements or agencies from dealing with such matters relating to the maintenance of inter-national peace and security as are appropriate for regional action."

Still, a qualifying clause—"provided that such arrangements or agencies and their activities are consistent with the Purposes and Principles of the United Nations"—adds some ambivalence as to the enforcement power of regional organizations and their relationship to the United Nations. According to the interpretation of U.S. ambas-sador to the United Nations Henry Cabot Lodge Jr., it was manda-tory that the regional organization discuss a situation before the Security Council acted.

For his part, the Guatemalan representative insisted that since aggression, not merely a dispute, was involved, Charter articles 34, 35, and 39 empowering the Security Council to restore international peace and security were applicable, giving his country an unchal-lengeable right to appeal to the UN organ. The Guatemalan delegate rejected Lodge's refuge behind article 33, which states, "The parties to any dispute, the continuance of which is likely to endanger the maintenance of international peace and security, shall, first of all, seek a solution by . . . resort to regional agencies or arrangements." In turn, Hammarskjöld pointed to paragraph 4 of article 52: "This Article in no way impairs the application of Articles 34 and 35" per-mitting the Security Council to intervene, despite the existence of a pertinent regional organization to which both disputant govern-ments belonged. In Hammarskjöld's opinion there was no basis in law or practice for the U.S. proposition that Guatemala first had to seek a remedy at the OAS, the regional organization, before it could turn to the United Nations. This view was consistent with Hammarskjöld's constant efforts to keep the world body in the picture in international political affairs.

Historically, however, the United States has preferred to have hemispheric disputes discussed in the OAS rather than in the world body, and Guatemala was no exception. The reason has had little to do with the constitutional fine points raised by Hammarskjöld and much to do with the political fact that the United States has been able to exert greater leverage in the OAS than in the veto-threatened Security Council and could promote its policies better in the regional forum. For this reason, the motion to transfer the issue to the OAS was vetoed by the Soviets at a second council meeting on June 20. But the Security Council did then pass a French resolution calling for the termination of any action likely to cause further bloodshed and requesting all members involved in the dispute to abstain from providing any assistance to such action that might prejudice the outcome of the case.

On June 22, the Guatemalan government addressed a message to Hammarskjöld, advising him that the council resolution of June 20 was not being observed and that the Honduras-based invasion was continuing. Guatemala and the Soviet Union requested Security Council President Lodge to call another meeting, which he finally agreed to do on June 25. But Lodge placed only the second Guatemalan complaint of June 22 on the council's agenda, not its earlier protest. Hammarskjöld objected to the omission (and was annoyed at Lodge's procrastination in calling the meeting). But the latter won a vote to prevent the adoption of the agenda item proposed by Guatemala: "Cablegram dated June 19, 1954, from the Minister of External Relations of Guatemala addressed to the President of the Security Council and letter dated June 22, 1954, from the representative of Guatemala addressed to the Secretary-General."

When Hammarskjöld saw how things were going, he prepared the draft statement mentioned earlier discussing the respective jurisdiction of the United Nations on one hand and regional organizations like the OAS on the other. But the U.S., British, and French delegates who read the draft felt that it would be unwise for the secretary-general to open a constitutional can of worms by circulating it among all the Security Council members, as Hammarskjöld had intended. Recognizing that public discretion is the better part of valor or that this was a case where power politics had it over principle, Hammarskjöld desisted.

United Nations action on Guatemala became moot after June 27, when the Arbenz government fell. On July 9, the new Armas regime informed the president of the Security Council of the restoration of law and order in Guatemala and that therefore "the occurrences that prompted the previous Government to appeal to the Security Council in the communication of June 19 and subsequent correspondence" had ceased. However, Hammarskjöld discreetly returned to the matter of legal principle. On June 30, he wrote Lodge that the line adopted by his government preferring article 52 to articles 34 and 35 could have serious consequences for the future constitutional development of the United Nations. The secretary-general noted that he considered it his duty to state his views on Charter principles and to provide consistency in the practices to be followed in the future. He appended the relevant records from the San Francisco conference of 1945 when the Charter was drafted and subsequent Security Council debates on the matter.

He reiterated that regional action was complementary to universal action and that, according to article 103, "In the event of a conflict between the obligations of the Members of the United Nations under the present Charter and their obligations under any other international agreement, their obligations under the present Charter shall prevail." He added that regional agreements also recognized the paramount nature of the UN Charter, where international peace and security were concerned. Hammarskjöld came back to this view in his introduction to the *Annual Report, 1953–1954* when he wrote on July 21, 1954, that "a policy giving full scope to the proper role of regional agencies can and should at the same time fully preserve the right of a Member-nation to a hearing under the Charter."

The U.S. delegation rejected Hammarskjöld's analysis of the relationship between the world body and regional organizations. Its response also reminded Hammarskjöld that the transfer of the Guatemalan case to the OAS had only been frustrated by the Soviet veto. But in the meantime, while this discussion of chapter and verse in the Charter was proceeding, a new autocracy became ensconced in Guatemala. Armas soon became the country's new president but was assassinated three years later.

Hammarskjöld "lost" on the Guatemalan issue for three basic reasons. First, 10 of the 11 Security Council members bought the U.S.

argument that the Security Council was first obliged to promote peaceful settlement through a regional organization; it was not its duty to solve a dispute right from the start although that interpretation was implied by the Soviet veto. Second, the fall of the Arbenz regime during the haggling over the meaning and priorities of the Charter made the outcome of the debate academic. Finally, a determined great power, willing to use its guns and influence to achieve its goals, was able to win support for its policy. In short, the case evidenced the triumph of politics over constitutionalism and showed Hammarskjöld the limits of his own authority.

HUNGARY

The Hungarian crisis of October 1956 provides an almost complete contrast to the one at Suez though occurring simultaneously with it. In the Middle East, the United Nations found a resolution to the Anglo–French–Israeli invasion, allowing all the parties to save face in the process and withdraw gracefully. Thus, at Suez, the United Nations was a focus for rallying support for viable policies to which sufficient member governments, including the two superpowers, committed their resources and influence to make the organization's policies successful.

In Hungary, the political and especially military realities were far different. There, the United States failed to counter the Soviet invasion because of the predictable Soviet veto in the Security Council, Moscow's unconcern for American opposition or international public opinion, and its greater determination to use the extensive force it needed in a logistically favorable situation enabling the Soviets to prevail. Hammarskjöld bore the brunt of the blame for the organization's seeming double standard, even though there was little he could do to alter the course of events.

Hungary's momentous revolution had begun very casually on October 23, 1956, when students at Budapest's Technological University drew up a list of 16 demands that included greater political rights and the evacuation of Soviet forces from Hungary. Later that evening, a student delegation at the Budapest radio station asking for broadcast time to read their requests were arrested. Crowds gathered to demand their release but were met with tear gas and then bullets fired by the security forces. Following the violence, the Central

Committee of the Hungarian Communist Party panicked and sought Soviet help in quelling the uprising. Soon thereafter, the intervening Soviet forces came under the fire of the hastily organized Hungarian "freedom fighters" that included students, workers, intellectuals, and defecting soldiers. In short order, although the Soviets had the upper hand, what had started as an internal rebellion against an unpopular Hungarian Stalinist regime became a struggle for independence against the Soviet occupiers.

On Sunday, October 27, an emergency Security Council meeting was convened in New York. Both Soviet and Hungarian delegates insisted that the matter was an internal affair triggered by "counter-revolutionaries" and fanned by Western imperialists. Hence, the Security Council had no jurisdiction. Did not article 2, section 7, of the Charter clearly exempt "matters which are essentially within the domestic jurisdiction of any state" from the purview of the world organization? Although the Security Council had approved the discussion of the "situation in Hungary" by a 9–1–1 vote, no resolution could be passed since a Soviet veto, inapplicable in the procedural adoption of the agenda, was certain on the substantive part. Equally impossible was any decision that included condemnation of aggression or repression. Besides, who would enforce such a decision against a superpower, especially as the United States seemed unwilling to do so? But perhaps nothing would be needed. By October 28, when a cease-fire took effect, the Soviets appeared to start withdrawing their troops from Hungary.

However, by November 2 it became clear that the Russians had merely regrouped and were now crossing into Hungary in great force and with heavy armor. The new Hungarian premier, Imre Nagy, immediately requested the Security Council to have the great powers recognize Hungary's neutrality. But the five permanent members were divided, and the Security Council meeting closed without submission of a formal resolution despite several suggestions for decisive action during the debate. Hammarskjöld did not even attend the session, ostensibly giving priority to the still dangerous Suez crisis. But even at the previous council meeting of October 27, he had said not a word publicly. His defenders assert that he hoped to maintain his credibility as a mediator between the two power blocs and that he realized the futility of a more outspoken role.

The Security Council held still another meeting on November 3 but only agreed to further study. The world watched as Soviet forces reached Budapest by November 4. That same day, the Soviet Union vetoed a U.S. resolution condemning its invasion of Hungary. Thereafter, the council voted to move the agenda item to the General Assembly where the veto was inoperative.

Thus, on November 4, the General Assembly adopted an American resolution similar to the one made in the veto-bound Security Council by a vote of 50–8–15. Hammarskjöld was instructed to report on the Hungarian situation and "as soon as possible suggest methods to bring an end to foreign intervention in Hungary." Hammarskjöld did not seize responsibility for filling in space, as he had done in Peking and at Suez, even though the matter was placed in his hands by an impotent political organ that seems to have empowered him to achieve what it had itself failed to do. In any event, the rebellion was totally crushed by November 8. Belatedly attempting to fulfill the Assembly mandate, Hammarskjöld sought to place observers inside Hungary.

Despite the clear wishes of the majority in the world body and all of Hammarskjöld's efforts, the newly created pro-Soviet regime of János Kádár in Budapest refused to grant access to UN observers. Further General Assembly resolutions, passed during this special session on November 4–10, 1956, became meaningless in the face of the ensconced Soviet might in its satellite country. The Hungarian government, supported by Moscow, delayed responding to Hammarskjöld's request for a personal visit to Budapest and eventually rejected his suggestion to send members of the UN Special Committee on the Problem of Hungary. Although additional Assembly resolutions passed (November 19–21, December 3–5, and December 10–12), all condemning the Soviet intervention in Hungary, they only managed to provide humanitarian aid. The latter, in the form of a UN–Red Cross relief program, was accepted by the Communists for shipment to Hungary.

Approximately 200,000 Hungarian refugees streamed across the Austrian and to a lesser extent Yugoslav borders after the outbreak of the uprising. Hammarskjöld followed up on the General Assembly's call for their assistance by requesting the office of the United Nations High Commissioner for Refugees to coordinate the international response. Reacting to UNHCR appeals for aid and resettlement, the world community was very generous. Countries on four continents opened their doors to the escapees. Extensive television coverage of Hungarian students hurling stones and homemade

Molotov cocktails at Soviet tanks brought home dramatically the brutality of the Russian repression. Those who fled were accepted in the West pell-mell, their refugee status and therefore eligibility for assistance recognized regardless of the differing motivations of their flight. Eventually the UNHCR managed to negotiate the return of some 18,000 refugees with Hungary. This was the first successful repatriation program of its kind, and the episode catapulted the UNHCR to the greatest prestige it had enjoyed since its establishment in 1951.

But overall, in contrast to his activist role in the Suez crisis, Hammarskjöld seemed ineffective in bringing the Hungarian situation to an end. He even refused to meet a Hungarian government representative in Rome for fear that the prestige of the United Nations would be excessively compromised. The reasons given for the secretary-general's laid-back approach to the Hungarian crisis included the following: This was strictly a dispute involving one of the two superpowers, unlike the case at Suez where both superpowers were united against two lesser great powers, Britain and France. The Soviet and Hungarian governments would not relent from their position that this was exclusively a matter of "domestic jurisdiction," and Hungary was not a threat to any UN effort at international peace and security. Another reason for Hammarskjöld's apparent inaction was that the United States and the rest of those members who vociferously condemned the Soviet action in Hungary were not themselves willing to use force to remove the Russians.

Furthermore, during the first few days of the uprising and certainly until the Soviets crossed the Hungarian border in force in early November, the insurgent Hungarian freedom fighters seemed to have the upper hand. Finally, despite his own disclaimers, Hammarskjöld may indeed have given priority to the Suez crisis because he may have believed that it represented a greater threat to world peace than the Soviets throwing their weight around in their own sphere of influence. At any rate, under these circumstances, Hammarskjöld may reluctantly have concluded that there was nothing he could do to alter the situation.[1]

On January 5, 1957, he recommended that the General Assembly set up the UN Special Committee on the Problem of Hungary to continue investigating and reporting on the situation. It did so five days later. But the adamant attitude of the Soviet and Hungarian regimes did not lend itself to new approaches. Despite a series of General

Assembly resolutions passed by overwhelming majorities for many months after the Soviet invasion, none were complied with. Merely, for its propaganda value, the United States kept the question of Hungary on the General Assembly's agenda long after the outcome of the case became obviously irreversible. The Assembly did approve in September 1957 the highly condemnatory report of its Special Committee on the Problem of Hungary by a vote of 60–10–10.

The Hungarian Revolution of 1956 was a major historical event, the first rising of a people in large numbers against Communism and Soviet domination. Some 30,000 Hungarians were killed in the uprising, and about 2 percent of the population fled the country as refugees. Premier Imre Nagy, who had sought the evacuation of Soviet forces and declared Hungary was pulling out of the Warsaw Pact, was executed by the Kádár regime—together with three associates—in June 1958.

In a broader perspective, both the Suez and Hungarian crises assumed a form not envisioned by the authors of the UN Charter. The latter was intended as an instrument to prevent forceful change of the status quo by an "aggressor" in what the framers envisioned as a static world system. But both Suez and Hungary involved unilateral actions by major powers to preserve a status quo threatened by disruptive change. Britain and France, holding untenable colonial positions at Suez, failed to turn the imperial clock back. The Soviet Union, a superpower enjoying a logistical and especially a psychological advantage over American unresolve, succeeded. But neither the United Nations nor Hammarskjöld managed to deal with the age-old puzzle of who was to guard the guardians when they decided to misbehave.

ALGERIA

The question of Algeria, like that of Bizerte (discussed below), indicates that power politics often triumphed over principle, especially in a Cold War environment. In both cases involving French decolonization, the United States did not wish to offend the stated interests of France, an important NATO ally. Accordingly, in both instances Hammarskjöld was unable to demonstrate that an aspiring state (in the case of Algeria) or a smaller independent state (in the case of Tunisia) could depend on full UN support even if its cause was just.

In the short run at least, the UN failure in Hungary repeated itself in an alternate version on the other side of the Iron Curtain.

On January 5, 1955, Saudi Arabia informed the Security Council that the situation in Algeria, where a rebellion against French rule had broken out in November 1954, was likely to endanger international peace and security. The Saudis characterized French action in Algeria as military operations to liquidate a nationalist uprising against colonial rule. In July, the question of Algeria was placed on the General Assembly's agenda at the request of 14 Afro-Asian states, but after some discussion the item was not considered further.

France objected to any discussion of the item by the United Nations, arguing that Algeria, a regular French department and an integral part of metropolitan France since 1834, was essentially within France's domestic jurisdiction under Charter article 2 (7). It followed, therefore, that the United Nations was not competent to intervene.

However, on June 13, 1956, a meeting of the Security Council was requested by 13 UN members on the grounds of the worsening situation in Algeria. They informed the council that it had deteriorated to such an extent that the United Nations could no longer remain indifferent to the threat to peace and security, to the infringement of the rights of self-determination, and to the flagrant violation of fundamental human rights by France. The council, however, would not place the question on its agenda, any more than it was to do in July 1959 when the seriousness of the matter was again brought to its attention by 22 members.

But the General Assembly did so, and on February 15, 1957, expressed its wish that in a spirit of cooperation, a peaceful, democratic, and just solution should be found, in conformity with Charter principles. The Assembly repeated this hope on December 10, 1957, when Morocco and Tunisia offered their good offices.

Charles de Gaulle became France's premier in May 1958—primarily because the public believed that he alone could deal with the bloody issue of Algeria. By 1958, the war between the French army, some half a million strong in Algeria and supported by French colons (settlers), and the Algerian National Liberation Front (FLN) had escalated in brutality. Few paid attention to numerous urgings to negotiate made by the Afro-Asian bloc. Only in September 1959, following the earlier French stonewalling, did de Gaulle, now president of the Fifth Republic, start to mention the possibility of Algerian independence.

Early in 1960, an attempt in the General Assembly to pass a resolution calling for a UN-sponsored referendum in Algeria nearly
passed. In the meantime, after a temporary suspension, negotiations
between the FLN's political arm—the Provisional Government of the
Algerian Republic (GPRA)—and the French government were
resumed. By January 1961, when a policy of self-determination was
endorsed in a French referendum, even the newly sworn-in Kennedy
administration had begun to move perceptibly toward the anticolonial bloc's position stressing the right of the Algerians to self-
determination. Earlier U.S. positions had backed France, but America's need for Cold War support from developing nations was becoming equally important. It was not until March 19, 1962, that an
Algerian cease-fire was signed. Within months, the Evian agreements
ended the war and granted Algeria its independence as of July 1, 1962.

The General Assembly had urged this outcome and served as a
pressure group to end the exorbitantly costly colonial conflict. But
neither the Assembly nor the United Nations in general determined
the final settlement. It was an essentially bilateral affair in which the
other great powers, especially the United States and Britain, played
an ambivalent role for fear of antagonizing or weakening their
NATO ally, France. Only the Soviet Union, by siding with the Afro-
Asians and urging Algeria's independence, emerged creditably from
the fray. Hammarskjöld, whose death occurred before the settlement, knew that his influence was minor and kept a relatively low
profile in the matter. Nonetheless, it was still large enough to dis-
please the French. The consequences of this fact will be evident in the
discussion of the Bizerte crisis.

BIZERTE

Following Tunisia's independence in 1956, all French troops were
gradually removed from its former protectorate except for a few
posts, garrisons, barracks, and especially the naval base near the city
of Bizerte. But after the French bombed the Tunisian border town of
Sakhiet-Sidi-Youssef on February 8, 1958—allegedly for allowing
Algerian rebels to operate from Tunisian territory—relations
between the two governments deteriorated.

On July 6, 1961, President Habib Bourguiba raised the question of
total French evacuation from the naval base at Bizerte, complaining

that French armed forces had violated Tunisian territory. Tunisian forces now blockaded the naval base, forbidding French aircraft from overflying the Bizerte area and the disputed zone at the country's southern border. President Charles de Gaulle, declaring that France would not negotiate under pressure and threats, sent French reinforcements, and French armored units occupied much of the city of Bizerte proper in bloody fighting.

On July 21, Tunisia asked the Security Council to put an immediate end to "acts of aggression" in Bizerte, then under attack by French forces. On its part, France maintained that it had abided scrupulously by the 1958 French–Tunisian agreement regarding Bizerte and that Tunisia bore full responsibility for the events there. Paris explained that its actions were intended to ensure the safety of the base and freedom of French communications.

On July 22, the Security Council held its first meeting to discuss the complaint. Hammarskjöld urged an immediate cease-fire and the withdrawal of all forces to their original positions until a final settlement could be reached. The council then adopted an "interim" resolution based on Hammarskjöld's proposals. The vote was 10–0–0, with France being absent as it was consistently during the debates. But a few days later, Tunisia complained that the French military forces had not complied with this council resolution.

In the meantime, in response to an appeal from President Bourguiba for a direct and personal exchange of views between himself and the secretary-general, Hammarskjöld left for Tunisia. He visited there from July 24 to July 27, 1961, entirely on his own authority. Hammarskjöld's hasty trip did not please the French. In fact, during the previous months, President de Gaulle had made it clear (except to Hammarskjöld) that he did not wish to share policy making with the secretary-general, whom he considered an interloper. Indeed, de Gaulle believed that the United Nations, which he derogatorily dubbed "the thing," had been intruding on France's sovereign rights. Even the minimally activist leadership of Hammarskjöld regarding the issue of Algerian independence was annoying to the "grand Charles."

After consulting with President Bourguiba in Tunis and being apprised of serious Tunisian losses in men and property, Hammarskjöld decided to visit the naval base at Bizerte. On July 26, he took the initiative without prior permission from the French authorities and contrary to spirited advice from Pier Spinelli, the UN European Office chief, who had joined Hammarskjöld on the way.

Although the secretary-general claimed his trip was intended to get the French side of the story, Hammarskjöld and his party were halted by French paratroopers at the outskirts of the city of Bizerte. Their automobiles were searched, and further humiliations included the commanding officer's "failure" to "recognize" Hammarskjöld. Only then were they allowed to proceed to the governor's residence in the city. But the French commander of the Bizerte naval base, Admiral Amman, refused to meet with Hammarskjöld. All Hammarskjöld could do was to ask Andrew Cordier, his executive assistant, to complain to the French UN ambassador in New York, not so much about his country's discourtesies to the secretary-general but about its disregard for the world organization.

When the French Foreign Ministry's reply was received by Hammarskjöld, the communication added insult to injury. It ignored Hammarskjöld's request for information on the French government's views, failed to respond to the secretary-general's offer to meet Foreign Minister Maurice Couve de Murville in Paris, and dismissed the Security Council's cease-fire resolution as inapplicable. The French note insinuated that Hammarskjöld had sounded like a spokesman of the Tunisian government and was hardly neutral.

Back at headquarters, Hammarskjöld reported to the Security Council on July 28. He explained that he had gone to Tunisia to fulfill his duty under article 99 of the Charter to collect all the relevant facts in the case. Only for that purpose had he accepted President Bourguiba's invitation. However, while he had received full Tunisian cooperation, he reported that he had failed to establish contact with both parties to arrange for a mutual withdrawal of their armed forces. Clearly, the secretary-general blamed France, which was still exercising sovereign rights in the Tunisian city of Bizerte. But because of U.S. and British reluctance to cast a negative vote against a fellow NATO member, none of Hammarskjöld's proposed three draft resolutions were adopted by the council. As usual, the French boycotted the Security Council meeting. Hammarskjöld urged U.S. Ambassador Adlai Stevenson to pressure the French to withdraw their troops from Bizerte, but the secretary-general was clearly irked by the lack of American support.

This failure of the Security Council to take action led 38 Afro-Asian members to request a special session of the General Assembly to consider the Bizerte crisis. The Assembly met from August 21 to August 25, 1961, and adopted a resolution (66–0–30) reaffirming the council's "interim" resolution of July 22. The membership urged France to carry out fully its provisions regarding "an immediate cease-fire and return of all armed forces to their original positions." The Assembly recognized Tunisia's right "to call for the withdrawal of all French forces present on its territory without its consent" and encouraged both parties "to enter into immediate negotiations to devise peaceful and agreed measures in accordance with the principles of the Charter."

Five weeks later the French began to withdraw their forces from positions in the city of Bizerte proper and return to their naval base. The process resulted from direct French–Tunisian negotiations, not a UN initiative. The French finally evacuated the naval base on October 15, 1963, some two years after Hammarskjöld's death and as part of the decolonization process he had supported but so often failed to hasten. The less empowered were often sacrificed on the altar of great power politics. In the Cold War, the viability of one's allies was often upheld regardless of who was on the side of the angels! Hammarskjöld seemingly again failed to grasp this Cold War reality.

LAOS

In the latter part of 1957, the Laotian government, supported by the United States, began shifting away from a neutralist Cold War position toward a pro-Western, anti-Communist one. The Pathet Lao (Communist) members of the coalition Government of National Unity and military units not integrated into the Royal Laotian Army were being squeezed out of political life. The army-dominated Laotian government crackdown on Pathet Lao members fostered a traditional Cold War scenario. Thus, on January 16, 1959, the Laotian government informed Secretary-General Hammarskjöld that armed units, presumably from North Vietnam, were operating on Laotian territory. Other official Laotian complaints followed that summer and were countered by threats from North Vietnam to the effect that any foreign (i.e., American) troops in Laos would bring a spirited response by Hanoi.

Hammarskjöld was sufficiently alarmed by these developments to have included in his introduction to his *Annual Report* to the General Assembly in 1959 a warning that "difficulties have developed at the north-eastern border of Laos." However, he added that he was pursuing "fairly modest . . . diplomacy" to smooth things out and prevent escalation. The secretary-general carefully recommended minimal possible alternatives—the dispatch of observers or of a fact-finding mission—to deal with what eventually turned out to be exaggerated reports from the Laotian and U.S. governments. Nevertheless on September 4, 1959, the Laotian government requested "prompt dispatch of an emergency force to halt aggression" and to prevent its spread. This emergency peacekeeping force, like the one at Suez, would consist of blue-helmeted troops positioned as a buffer between Laos and North Vietnam. On September 5, Hammarskjöld requested that the Security Council convene urgently to consider the Laotian complaint and request.

At its meeting of September 7, the council adopted a resolution after deciding 10–1, over Soviet objections, that the subject matter of the resolution was of a procedural nature and that therefore the veto was not applicable. The resolution asked that a subcommittee consisting of Argentina, Italy, Japan, and Tunisia conduct inquiries and report to the council. The Soviets continued to object to the entire proceedings, which they regarded as illegal and therefore not binding on anyone. Hammarskjöld probably remembered this to-do when he announced his unilateral decision to visit Laos "with the consent of the Government, temporarily stationing a personal representative in Vientiane."

The subcommittee of inquiry on the situation in Laos visited Laos between September 15 and October 13, 1959, at the invitation of the Laotian government. Its report of November 5, 1959, noted that the military action in Laos had been "of a guerrilla character" even though it appeared from the testimony of the Laotian government officials and a few witnesses that some of the hostile operations "must have had a centralized coordination."

Because of the "half-hearted and inconclusive" inferences in the report, Hammarskjöld visited Laos at the invitation of its government between November 12 and November 19 in order to give himself the "opportunity to get, at first hand, as complete a picture as possible of conditions and developments in Laos of relevance from the point of view of the general responsibilities of the secretary-general." He explained that his mission followed on threats to international peace and security as well as his administrative authority under the Charter. The mission neither sought nor received approval from the Security Council but was another of Hammarskjöld's self-appointed crisis mediation efforts.

In Vientiane, he urged the Laotian government to pursue an "independent" path, that is, one more neutralist and less pro-Western. In short, he encouraged the formation of a neutralist coalition government. After discussions with Laotian officials, Hammarskjöld also instructed Sakari Tuomioja of Finland, executive secretary of the Economic Commission for Europe, to review the economic situation of the country, a task completed by December 17, 1959. On the basis of that report, Hammarskjöld requested UN Commissioner for Technical Assistance Roberto M. Heurtematte to go to Laos and discuss the implementation of the Tuomioja recommendations on Laotian needs for economic development.

But there was a sequel to the question of Laos. After a coup by right-wing Laotian generals in early 1960, Hammarskjöld communicated to King Savang Vathana his hope that the country's evolution toward neutrality, democracy, and national reconciliation would not be interrupted but that "the line of independent neutrality . . . [should] be firmly maintained." Such gratuitous interference in the internal political life of a member state was unprecedented and went way beyond "filling space."

But Hammarskjöld's heavy-handedness was offset by further evidence of his diplomatic skill. Three days before the scheduled general elections of April 24, 1960, he was asked whether Laotian policies were trending left or right, East or West. The secretary-general merely replied, "Forward." Before Hammarskjöld's tenure was over, Laos would drift into a civil war between pro-Western and pro-Communist forces. With each side getting assistance from its superpower sponsor, the crisis was another in a series of proxy wars. But by then, Hammarskjöld virtually ignored the Laotian issue as the Congo crisis consumed most of his time and attention. The Soviets, who had opposed Hammarskjöld's fact-finding trip in November 1959, were increasingly hostile, further reducing the secretary-general's effectiveness. The situation continued to unravel in Laos and was to await Hammarskjöld's successor.

HAMMARSKJÖLD'S ACHILLES' HEEL: NOT ONLY POLITICAL BUT ADMINISTRATIVE

So far, this chapter has suggested that in cases where the Cold War intruded directly, as in Guatemala, Hungary, and Laos, Hammarskjöld's space for maneuver was highly circumscribed and all his diplomatic skills proved of little avail. In instances involving decolonization—also overlapping Cold War issues—as in Algeria and Bizerte, Hammarskjöld's influence was also limited.

The following case study presents an administrative problem (admittedly, also colored by the Cold War) involving insubordination and lack of professionalism in one of Hammarskjöld's staffers— seemingly, a disturbed man. Even though the secretary-general managed to assert his authority over his subordinate, he did not emerge completely unblemished from the confrontation.

CASE STUDY 5: POVL BANG-JENSEN

The limits of Dag Hammarskjöld's reach may be illustrated, then, not with reference to any international political event, but in his performance as chief administrative officer of the United Nations. An example involved confrontation with a member of his secretariat who was as highly principled, sensitive, and vulnerable as Hammarskjöld himself.

Povl (Paul) Bang-Jensen, a lawyer, was a successful Danish civil servant who had worked in the Danish foreign service in Washington and several Latin American countries before joining the Department of Political and Security Affairs in the UN secretariat in 1949, four years before Hammarskjöld. The two men were casually acquainted before joining the United Nations, but conflict between them flared up in the aftermath of the Hungarian crisis in November 1956. On January 5, 1957, Hammarskjöld recommended that the General Assembly establish the UN Special Committee on the Problem of Hungary to investigate the causes and implications of those events. The Assembly approved its establishment on January 17, but the Budapest regime of János Kádár would not permit this committee (any more than it had allowed Hammarskjöld or his personal representative) to visit Hungary to gather facts. Accordingly, the special committee was forced to work on its assignment outside of Hungary and other Soviet bloc countries, always remembering Hammarskjöld's caution that "hearings must be extensive and organized in a juridically satisfactory form."

The committee's chairman was Alsing Andersen of Denmark, the deputy chairman was Bang-Jensen, and the rapporteur was K. C. O.

Shann of Australia. There were three other members from Ceylon (now Sri Lanka), Tunisia, and Uruguay. The committee perused press reports and those of foreign embassies with missions in Budapest, official Hungarian documents, and even Soviet army orders where available. Especially, it heard the testimony of witnesses, mostly Hungarian refugees now resident in neighboring countries.

It was the duty of the committee's deputy chairman, Bang-Jensen, to make administrative arrangements for the appearance of such witnesses, and he held preliminary interviews with refugees in New York, London, Geneva, Rome, and Vienna. Whether authorized or not, Bang-Jensen assured prospective witnesses that their names and addresses would be held in secrecy to prevent retaliation by Hungarian authorities against their kin and friends who had stayed behind. The refugees were so fearful of such retribution that 81 of 111 witnesses before the committee requested anonymity. Bang-Jensen assured them all that Soviet bloc secretariat staff members would have no access to the names. The list of witnesses was kept by Bang-Jensen, even though inevitably some of their identities came to be known to a few of his colleagues on the committee.

The Special Committee on the Problem of Hungary returned to New York in April 1957 and published a preliminary report on June 18, 1957. It was a vigorous indictment of the Hungarian–Soviet Communist repression of the uprising that crushed the country's freedom, imposed the Kádár regime on it, and carried out a mass deportation of "subversives." However, Bang-Jensen, charging "sabotage" and "dishonesty" by his colleagues, took exception to the report as both incomplete and distorting facts. The chairman and the rapporteur of the special committee went over Bang-Jensen's objections point by point but found no justification for most of them. Thereupon Bang-Jensen wrote letters of complaint to Hammarskjöld and Andrew Cordier, the secretary-general's executive assistant. Bang-Jensen then became very emotional and threatened to make the matter public. Hammarskjöld refused to grant Bang-Jensen an interview, explaining, "I did not know that there is any obligation on the part of the secretary-general to go into such matters personally." But he did send Ralph Bunche to investigate. The secretary-general's confidant found no evidence to support Bang-Jensen's allegations of suppression and distortion of facts by his colleagues on the special committee on Hungary.

Then, in October 1957, a minor incident occurred that had serious consequences. A Hungarian refugee who had testified before the special committee requested the United Nations to issue a certificate to that effect. The individual was facing deportation from the United States and wished to prove, in his own defense, that he had testified anonymously before the committee.

The special committee cooperatively asked Hammarskjöld to authorize the issuing of such a document and discovered only then that Bang-Jensen had kept it in his personal possession and had concealed highly confidential papers at his home and in hotel rooms while on mission, including the register of anonymous witnesses. Angered by this violation of standard operating procedures, Hammarskjöld first requested and then instructed Bang-Jensen to deliver this documentation to the secretariat for safekeeping in a secure, locked place where other sensitive papers were also being stored. Bang-Jensen refused, and in December 1957 Hammarskjöld suspended his subordinate in the secretariat with pay and without prejudice. Hammarskjöld named a special investigating committee headed by Ernest A. Gross, an international lawyer and a former U.S. deputy representative to the United Nations, who acted as an occasional consultant to Hammarskjöld, to investigate the entire matter.

After interviewing Povl Bang-Jensen, the Gross committee found him very remiss in matters of security. Bang-Jensen admitted that he had carried confidential documents on his person when traveling and that he had concealed them in hotel rooms where he stayed. The committee concluded that because of such "ignorance of rational security procedures," the confidential documents had probably already been compromised and should be destroyed. Hammarskjöld accepted its recommendation, but the Gross committee had also determined that Bang-Jensen's allegations were "largely puerile and without foundation." It noted his irrational behavior when instructed not to attend special committee meetings because of his previously disruptive and aggressive conduct. Moreover, he had exceeded his authority when he gave assurances on his own to prospective witnesses before the special committee on Hungary.

In its final report, the Gross committee advised the secretary-general that "the continued employment of Mr. Bang-Jensen would be incompatible with the best interests of the United Nations," since he had "departed markedly from normal and rational standards of behavior." The committee also recommended a psychiatric examination for Povl Bang-Jensen.

The Danish secretariat official refused to see a psychiatrist and, at first, even to surrender the documents. However, as the only solution to the impasse, he finally accepted the suggestion that his list of confidential witnesses should be destroyed in a sealed envelope. On January 24, 1958, this was done on the roof of UN headquarters in the presence of Bang-Jensen, Ed Begley, the chief UN security officer, and other officials. But the imbroglio continued, since on February 19, 1958, formal charges of grave misconduct and insubordination were filed against Bang-Jensen. After review by the UN Joint Disciplinary Committee, it was unanimously recommended to the secretary-general that Bang-Jensen be dismissed from UN service.

Hammarskjöld wrote to Bang-Jensen on July 3, 1958, terminating his employment with three months' pay and an indemnity of $29,000. It is not known whether the secretary-general worded this 12-page communication himself or merely signed it. Essentially, the letter reiterated the Joint Disciplinary Committee's determination that Bang-Jensen's "grave errors of judgement and serious acts of undiscipline" made him unfit for continued employment at the United Nations. The letter's tone of gratuitous rudeness was almost insulting. Among other things, Hammarskjöld asserted that Bang-Jensen was

> guilty of behavior even more reprehensible than that reviewed by the Joint Disciplinary Committee. . . . The Rapporteur [of the Special Committee on Hungary] states that he regards your behavior 'as unbecoming a member of the Secretariat,' that he is of the opinion that you did considerable harm and that your allegations were largely childish and without foundation, and that he reserved the necessity of raising the situation 'at a higher level so that proper disciplinary action may be taken to see that it stops,'. . .
>
> While it is not necessary to my decision . . . I wish nevertheless to lay particular stress on my conclusion that the charges . . . are borne out by the evidence. I need hardly emphasize that your behavior towards the Rapporteur [whom Bang-Jensen had at one point jostled and pushed] by itself constitutes sufficient grounds for dismissal for misconduct by any member of the Secretariat. It is unthinkable . . . and cannot be countenanced.[2]

Most press commentary supported Bang-Jensen's view that surrendering the names of 111 Hungarian witnesses to the secretariat for safekeeping, as per the secretary-general's directive, "would have been tantamount to handing them to the Russians and Communist Hungarians." The critics also noted that if Bang-Jensen was emotionally disturbed as charged, it had been a serious error to have appointed him deputy chairman of such a politically sensitive body as the special committee on Hungary in the first place. If he was really as deranged as he was made out to be, he should have been treated more sympathetically. At any rate, Bang-Jensen appealed his dismissal to the UN Administrative Tribunal, the final court of appeal for UN personnel, which unanimously turned down his petition on December 5, 1958.

On November 23, 1959, Bang-Jensen went out to a park in Queens, New York. His body was discovered there three days later. A few right-wing zealots alleged a Communist "hit" against an anti-Communist crusader, but most accepted his death as a suicide. On December 1, Hammarskjöld, writing to a Swedish friend, noted that "it is . . . sad to see the curious blend of sentimentality, wishful thinking and McCarthy-ish hysteria which his [Bang-Jensen's] suicide has stirred up."

The case of Povl Bang-Jensen reads like a Greek tragedy. The two major characters were both strong-willed and guided only by highest principle. Bang-Jensen insisted consistently that his pledge of confidentiality to prospective witnesses might be compromised if he surrendered the list to the secretariat. He did not feel that UN safekeeping was very secure. Hammarskjöld was equally insistent that UN staff regulations must be followed and that all officials should subordinate personal views to the decisions of their superiors—or else resign. When one of the principals died in the process, leaving a wife and three children, the tragedy was complete.

The Gross committee reported that Bang-Jensen had exhibited a "marked inclination to see duplicity everywhere," while Bang-Jensen had characterized Hammarskjöld's letter of dismissal as "sheer libel" and the indemnity paid to him as a "bribe." He found a number of sympathizers, including the right-wing press and American conservatives such as Robert Morris, former chief counsel of Joseph McCarthy's U.S. Senate Internal Security Subcommittee, and Senator Thomas Dodd of Connecticut. They were joined by those who felt guilty about letting the Hungarians down in the face of raw Communist aggression. For all these, the United Nations was a convenient scapegoat for their frustrations.

On December 22, 1959, trying to set the record straight, the secretariat issued a mimeographed background paper giving its version of the story. The document was titled "A Chronological Record of Facts concerning Mr. Povl Bang-Jensen's Period of Duty in the Secretariat Assigned to Serve the Special Committee on the Problem of Hungary and Subsequent Developments Ending in His Dismissal." The paper explained, "It has not been the wish of the United Nations to reopen the record concerning a man who has died. However, there is also a duty to the Organization itself, to those who serve it, and to all who believe in its aims." These lines clearly reflected the position of Hammarskjöld himself.

NOTES

1. When the author of this work visited the National Library in Budapest to find sources on the Hungarian crisis, the librarian from whom he sought assistance, a middle-aged lady who had been there in 1956, asked rhetorically about Hammarskjöld: "And what has he done for us?" While this account is admittedly anecdotal, the attitude about Hammarskjöld's role in the event where it actually happened may have been more generalized. As it turned out, the index under Hammarskjöld's name listed only two sources. The first was a translation of the report by the UN Special Committee on the Problem of Hungary published in 1983 under the Hungarian title, "What Happened in 1956?" The second was a book by Tibor Zábor; the translated title was *United Nations Secretaries-General: Lie, Hammarskjöld, U Thant, Waldheim* (1984). These were lean pickings indeed!

2. Letter of dismissal of July 3, 1958, from Hammarskjöld to Bang-Jensen, reproduced in UN press release SG/700 of July 3, 1958.

5

Breaking New Ground

During the Hammarskjöld years, the agenda of the United Nations expanded sharply as the world organization came to address an increasing number of global issues. The enlarged agenda increasingly reflected the concerns of the world body's newest members— independent but still developing countries—which faced major post-colonial problems. These new nations struggled to consolidate their sovereignty; organize their political, military, economic, and social institutions; and survive the initial years of hardships involved in the nation-building process. They also strived to hasten the process of independence of the territories still under colonial rule.

But there were other issues as well, not so directly related to Third World decolonization and development but rather to Cold War problems of high politics, of security and control. This is not a neat dichotomy inasmuch as the two sets of issues frequently tended to interact. And no matter what the categorizations or how accurate, in the meantime the United Nations tried to serve the interests of its new members, its incipient new majority.

DECOLONIZATION

The pre-World War II colonial situation whereby seven Western European countries with a population of 200 million controlled dependencies with 700 million natives became increasingly problematic after the conflict. The tone of several delegates at the San Francisco conference of 1945 drafting the UN Charter had been anticolonialist.

Accordingly, shortly after its creation, the United Nations became deeply involved with the emancipation and national liberation movements agitating these possessions. However, it was not until 1960 that the General Assembly passed its Declaration on the Granting of Independence to Colonial Countries and Peoples (89–0–9). The following year, an Assembly resolution declared apartheid in South Africa to be a flagrant violation of the Charter (97–2–1). Hammarskjöld was the first secretary-general who had to contend with the implications of these General Assembly actions.

The UN Charter approached the colonial issue from two perspectives. One Charter provision continued the League of Nations mandate system but renamed it the trusteeship system. Under Chapters XII–XIII, a UN Trusteeship Council would supervise three types of territories that were nonself-governing, namely, (1) those still under mandate, (2) those detached from enemy states after World War II, and (3) those voluntarily placed under the system by states responsible for their administration. The Trusteeship Council, a principal UN organ, was to consider reports by the administering power, accept petitions from local inhabitants, and make periodic visits to trust territories to ensure that the political, economic, social, and educational advancement of the inhabitants was in fact occurring.

From the perspective of decolonization, however, much more important was Chapter XI, which mandated member states controlling nonself-governing territories to promote the well-being of the latter's inhabitants, to develop self-government, to assist in the progressive growth of free political institutions, and to transmit regularly to the secretary-general information on the economic, social, and educational status of these territories.

The Charter's provisions for UN supervision of nonself-governing territories are vague, and even in 1960 the Assembly had found no effective means of doing so. Still, interest in colonial problems had grown in the first decade and a half of UN existence. By 1960, this evolution led to the formation of a majority opinion in the General Assembly hostile to the prolongation of colonialism in Africa and Asia. This was true even in the case of territories that did not fall under Chapters XI, XII, and XIII of the Charter, as the case of Algeria will have suggested. Accordingly, for the first time, an international organization was starting to assert its interest in affairs of colonies outside either the League of Nations mandate system or the successor UN trusteeship system. Hammarskjöld would have to deal with this overriding Third World concern.

In 1960, 18 colonial territories, including 17 in Africa, were scheduled to gain their independence. Their presence at the 15th session of the General Assembly would tip the voting balance there to the Afro-Asian or the Afro-Asian–Latin American bloc.

But in the meantime, when Soviet Premier Nikita Khrushchev arrived in New York to attend the Assembly session that September, he tried to recruit these new UN members behind Soviet leadership. He issued a draft for dependent countries and peoples, blaming the capitalist West for colonialism and its harmful effects. He attributed the numerous injustices flowing from imperialism to Western malevolence. He went on to demand immediate and complete independence for all colonies and the elimination of foreign overseas bases. The Soviets not only managed to have their new item added to the agenda but also succeeded in bypassing the First (Political and Security) Committee of the Assembly to which it had been assigned and in having their resolution debated at the outset at the General Assembly's plenary session with strong support from the new member states and in the face of great reluctance from the older ones. Accordingly, the issue of decolonization led to a major debate in the fall of 1960. As the first item on the Assembly's plenary agenda, it could not be muscled out by time considerations and would receive maximum press coverage. Eventually, a slightly modified draft was proposed by 43 Afro-Asian countries and adopted by 89–0, with nine abstentions, on December 14, 1960. This was the famous Resolution 1514 (15), also known as the Declaration on the Granting of Independence to Colonial Countries and Peoples. Its seven provisions had the effect of elevating self-determination, mentioned as a principle in the UN Charter, to a right. It was, in effect, an informal amendment of the Charter.

Even though the Afro-Asian draft that passed muster was less intemperate in its language and less extreme in its demands for impossible deadlines than the Soviet version (proposing, for example, 1961 as the target date for the complete elimination of colonialism), the United States was at first cool to the entire endeavor. But not wishing to alienate the new African members and planning to turn the tables on the Soviets by referring to their own form of colonialism in Eastern Europe, Washington finally voted to abstain, together with the colonial powers. In fact, under great pressure from Britain, a direct order from President Dwight Eisenhower overrode the American delegation's wish to vote for the draft. The United States would long feel the effects of its action! But clearly, the balance of forces in the General Assembly had shifted to reflect the concerns and political influence of the Third World. The decolonization resolution gave the world organization a new dimension that would have great impact in the subsequent decades.

As it turned out, despite Hammarskjöld's belief in the benefits of pluralism and innovation in the primary UN functions, the new member states exhibited an intense but limited range of concerns. They became almost exclusively devoted to the issues of decolonization, the human rights of nonwhite peoples, and economic and social progress and aid. They evidenced much less interest in East–West issues such as the perennial question of the recognition of the People's Republic of China by the United Nations or matters of international law.

The major exception to this generalization was the issue of arms control and disarmament. Linking economic and social development with disarmament as a source of funding the former—say, through the suspension of nuclear weapons testing—became a constant theme of these new members. Developing countries recognized the insufficiency of UN financing to meet their needs, but a vast revolution of rising expectations was already sweeping the recent arrivals, with requests, demands, and hope now replacing their earlier fatalism and resignation.

Inevitably, their major interests were also reflected in the voting patterns of new members. Beginning in 1960, on issues of decolonization, these countries tended to vote as almost a solid bloc. Since the large and consistent majorities on decolonization issues gave the underlying principles added weight, in time they became established elements in international law. Just as self-determination was transformed from a principle to a right, so human rights as in South Africa would witness a similar metamorphosis. The growth of Third World UN membership was clearly translated into political influence.

Tables 5.1 and 5.2 list the major issues discussed and voted on at the 15th session of the General Assembly in 1960, broken down according to whether they were decolonization issues (table 5.1) or East–West issues (table 5.2). The voting numbers refer to approval, opposition, and abstention, respectively.

These records suggest that decolonization issues almost consistently involved a larger set of yes votes (the initial numbers) than East–West

Table 5.1   Major Decolonization Issues at the 15th Session of the General Assembly in 1960

Resolution		Vote
1514 (XV)	Declaration on the Granting of Independence to Colonial Countries and Peoples, December 14, 1960	89–0–9
1536 (XV)	Racial discrimination in nonself-governing territories, December 14, 1960	88–0–2
1541 (XV)	Principles that should guide members in determining whether or not an obligation exists to transmit information called for under article 73 (e) of the Charter (regarding the transmission of information to the secretary-general by administering powers of nonself-governing territories) December 14, 1960	69–2–21
1542 (XV)	Transmission of information under article 73 (e) of the Charter December 14, 1960	68–10–17
1565 (XV)	Legal action to ensure the fulfillment of the obligation assumed by South Africa in respect to South-West Africa December 18, 1960	86–0–6
1568 (XV)	Question of South-West Africa: Separate vote on operative paragraph 3 deprecating the policy of apartheid December 18, 1960	90–0–3
1568 (XV)	Question of South-West Africa December 18, 1960	78–0–15
1579 (XV)	Question of the future of Ruanda–Urundi (now Rwanda and Burundi) December 20, 1960	61–9–23
1593 (XV)	Appeal to member states that have particularly close and continuous relations with South Africa March 23, 1961	70–0–9
	Procedural proposal to include the situation in Angola on the agenda March 23, 1961	79–2–8
1596 (XV)	Question of South-West Africa April 13, 1961	95–1–0
1605 (XV)	Question of the future of Ruanda–Urundi April 21, 1961	86–1–4
1607 (XV)	Dissemination of information on the United Nations in the trust territories April 21, 1961	78–0–9

issues. The latter brought the largest tally of no (second numbers) votes or abstentions (third numbers). This pattern reflects the intense interest of the newly independent UN members in decolonization in contrast to Cold War issues, except when they could see some relevance to their own cause, as in the suspension of nuclear testing.

Table 5.2 Major East–West Issues at the 15th Session of the General Assembly in 1960

Resolution		Vote
1576 (XV)	Requests all governments to make every effort to prevent the wider dissemination of nuclear weapons December 20, 1960	68–0–26
1577 (XV)	Urges continuation of the voluntary suspension of the testing of nuclear weapons December 20, 1960	88–0–05
1498 (XV)	Accepts the credentials of the Congo delegation issued by President Joseph Kasavubu, the head of state November 22, 1960	53–24–19
1600 (XV)	Urges the immediate release of all members of the Congolese parliament and its convening without delay, and appoints a Commission of Conciliation April 15, 1961	60–16–23
Document A/C.5/L.638/ Rev. 1.	Draft resolution recognizes that the Congo expenses "constitute 'expenses of the Organization' within the meaning of Article 17, paragraph 2, of the Charter" and apportions the 1960 expenses, Fifth (Administrative and Budgetary) Committee, December 15, 1960	45–15–25
1590 (XV)	Authorizes the secretary-general to incur $24 million in commitments in 1961 for the Congo operation December 20, 1960	39–11–44
1493 (XV)	Rejects the Soviet request for inclusion of an agenda item on Chinese representation and decides not to consider any proposals to seat the People's Republic of China at this (15th) session October 8, 1960	42–34–22
Document A/C.5/L.275.	Draft resolution calling on all states to ensure that their territories are not used to promote a civil war in Cuba and asking them to cooperate, in the spirit of the Charter, in a search for a peaceful solution to the problem, First (Political and Security) Committee April 21, 1960	42–31–25

CASE STUDY 6:
APARTHEID IN SOUTH AFRICA
AND SOUTH-WEST AFRICA

For several decades, various UN bodies devoted more effort to the issue of apartheid (literally, separateness) than any other human rights problem. During these years, racial separation in South Africa was the only deliberately created, legally based system of racial discrimination in the world and was an affront to the increasing nonwhite membership of the world organization. Accordingly, ever since 1946, when India first filed a complaint about discriminatory laws directed against Indian ethnics in South Africa, the General Assembly has vocally condemned racial discrimination against the black majority, "coloreds" of mixed blood, and Asians living in the Union of South Africa. Designed to segregate the races in many and complex ways and preserve white minority domination in all spheres of life, apartheid became a major UN concern during Hammarskjöld's tenure.

The policy began to be implemented after the Afrikaner (Boer) National Party won the elections in 1948. Thus in practice apartheid meant that some four-fifths of the country's total population of 13 million were confined mainly to black reservations outside of the large cities such as Johannesburg. There blacks were housed under deplorable conditions in ghettoes like Soweto. Or they lived in black settlements, later designated as independent "African homelands," or Bantustans, by the South African government. Everywhere the blacks were restricted in terms of pass laws and labor contracts and suffered from low wages and a lack of educational and health facilities. In short, there were two distinct societies in this wealthy, industrialized country, kept apart by customs and especially laws. There were no mixed neighborhoods, schools, churches, sports clubs, and, especially, government.

In those days, the Charter's principle of state sovereignty, enshrined in article 2 (7) and implying a government's absolute rights over its citizens, was still given priority over another Charter principle "encouraging respect for human rights and for fundamental freedoms for all without distinction as to race" mentioned in article 1 (3) among others. Accordingly, because of these contradictory principles, actions by a government against its own citizens were still not widely viewed as an offense against international law. Besides, several governments, not just that of South Africa, considered that the treatment of their own citizens was not subject to negotiation with other governments or international organizations.

All of this changed from 1960 on. In that "year of independence," Cameroon, the Central African Republic, Chad, Congo (Brazzaville), Congo (Leopoldville, or the Republic of the Congo, now Zaire),

Dahomey (now Benin), Gabon, Ivory Coast, Madagascar, Mali, Niger, Nigeria, Senegal, Somalia, Togo, and Upper Volta (now Burkina Faso) were admitted to the United Nations. By the end of that year, the General Assembly had 26 African members, compared to only four when Hammarskjöld assumed his duties in 1953. Three more African states joined the organization in 1961. Consequently, the General Assembly began to move from general to specific resolutions. The Africans had no qualms about requesting member states to take individual as well as collective measures against South Africa to force it to terminate its hated apartheid policies.

The situation was exacerbated by the Sharpeville massacre in a Johannesburg suburb on March 21, 1960. In that incident, the South African police killed 56 blacks protesting the country's pass laws and wounded 156. As a result, the matter was discussed in the Security Council on April 1. It passed a resolution (9–0–2) calling for the end of apartheid and greater racial justice in South Africa. Britain and France, the former colonial masters of much of Africa, abstained as the council requested Pretoria to "initiate measures aimed at bringing about racial harmony based on equality." Furthermore, the council directed Secretary-General Hammarskjöld to consult with the South African government in order "to make such arrangements as would adequately help in upholding the purposes and principles of the Charter in the Union of South Africa."

Hammarskjöld tried to get around the inherent difficulty of tackling an issue that South Africa considered a matter of its "domestic jurisdiction." In his meetings with South African officials in New York, London, and, much later, Pretoria, he used a surgical scalpel to bypass article 2 (7) by reviving the ambiguous Peking formula, which he had used in 1955 to get Premier Chou En-lai to discuss with him the release of imprisoned American airmen of the United Nations Command in Korea. This "formula," it will be recalled, consisted of using the secretary-general's "authority under the Charter" to discuss what could be considered a "domestic" issue without prejudging whether it was or not. Hammarskjöld stressed that Pretoria's willingness to discuss apartheid and other human rights issues affecting nonwhites in that country would not imply that South Africa acquiesced that these issues in fact fell under UN jurisdiction.

Right from the start, Hammarskjöld emphasized that he was merely concerned with the international consequences of these policies. For instance, as regards the pass system, which required all

Africans to carry identification cards at all times, his interest was not in South Africa's internal rules but only in the fact that this measure produced international friction. Only when Hammarskjöld, long delayed by the Congo crisis, finally visited Pretoria from January 6 to January 12, 1961, did he point to the cruel inconsistencies of apartheid. He noted that on the one hand the government's economic policy was based on integration because the gold and diamond mines, among others, depended heavily on unskilled black labor. Yet that same government simultaneously prohibited any involvement or representation of the Bantus and other tribesmen in the country's political life.

During his six-day visit, Hammarskjöld challenged Prime Minister Hendrik Verwoerd to consider under what circumstances apartheid—if it had to be that—would work. He himself mentioned two options. First, sufficient land for black reservations would allow them to become economically viable and permit the ingathering of Bantus scattered around the country. This would encourage voluntary return to the "homelands." Second, the blacks would be integrated into South African life with the prerogatives of citizenship. Hammarskjöld had no illusions at the conclusion of his trip that what he had said would change South Africa's policies of apartheid and the wider issue of racial conflict. Still, on his return to New York he informed the Security Council that even though no mutually acceptable arrangement had been achieved with Pretoria, he looked forward to continued consultations, to which the South African government remained amenable.

However, his subsequent preoccupation with the Congo issue and his death that same year precluded further action in what, beginning in 1962, came to be designated simply as "the policies of apartheid of the government of the Republic of South Africa" on the General Assembly's agenda. In subsequent years, attempts to change the apartheid system would witness an entire gamut of UN methods, ranging from diplomacy to legal steps and coercive actions. But it was not until July 1993 that the pressure yielded dramatic results; multiracial elections were held in April 1994 and a black president voted into office.

General Assembly resolutions also dealt with the territory of South-West Africa, seized from Germany during World War I and entrusted to South Africa in the 1920 peace settlements as a Class C mandate. In 1946, the General Assembly had rejected South Africa's request to incorporate the territory. Pretoria had asked for this right on the grounds that with the demise of the League of Nations, officially only in June 1946, its former obligations had also lapsed, and it alone should determine the future status of South-West Africa. In 1948, South Africa reiterated that the mandate had ended with the League and that the United Nations had no authority in the matter. Thus the National Party government of Daniel Malan ceased reporting to the United Nations and started to install features of the apartheid system in South-West Africa itself. The two issues were inseparably joined from that point on.

In November 1960, Ethiopia and Liberia—the only two African members of the defunct League of Nations—complained to the International Court of Justice that South Africa had violated its League mandate by extending apartheid into that territory, unilaterally changing its legal status, and for failing to submit reports on its administration to the General Assembly as a UN-supervised trust territory. Surprisingly, South Africa responded to the charges in court, implicitly acknowledging the latter's jurisdiction and that it would be bound by its decision. However, on July 18, 1966, the World Court determined that the petitioners had no legal standing to bring the case or any direct interest in it. Therefore, it was unnecessary for it to rule on the substantive merits concerning South Africa's further obligations.

In reaction to this adverse World Court decision, the General Assembly declared South Africa's mandate terminated on October 27, 1966, and made South-West Africa the direct responsibility of the United Nations. In 1968, the Assembly renamed the territory Namibia, but its future was not decided until 1990. South Africa, weakened by numerous sanctions and multinational corporation disinvestments, then relented and the territory became the independent state of Namibia and the 160th UN member. Accordingly, issues that were just gathering momentum in Hammarskjöld's time are now largely a matter of history.

TECHNICAL ASSISTANCE
AND DEVELOPMENT

Technical assistance nowadays includes both hardware, such as equipment, and software, such as advice, training, organization, management, and demonstration. It is often known as technology transfer and involves the movement of gadgets, knowledge, and skills from more advanced to less advanced societies to meet their developmental needs. This means speeding up social, economic, and technical transformation (or any of these) for the purpose of change for the better, however interpreted. In the United Nations, the term "technical assistance" is more closely identified with software. As the General Assembly itself defined it, technical assistance is the "cooperative pooling of wits, wisdom, and skills in economic development in which all countries are able to participate, that all may give as well as receive."

The rationale for multilateral technical assistance, as articulated by various UN organs, is that when an international organization provides it, the often distrustful underdeveloped recipients are less likely to suspect colonialist or neocolonialist exploitation. Moreover, many technical problems—say, a locust epidemic—are transnational in nature and solution. The third reason advanced for technical assistance by the United Nations is that an international organization's program combines and makes use of the experience of many societies that have different social patterns and different cultural traditions, and are at different stages of development.

In the early 1950s, the technical, economic, and social problems of underdeveloped countries began to dominate the focus of the UN agenda. Secretary-General Trygve Lie had said that "poverty remains mankind's chief enemy," and misery, ignorance, hunger, and disease applied to about half the world at the time. In July 1952, the Economic and Social Council recommended that the overriding goal of UN economic and social programs should be the rapid development of these backward areas. Fittingly, just after Hammarskjöld's tenure ended in 1961, the General Assembly designated the 1960s as the first "United Nations development decade."

Throughout Hammarskjöld's administration, there was growing sensitivity about development issues. For one thing, the Charter itself—in articles 1 (3), 55, 56, and 57—committed the organization to improve the economic and social well-being of all peoples, a goal promoted by technical assistance. Second, as more Afro-Asian members were being admitted into the United Nations, the General Assembly and the Economic and Social Council began to exert increasing pressure on the developed states for greater aid of all kinds. As advanced states began to perceive the linkage between development on the one hand and political stability on the other, East and West would eventually assign moderate financial resources to cope with Third World underdevelopment. Western states came to use development assistance as one of the ways to blunt the advance of Communism by trying to reduce hunger, anger, and the need for leftist revolutions, a contest in which both power blocs tried to recruit client states.

Politics already had a lot to do with the amount of aid granted and who got it. For that reason, the overwhelming proportion of such assistance was given on a bilateral basis and not multilaterally, as through UN programs. This was a source of constant irritation to Hammarskjöld, since he believed that technical assistance was best provided in an integrated, not piecemeal, fashion. The United Nations must not be excluded from this important function. As the secretary-general constantly reiterated, only the United Nations could successfully remove technical assistance from the influence of bilateral or Cold War politics.

When Hammarskjöld learned in 1960 that the Organization for European Economic Cooperation (OEEC) had decided to transform itself into the Organization for Economic Cooperation and Development (OECD), he became very upset. The new organization claimed to have a major responsibility to develop the Third World. Brian Urquhart, Hammarskjöld's aide, remembered that the secretary-general regarded the OECD "as the intrusion of a rich man's club into problems that were within the rightful jurisdiction of the more democratic and broadly based United Nations." It seemed to Hammarskjöld that the 24 Western countries of the OECD were interested in "going it alone" on Third World development rather than in using prior UN experience or its existing machinery.

Significantly, when Hammarskjöld created a UN presence, as he did in Jordan, Guinea, Togo, Somalia, or elsewhere, he made it an important part of the duties of his personal representative to identify developmental needs and not just keep a political weather eye. Since his anger at OECD presumption was shared by some new developing states, Hammarskjöld made use of the resentment. For instance, in September 1958, after Guinea voted to leave the French African Community, the secretary-general went out of his way to provide this poor African nation with UN assistance and offset French President de Gaulle's threat of reducing aid from Guinea's former mother country. To maintain contact with developing states, Hammarskjöld also made extensive visits to Africa in 1959 and 1960. He felt the next decade would belong to that developing continent—if there was no nuclear war—and wanted it to look to the world body for leadership. He preached that the United Nations, because it was free from colonial blemish and thus suspicion—unlike several major powers with colonial pasts—could play an important role in the Dark Continent. In contrast to the fears of some Western statesmen, Hammarskjöld was impressed with the political maturity of several African leaders and believed that they could make valuable contributions to the world organization.

For all that, this dramatic growth in UN technical assistance was far from excessive. Developing countries needed more and better infrastructure such as energy grids, communications networks, schools, hospitals, and other social, commercial, and financial institutions. While a number of specialized agencies had participated in technical assistance right from the start—the United Nations Children's Emergency Fund (UNICEF), the Food and Agriculture Organization (FAO), the United Nations Educational, Scientific, and Cultural Organization (UNESCO), the World Health Organization (WHO), and the World Bank (IBRD)—the Expanded Program of Technical Assistance (EPTA) created in 1950 provided some coordination mechanism for projects in population control, refugee assistance, transportation, and other matters. During the 1960s, specialized agencies funded anticholera inoculations of schoolchildren in Saudi Arabia (UNICEF), studied the swollen shoot blight affecting cocoa trees in West Africa (FAO), recruited student nurses for South Vietnam (WHO), provided portable film units for adult education in Pakistan (UNESCO), and resettled Iron Curtain refugees in host countries (UNHCR), among a myriad of other good works.

Hammarskjöld was always hopeful that technical assistance would grow into the paramount UN responsibility after order was achieved. During his early years, he encouraged the establishment of two new programs: Operational Executive and Administrative Personnel Services (OPEX) and the Special United Nations Fund for Economic Development (SUNFED). The latter would finance large preinvestment projects likely to contribute substantially to a developing country's growth—for instance, resource surveys, training programs, and applied research projects enhancing investment and the expansion of the productive base.

As for OPEX, approved by the General Assembly on November 14, 1958, it sought to recruit experts and administrators to serve in developing countries and train native counterparts. OPEX personnel would go not as advisers but as employees of the government receiving the assistance. When necessary, the United Nations would make up the difference between the salary of the seconded expatriate paid by the local government and what the OPEX staffer would normally earn in his home country. But the scheme was opposed by several advanced and less developed countries. The former feared the additional cost of a new and untried international program and continued to prefer bilateral aid. The latter were leery of a new form of "neocolonialism." While Hammarskjöld had managed to win approval for the program in the General Assembly, it remained at a very modest experimental scale.

Hammarskjöld's enthusiasm for greater aid to developing nations was not merely driven by his desire to see them enjoy more of the good life. Reducing the inequity between the developing and the more advanced nations would establish a more stable political order. Like Franklin Roosevelt, Hammarskjöld was aware that "freedom from want" was a prerequisite to a more peaceful world. Accordingly, his reports to the General Assembly and the Economic and Social Council talked of "closing the large divide between productive capacity and human requirements in underdeveloped countries." The secretary-general was especially mindful of what fluctuations in world commodity prices could do to a country dependent on the export of a single crop for revenues and foreign exchange. He therefore strived to forge the autonomous and specialized agencies into a coordinated machine for economic and social assistance that would overcome the natural divisiveness of the system. Generally speaking, his attempts at coordination were frustrated, often by agency heads jealous of their independence. Perhaps that is what underlay Hammarskjöld's great interest in the OPEX program.

During his tenure, Hammarskjöld's efforts to spur progress in the developing countries also suffered grievously from a shortage of financial resources, especially after the United States reduced its pledge from 60 percent of the total at the outset in 1950 to 40 percent by 1961. The Expanded Program of Technical Assistance, while concentrating its efforts on supplying individual experts for work in developing countries and on fellowships for training native personnel, tried to spread its limited funds among so many countries that any one project made little impact. There was always pressure to escalate the amount of aid and coordinate it better. A new start was tried with SUNFED, somewhat better funded than EPTA and willing

Table 5.3   Core Technical Assistance Expenditures in the Hammarskjöld Years, 1953–1961 (in thousands of dollars)

	1953	1954	1955	1956	1957	1958	1959	1960	1961
Expanded Program of Technical Assistance (EPTA)	22,662	19,465	25,405	30,483	31,574	33,825	32,829	34,413	43,737
Special United Nations Fund For Economic Development (SUNFED) (began operations in 1959)	—	—	—	—	—	—	694	2,771	31,531

Source: Inis L. Claude Jr., *Swords into Plowshares,* 3d ed. (New York: Random House, 1968), pp. 450–451; based on U.S. government sources.

to deal with larger projects than EPTA had done. After it created the groundwork through its survey, pilot projects, and training programs, SUNFED's concern, in addition to coordination of technical assistance activities, was to stimulate investments from internal and external, private and public, sources for development. Yet the $32 million budgeted to SUNFED in 1961 did not begin to meet the gigantic needs of the developing world, and voluntary contributions often remained below pledged amounts. As Hammarskjöld lamented, "Such are, of course, the hazards of voluntary programs." Not surprisingly, the equally modest (first) development decade, which got under way that same year, consisted mostly of rhetoric and promises.

Table 5.3 presents figures for core technical assistance outlays from 1953 to 1961. It should be borne in mind, however, that in addition to EPTA and SUNFED, there was also a technical assistance component in the regular UN operating budget and those of several subsidiary organs and specialized agencies. There was also bilateral aid from various governments. That is, more was spent for this purpose than is immediately apparent.

ARMS CONTROL AND DISARMAMENT

Arms control involves agreed-on restraints at any level of weaponry, whether qualitative or quantitative. Disarmament refers to real reductions in the means to engage in warfare. The writers of the UN Charter believed that the creation of a stable international society would reduce the need for national armaments. To the extent that the Security Council and the General Assembly could bring about international peace and security, worldwide arms control would result.

Accordingly, in compliance with articles 11 and 26 of the Charter, both political organs have taken a long series of steps—however limited the results—to carry out their duties. Article 11 requests the General Assembly to "consider the general principles of cooperation in the maintenance of international peace and security, including the principles governing disarmament and the regulation of armaments." Article 26 directs the Security Council, "in order to promote the establishment and maintenance of international peace and security with the least diversion for armaments of the world's human and economic resources," to draw up plans "for the establishment of a system for the regulation of armaments."

The organization's founders knew that greater trust among states and their willingness to reduce the use of force in settling their differences must precede any substantial limitation on national armaments. The early establishment of the United Nations Atomic Energy Commission in 1946 by the General Assembly and the Commission on Conventional Armaments in 1947 by the Security Council were efforts to create effective control systems. But as soon as the East–West confrontation got under way, the United States was unwilling to yield its atomic superiority and the Soviet Union would not renounce its efforts to reach atomic parity, even though it was retaining its advantage in conventional weaponry. In short, the arms race was on.

Hammarskjöld believed that the process of states arming themselves was a symbiotic one, that is, that the political environment and disarmament were completely interacting instead of one being dependent on the other. As he explained, "disarmament is never the result only of the political situation; it is also partly instrumental in creating the political situation." Accordingly, after experiencing earlier disappointment at not making more headway in the matter, the secretary-general changed his tactics. By promoting technical study and exchange of information among experts on the implication of a cessation of nuclear tests, he hoped to build a consensus for mutual disarmament. So, in August 1958, a conference of experts from East and West met in Geneva to exchange nuclear information and agreed that a test ban was both feasible and could be monitored. Hammarskjöld was elated, believing that such openness in the scientific field would reduce distrust and suspicion. In an improved political atmosphere, the larger goal of general disarmament could advance.

By 1957, the United Nations International Atomic Energy Agency (IAEA) had begun operations with the major aim of assisting countries and disseminating information on the use of atomic energy for peaceful purposes. Following joint efforts in the South Polar region during the International Geophysical Year (IGY) of 1957–1958, 12 countries with territorial or scientific interests in the area signed the Antarctic Treaty in 1959, which opened that continent to all countries for research. At the same time, the Antarctic Treaty prohibited military activities of all kinds, including those involving nuclear technology or the dumping of radioactive wastes. This treaty set a precedent for the creation of later demilitarized and nuclear-free zones in specific regions.

The Antarctic Treaty was successfully completed because there were no existing armaments in place in the South Polar region, and thus no state would have to give up more than any other. Too, it was not self-evident at the time that there was any value in hanging on to what the agreement prohibited.

Even though few issues occupied so much UN time and effort, to Hammarskjöld's chagrin many negotiations and much activity involving arms control and disarmament took place outside of the world organization. The reason for this extracurricular endeavor was that the great powers felt that they were the most important players in this highly politicized game. Accordingly, until the late 1980s, nearly all international agreements on armaments either concerned secondary issues or were arranged outside of the UN framework between the two superpowers. The British and French were nearly as exclusivist. Another reason was that by discussing weapons limitation outside the world body, nonmembers of the nuclear club could participate. Weighted voting rather than the one-state, one-vote arrangement of the principal UN organs could be used. In such a setting, unlike the Security Council, resolutions would be veto-proof and thus more likely to pass.

Hammarskjöld fought hard against this practice, since he perceived it as a tendency to circumvent the United Nations. He held a vision of a future world in which state sovereignty would be greatly subordinated to the general good. His viewpoint was that organizational arrangements do not alter political realities. "The moment these . . . questions could be resolved . . . in a new organ, they could just as well be resolved within the UN itself," he once observed.

Still, his perspective did not always prevail, and arms negotiations took place in a number of forums with alternately rising and falling membership. For instance, in August 1959, the major powers created a Ten-Nation Disarmament Committee (TNDC) composed of an equal number of states from East and West. Its first session was held on March 15, 1960, completely outside of the UN framework. But the body atrophied when, later that spring, the Communist bloc countries withdrew after a CIA plane flown by Gary Powers was shot down over Soviet territory. Similarly, the Conference on the Discontinuance of Nuclear Weapons Tests involving the United States, the Soviet Union, and Britain had started work in 1958, also outside the United Nations, to determine the feasibility of establishing an effective control system for the detection of violations of a test ban agreement. Even after the destruction of Gary Powers's U–2 spy plane, the entity continued to function. Later, following bilateral U.S.–USSR talks, the Partial Nuclear Test Ban Treaty covering all but underground tests was signed in Moscow in August 1963. But Hammarskjöld was no longer around.

Progress within the United Nations was much less notable. On November 1, 1953, the General Assembly suggested that the Disarmament Commission, which it had created on January 11, 1952, establish a subcommittee of the powers principally involved to seek an acceptable solution to the disarmament problem in private. The Subcommittee on Disarmament established in April 1954 consisted of the United States, Britain, France, the Soviet Union, and Canada. Between May 1954 and September 1957, many proposals were exchanged and some mutual concessions were made. The proposals included phased and synchronized general disarmament along with a ban on nuclear weapons and a ceiling on conventional weapons; new forms of inspection against surprise attack, such as ground control posts and the "open skies" or aerial inspection plan; as well as partial or required disarmament.

In 1957, the subcommittee discussed all aspects of the disarmament problem, including the question of nuclear weapons tests about which members had voiced concerns in General Assembly discussions in 1956. During 1957, the emphasis shifted from comprehensive plans to efforts toward partial agreements as preliminary steps.

After considering the reports of the Subcommittee on Disarmament, in 1957 the General Assembly urged that priority be given to reaching a package agreement sponsored by the Western powers that would provide for immediate suspension of nuclear weapons with prompt installation of effective international control; cessation of the production of fissionable materials for weapons purposes; reduction of nuclear weapons stockpiles through transfer to peaceful purposes; reduction of armed forces and armaments; progressive establishment of ground and aerial inspection to guard against surprise attack; and joint study of an inspection system designed to ensure that outer space would be used exclusively for peaceful and scientific purposes.

On November 19, 1957, the General Assembly expanded the size of the Disarmament Commission to 25 states following a Soviet complaint that both the commission and its subcommittee were weighted in favor of NATO powers. Still displeased with the enlarged Disarmament Commission, the Soviets now refused to participate in the work of the commission and its subcommittee.

Accordingly, in 1958, the General Assembly resolved that the commission should, for 1959 and on an ad hoc basis, include all UN members. It met in September 1959 to consider a communication from the Conference of Foreign Ministers of the United States, Britain, France, and the Soviet Union to the effect that the four major powers had agreed on the creation of the new Ten-Nation Disarmament Committee mentioned earlier.

On September 17, 1959, the British Foreign Office submitted to the General Assembly an outline of a comprehensive plan aimed, in three balanced stages, at scrapping all weapons of mass destruction and reducing other arms and armed forces to levels that would rule out the possibility of aggressive war. The next day, the Soviets submitted their own three-stage plan on general and complete disarmament. This "Declaration of the Soviet Government on General and Complete Disarmament" called for violations to be submitted to the Security Council or the General Assembly in accordance with their respective spheres of competence. Finally, it provided for a series of partial measures if the Western powers were not willing to accept the Soviet disarmament proposals. On November 20, 1959, the General Assembly unanimously adopted a resolution asking governments to achieve a constructive solution of the problem of general and complete disarmament and sent to the TNDC all the proposals made in the Assembly.

The TNDC then took up the issue, but talks collapsed, and on August 18, 1960, the Disarmament Commission to which the discussions were transferred urged a resumption of negotiations. At the 15th session of the General Assembly that year, it looked as if the United States and the Soviet Union might be able to resume negotiations in an appropriate forum to be agreed upon by them. Accordingly, the Assembly resolved to take up the question in 1961, at its 16th session, after Hammarskjöld's passing.

Hammarskjöld never stopped arguing that disarmament was intimately linked to the peace enforcement provisions of the UN Charter and that "to get the proper kind of policy integration," it should happen in that context. And as already mentioned, he never tired of reasoning that "what at a given time politically is attainable on one organizational basis is equally attainable on another one."

PEACEFUL USES OF ATOMIC ENERGY

The international regulation of atomic energy was first placed on the General Assembly's agenda in the early days of the organization. On January 24, 1946, the Assembly established the United Nations Atomic Energy Commission to make proposals in this regard. However, the original international control plan submitted by the United States became a victim of worsening East–West relations and ended up getting engulfed in the general problem of disarmament.

Even so, countries were aware that besides yielding weapons of mass destruction, the atom could also be an unlimited source of energy for peaceful purposes. However, since the technology involved in the development of atomic energy for war or peaceful use is largely interchangeable, the possibilities of diversion from one to the other have confined the production of atomic energy to a relatively few countries. These fortunate few, under strict safeguards, have managed to acquire the raw materials and the expertise to apply the atom to peaceful purposes.

Hammarskjöld's efforts in promoting international cooperation in the use of atomic power for peaceful purposes is possibly the least known but potentially most important of his endeavors. He certainly thought so. His accomplishments there demonstrated that functionalism could triumph over high politics—at least in the short term.

Too, events favored his position. On December 8, 1953, President Dwight D. Eisenhower proposed to the eighth session of the General Assembly that governments jointly contribute uranium and fissionable materials to an international atomic energy agency to be set up under the aegis of the United Nations. Thus, at its ninth session on December 4, 1954, the General Assembly resolved that such an agency be established without delay and that to this end an international technical conference be held under UN auspices to explore the means of developing the peaceful uses of atomic energy through international cooperation and in particular to study the development of atomic power. The agency also considered other related technical areas such as biology, medicine, and protection from radiation. Accordingly, the United Nations International Conference on the Peaceful Uses of Atomic Energy met in Geneva from August 8 to August 20, 1955. The statute of what came to be the International Atomic Energy Agency (IAEA) was drafted there and later circulated among all members. After some changes, the statute was unanimously approved on October 26, 1956, and signed by the representatives of 70 countries. Another 10 signed within the deadline. Thus the IAEA legally came into being on July 29, 1957, with the deposit of the necessary ratifications of its statute.

Hammarskjöld had played an important role in organizing this atoms for peace conference with the help of the Atomic Advisory Committee of seven scientists appointed by member governments. Even though he had tried hard to have the IAEA made part of the United Nations proper, in fact it became a structure akin to a specialized agency reporting to the General Assembly. In short, the Vienna-based body came to function at a distance from the core organization—and from Hammarskjöld.

In the meantime, the "Geneva spirit" that had witnessed the IAEA's creation gave rise to optimism about the possibilities of the atom for human progress, especially as, also in 1955, the General Assembly established the United Nations Scientific Committee on the Effects of Atomic Radiation. These various events renewed Hammarskjöld's faith in the exchange of scientific data as a means of improving the political atmosphere and reducing distrust among nations. It was widely felt that the subsequent nuclear test ban negotiations flowed from the atoms for peace conference.

Thus, at its 10th session in 1955, the General Assembly recommended that a second conference be arranged within two or three years. This second United Nations International Conference on the Peaceful Uses of Atomic Energy, held in Geneva from September 1 to September 13, 1958, was wider in scope than the first conference since it covered a new field—the possibility of controlled fusion. After considering Hammarskjold's report on the second conference, the Assembly unanimously approved a resolution whereby the advisory committee established at the ninth session of the Assembly to assist the secretary-general in the organization and convening of both conferences be extended. It became the United Nations Scientific Advisory Committee, and it advised and assisted the secretary-general on all matters relating to the peaceful uses of the atom with which the world organization might be concerned. One of the last things that Hammarskjöld did in this regard was to recommend, in his report to the 15th session of the General Assembly in 1960, that a third conference be held in two or three years. This did not occur until the fall of 1964.

The Scientific Committee on the Effects of Atomic Radiation had been established by the General Assembly on December 3, 1955. The committee's first substantive report to the Assembly was made in 1958. It provided a broad, comprehensive evaluation of existing knowledge of the levels of ionizing radiation on human beings exposed to its effects. Its subsequent report to the Assembly was made in 1962. But in the meantime, its endeavors—as well as President Eisenhower's invitation to the United Nations on March 26, 1958, to send a group of qualified observers to witness a large American nuclear explosion in which radioactive fallout was to be reduced—produced the Conference on the Discontinuance of Nuclear Weapons Tests in Geneva in the summer of 1958. This was followed by similar ones in later years.

PEACEFUL USES OF OUTER SPACE

The question of the peaceful uses of outer space was first considered by the United Nations in 1958. A Soviet proposal recommending "the establishment within the framework of the United Nations of an international committee for cooperation in the study of cosmic space for peaceful purposes" and an American proposal "to obtain fullest information on the many problems relating to outer space" led to the General Assembly's decision, at its 13th session in that year, to include both proposals on its agenda as the "question of peaceful uses of outer space."

The Assembly created an ad hoc committee of 18 states to report on the activities and resources of the UN network on various matters dealing with international cooperation in the peaceful uses of outer space. In December 1959, recognizing the need for a special organ to further progress in this area, the General Assembly created a 24-member committee to study practical and feasible means for giving effect to such outer space programs under UN auspices. The Committee on the Peaceful Uses of Outer Space, later enlarged to 28 members, thus provided a forum for considering the political and legal issues arising in the peaceful exploration of outer space. And indeed, in subsequent years, the committee has presented a series of recommendations, a number of them implemented, on the exchange of information, encouragement of international programs, potentially harmful effects of space experiments, and education and training. These have laid the groundwork for further practical action in the development of international cooperation regarding outer space.

Despite numerous setbacks in the interim that witnessed Cold War deadlocks in and out of the committee, Hammarskjöld's vision finally materialized in October 1967 when the Treaty on Principles Governing the Activities of States in the Exploration and Use of Outer Space came into force. In accordance with his hope to protect "the overriding interest of the community of nations in the peaceful and beneficial uses of outer space," the treaty prohibits the placing or orbiting of nuclear weapons or other means of mass destruction in outer space, on the moon, or on celestial bodies.

DIVERSIFICATION AND EXPANSION

Table 5.4 compares the several budgets of the UN network in the initial and final years of Hammarskjöld's tenure. They highlight the more diversified and stepped-up activities of the world body—the breaking of new ground—as well as the UN serving its expanding membership. Hammarskjöld was instrumental in both processes.

Table 5.4   Total Expenditures of the UN System for Calendar Years 1953 and 1961 (in thousands of dollars)

		1953	1961
United Nations			
Operating budget		48,328	72,969
Supplement/Reduction		1,542	−1,320
		49,870	71,649
UN Specialized Agencies			
Food and Agriculture Organization (FAO)		5,064	10,872
Intergovernmental Maritime Consultative Organization (IMCO)			233
International Civil Aviation Organization (ICAO)		3,150	4,880
International Labor Organization (ILO)		6,510	10,414
International Telecommunication Union (ITU)		1,456	2,920
United Nations Educational, Scientific, and Cultural Organization (UNESCO)		7,973	15,095
Universal Postal Union (UPU)		435	798
World Health Organization (WHO)		8,113	18,975
World Meteorological Organization (WMO)		272	671
Subtotal		32,973	64,858
Peacekeeping Forces			
United Nations Emergency Force (Egypt) (UNEF)		—	19,000
United Nations Operation in the Congo (ONUC)			
Military	100,000		
Economic	35,000	—	135,000
Subtotal		0	154,000
Special Programs Financed by Voluntary Contributions		1953	1961
International Civil Aviation Organization (ICAO) (joint support program)		1,604	1,984
United Nations Children's Fund (UNICEF)		12,506	27,000
UNESCO Aid to Africa		—	1,504
United Nations Expanded Program of Technical Assistance (EPTA)		22,662	43,737
United Nations High Commissioner for Refugees (UNHCR)		848	6,000
United Nations Korean Reconstruction Agency (UNKRA)		58,219	—
United Nations Relief for Hungarian Refugees		—	253
United Nations Relief and Works Agency for Palestine Refugees in the Near East (UNRWA)		29,192	39,334
Special United Nations Fund for Economic Development (SUNFED)		—	31,531
World Health Organization (WHO), Community Water Development Program		—	300
World Health Organization, Malaria Eradication Program		—	5,769
World Health Organization, Medical Research Program		—	1,620
Subtotal		125,031	159,032
Grand total		207,874	449,539

Source: United Nations, Office of Public Information, *Everyman's United Nations 1945–1965,* 8th ed. (New York: United Nations, 1968), pp. 475–476; Inis L. Claude Jr., *Swords into Plowshares,* 3d ed. (New York: Random House, 1968), pp. 450–451; based on U.S. government sources.

6

Hammarskjöld's Last Hurrah: The Congo

The process of decolonization, anticipated by the UN founders in Chapter XI of the Charter, had been expected to be gradual, orderly, and peaceful—evolutionary rather than revolutionary. Yet the 1960 Declaration on the Granting of Independence to Colonial Countries and Peoples in fact transformed the process into a disorderly and often violent rout. It called for the colonial powers to hand over self-governing authority to peoples not enjoying independence regardless of their state of preparedness. It also placed the prestige of the United Nations behind the cause of lifting the nonself-governing territories out of a dependent status and fulfilling their twentieth-century nationalist aspirations. For, as mentioned earlier, the United Nations was by now deeply involved in the process of decolonization. But it had yet to learn that nation building was a far more difficult process.

Beginning in 1960, the nascent Afro-Asian majority, or at least plurality, in the General Assembly often shunned moderation. After November 1961, it used the Special Committee on the Situation with Regard to the Implementation of the Declaration on the Granting of Independence to Colonial Countries and Peoples (the Committee of Twenty-Four) to implement this program. No case of decolonization epitomized better the departure from a deliberate and orderly evolution toward sovereignty than that of the former Belgian Congo, one of 17 colonies to become independent that year.[1] Perhaps because of this, Hammarskjöld's goal of filling constitutional, legislative, and precedential space with UN authority met its greatest challenge in what came to be known as the Congo crisis.

Dag Hammarskjöld's interest in Africa began soon after he took office. His introduction to the *Annual Report of the Secretary-General, 1955–1956* focused on Africa's "crucial stage of transition." His understanding of that continent's problems was enhanced during a six-week tour of the sub-Saharan region in 1960. He was struck by the extent of balkanization that took place when nineteenth-century imperialists carved up the area for the European colonizers' purposes and without regard to tribal, religious, linguistic, or any other criteria. As colonial rule waned, Hammarskjöld sensed the dangers of premature self-government and the possibilities of superpower clashes as they rushed to fill the vacuum created by the end of empire. Although he was impressed by the poverty south of the Sahara, Hammarskjöld was optimistic about the area's future and believed that the United Nations could play a useful role in the Dark Continent through assisting its many weak and inexperienced countries. At one point he even said, "We are at a turn of the road where our attitude will be of decisive significance, I believe, not only for the future of this organization but also for the future of Africa. And Africa may well in present circumstances mean the world."

As it turned out, Hammarskjöld's endeavors in the Congo became the most complex and controversial cause to which he devoted much of the final 14 months of his life. In that vast territory, Belgium's jewel in the crown, he would soon have to deal with the collapse of internal law and order, multitribal hostility, several secessionist movements, the interplay of adversarial personalities in the country's power structure, renewed Belgian political and military intervention, the presence of foreign mercenaries, and the scheming and intrusion of the great powers. He had indeed met his Waterloo.

Unlike the Suez crisis, in which clear enemies were aligned on two sides, in the Congo the parameters of conflict were always nebulous. Alignments shifted endlessly in kaleidoscopic manner. Neither was it always obvious who was in charge or even which of the competing authorities was legitimate and thus worthy of involvement with the United Nations. Additionally, in short order the divisiveness in the Congo was reechoed in the world body itself, and Hammarskjöld came under abusive and repetitive attacks from the Soviet bloc but also others.

More than anywhere else, the Congo forced the secretary-general to implement his technique of preventive diplomacy, an alternative to other forms of conflict management. In his introduction to the *Annual Report of the Secretary-General, 1959–1960,* Hammarskjöld explained that his approach tried to discourage the major power blocs from intruding in a particular area, that it was a way of containing the East–West struggle in a specific situation. As he also indicated, he had used this technique of useful UN activity in the Middle East in 1956 and again in 1958 and in Laos in 1959. As it turned out, he was going to employ it on a larger scale than ever in his last hurrah, the Congo.

THE CRISIS

The former Belgian Congo, colonized in the nineteenth century, became the independent Republic of the Congo[2] on June 30, 1960. The transformation was done in great haste and with practically no preparation. This huge and potentially wealthy country had essentially no native personnel trained in administrative, political, and technical skills. On Independence Day, the Congo had fewer than two dozen native university graduates. This had not been a problem as long as the Belgian cadres completely controlled the economy, the civil service, the army, and political life. It became a monumental dilemma on the day when the Republic of the Congo came into being.

Not until January 1960 was a Roundtable Conference held in Brussels, bringing together Belgian and Congolese leaders to discuss the territory's future. The incipient Congolese nationalist movement boasted leaders like Joseph Kasavubu, Patrice Lumumba, and Joseph-Désiré Mobutu, but there was little unity among them except about the need for independence. At the Brussels conference the leaders agreed on January 27, 1960, to hold general parliamentary elections in May 1960. But this did not mean much, since the Congolese had enjoyed no right to vote before December 1957, and the very concept of democracy and its implications was strange. Still, a new Congolese constitution, the Loi Fondamentale, was drawn up to serve as the blueprint for the new political system.

On short notice, then, the second largest country of Africa, nearly five times the size of France, with 14 million inhabitants divided among hundreds of intermittently hostile and violent tribes and bickering leaders, became free. A few weeks before independence some copies of the new constitution were available. Only days prior to June 30, there was no Congolese president, premier, or cabinet. Any premier's election required a two-thirds majority in both houses of the legislature by parliamentarians inexperienced in the art of political compromise. These neophytes had to decide between two bitter opponents whose rival ambitions had already been evident at the Brussels conference. The two political foes were Joseph Kasavubu and Patrice Lumumba, but there were others, especially Moise Tshombe.

From the start, the political spotlight focused on Lumumba, a fiery anticolonialist who had precipitated independence by the anti-Belgian riots that followed his anticolonial speeches in 1959. He advocated a strong central government to control the various provincial administrations. Lumumba had many loyal supporters—and possibly as many detractors. His election as premier of the national government in Leopoldville (now Kinshasa), the capital, just before independence, was made possible by a shifting majority backing in parliament. In a gesture of reconciliation, Joseph Kasavubu, his more moderate challenger, was installed in the presidency, a largely ceremonial post. What came to be known as the Congolese "cha-cha" had begun.

Lumumba's policy alternated between support for a strong UN presence in the Congo (to help him throw out the Belgians and impose centralized rule on the dissident provinces) and connivance with the Soviets to oust both of these and provide him with military and economic aid. Tshombe, who headed the richest province, Katanga (now Shaba), was promoting a weak central government and great provincial autonomy, if not outright sovereignty. In fact, by July 11, 1960, Tshombe had declared Katanga's "total independence" from the Congo, terming himself "president" of the new "state." He was soon emulated by other leaders in Kasai and Orientale Provinces. Alone among Congolese, Tshombe sought more Belgian troops and assistance of all kinds, just when the UN Security Council asked the former colonial power to withdraw so that it might replace the latter during the interregnum while the Congolese learned to govern themselves.

Tshombe refused to deal with Lumumba, who sought to speed the departure of approximately 10,000 Belgian civil servants and 1,000 Belgian officers in the 25,000-man Force Publique, the colonial Congolese army. While Tshombe attacked Lumumba's alleged Communist ties and his central government as "neo-Communist," the Katangan leader's version of the cha-cha consisted of intermittently agreeing with the central government in Leopoldville and then just as abruptly reversing himself, especially in his own provincial capital of Elisabethville (now Lubumbashi), where the Belgians had been asked to stay. Tshombe's double-talk and incorrect attributions—including to Hammarskjöld—tended to make a bad situation worse.

At first Brussels hoped that the Congolese would be unable to rule themselves and delayed withdrawing. But as it became evident that, in the face of Congolese, Soviet, and UN pressure, the Belgians would in fact have to leave their former prize colony, they used Tshombe's ambitions to maintain their position at least in the mineral-rich province of Katanga.

A major motivation for Belgian support of the Katangan leader was its resources of copper, tin, cobalt, manganese, zinc, and uranium mines. Katanga accounted for some 60 percent of the Congo's entire revenues, and many of the mines were owned by the Union Minière du Haut Katanga (UMHK). This Belgian company's shareholders feared that a different regime would depreciate the value of their assets or would nationalize them. Partly for that reason, Tshombe was represented by the Soviets and his other adversaries as the stooge of Western mining interests.

Tribal violence broke out on July 2 in Leopoldville and Luluabourg and on July 4 in Coquilhatville as old scores were settled. On July 8, Premier Lumumba dismissed all Belgian officers from the Force Publique after a mutiny against them broke out on July 5. He appointed Sergeant Victor Lundula as a major-general and army chief and Sgt. Maj. Joseph-Désiré Mobutu as colonel and chief of staff. Belgian administrators and their dependents started to flee the chaos even as fresh Belgian paratroopers arrived from metropolitan bases, ostensibly to protect Belgian lives and property. They ensconced themselves in Elisabethville in Katanga, where they were welcomed by Tshombe, and eventually in other Congolese cities. Lumumba characterized the dispatch of these Belgian forces as an act of aggression against the nation. Moreover, sporadic tribal violence, incited by rival leaders with shifting policies, alignments, and personal relations, continued to plague the newly independent state and cause great loss of life and flights of European, mostly Belgian, refugees.

On July 12, Kasavubu and Lumumba attempted to fly to Elisabethville to get Tshombe to rescind his declaration of Katanga's secession made the previous day. The effort failed when their plane was barred from landing. That same day the Congolese president and his premier cabled Hammarskjöld as follows: "The Government of the Republic of the Congo requests urgent dispatch by the United

Nations of military assistance. This request is justified by the dispatch to the Congo of metropolitan Belgian troops in violation of our treaty of friendship . . . to protect the national territory of the Congo against the present external aggression which is a threat to international peace."

On July 13, using his authority under Charter article 99 for the first time, Hammarskjöld called the Security Council into urgent session. The provision allows the secretary-general to bring to the council's attention any matter that in his opinion may threaten the peace. Until now, Hammarskjöld had been reluctant to use article 99, since to do so "would necessarily involve a judgement as to the facts" for which on other occasions he had conceded not to have a sufficient basis. But this time, skillfully avoiding reference to charges of Belgian aggression made by Leopoldville and Moscow, Hammarskjöld was requesting from the council that he had convened a UN force to be guided by the earlier UNEF principles of "self-defense and noninterference."

Thus, on July 14, by a vote of 8–0–3 (with Britain, France, and Nationalist China abstaining), the Security Council adopted a Tunisian motion and called on Belgium to withdraw its troops "speedily." It also authorized Hammarskjöld "to take the necessary steps, in consultation with the Government of the Republic of the Congo, to provide the Government with such military assistance as may be necessary until, through the efforts of the Congolese Government with the technical assistance of the United Nations, the national security forces may be able, in the opinion of the Government, to meet fully their tasks." Simultaneously, the council rejected three Soviet amendments that would have condemned armed aggression by Belgium, called for the immediate withdrawal of Belgian troops, and limited the military assistance to be provided to that country to exclusively African member states. The secretary-general was now launched on what he soon called the UN's "biggest single effort."

Hammarskjöld's "necessary steps" to provide the Congo with the Security Council's authorized military and technical assistance (but not the use of force) focused on the creation of a peacekeeping body that came to be known as the United Nations Operation in the Congo, or ONUC. Hammarskjöld explained to the council that his goal was to make the Force Publique and Congolese police able "to meet fully their tasks"—a long-term solution to the crisis—and that ONUC would be a stopgap measure for the maintenance of law and order.

At the same time, the UN force would obviate the need for Belgian troops in the Congo. A parallel civilian assistance program would help restore essential administrative and public services.

According to Hammarskjöld, the operating principles would be to obtain "the consent of all interested parties regarding the force; that it should be used exclusively under United Nations control and serve the organization's purpose alone; that it should not interfere in the Congo's internal affairs; that it should be for self-defense only; and that it should have freedom of movement in the Congo and have access to its facilities." Troops from the permanent Security Council members would be excluded. These rules paralleled those applying to UNEF at Suez in 1956. Subsequently, Hammarskjöld specified that ONUC could not be used in joint operations with the Congolese government.

By July 15 some 1,300 ONUC soldiers from Ghana and Tunisia had arrived in the Congo, and within a month there were over 14,000 military and civilian personnel from several states. Both the Security Council's resolution and Hammarskjöld's implementation fudged the essential issue of how to keep a country in chaos from unraveling. In the Congo as in several other decolonized areas, the principle of national unity and territorial integrity was on a collision course with the other principle of the self-determination of peoples, especially when they had different loyalties. The answers to this fundamental problem were to be provided on an as-you-go, day-to-day, case-by-case basis, leaving many participants and observers discontented and Hammarskjöld in a constant dilemma.

In the Congolese context, this neutralist, hands-off policy pursued by Hammarskjöld on the basis of the council's deliberately vague mandate proved to be counterproductive and in fact impossible. The Congo's chaotic internal conditions, flowing from incomplete and faulty nation building, the roles played by various outside powers, and the personal cha-chas of the native leaders, caused turmoil and delayed the return of the relative political stability that had existed under the authoritarian Belgian colonial rule. The unpredictable and politically inexperienced Lumumba was described by his detractors as a rabble-rouser interested primarily in his political self-aggrandizement. The Eisenhower administration considered him messianic and irrational. By now he was threatening to call in the Soviets if the UN force did not oust the Belgians and forcefully sub-

Map 6.1   ONUC Deployment as of June 1961

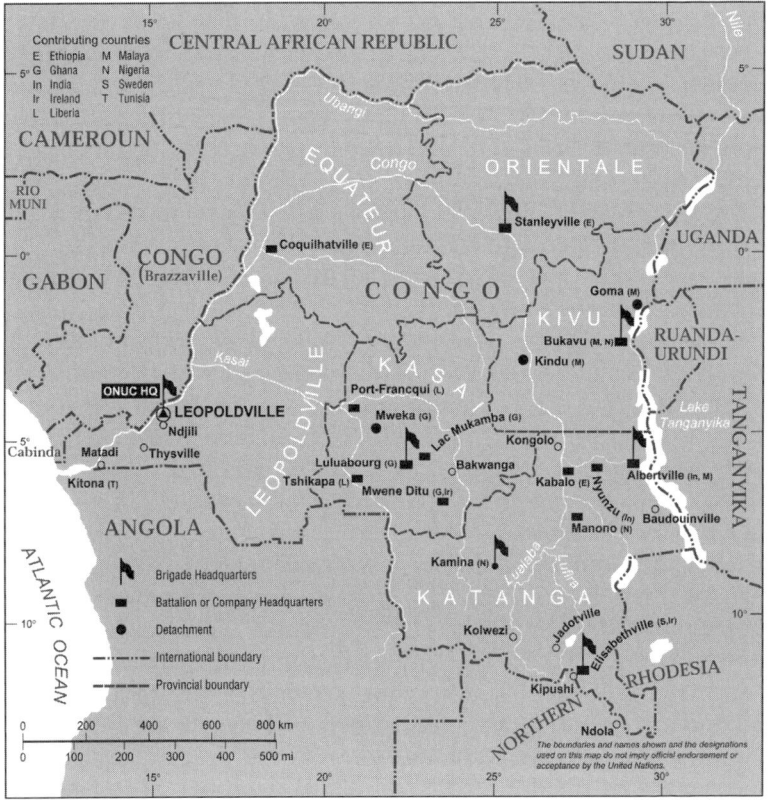

Map No. 3952.13 UNITED NATIONS
September 1996

Department of Public Information
Cartographic Section

Source: UN Cartographic Section.

due Tshombe's secession. And earlier, the Congolese premier had indicated he would appeal to the neutralist, nonaligned Bandung Treaty powers if the United Nations did not provide his requested aid.

Lumumba, like Tshombe, practiced his cha-cha on Hammarskjöld himself. For instance, on July 25 in New York, the Congolese leader assured the secretary-general that a UN shadow administration would receive Leopoldville's full cooperation in the nonpolitical field. On that occasion, Lumumba barely mentioned Katanga. Yet after meeting the Soviet ambassador in Ottawa, Lumumba executed his customary volte-face. Thus, by July 28, when Hammarskjöld arrived in the Congo, Vice Premier Antoine Gizenga (Lumumba only returned on August 2) informed the secretary-general that his government expected ONUC to move immediately into Katanga. Although Hammarskjöld had made it clear that he regarded the secessionist province and the significant Belgian presence there as a legitimate UN concern, he also urged patience in replacing them. For Hammarskjöld kept insisting that ONUC was a neutral force that should not get involved in the country's internal disputes but only try to balance the contending powers.

In separatist Katanga, "President" Tshombe (as he styled himself), encouraged covertly by the Belgians, relentlessly rebuffed the overtures of Ralph Bunche, an African-American and Hammarskjöld's first personal representative in the Congo. Early in August, Bunche had tried to negotiate the peaceful entry of ONUC units into Katanga and the removal of the Belgians. Hammarskjöld in turn attempted to reassure Tshombe that UN troops were independent of the central government in Leopoldville and would not be used to bring Katanga under its control. But Tshombe could not be persuaded. After hearing Bunche's account of his meeting with Tshombe, Hammarskjöld canceled his orders that ONUC contingents move into Elisabethville. In New York, the Security Council commended him for his "prompt action" and again urged Belgium to withdraw speedily.

On August 9, by a 9–0–2 vote, the Security Council, with France and Italy abstaining, resolved that compliance was mandatory and that the ONUC entry into Katanga was "necessary for the full implementation of this resolution." The first ONUC troops made their appearance within minutes of Hammarskjöld's arrival in the Katangan capital on August 12. The secretary-general having just landed at Elisabethville airport, two planeloads carrying 240 Swedish soldiers followed. It is not clear how Tshombe had allowed that to happen. Perhaps the council's affirmation that ONUC "will not be a party to or in any way intervene in or be used to influence the outcome of any internal conflicts, constitutional or otherwise" was credible. Possibly, in the midst of both men's ambiguities, at which Hammarskjöld was a past master, the secretary-general may have surprised Tshombe by his unexpected move, and the Katangan guards at the airport had received no specific instructions to bar the landing. Or Tshombe, like Hammarskjöld, may have known that the Belgian troops were under strict orders to neither delay nor oppose the entry of ONUC troops into Katanga. Or conceivably, Tshombe may have become intimidated by Lumumba's threats—made both to him and to Hammarskjöld—that he would use the Congolese army to invade Katanga if ONUC did not. Or this may have been just one of the many 180-degree turnarounds so typical of Tshombe. To the very end, it was difficult to reconcile what was in the mind of this wily politician in the first place, what he said in the second place, and what he did in the third place.

At any rate, other ONUC units reached eastern Katanga that same day, and within 48 hours there were some 2,000 UN troops in the secessionist province. After more delay and evasive maneuvers, on August 15–16 the 1,600 Belgian troops in Elisabethville apparently withdrew to their Kamina and Kitona treaty bases in Katanga and Leopoldville Province, respectively. In fact, by the end of that month, Belgian military personnel had seemingly pulled out of their final strongholds in Katanga as well as from the two bases. However, it was soon discovered that individually recruited or other military personnel as well as civilian advisers, shipments of weapons, and financing by the Union Minière du Haut Katanga and Belgian banks continued the Belgian presence and influence in the province. But for now, the ostensible Belgian withdrawal from Katanga represented a diplomatic victory for Hammarskjöld, since on July 27, when he had talked to Premier Gaston Eyskens about the matter in Brussels, the Belgian leader had given him to understand that his forces needed to stay to protect Belgian lives and property—and that they would.

Eventually, Hammarskjöld's rigid anti-Belgian policies were sharply criticized by many, both inside and outside of Belgium. The secretary-general insisted on the withdrawal of Belgian civilian advisers, technicians, and administrators working throughout the Congo, as well as Belgian forces and, later, mercenaries hired directly by the Katanga authorities. The critics opined that the United

Nations could not begin to provide the physicians, teachers, planners, and other personnel that the Congo needed, not only in terms of quantity but also quality. They pointed to Belgium's 80 years of experience in its former colony. At any rate, Hammarskjöld's stated purpose (October 1960) to "fully circumscribe the Belgian factor and eliminate it" failed. In some way or other, the Belgians continued to be a presence in the country throughout the episode.

The events of mid-August did not satisfy an impassioned Lumumba in Leopoldville. He was angry at not having been more fully involved in the "taking" of Elisabethville. He objected to Hammarskjöld's "neutralist" interpretation of the Security Council's resolution of August 9. Lumumba was infuriated by Hammarskjöld's clarification that ONUC was entering Katanga merely to replace the Belgians and not to bring Tshombe's administration under central government (i.e., Lumumba's) control. Lumumba viewed such reluctance as "unilateral and erroneous" despite the council resolution's reaffirmation of neutrality in any internal conflict. Whatever the merits of the argument, the Congolese premier thenceforth refused to cooperate with the secretary-general, declaring that his government had lost confidence in Hammarskjöld and demanding that ONUC leave the Congo "at once." Lumumba's position enjoyed the full support of the Soviet Union which, after the council's resolution of August 9 was approved by Moscow, became increasingly critical of Hammarskjöld, his policies, and the very nature of his office.

Lumumba now decided to use the Congolese army to invade Katanga, secretly requesting and receiving 17 Soviet transport aircraft and 100 trucks for the purpose without consulting President Kasavubu or the other moderate Congolese cabinet members. Actually, the threatened invasion by the Congolese National Army (ANC)—successor to the Force Publique—never materialized in this instance. Only in January 1961 did 400 to 600 ANC troops enter a town in northern Katanga.

The ONUC Advisory Committee, chaired by Hammarskjöld with heavy Afro-Asian representation to mollify Soviet and Third World demands, met on August 24 for the first time. This committee, with representatives from Canada, Ethiopia, Ghana, Guinea, India, Indonesia, Ireland, Liberia, Mali, Morocco, Pakistan, Sudan, Sweden, Tunisia, and the United Arab Republic—reflecting the makeup of ONUC—selected the members of the UN Congo Conciliation Commission, whose purpose was to visit the country and try to bring the feuding parties together. Lumumba fleetingly declared himself "satisfied" with the turn of events, as he was now fully occupied with suppressing the rebellion in Kasai, a rich agricultural province also bent on secession. On this very day, following the installation of "President" Albert Kalonji, Lumumba sent Congolese army troops (later withdrawn by Mobutu) to Luluabourg, Kasai's capital. By way of response, Kasai declared its federation with Katanga on August 25, and Tshombe pledged his military aid against Lumumba. Months of disturbance followed.

CONSTITUTIONAL EVOLUTION

In the meantime, Leopoldville had its own internal problems. The breach between the Congolese president and his premier came to a head on September 5. The relationship between these two leaders had been tense even before independence because of tribal and political rivalry. After independence on June 30, 1960, fundamental rifts over policy, especially Lumumba's "overreliance" on the Soviets from President Kasavubu's and the moderates' perspectives, raised the political temperature in Leopoldville. When Lumumba disclosed that in addition to 14 Ilyushin transport planes the Soviets had also provided him with 100 trucks to put down the secessionist movement in Kasai, Kasavubu openly challenged Lumumba's leadership.

The constitutionally "weak" president abruptly dismissed his mercurial premier and replaced him with Joseph Ileo. Within hours, Lumumba returned the compliment and "fired" Kasavubu. The Congolese parliament refused to ratify either dismissal, and for a few days there were two rival governments in Leopoldville. It took ONUC forces a week to quell the ensuing clashes between Kasavubu and Lumumba supporters.

The constitutional crisis of September 5 precipitated another one between Lumumba and ONUC. On that very night the UN force closed all the major Congolese airports to non-UN traffic in the interest of peace and security—that is, to prevent Soviet supply and troop transport aircraft from using them on Lumumba's behalf. The following day, ONUC temporarily closed down the Leopoldville radio station, just as Lumumba was trying to address the Congolese people to seek their support in his power struggle with Kasavubu. The premier was barred from entering the premises by ONUC troops, and he charged that this action helped his rival, who had access to Radio Brazzaville across the Congo River. All the facilities were reopened on September 12, but in the meantime the disturbances continued and the UN move provoked disaffection in its own ranks. The United Arab Republic charged "a flagrant violation of the Congo's sovereignty" and soon removed its contingent from ONUC, as did other contributing states.

Into this mess and power vacuum stepped a new Congolese strongman, Joseph-Désiré Mobutu, the 29-year-old former noncommissioned officer in the Force Publique and now chief of staff of the Congolese army. On September 14, Mobutu declared Kasavubu, Lumumba, and Joseph Ileo, Kasavubu's newly appointed premier, "neutralized" as he did the two rival cabinets and parliament until December 31, 1960. A violent cha-cha among the leaders ensued, and Mobutu placed Lumumba under house arrest. Through Kasavubu, who remained a figurehead president, Mobutu gave all Soviet and Czechoslovak diplomatic personnel 48 hours to leave the Congo. Naturally, all of these events ran counter to the stated UN purpose of trying to reconcile the feuding factions.

But Mobutu did not wish to assume the reins of government officially yet. Rather, for the subsequent several months, a form of makeshift caretaker government was in charge. It was a College of High Commissioners chaired by Minister of Foreign Affairs Justin Bomboko, who also continued as high commissioner for external affairs. Most commissioners were young, educated, and inexperienced. Since Kasavubu was still the nominal head of state, Hammarskjöld continued to deal with him. But the secretary-general had strong reservations about the legitimacy of the College of High Commissioners' government and clashed sharply with the views of the Eisenhower administration, rumored to have aided and abetted Mobutu's coup, on this score. There is no question that Hammarskjöld's representative in the Congo, Rajeshwar Dayal, urged the secretary-general to regard Lumumba as the legal prime minister, prompting Washington to pressure for Dayal's replacement.

GENERAL ASSEMBLY DELIBERATIONS

On September 9, the Soviets had vetoed a Security Council resolution that explicitly directed members not to intervene in Congolese domestic affairs and to channel all assistance to the country through the United Nations. Because of this deadlock ending the council's efforts to deal with the crisis, the latter summoned the General Assembly under the Uniting for Peace resolution over the strong opposition of the Soviets. The Assembly's special session—its fourth during Hammarskjöld's tenure—ran from September 17 to September 20, 1960. Its resolution reiterated all the provisions of the vetoed Security Council's motion.

But by now the Soviets realized that in addition to their unilateral supply of equipment, technical assistance, and "political experts" running afoul of the directive that all aid be funneled through the United Nations, their probable game plan was also in jeopardy. The same motions that targeted the Belgians' intrusion in Congolese affairs could also keep the Soviets from projecting themselves further in Central Africa. Indeed, they perceived that while ONUC was not engaged in collective security against Belgian "aggression," it was involved in preventive diplomacy that had not played into the hands of their protégé, Patrice Lumumba, or their own. For these and possibly other reasons, the Soviets were now ready to play their trump card.

On September 23, at the regular 15th session of the General Assembly in New York, Soviet Premier Nikita Khrushchev accused the Western "colonialists" of "doing their dirty work in the Congo through the secretary-general and his staff." The Russian leader added that Hammarskjöld should be called to order so that "he does not misuse the position of the secretary-general." The next day, Khrushchev unveiled the Soviet troika plan. Since there were no "neutral men," he said, the colonialists had been aided and abetted by "Mr. Hammarskjöld and his staff." The Soviet premier explained that the secretary-general's use of ONUC "disorganized the life of the state and paralyzed . . . the legitimate government." Thus the post of secretary-general "should be abolished." Because the United Nations included "the military blocs of the Western powers, socialist states and neutralist [nonaligned] countries . . . we consider it reasonable . . . for the executive body . . . to be constituted not as one person—the secretary-general—but as three representatives," one from each bloc. In fact, this was not a completely novel Soviet idea.

At the United Nations Conference on International Organization in San Francisco in 1945, Moscow had already proposed a representative collegium to run the secretariat. And even though the Soviets had lost out on that point then, they had continued to promote a very conservative and restricted view of the secretary-general's authority and functions. For by now it had become clear to the Russians that Hammarskjöld was trying to act as an independent executive and so they attempted to slice his position and thus his authority into thirds. Their present demand would have imposed a potential veto on the secretary-general's implementation and interpretation of Security Council decisions and General Assembly resolutions.

As in 1945, the Soviets received very minor support among the members for a collective UN executive. Although the neutralist countries would have stood to gain representation in the three-man secretary-generalship proposed by the Russians, the majority backed Hammarskjöld. Even the more radical African states such as Ghana and Guinea, unhappy about ONUC's refusal to forcefully bring Tshombe's Katanga under Lumumba's government, supported Hammarskjöld's leadership. Admittedly, the latter may have hit a sympathetic chord when, responding to Khrushchev's urging that he resign and be replaced by a threesome, the secretary-general declared that he would remain in office so long as the small- and middle-ranking member states desired. He explained, "It is not Soviet Russia or any of the great powers that need the vigilance and protection of the United Nations; it is all the others." Hammarskjöld also observed that "this is a question not of a man but of an institution." He refuted the charge that he had abused the power granted to him by the UN political organs and had mismanaged ONUC. "I have the right to expect guidance, but if the Security Council says nothing, I have no other choice than to follow my convictions," he explained.

Still, Khrushchev was not pacified. On October 3, he repeated his charge that Hammarskjöld was a colonialist stooge biased against the socialist countries. He now warned that if Hammarskjöld "does not muster enough courage to resign, so to say in a chivalrous manner, then the Soviet Union will draw the necessary conclusions." Hammarskjöld responded that same afternoon, saying the he had "no right to do so," for to comply would be to "throw the Organization to the winds."

For all the ovation he received following his remarks, the secretary-general won only a pyrrhic victory. From September 1960 until his death a year later, his effectiveness was diminished by active Soviet hostility, just as Trygve Lie's had been. And the Soviet criticisms did not abate. Rather, Hammarskjöld continued to be accused of "usurpation of power." Soviet Foreign Minister Andrei Gromyko even characterized him as a "United Nations Field Marshal" and said he suspected that the secretary-general fantasized himself to be the "Prime Minister of a World Government." It was only after U Thant had succeeded Hammarskjöld that the Soviets quietly dropped their insistence on a triumvirate executive arrangement in the secretariat.

THE CONGO AFTER LUMUMBA

There were now at least four governments claiming legitimacy in the Congo: the government of Kasavubu (and behind the scenes, Mobutu) in Leopoldville, recognized by most UN members, especially in the West; that of the leftist Antoine Gizenga in Stanleyville (now Kisangani), Orientale Province, recognized by the Soviet bloc and some of the more radical African states as the rightful heir to Patrice Lumumba; that of Albert Kalonji in Kasai Province, recognized primarily by his tribal followers; and of course that of Tshombe in Elisabethville, Katanga Province. After a visit to the Congo early in 1961, the UN Conciliation Commission reported that its efforts had failed. In its opinion, the country was "on the verge of catastrophe" because of civil war, famine, near financial bankruptcy, and the threat of foreign intervention. Such warning was reminiscent of one made a few weeks earlier—on December 14, 1960—by Hammarskjöld reechoing his special representative in the Congo, Indian diplomat Rajeshwar Dayal, who had taken Ralph Bunche's place on September 8.[3] Hammarskjöld noted ominously on that occasion that if the United Nations were forced to end its mission in the Congo because of the withdrawal of possible additional ONUC contingents from the force, "the consequences would be immediate civil war, degenerating into tribal conflicts fought in the most uninhibited manner," which he compared with "a Spanish civil war situation."

In the meantime, the Congo's political life continued to evolve, part tragedy and part soap opera. For instance, two separate Congolese delegations had shown up in New York in September 1960, each seeking to represent its country at the 15th session of the General Assembly. Justin Bomboko headed the Kasavubu delegation while Thomas Kanza led the Lumumba faction. Kasavubu's personal plea in the Assembly, strongly supported by the West and especially the United States, which considered him moderate and sufficiently anti-Soviet, resulted in the seating of the latter's delegation by a split vote of 53–24–19. Hammarskjöld had advised leaving the seat open to give African members more time to work out a reconciliation, but his counsel was not followed. Accordingly, the event was a political setback for the secretary-general. In contrast, on his return to Leopoldville, Kasavubu was hailed as a hero, and he was clearly on the way to winning his power struggle with Lumumba—and more.

The last four months of Patrice Lumumba's short life were marked by a number of arrests beginning on September 12, escapes from house confinement, renewed arrests, further escapes, and finally recapture and transfer to Katanga, where he and two associates were executed on January 17, 1961. What had started the sequence of events that led to this denouement was Lumumba's final escape from his home on November 27, 1960. Since September, ONUC had maintained a security guard at Lumumba's residence (and that of Kasavubu and other political and military leaders) at Kasavubu's request. The guards neither interfered with his comings and goings nor provided protection outside Lumumba's home. Some distance away, the Congolese army had maintained its own outer ring of guards loyal to General Mobutu.

On November 27, the day Kasavubu returned in triumph from New York, Lumumba slipped through an inattentive ANC guard. His plan was to flee from his enemies in Leopoldville to his political base in Stanleyville, Orientale Province, where Gizenga had preceded him in October, in order to establish an alternative central government rivaling the Kasavubu–Mobutu regime. But on December 1, Mobutu's men caught up with Lumumba in Kasai Province, as the latter delayed his final escape waiting for his wife and children. Lumumba was arrested, beaten up, and returned, this time to the ANC military prison in Thysville, near Leopoldville, where he was held for some six weeks. Kasavubu announced that he would have Lumumba tried for serious crimes against the state's security.

Hammarskjöld dispatched two letters to Kasavubu appealing for legality and humane treatment of the prisoners (Lumumba's aides were also interned). In turn, the Soviets led the attack on the secretary-general's insistence on his "neutral mandate" from the Security Council and his refusal to use ONUC to have the prisoners freed on account of his "neutrality."

Kasavubu's reply, countersigned by Justin Bomboko, commissioner-general for external affairs, placed all the blame on Lumumba and urged noninterference in the country's domestic affairs. The

Security Council meetings of December 7 and December 13 ended in deadlock. So Antoine Gizenga now proclaimed "the reestablishment of the legal government of the Republic of the Congo" at Stanleyville, Orientale Province. And the General Assembly meeting of December 16 was no more successful at finding a solution.

In the meantime, as the chorus of protests was rising, Lumumba's captors were becoming apprehensive that the ANC military camp at Thysville might not be all that secure, given the existence of Lumumba sympathizers within the Congolese army's ranks. Accordingly, they arranged that on January 17, 1961, Lumumba, together with Joseph Okito, vice president of the senate, and Maurice Mpolo, minister of youth in the previous Lumumba cabinet, be secretly flown to Katanga. Hammarskjöld's protests and appeals on hearing of the transfer brought only negative responses from both Kasavubu and Tshombe. The secretary-general's efforts to have the prisoners visited by ONUC representatives, the Red Cross, or members of the UN Conciliation Commission were all rebuffed. Unknown to him, Lumumba and his associates had been executed that same night.

The confrontation both inside and outside the United Nations following the announcement of the threesome's death on February 12 became especially virulent when evidence that Lumumba had been tortured in captivity by the Congolese National Army came to light. The pro-Lumumba Afro-Asian states—especially Ghana, Guinea, Morocco, and the United Arab Republic—expressed outrage, and several of them indicated their intention to withdraw their ONUC contingents. The perpetrators of the deed were never clearly identified, but a number of conspiracy theories, charges, and counter-charges made the rounds. There was strong suspicion of Tshombe's connivance. The Soviets renewed their attacks on Hammarskjöld and the West, demanded the total disarming of "Mobutu's band of terrorists," and demanded the removal of all Belgian officials and troops from the entire Congo. In a letter to the president of the Security Council, the Soviet UN representative, Valerian Zorin, referring to Hammarskjöld, declared, "The blood of Patrice Lumumba is on the hands of this henchman of the colonialists and cannot be removed." The Soviets argued that the man who hands another a weapon is just as guilty as the one who uses it. From then on, the members of the Communist bloc refused to recognize Hammarskjöld as a UN official. But even worse for him was the setback in the secretary-general's efforts to restore African solidarity behind ONUC. For these members now split in support or opposition to Hammarskjöld's interpretations of previous Security Council resolutions. The left-leaning ones openly sided with the Soviets.

On February 9, 1961, a new provisional Congolese government chosen by Kasavubu and installed by Mobutu was formed. Joseph Ileo was confirmed as premier and Justin Bomboko as foreign minister. The cabinet replaced the military regime and the College of High Commissioners that Mobutu had proclaimed on September 20, 1960. But still the country continued to unravel.

Members who had contributed forces to ONUC were displeased because their troops were being ridiculed, slandered, manhandled, and prevented from performing duties normally associated with soldiering. In one of the worst incidents, 12 Italian airmen who had flown planes into Katanga were captured, killed in cold blood, and mutilated. On occasion, ONUC troops had to stand by helplessly in their role as neutral policemen while the Congolese were settling scores among themselves. Eventually, the ONUC contingents from Guinea, Morocco, the United Arab Republic, Ceylon (now Sri Lanka), Indonesia, and Yugoslavia were pulled out of the Congo by their governments in protest against Hammarskjöld's policies and/or ONUC's alleged favoritism toward Kasavubu and Mobutu.

Indeed, even men like Ghana's President Kwame Nkrumah and Guinea's President Ahmed Sékou Touré, with whom Hammarskjöld had entertained cordial relations, failed to understand how the secretary-general's mandate to restore order in the Congo could be achieved through his exaggerated neutrality and nonintervention in the country's internal affairs. They also resented Lumumba's fate and tended to blame Hammarskjöld for it. They remained unpersuaded by the secretary-general's self-defense, which consisted of several points. First, Hammarskjöld quoted the UN Charter to document the incompatibility of any UN intrusion into a member's domestic affairs (a principle that Hammarskjöld managed to twist to his purposes on other occasions as in South Africa in connection with that government's racial policies). He also noted that the Security Council had not granted him authority to disarm the mutinous and ill-behaved rank and file of the Congolese National Army. Indeed, an eight-member resolution in the General Assembly on December 20, 1960, authorizing the disarming of the ANC and the use of force to free Lumumba, had been defeated 28–42–27.

LIGHT AT THE END OF THE TUNNEL?

On February 21, 1961, the Security Council voted 9–0–2 (with France and the Soviet Union abstaining) "that the United Nations take immediately all appropriate measures to prevent the occurrence of civil war in the Congo, including arrangements for cease-fires, the halting of all military operations, the prevention of clashes, and the use of force, if necessary, in the last resort."

The resolution also called for the insulation of the Congolese National Army from politics; the removal of all Belgian and other foreign military and political personnel not employed by the United Nations; and the settlement of political strife by the reconvening of the Congolese parliament and reconciliation of opposing political factions. Finally, the council ordered the determination of responsibility for Lumumba's assassination and rejected the Soviet proposal to disband ONUC and dismiss Hammarskjöld. The latter applauded this council resolution as "a stronger and more clear framework" for UN action in the Congo, even though in fact none of its provisions created a broader legal basis or new methods for implementation. Yet Kasavubu and Tshombe denounced the resolution as an attempt to impose a UN trusteeship on the Congo.

But even without this formal change in its mandate, perhaps because of the spirit of the times or because of Hammarskjöld's positive assessment of the resolution, ONUC was gradually being transformed from a peacekeeping force into a combatant one of 20,000. In March 1961 India contributed some 5,000 men to replace the withdrawing members of the coalition.

It was around this time, too, that the United States under the new administration of President John F. Kennedy became a stronger supporter of ONUC. This fact intensified the Soviets' attacks and criticism, not only of the United States but of Hammarskjöld as well. On February 15, the newly appointed U.S. ambassador to the United Nations, Adlai E. Stevenson, told the Security Council: "The only way to keep the cold war out of the Congo is to keep the United Nations in the Congo."

But the Soviets were unmoved. On March 21, Foreign Minister Andrei Gromyko repeated the Soviet agenda for the condemnation of Belgium, the arrest of Kasavubu and Mobutu, the disarming of their troops, and the termination of ONUC "within one month." Gromyko also reiterated that his country would give assistance only "to the legitimate government of the Congo headed by Antoine Gizenga" and had "ceased all relations with him [Hammarskjöld] and does not recognize him as a United Nations official."

The spring and summer of 1961 witnessed some movement in the restoration of constitutional life in the Congo and provided further evidence of the chameleon-like character of Moise Tshombe and others, and consequently, the difficulty of bringing about the integration of the country sought by Hammarskjöld. Around the end of February, Ileo of the central government in Leopoldville, Kalonji of Kasai, and Tshombe of Katanga agreed to join against Gizenga in Orientale Province as well as against the tighter demands of the Security Council resolution of February 21. To forestall further UN intervention, they decided to call a conference of Congolese leaders. At Tshombe's insistence, it was held in Tananarive (now Antananarivo), Madagascar, from March 8 to March 12. In fact, he was the moving spirit there.

The leaders declared the Security Council resolution of February 21 to be a violation of the Congo's sovereignty and even the UN Charter. They also agreed to transform the Congo into a confederation of virtually independent states with Kasavubu as titular president—but without effective central authority.

On April 17, Kasavubu signed a compromise agreement with the United Nations accepting the operative provisions of the Security Council resolution, which Tshombe forthwith urged him to renounce. On April 24, a second Congolese conference attended by 200 political and tribal leaders at Coquilhatville, Equateur Province, was held, again with Gizenga absent. Tshombe demanded that Kasavubu abrogate his April 17 agreement with the United Nations. When Kasavubu refused, Tshombe walked out. But ANC troops at the airport refused to let him return to Elisabethville on April 26, insisting that no one should leave until a coalition government for a united Congo had been formed. The comedy continued as Kasavubu had Tshombe placed under house arrest and ordered the Belgian advisers who had accompanied the Katangan leader expelled. Finally, the conference endorsed Kasavubu's April 17 agreement with the United Nations and annulled the decision of the earlier Tananarive meeting.

The confederal arrangement was now replaced with a federal solution involving a fairly strong central government. The conference also called for the reconvening of the Congolese parliament under UN protection without delay. By June 24, two days after being released from detention in Leopoldville, even Tshombe had signed a protocol agreeing to place Katanga under central government control. He repudiated the agreement as soon as he was back in Elisabethville, claiming that he had signed it under duress.

Regardless of the results achieved, these developments had a salutary effect on Leopoldville's relations with the United Nations. Kasavubu moved from hostility toward ONUC to full cooperation with it. He had been angered by Hammarskjöld's refusal to recognize the legitimacy of the shadow cabinets of Mobutu as well as by Hammarskjöld's reluctance to replace Rajeshwar Dayal as his personal representative in the Congo. But Kasavubu now supported UN efforts to promote reconciliation among the various political leaders and the reconvening of the parliament under UN protection so that a constitutional regime could be installed.

On August 1, when parliament reconvened, it confirmed Kasavubu's appointment of Cyrille Adoula as the new premier and of Antoine Gizenga, his long-time pro-Lumumba foe, as deputy prime minister. Adoula said on that occasion, "We have achieved what Lumumba wanted—one Congo." Accordingly, Hammarskjöld was able to report on August 10 that "the Congolese Parliament . . . has ended the Congolese constitutional crisis by unanimously placing its confidence in a government of national unity and political reconciliation." Of course, neither man was completely right. Tshombe, his senators, and deputies again changed their minds and finally refused to attend the reconvening of this "unified" legislative body. Still, after his appointment of Premier Adoula and strongly encouraged by Hammarskjöld, Kasavubu again tried to win Tshombe over, only to be frustrated time after time.

It became apparent that hope for such a rapprochement depended first on removing the 500 or so Belgian officers and paramilitary personnel serving in the Katangan gendarmerie (auxiliary police) whose vested interest was to encourage Tshombe to resist integration. Accordingly, at Hammarskjöld's suggestion and using his language, Kasavubu issued Ordinance 70 on August 24 for the immediate expulsion of all non-Congolese officers and mercenaries in Katanga who did not have a contract with the central government. Simultaneously, Adoula requested ONUC to help enforce the ordinance. On August 28 Conor Cruise O'Brien, the new UN representative in Katanga, failed to persuade Tshombe to go to Leopoldville under ONUC protection to reach a compromise with Adoula. O'Brien and

his aides then decided to have ONUC occupy the gendarmerie headquarters, the radio station, the post office, and other key points in
Elisabethville, and to arrest Belgian officers and mercenaries wherever they were found in Katanga. Within hours, Tshombe, taken by
surprise, agreed to their dismissal and expulsion. Some 338 mercenaries were rounded up in Elisabethville and northern Katanga and
273 of them were deported in short order while the rest promised to
leave peacefully. But despite Tshombe's expression of desired cooperation, his government launched a violent propaganda campaign
against ONUC—perhaps as a cover for the fact that many of the
remaining mercenaries were declared "missing" or disappeared
from public view or were quietly rejoining the gendarmerie and the
sureté (secret police).

On September 13, O'Brien decided to move once more as he had
done on August 28 in Operation Rumpunch and effect a second
roundup of Belgian officers and mercenaries. Before ONUC could
implement this directive, its units were allegedly attacked by the
Katangan gendarmerie. O'Brien then ordered ONUC to occupy
several strategic points in Elisabethville and attempted to disarm
the gendarmes. It seems that Hammarskjöld's new personal representative in Kantanga, an Irish diplomat, was exasperated with the
wily Katangan and his constant shilly-shallying and reneging on
promises about accepting the integration of his province into a
united Congo. Even though Antoine Gizenga had accepted the
federal arrangement, Tshombe, despite his gyrations and rhetoric,
had not.

The fighting between ONUC and the Katangan gendarmerie was
bloody. Within a week, during which it became evident that non-
Katangans were in military command, 20 ONUC troops were killed
and 63 wounded. Additionally, 186—most of them Irish soldiers—
were captured when the ill-defended Jadotville surrendered and also
in Elisabethville, Kamina, and Albertville. As usual, there was a del-
uge of fresh criticism of Hammarskjöld's Congo policies, but even
among his detractors there was disagreement on how to settle the
violence and end the crisis. For the last time, Hammarskjöld, who
had arrived in Leopoldville at Adoula's invitation the day before the
fighting broke out, got in touch with Tshombe. The secretary-general
made plans to meet with the Katangan leader to end the fighting and
persuade him adopt a more moderate policy vis-à-vis the new central government and the United Nations itself.

In the meantime, in Elisabethville, O'Brien was announcing that he had acted in accordance with the Security Council resolution of February 21, which had authorized ONUC's use of force to prevent civil war, and that "the secession of Katanga is ended" and the province was now under central government control. These declarations strengthened the impression that the UN force had worked on behalf of the Leopoldville government and ran contrary to Hammarskjöld's continued insistence on ONUC neutrality. When Tshombe resurfaced on September 16, O'Brien arranged to meet him the next day just across the border in Northern Rhodesia, where the Katangan had fled during the fighting. However, Hammarskjöld may have had reservations about O'Brien's performance and decided to go in his stead. The secretary-general changed the meeting place from Bancroft to Ndola because the latter happened to have an airport.

The rest is history. Hammarskjöld's plane crashed after the Ndola airport came into view, killing all 16 aboard on the night of September 17–18, 1961. The UN Commission of Investigation, appointed by the General Assembly on December 8, 1961, submitted its final report on May 2, 1962. It concluded that while the cause of the disaster did not appear to be sabotage, an attack by a hostile aircraft, mechanical trouble, or even pilot error could not be definitively excluded. For whatever reason, Hammarskjöld's plane, flown by a Swedish crew that had never landed in Ndola, was a few feet too low on its approach to the runway and hit the trees on a nearby mountain slope. Unlike all the others with him, who were severely burned after the aircraft's impact, Hammarskjöld, who had an aversion to using seat belts, was thrown clear of the plane. Despite his lethal internal injuries, he managed to prop himself up against a rock before dying. A UN guard on the plane was found alive many hours later when the rescue team finally arrived. But he was delirious and incoherent and died shortly thereafter.

Almost immediately, a UN–Katangan cease-fire was signed on September 21 by Mahmoud Khiari, the Tunisian head of the UN civilian operations in the Congo who went in Hammarskjöld's place, and Moise Tshombe. Characteristically, the cease-fire was soon flouted, as were several subsequent ones. Tshombe's intrigues, aided and abetted by groups in Belgium, Britain, France, the Rhodesias, and even the United States, continued to make the Congo and chaos synonymous.

Accordingly, on November 24 the Security Council, with only Britain and France abstaining, gave Acting Secretary-General

U Thant the sweeping mandate "to take vigorous action, including the use of a requisite measure of force, if necessary, for the immediate apprehension, detention pending legal action and/or deportation of all foreign military and paramilitary personnel and political advisers not under the United Nations Command, and mercenaries." It was now official: ONUC would no longer be a neutral policeman. Its forces could now engage in military operations within the framework of this new mandate.

After several provocations by the Katangan gendarmerie involving the manhandling, abduction, and killing of ONUC personnel, the UN force renewed military pressure on Tshombe. The fighting, which began on December 5, lasted until December 19. Known as Round Two, it ended as inconclusively as Round One. That day, at Tshombe's request, he met Premier Adoula at the UN base at Kitona in Leopoldville Province. This led to Tshombe's acceptance two days later of the eight-point Kitona Declaration in which the Katangan leader acquiesced to Congo's Fundamental Law (constitution), recognized the central government's authority, and agreed to other steps terminating his province's secession.

Yet the cha-cha was far from over. Even after U Thant proposed a plan of national reconciliation in August 1962, a new federal constitution drafted by UN experts, and a proclamation of amnesty issued by President Kasavubu, Tshombe did little to put integration into effect and continued his refusal to abide by his promises. On December 13, 1962, the acting secretary-general requested member states to halt their imports from Katanga, especially copper and cobalt, in his effort to put economic pressure on the recalcitrant leader. Meanwhile, the Katangan gendarmerie continued to harass ONUC units, and Tshombe even threatened the massive destruction of the mining and power facilities in South Katanga in a kind of scorched-earth policy.

Perhaps not surprisingly, beginning in January 1963, Tshombe again changed his tune and made a number of conciliatory gestures, especially after ONUC neutralized Kolwezi, the last stronghold of the Katangan gendarmerie and thus of Tshombe in Round Three. Tshombe (again) announced the end of his secessionist activities. On January 23, Joseph Ileo arrived in Elisabethville as minister-resident of the central government in Katanga. On February 4, U Thant reported to the Security Council the end of Katanga's secession and the removal of most foreign personnel from the province. Katanga was finally part of a federal united Congo. The final irony was that in 1964, Moise Tshombe, recalled from exile, became president of the Congo he had opposed so virulently.

CASE STUDY 7: FUNDING THE UNITED NATIONS OPERATION IN THE CONGO

At first, the Soviet Union had agreed to the establishment of ONUC, but by the fall of 1960 it had reversed itself in light of several developments. Soviet displeasure took the form of vigorous attacks on Dag Hammarskjöld's Congo policies and more broadly the office of secretary-general as constituted, as well as on the United Nations Operation in the Congo and the way it was financed. It will be recalled that the Soviets (and the French) had energetically opposed shifting the Congo issue from the Security Council to the General Assembly in September 1960 because they considered such transfer a usurpation of power that properly belonged to the Security Council, where both enjoyed the veto. Thus Moscow and Paris characterized any financial assessment for ONUC as "unconstitutional." The United States, for its part, had insisted that the same formula be used to meet ONUC expenses as for other outlays of the organization. In short, the argument was really about whether the function of peacekeeping should be beyond the reach of the veto of permanent members such as the USSR and France.

Whatever the merits of the case, the Soviet Union and France refused to pay their share of the General Assembly's assessment to defray ONUC costs—some $39 million and $17 million, respectively—by the close of the operation. According to their contention, only the veto-equipped Security Council, after defining the nature, size, composition, duties, and direction of such a force, could decide the manner of its funding. But this was not the first time the Soviet Union had espoused such a position about funding peacekeeping operations. The earliest evidence of such a financial crisis had surfaced with the refusal of the Soviet bloc countries and several Arab states to contribute to UNEF outlays in 1956 and thereafter. They insisted that the perpetrators of the aggression that made it necessary to have such a force in the first place—Britain, France, and Israel in the case of UNEF, Belgium in the case of ONUC—should pay for the operation. But now, additional members balked at making their contribution to ONUC. France's refusal to pay its share of the assessment was essentially motivated by its lack of sympathy for the United Nations in general and for Hammarskjöld and his management of ONUC in particular. French President de Gaulle had been especially critical of Hammarskjöld and the UN and was not about to change his views or open his treasury for the Congo.

In contrast, the United States and several other members contended that all of them shared peacekeeping responsibilities and that under article 17 of the Charter, the General Assembly was empowered to make assessments for such operations as in the case of the general operating budget. Section 2 of that article provides: "The expenses of the Organization shall be borne by the Members as apportioned by the General Assembly."

As the political and financial debate continued and ONUC outlays were going through the roof, the General Assembly itself became increasingly ambiguous about the operation's funding. This trend reflected not only the lack of political consensus about the Congo but also other pressing financial problems of the world organization. Whereas at first the Assembly held that ONUC expenses were constitutional and therefore created a binding legal obligation on members to pay their assessed quota, by late 1960 and early 1961 the Assembly had discovered that "the extraordinary expenses for the United Nations Operation in the Congo are essentially different from the expenses of the Organization."

On April 21, 1961, the General Assembly, accepting a recommendation of its Fifth (Administrative and Budgetary) Committee, approved by 67–12–47 a compromise resolution that did not include an explicit affirmation of the application of articles 17 and 19. The latter provides for the loss of voting privileges for a member state two years or more in arrears in assessed financial contributions. Under the new formula, the Congo expenses were to be apportioned in accordance with the regular scale assessments but with a reduction of 80 percent for those whose contributions were under 1.25 percent and a cut of 50 percent for any member receiving technical assistance—that is, for the more underprivileged states. The shortfall was to be offset by voluntary contributions from the more affluent members.

On the basis of a U.S.-sponsored resolution, on December 20, 1961, the Assembly requested an advisory opinion from the International Court of Justice. The World Court responded on July 20, 1962, to the effect that such outlays were in fact "expenses of the Organization" within the meaning of article 17 (2) of the Charter. Indeed, the 9–5 vote of the court sustained the Assembly's broad discretion with regard to its functions in upholding international peace and security. Regardless of the World Court's ruling, by then three-quarters of UN members had failed to pay their full share (or any) of ONUC assessments. Yet its expenses were mounting. In 1960 (July to December), ONUC outlays were as follows: military, $60 million; economic assistance, $1.9 million. In 1961 (full year), the figures were $100 million and $35 million, respectively. By way of comparison, in 1961 UNEF (military only) cost $19 million and since its inception in 1956 through 1961, $110.9 million. The United States ended up paying the largest share of the expenses. Forty-four governments paid none of their assessed quota, totaling some $75 million over the four years of ONUC, terminated on June 30, 1964. The balance was eventually financed by a 25-year bond issue that the General Assembly had authorized in 1961. Some 85 percent of the $200 million was eventually subscribed, half of it by the United States. Since that time most peacekeeping projects have sought alternative means of financing.

REPORT CARD ON A MISSION IMPOSSIBLE

When the Congo crisis began in July 1960, ONUC was modeled on UNEF, since it was mistakenly assumed that functioning administration and other essential institutions existed in the newly independent state. In truth, there was little analogy with the Middle East. At Suez the superpowers agreed that UNEF would interpose itself between the three invading forces on the one hand and those of Egypt on the other and supervise their withdrawal from the combat zone. But in the Congo, ONUC had to cope with army mutinies, a civil war, several secessions, tribal hatreds, chaotic economic conditions, fleeing refugees, personal hostilities in the leadership, the self-serving designs of several powers, and Cold War tensions in a political game played with few rules. Receiving only vague directives and an open-ended mandate not subject to periodic reviews by UN political organs as the Security Council was tied up in deadlock, ONUC became a cropper as a result.

It was unable to exercise the neutrality that it had scrupulously observed in the Middle East because it had to maintain law and order in the Congo, prevent the country's fragmentation, expel foreign troops, and deal with the threat of outside intervention. Hammarskjöld aptly characterized the situation when he likened it to a political bordello with a number of foreign madams and compared the role of ONUC with trying to give first aid to a rattlesnake.

Whether by design or not, UN action tended to favor the pro-Western, moderate, Kasavubu elements over the leftist factions. ONUC also threw its weight behind the Kasavubu–Mobutu central government in Leopoldville in its confrontation with secessionist provinces such as Tshombe's Katanga. But only after the more activist Security Council resolutions of February and especially November 1961 authorized the use of force by ONUC did the United Nations manage to halt the centrifugal forces at home and the threat of international peace and security from abroad.

Hammarskjöld himself complained justifiably about the vague and ineffective Security Council and General Assembly mandates. In the secretary-general's mind, the task of ONUC was to reverse the Congo's internal political disruption and economic disintegration and to keep the Cold War out of the country. At first he tried to intervene without intervening, to uphold law and order without using force, to assist the "legitimate" government (whose identity itself was often a puzzle) without taking sides in domestic controversies, and to prevent civil war without suppressing dissident and secessionist movements. But he discovered that these contradictory goals were impossible to fulfill; and even if they had been possible, any action by ONUC had the effect of favoring one side or another. Thus it was in the very nature of things that ONUC's proclaimed neutrality was rarely possible. It was also in the very nature of things that Hammarskjöld could not perform to everyone's satisfaction. Yet he never considered inaction a viable alternative. Did he not say in *Markings* that the road to holiness passes through action?

Hammarskjöld admitted to some mistakes of his own. He botched some of his Congo appointments. For instance, he insisted on retaining Rajeshwar Dayal, his personal representative in the Congo, long after the outspoken Indian diplomat had become unacceptable to the Leopoldville regime. Dayal had refused to use ONUC troops to put down Antoine Gizenga's revolt in Orientale Province just as Ralph Bunche balked at employing ONUC units to terminate Tshombe's Katanga rebellion. In his reports, Dayal stigmatized Mobutu as a "usurper" and the Congolese National Army as "rabble," causing political chaos. In fact, Dayal even urged the restoration of Patrice Lumumba to the premiership as an essential step in the return of order in the Congo. Hammarskjöld was too loyal to his aide to replace him, even when Kasavubu and Mobutu came to insist on it. Only on May 25, 1961, when Dayal himself asked to be relieved in order to return to his senior position in the Indian Foreign Service, did Hammarskjöld select Sture Linner of Sweden. As for Conor Cruise O'Brien, the secretary-general's special representative in Katanga, his actions in that province turned out to be equally controversial. Hammarskjöld had known O'Brien largely through his literary works, and one may wonder whether this alone qualified him to be a "superintendent in a lunatic asylum," as former Undersecretary-General Brian Urquhart described the job.

Then there was Hammarskjöld's appointment of Maj. Gen. Carl Carlsson von Horn of Sweden as commander of ONUC on July 14, 1960. A former chief of staff of the United Nations Truce Supervision Organization in the Middle East, von Horn proved to be completely insensitive to the situation in his new command. On his appointment, instead of ferrying much needed UN supplies such as blue helmets, insignias, and communications equipment to the Congo, von Horn carried his personal automobile on board the aircraft. When Hammarskjöld asked him to draw up a standby plan for ONUC's move into Katanga, von Horn reportedly gave the secretary-general a list of reasons why this could not be done. In justification, he argued that civilians did not understand military operations. At several critical junctures of the crisis, von Horn, who went out into the field only reluctantly, was evident by his absence. Rumors were that he was ailing physically or psychologically. His relations with senior UN staff were often tense. Yet it was not until December 21 that Hammarskjöld replaced von Horn with Lt. Gen. Sean McKeown of Ireland.[4]

Although the Congolese operation led to Hammarskjöld's vilification by some Africans and calls for his ouster by the Soviets, most diplomats recognized that the secretary-general had taken preventive action with great skill. In the first 14 months of the crisis, thanks largely to his quiet diplomacy and shrewd strategy, Hammarskjöld managed to save a huge, ill-prepared new country from being recolonized by pro-Soviet and pro-Belgian factions, stall provincial secessions, and insulate the Congo from Cold War rivalry.

On the civilian side, he managed to mobilize all UN resources to keep the Congo operating, at least minimally, as a reasonably viable society. In the midst of great turmoil, the UN civilian operation provided technical assistance in transportation, communications, public health, education, agriculture, finance, and public administration. Emergency relief alleviated the famine that might have occurred following tribal massacres of various kinds. And indeed, the UN civilian assistance programs continued even after ONUC military contingents left the country. The deaths of Lumumba, Hammarskjöld, and many others were part of the birth pains of a newly independent country, but development efforts far outlasted that trauma.

ONUC, which nearly bankrupted the United Nations, was the largest, most complex international operation up to that time, and its history yielded valuable lessons for the future. Hammarskjöld did not live to assess any of its accomplishments. Perhaps his shortcomings in the Congo can be justified by quoting his own words, uttered on the happier occasion of his unanimous reelection to a second term as secretary-general in 1957: "If a mountain wall is once climbed, later failures do not undo the fact that it has been shown that it can be climbed."[5]

There remained a final ironic twist in the cha-cha. After ONUC completed its withdrawal from the Congo on June 30, 1964—four years exactly after its independence day—Moise Tshombe became premier of the united Congo. A subsequent power struggle between him and Mobutu ended the following November when the commander of the Congolese National Army assumed the reins of government and declared: "The race for the top is finished." Joseph-Désiré Mobutu, restyled Mobutu Sese Seko, remained the Congo's president until 1997, reportedly a much richer man but ruling over a still turbulent country. In that year he was ousted by Laurent Kabila and his rebel troops, only to die a few months later. But at the turn of the millennium, the process of nation building in this agitated country was still far from complete.

NOTES

1. The addition of the Congo brought the Afro-Asian bloc to 47 UN members out of a total of 100.

2. There have been many name changes since. The country itself, after becoming Zaire, is now back to Congo, officially, the Democratic Republic of

the Congo, but also known as Congo–Kinshasa after the name of its capital city, previously known as Leopoldville. This former Belgian colony should not be confused with the neighboring Congo Republic—officially Republic of the Congo—or Congo–Brazzaville, the former French colony. Name changes are indicated selectively, not exhaustively, in the chapter.

3. Andrew W. Cordier served in an interim capacity in that position from August 27 to September 6, 1960. He is the UN official who closed the Congo's major airports on September 5 and the Leopoldville radio station on September 6.

4. This paragraph relies heavily on information in Brian Urquhart, *A Life in Peace and War* (New York: Harper & Row, 1987), pp. 148, 155, 160.

5. Wilder Foote, ed., *Dag Hammarskjöld, Servant of Peace: A Selection of His Speeches and Statements* (New York: Harper & Row, 1962), p. 300.

7

Conclusion: Hammarskjöld—Flash in the Pan or Prophet of a New World Order?

At one point, Dag Hammarskjöld noted that the United Nations was "not created to bring us to heaven, but in order to save us from hell." On another occasion, he said that "the gap between aspiration and performance now, as always, makes the difference between civilization and chaos." And at another juncture still, in answer to the question of what, in his opinion, would the state of the world have been in his time if there were no United Nations, he responded, "The world would be in a state where everybody would agree that such organization had to be created."

The words of his own undersecretary-general, Ralph Bunche, seemed to run in the same vein: "If we in the United Nations could be as successful at peacemaking as we are at peacekeeping, then our problems would be greatly reduced." But since they served the world body at the height of the Cold War, these men understood that any UN action to maintain international peace and security was subject to the concurrence of the superpowers, possibly each of the five "perms," and other restraints as well.

As with an American president, the personality of the individual secretary-general determines his influence and performance. The UN Charter, like the U.S. Constitution, is a short, vague document that delineates very broadly and ambivalently the purposes of the organization but elaborates little on how these aims are to be implemented. How could it have done otherwise? Just as the U.S. Constitution was charting new territory by replacing the Articles of Confederation with a new federal system of government, so the authors of the UN Charter had to replace the discredited League of Nations Covenant—which they did only to a very small degree. But whatever the document provides, in the American case a long list of judges, congresses, and especially presidents have drawn more clearly the lines of authority dividing the powers of the national government from those of the states and the rights of the people. So too it took an activist internationalist such as Dag Hammarskjöld to probe the farthest limits of UN authority and the "elasticity" of the Charter.

During the eight and a half years of Hammarskjöld's tenure, his successes and failures were often of a particular phase in the Cold War. Sometimes his initiatives concerned a region where the major powers were less involved, where they had a smaller perceived national interest in seeing a settlement. These were areas of opportunity for Hammarskjöld, and there his character and actions determined the outcomes. He was a dedicated official who enjoyed his job tremendously—a type that Duke University political scientist James David Barber has categorized as active positive in his assessment of U.S. presidential character. Critics would even have opined that he was filled with missionary, if not messianic, zeal. Hammarskjöld insisted that judgment about his interpretation of his role within the limits set by the UN Charter, UN resolutions and decisions, and UN precedent—or his own initiatives in case of a vacuum—be rendered by the smaller states, which in his view needed the United Nations more. He felt that for the sake of both their security and their economic and social development, the small and especially new nations relied more on the world organization. But he made it clear that he did not envision this to be a patrimonial relationship in which the United Nations would give everything and the small member states would receive everything. Rather, he thought that the latter must bring their wisdom and experience and culture to bear on the world scene and that their diversity would in fact strengthen the United Nations.

Secretary-General Hammarskjöld also believed that a reliable and just world order could be built pragmatically on the basis of precedents, case by case. By this means, he hoped that the United Nations could eventually accumulate sufficient authority to be respected by all nations. In his view, the only way to bring this about was to adhere strictly to the Charter principles and try to prevent their subversion by national and individual self-interest.

By following this line, in his lifetime Hammarskjöld managed to give the United Nations and its secretaryship the kind of respect it may have lacked earlier. Minimally, he prevented the United Nations from following the League of Nations into well-deserved ignominy. Even in the face of great odds, such as tackling the U.S. government on McCarthyism and secretariat staff loyalty or the Soviet Union's desire to restructure his own job, Hammarskjöld hoped that world public opinion would make principle and justice triumph over power politics. In cases such as Guatemala and Hungary, his challenge to national sovereignty went beyond what the powerful were willing to tolerate. Unquestionably, his actions disturbed governments and leaders—especially the Russians and the French. To these he became persona non grata, as he did to a few subordinates as well. But to most, he remained what a newsman originally characterized as "the most charming oyster in the world" and continued to receive their support.

OUTCOMES

Still, one must distinguish between the short-term and long-term effects of Hammarskjöld's numerous endeavors, which is not an easy task. For instance, whereas peacekeeping is still followed—and in increasing numbers in the 1990s in such places as Somalia, Bosnia, Cambodia, El Salvador, and elsewhere—its long-lasting political effects have not always been as successful as, say, at Suez in 1956. Indeed, the presence of peacekeepers has made it less urgent for adversaries to solve the basic political problem that elicited creation of these forces in the first place. Thanks to peacekeeping, peacemaking has often been sidetracked. Hammarskjöld was not unmindful of the fact that the goal he always strived to attain—to make the UN Charter the ground rules by which all states regulated themselves—would not always be a straight path. For instance, in a speech at the University of Chicago Law School on May 1, 1960, he said:

> Working at the edge of the development of human society is to work on the brink of the unknown. Much of what is done will one day prove to have been of little avail. That is no excuse for the failure to act in accordance with our best understanding, in recognition of its limits but with faith in the ultimate result of the creative evolution in which it is our privilege to cooperate.

But in the meantime, "the safest climber is the one who never questions his ability to overcome the next difficulty." And "only he who
keeps his eye fixed on the far horizon will find his right road."

Another of Hammarskjöld's significant contributions to the development of the United Nations was to demonstrate that the organization could perform as an independent actor in a world consisting first
and foremost of states very protective of their national sovereignties.
In synergistic fashion, the international organization had a dynamic
of its own that was more than the sum of its members' wishes. Hammarskjöld promoted this trend by entering some disputes even without Security Council or General Assembly directives as, say, in the
Cambodian–Thai flap of 1959. Indeed, Hammarskjöld's activism had
led him to adopt procedures and tactics new to the United Nations,
such as the creation of peacekeeping forces of various UN "pres-
ences" in world trouble spots, which worked fairly well then and
later.

However, to place this fact into its proper perspective, it must be
recognized that already in Hammarskjöld's time and despite such
celebrated East–West crises as the Hungarian Revolution of 1956 and
the building of the Berlin Wall in 1961, the world was no longer as
bipolar as it had been during Joseph Stalin's dictatorship, which
ended just weeks before Hammarskjöld assumed his duties at the
United Nations. The Korean War, in which rival ideologies and
power politics caused the deaths of many Americans, South and
North Koreans, and Chinese Communists, was by now a thing of the
past. The great new reality was the emergent developing world, few
members of which were solidly aligned with either side in the Cold
War. Because of this the United Nations was becoming a different
place that now insisted on discussing issues outside the Cold War
context. By the close of the Hammarskjöld years, this mostly nonaligned bloc used its incipient majority in the UN General Assembly
and elsewhere to demand sweeping changes in the international
order. Third World self-determination and development, not just
East–West confrontation, was becoming another primary concern of
the United Nations.

At any rate, from a political perspective, Hammarskjöld was luck-
ier than his predecessor, Trygve Lie, who also had to bear the brunt
of Soviet attacks—and for this reason. Even though Hammarskjöld
was also finally boycotted by the Soviets, many of the poor, developing states stood at his side and prevented his ouster. Ham-

marskjöld was also more fortunate because, being more skillful at mobilizing public opinion for his purposes, UN political organs were more willing to "leave it to Dag." Subsequent secretaries-general with less prestige were more inhibited in their freedom to fill in space or lacked Hammarskjöld's personality to want to do so.

CONCLUSION

The late British political economist Barbara Ward (Lady Jackson) of the London School of Economics called Hammarskjöld "a man of the next generation" because she perceived him to have a vision of the future. Ward was intrigued by Hammarskjöld by virtue of his humanistic values, culture, and perceptive internationalism. Others have been more sensitive to his shortcomings. Even his admiring aide, Brian Urquhart, who found him "the most unusual and striking personality I have encountered in public life," goes on to add that "he was at the same time shy but demanding, modest but arrogant, quiet but with a formidable capacity for anger and indignation. I do not think he was accustomed to dealing with people at close quarters."[1]

Whatever the truth about this enigmatic man, Dag Hammarskjöld left a legacy of major problems. The East–West split and the arms race leading to a possible nuclear apocalypse continued to bedevil the world and siphon off valuable funds from Third World development aid, the new leitmotiv. Member states continued to balk at funding the new technique of conflict management, peacekeeping, so that the organization had to resort to all kinds of strategies and hope for voluntary financing.

Still, by its support for the independence of previously colonized nations, Hammarskjöld's United Nations was reducing tensions in some areas. The process was not always painless, as witness Hammarskjöld's confrontation with the French over Bizerte, with the Belgians and especially the Soviets over the Congo, and elsewhere. And some issues, already on the UN agenda in Hammarskjöld's time, remain unresolved to this day. Complete peace in the Middle East comes to mind, as does the Indian–Pakistani tension over Kashmir and political instability—still—in the Congo.

The Palestinian refugee problem is a perennial item on the agenda as well, and many Third Worlders at the millennium continue to die of hunger and violence. In the meantime, states are still spending enormous sums on armaments as the Third World itself is building huge arsenals of conventional weapons, weapons of mass destruction, and possibly nuclear devices.

It is a historical truth that no individual can impress any organization with his own indelible mark forever, for everything in the world is in a state of flux. Hammarskjöld recognized the inevitability of such change: "The United Nations is, and should be, a living, evolving, experimental institution. If it should ever cease to be so it should be revolutionized or swept aside for a new approach." As far as he was concerned, he played a role in promoting this evolution toward a more effective form of international organization. To that extent he was indeed the new style of secretary-general. But even he could not reinvent the United Nations for keeps. The interaction between any secretary-general and his various constituencies is a function of the times, the events, the circumstances, the personalities—in short, it is sui generis, of its own unique kind.

Hammarskjöld himself may have recognized that he had gone as far as he could. When he handed to Andrew Cordier, his loyal executive assistant, what turned out to be the draft of his final introduction to his *Annual Report of the Secretary-General, 1960–1961,* Dag Hammarskjöld reportedly told him, "I don't see what I can write after this one."

NOTE

1. Brian Urquhart, *A Life in Peace and War* (New York: Harper & Row, 1987), p. 126.

Chronology of Dag Hammarskjöld's Life, 1905–1961

1905   Born Dag Hjalmar Agne Karl Hammarskjöld in Jönköping, south central Sweden

1925   Earns bachelor's degree in the humanities

1928   Earns second degree in economics

1930   Earns bachelor of law degree

1930   Appointed secretary of the Unemployment Commission

1933   Earns doctorate in economics from the University of Stockholm

1936   Appointed permanent undersecretary in the Swedish Ministry of Finance

1940   Death of Agnes Almquist Hammarskjöld, mother

1941   Appointed chairman of the board of the National Bank of Sweden

1945   Appointed adviser in the Swedish cabinet on economic and financial matters

1947   Appointed undersecretary in the Swedish Ministry of Foreign Affairs

1947   Delegate to the Marshall Plan economic conference in Paris establishing U.S. aid to World War II–damaged Europe

1948   Appointed chief Swedish delegate to the Organization for European Economic Cooperation (OEEC)

1949   Appointed cabinet secretary in the Swedish Ministry of Foreign Affairs

1950   Elected chairman of the OEEC

1951   Appointed deputy minister of foreign affairs and member of the Social Democratic-controlled Swedish cabinet but without party affiliation

1951   Appointed vice chairman of the Swedish delegation to the UN General Assembly

1952   Appointed acting chairman of the Swedish delegation to the UN General Assembly

1953   Elected as the second UN secretary-general

1953   Death of Hjalmar Hammarskjöld, father

1954   Elected to membership of the Swedish Academy to take father's seat

1955   Visits the People's Republic of China for the release of captured American airmen

1956   Negotiates the end of the Suez crisis but fails to intermediate successfully in the Hungarian crisis

1957   Reelected UN secretary-general

1958   Negotiates the end of the Lebanese crisis

1959   Addresses the Laotian problem

1959   Tours 21 African countries

1960   Addresses the Congolese crisis

1961   Killed in plane crash in Northern Rhodesia (Zambia) during efforts to solve the continuing Congolese crisis

1961   Buried in Uppsala, Sweden

1961   Posthumously awarded the Nobel Peace Prize

Chronology of Events, 1953–1961

1953

January 1   The U.S. State Department releases a report listing 38 past and present American employees of the United Nations believed to be Communists or Communist sympathizers.

January 7   President Harry Truman, in his final State of the Union message to the U.S. Congress, declares that the United States has entered a new age of atomic power. He warns Soviet Premier Joseph Stalin against starting an unprovoked war.

January 11   UN headquarters in Tokyo reports that relief and reconstruction aid to South Korea between June 1950 and November 30, 1952, totaled $599,365,660.

January 14   Josip Broz Tito is elected first president of the Socialist Federal Republic of Yugoslavia under its new constitution.

January 18   A U.S. Navy patrol plane is shot down off the southern China coast, one of many similar incidents in the Cold War environment.

January 20   Dwight D. Eisenhower is sworn in as president of the United States and Richard M. Nixon as vice president.

January 25   Secretary-General Trygve Lie orders non-American UN employees to answer questions by the U.S. Federal Bureau of Investigation (FBI) regarding the loyalty of 375 professional and policy-making American citizens working in the secretariat.

January 30   Czechoslovakia withdraws from the Economic and Social Council (ECOSOC), the last Soviet bloc member to leave that UN organ.

February 3   British Foreign Minister Anthony Eden reports that London has protested the unilateral U.S. deneutralization of Formosa (a.k.a. Taiwan, or Nationalist China).

February 4   U.S. Secretary of State John Foster Dulles responds that such deneutralization does not imply a full-scale attack on the People's Republic of China (PRC) (a.k.a. Communist China, or mainland China) or a coastal blockade.

February 11   President Eisenhower refuses to grant executive clemency to Julius and Ethel Rosenberg, convicted U.S. atomic spies under death sentences.

February 12   In a move to gain Arab support, the Soviet Union breaks diplomatic relations with Israel.

February 13   Soviet Premier Joseph Stalin and Chinese Communist Party secretary Mao Tse-tung pledge continued cooperation on the third anniversary of the Sino–Soviet Treaty of Friendship.

February 14   The General Agreement on Tariffs and Trade (GATT) recommends Japan's admission as a member to prevent a revival of its pre-World War II trade practices.

February 23   The members of the European Coal and Steel Community (ECSC) ratify the European Defense Community (EDC) and tentatively approve a proposal to create a single European market.

February 24   The South African parliament grants Prime Minister Daniel F. Malan extensive powers to resist black and Indian opposition to apartheid (separation of the races) laws.

February 26–27   At its third pledging conference, the UN General Assembly approves $22,395,687 for technical assistance to developing nations.

March 5   Joseph Stalin dies of cerebral hemorrhage after 25 years as absolute ruler of the Soviet Union. Georgi M. Malenkov succeeds him as chairman of the Soviet Council of Ministers.

March 10   Trygve Lie defends his personnel policies in the face of rising McCarthyism in the United States and charges of Communist infiltration in the UN secretariat. The Soviet Union continues its refusal to recognize Lie as the chief UN administrative officer because of the secretary-general's support of the Korean War under U.S. command.

March 10   Czechoslovak Soviet-built fighters shoot down a U.S. Air Force jet over the U.S. Zone in Germany.

March 11   The Security Council begins selection of a successor to Trygve Lie, who announced his resignation in November 1952. Carlos Romulo of the Philippines, Stanislaw Skreszewski of Poland, and Lester B. Pearson of Canada emerge as leading candidates.

March 12   Soviet jet fighters shoot down a British bomber in the Berlin–Hamburg air corridor, killing seven crew members.

March 13   In secret session, the Security Council rejects for political reasons the three candidates proposed as the new secretary-general. After the three original candidates are rejected, the Soviet Union indicates it would accept Mrs. V. L. Pandit, the sister of Prime Minister Jawaharlal Nehru, or Sir Benegal Rau, both of India, for the position.

March 21   Premier Malenkov voluntarily relinquishes his position as first secretary of the Communist Party of the Soviet Union in favor of Nikita S. Khrushchev.

March 23   The Soviet Union rejects an American protest for its shooting down of a U.S. reconnaissance aircraft that allegedly violated Soviet airspace.

March 24   The Soviet Union signs a major trade agreement with the People's Republic of China.

March 27   A U.S. resolution in the General Assembly requests that a UN-appointed commission investigate Communist charges that it used germ warfare in the Korean War.

March 28   Chinese and North Korean commanders accept a long-standing UN proposal for an immediate exchange of sick and wounded prisoners of war (POWs).

March 31   Eighteen UN members, including the Soviet Union, France, and Yugoslavia, sign the Convention on the Political Rights of Women.

March 31   In a surprise compromise following earlier disagreements, the Security Council, by a vote of 10–0–1 (Nationalist China abstaining,) recommends that Dag Hammarskjöld, Sweden's deputy foreign minister, become the second UN secretary-general.

April 1 Dag Hammarskjöld accepts his appointment as the second UN secretary-general. On the same day, the General Assembly requests a full report on secretariat personnel policies, a controversial task that becomes Hammarskjöld's first major assignment.

April 4 On the fourth anniversary of the creation of the North Atlantic Treaty Organization (NATO), President Eisenhower lauds it as "the central force of strength for defense of the Western world."

April 6 Secretary of State Dulles announces that the Eisenhower administration will sign neither the proposed UN Human Rights Covenant nor the UN Convention on the Political Rights of Women.

April 7 Berlin hosts the first Big Four parley in two years as U.S. and French delegates join Soviet–British talks on ways to avoid clashes between Soviet and Western aircraft over Germany.

April 7 A UN liaison group accepts a Communist proposal for the exchange of all sick and wounded prisoners in the Korean War on condition that none be returned against his will.

April 7 By a vote of 57–1–1, the General Assembly elects Dag Hammarskjöld UN secretary-general.

April 8 Soviet Deputy Foreign Minister Andrei Y. Vichinsky offers the General Assembly a modified world disarmament plan, omitting long-standing Soviet demands for an immediate ban on atomic weapons and a uniform percentage reduction of conventional armaments.

April 9 Trygve Lie welcomes Dag Hammarskjöld, his successor, at New York's Idlewild International Airport.

April 10 Hammarskjöld is officially installed by the General Assembly as the second UN secretary-general.

April 11 The U.S.-led United Nations Command in Korea and North Korea sign a formal agreement for the exchange of sick and wounded prisoners of war.

April 15 U.S. Narcotics Commissioner Harry Auslinger tells the

UN Commission on Narcotic Drugs that the People's Republic of China exports large shipments of illegal drugs to the United States to undermine its public health.

April 15 South Africa's Daniel F. Malan of the Nationalist Party wins election, which confirms apartheid as national policy.

April 15 Laos appeals to the United Nations for a formal condemnation of aggression against it by Communist-led Vietminh (Vietnamese) forces.

April 16 President Eisenhower urges the Soviet Union to promote an "honorable" armistice in Korea, an Austrian peace treaty, German reunification under a democratic government, and gradual disarmament.

April 18 The General Assembly unanimously calls for an armistice in the Korean War, now almost three years old.

May 2 King Hussein I accedes to the throne of Jordan while his cousin, Faisal II, rules as king of Iraq.

May 3 The World Health Organization (WHO), a specialized UN agency, reports a 50 percent drop in respiratory tuberculosis between 1938 and 1950 in 21 countries. The exchange of sick and wounded POWs in Korea is completed.

May 6 Hammarskjöld visits Washington to meet President Eisenhower and U.S. Secretary of State John Foster Dulles.

May 8 President Eisenhower announces that the United States is providing $60 million to France for its Indochina War. By 1954, Washington is defraying three-quarters of the costs of that ill-fated conflict.

May 8 Former Secretary-General Trygve Lie sails from New York for his native Norway (where he died at age 72 on December 30, 1968).

May 19 The International Court of Justice (World Court) adjudicates the Ambatielos case, mandating that Britain submit its dispute with Greece pleading on behalf of Mr. Ambatielos, a Greek ship owner, to arbitration.

May 26 Soviet Deputy Foreign Minister Andrei Vichinsky agrees to Hammarskjöld's appointment of Ilya S. Tchernychev, former Soviet ambassador to Sweden, as UN assistant secretary-general for security and political affairs. The Soviets had at first proposed a much less experienced man as their top secretariat official.

May 29   In Geneva, Hammarskjöld first chairs the Administrative Committee on Coordination (ACC), a meeting of specialized agencies of the UN system. While in the city, he tries to restore the morale of UN staff after the McCarthy–McCarran investigations on the loyalty of American personnel.

May 31   U.S. Mutual Security Administration director Harold Stassen urges continued "nonstrategic" trade with the Eastern bloc to improve East–West peace prospects.

June 2   Queen Elizabeth II is crowned in Britain's Westminster Abbey, and the six-and-a-half-hour ceremony is televised across the world.

June 2   President Eisenhower orders the creation of an International Organizations Employee Loyalty Board to evaluate as security risks U.S. citizens employed by or applying for positions with the United Nations.

June 8   UN and Communist truce negotiators sign an agreement on the exchange or release of prisoners of war in Korea. But the following day these truce terms are rejected by South Korea.

June 9   Hammarskjöld appoints Maj. Gen. Vagn Bennike (Denmark) to lead the United Nations Truce Supervision Organization (UNTSO) in the Middle East.

June 16   Workers in East Berlin demonstrate against their Communist government; their call for a general strike is one of the first acts of dissidence in Soviet-controlled Eastern Europe.

June 17   Soviet tanks and troops repress thousands of rioting East Berliners, killing 16. The East German (German Democratic Republic) government declares martial law.

June 18   Hammarskjöld criticizes the Republic of Korea (South Korea) for its "premature" release of enemy prisoners of war without approval by the United Nations Command.

June 19   Egypt's military junta, which toppled King Farouk in July

1952, proclaims a republic as Maj. Gen. Mohammed Naguib is named president and premier.

June 19   A group of private Western businessmen representing 50 firms arrives in Peking to negotiate an $84-million agreement with the People's Republic of China. They pledge no violation of the UN ban on the shipment of strategic goods to Communist China.

June 19   American atomic spies Julius and Ethel Rosenberg are executed for espionage and treason after President Eisenhower again refuses to grant them executive clemency.

June 23   President Syngman Rhee of South Korea reiterates his refusal to accept the proposed Korean truce terms after unilaterally ordering the release of non-Communist prisoners of war.

June 27   Hammarskjöld asks the United Nations to accept new conditions of warfare under which fighting "ends without vengeance," hopefully as in Korea.

July 4   Moderate Imre Nagy replaces Communist hardliner Mátyás Rákosi as Hungarian premier.

July 8   Communist commanders accept a suggestion by UN Commander Gen. Mark W. Clark of the United States to proceed with final arrangements for signing a Korean armistice without South Korean participation.

July 10   Soviet First Deputy Premier Lavrenti Beria is dismissed as an "enemy of the people" in a post-Stalin purge.

July 11   The U.S. State Department announces that South Korean President Syngman Rhee has accepted the proposed armistice terms.

July 14   The Big Three (U.S., British, French) foreign ministers conclude their Washington conference after agreeing to meet with Soviet Foreign Minister Vyacheslav Molotov to discuss an Austrian peace settlement and German reunification.

July 20   The Economic and Social Council establishes the United Nations International Children's Fund (UNICEF) as a permanent agency, dropping the term "Emergency" from its official title.

July 24   Hammarskjöld requests a UN operating budget of $48,123,400 of which the U.S. share would be $13,747,866.

July 26 The government of President Fulgencio Batista crushes an attack by 170 rebels on its Moncada army barracks in Santiago, Cuba. The leader of the attack, Fidel Castro Ruz, is captured, tried, and sentenced to a 15-year prison term. He is released in 1955 and exiled to Mexico.

July 27 An armistice agreement is signed in Panmunjom, Korea, to end the three-year-old conflict. It calls for a cease-fire and a demilitarized buffer zone (DMZ) separating North and South Korea at the 38th parallel. A Neutral Nations Supervisory Commission (NNSC) and a Neutral Nations Repatriation Commission (NNRC) will supervise the settlement terms.

July 27 Acting U.S. Senate Majority Leader William Knowland rejects the Eisenhower administration's contention that the Korean peace represents "effective collective security," given that the United States and South Korea provided 95 percent of the 16-member United Nations Command force.

July 29 Soviet fighters shoot down a U.S. B–50 bomber over the Sea of Japan near the Russian Far Eastern port of Vladivostok, claiming violation of Soviet airspace.

July 30 Troops belonging to the United Nations Command withdraw behind the demilitarized zone (DMZ) at Korea's 38th parallel.

July 31 The United States rejects a Soviet claim that its B–50 aircraft shot down near Vladivostok had violated Soviet airspace and had opened fire first.

July 31 Ending a controversy between the U.S. State Department and the United Nations over interpretation of a provision of the UN Headquarters Agreement of June 26, 1947, Hammarskjöld reports that Alva Myrdal, the Swedish director of UNESCO's Social Science Department and wife of the distinguished economist Gunnar Myrdal, has been granted "unimpeded access" to the United States. Originally, the U.S. State Department had restricted her entry visa to only UN headquarters in New York on account of her allegedly leftist sympathies.

August 3 Hammarskjöld asks UN members to use the organization less for the "voicing of complaints" and more for "proposals furthering the common end."

August 5 "Operation Big Switch" to exchange prisoners of war in Korea gets under way at Panmunjom and is completed by September 6.

August 7 Six UN members with forces in Korea warn that they will resist any armistice-breaking Communist attack.

August 8 Premier Georgi Malenkov tells the Supreme Soviet (parliament) that the USSR has the hydrogen bomb (H-bomb).

August 8 The UN International Conference on the Peaceful Uses of Atomic Energy opens in Geneva.

August 12 U.S. scientists report a Soviet H-bomb blast in Siberia; "a balance of terror" in the Cold War is thus initiated.

August 13 Mohammed Reza Pahlavi, the shah of Iran, dismisses Premier Mohammed Mossadegh because of the latter's radical reform program. Three days later, the shah flees to Iraq as Mossadegh rules.

August 14 British Prime Minister Winston S. Churchill declares that his country is not bound to resume fighting if South Korea breaks the armistice in the Korean peninsula.

August 16 The Soviet Union proposes a Big Four conference to discuss a German peace treaty to reunite the nation.

August 18 U.S. Senator Alexander Wiley warns that admitting Communist China into the United Nations would be a "very serious matter as far as the American public and the Congress of the United States are concerned."

August 19 Troops loyal to Shah Mohammed Reza Pahlavi of Iran remove Premier Mossadegh from office.

August 20 The Soviet Union announces a hydrogen bomb test for experimental purposes.

August 21 The UN Administrative Tribunal, the secretariat's highest court of appeal, hands down decisions in 21 cases where American personnel challenged their terminations or dismissals by Secretary-General Trygve Lie in December 1952 (all had invoked the Fifth Amendment of the U.S. Constitution against self-incrimination during loyalty investigations by the U.S. authorities). The tribunal absolves 11 of the appellants, awarding compensation to seven of them and calling for the reinstatement of four.

August 22   The shah of Iran returns to Tehran, with full support from the United States.

August 26   The Soviet Union informs the United States that it has no information on the fate of the American B–50 bomber crew shot down near Vladivostok.

August 27   The United States, Britain, and France relax travel restrictions on Soviet diplomats and newsmen in their respective countries.

August 28   The General Assembly recommends that a conference on Korea be held no later than October 28; it rejects a Soviet proposal that the People's Republic of China, whose "volunteers" fought on the side of North Korea, attend the parley.

August 28   The U.S. government criticizes Guatemala for offering inadequate compensation to the United Fruit Company for expropriated holdings.

August 29   Italian troops are alerted that Yugoslavia is planning to annex the Yugoslav-occupied zone of Trieste.

September 2   Hammarskjöld declares that, despite the UN Administrative Tribunal's ruling, reinstatement of dismissed American secretariat employees at the United Nations would be "inadvisable;" the secretary-general approves financial compensation in lieu of reinstatement. Indemnities ranging from $6,000 to $40,000 are paid to seven employees who had not sought reinstatement and Hammarskjöld's right to dismiss temporary personnel at his own discretion is also upheld.

September 4   Maj. Gen. William F. Dean (U.S.), the highest ranking UN prisoner of war in Korea, is released at Panmunjom.

September 8   President Eugene Black of the International Bank for Reconstruction and Development (IBRD, or World Bank), a specialized agency of the United Nations, is reelected to a second five-year term by the General Assembly.

September 8   Speaking on Staff Day, Hammarskjöld advises 3,000 members of the UN secretariat in New York to abstain from unsuitable political activities lest the problem of maintaining personnel independence become more acute.

September 10 The Neutral Nations Repatriation Commission (NNRC) begins to assume custody of prisoners of war in Korea.

September 13 Communist China advises Hammarskjöld that it rejects the UN plan for a "two-sides" political conference on Korea and insists on a broader "roundtable" conference.

September 13 Nikita S. Khrushchev is elected first secretary of the Central Committee of the Communist Party of the Soviet Union.

September 14 Moscow approves economic aid for Communist China's heavy industry.

September 15 At the opening of the eighth session of the General Assembly, debate on seating the People's Republic of China in the world body is postponed by a vote of 44–10–2. Annual adoption of U.S. resolutions to prevent the discussion regarding China's representation is to continue as a yearly occurrence.

September 17 Dulles complains that the Security Council has been rendered "unworkable" by the use of the Soviet veto, and he suggests a Charter revision conference to make the United Nations "more responsive to the needs of our peoples."

September 22 The General Assembly defeats a Soviet resolution to debate which states should attend a political conference on Korea.

September 23 The United Nations Command completes the transfer to the custody of the Neutral Nations Repatriation Commission of North Korean and Chinese war prisoners refusing repatriation.

September 26 After Spain grants the United States the right to establish air and naval bases, U.S. political leaders call for its admission into the North Atlantic Treaty Organization (NATO).

September 28 Yugoslavia rejects a plebiscite over the future of the Trieste region, which it is contesting with Italy.

October 10 The People's Republic of China and North Korea accept a U.S. proposal for a preparatory meeting prior to a Korean political conference.

October 12 Knut Hjalmar Leonard Hammarskjöld, the secretary-general's father, dies in Stockholm.

October 12 The Soviet Union proposes simultaneous admission of Hungary, Bulgaria, Romania, Finland, and Italy into the United Nations.

October 13 The United States and Britain reject the Soviet proposal for group admission into the United Nations, insisting that each application must be considered on its own merits.

October 13 The Soviet Union requests a Security Council meeting on the status of the Trieste region, in effect strengthening Yugoslav President Josip Broz Tito's call for an international conference to settle the dispute with Italy.

October 14 U.S. Assistant Secretary of State Henry Cabot Lodge Jr. accuses Guatemala of being pro-Communist and announces suspension of American aid.

October 15 Britain's second announced atomic explosion is set off at the Woomera testing range in Australia, and a third test is held on October 26.

October 15 The UN Mixed Armistice Commission reports that Israeli forces have attacked Qibya, Budrus, and Shagba in Jordan near the Israeli border.

October 18 The Big Three again urge the Soviet Union to attend a foreign ministers conference on Austrian and German problems.

October 19 The UN Administrative Tribunal awards compensation of $48,230 to the remaining four American secretariat employees (dismissed by former Secretary-General Tryve Lie) who refused to answer questions about their alleged Communist ties at U.S. federal loyalty hearings. Total compensation to the 11 permanent staffers amounts to $179,420.

October 22 France recognizes the independence of Laos, its former colony in Indochina.

October 27 The Security Council approves Israel's suspension of work on the diversion of water from the River Jordan. Because of it, the United States resumes economic aid to Israel.

October 29 The Burmese government consents to a temporary cease-fire with Chinese Nationalist troops on its territory to permit their repatriation to Formosa (Taiwan) via Thailand.

November 1 Yugoslavia and Italy agree to attend a conference proposed by the Big Three and withdraw their troops from the disputed areas of Trieste.

November 2 The General Assembly resolves to investigate atrocity charges leveled by the United States against North Korea.

November 3 Hammarskjöld requests the General Assembly to broaden his powers to dismiss UN employees.

November 11 By a vote of 53–5, the General Assembly overrides Soviet objections to its investigation of North Korean atrocities during the war.

November 16 The International Labor Organization (ILO), a specialized agency of the United Nations, rejects a Soviet application for membership.

November 17 The International Court of Justice rules unanimously that the Minquiers and Ecrehos Islands between the English Channel and the French coast belong to Britain, not France.

November 18 The General Assembly's First (Political and Security) Committee calls on the major powers to hold private talks on disarmament and the control of atomic weapons.

November 20 French forces seize the Vietminh stronghold of Dien Bien Phu, 10 miles from the Laotian border in northwestern Vietnam.

November 21 Hammarskjöld reports on personnel policy to the General Assembly, clarifying the line between his authority and that of the U.S. government regarding American secretariat staff.

November 24 Dulles agrees with Vice President Richard M. Nixon's comment that the United States "made a mistake" in disarming Germany and Japan after World War II.

November 24 The UN Security Council adopts, 9–0, a resolution expressing strong censure of the Israeli raid on the Jordanian town of Qibya in which 53 villagers were killed.

November 26 The Soviet Union proposes a four-power foreign ministers meeting without preconditions to discuss European problems.

November 27 The General Assembly authorizes a budget of $24.8

million for the year ending June 30, 1954, and $18 million for the following year to fund the United Nations Relief and Works Agency for Palestine Refugees (UNRWA). The General Assembly reduces the U.S. share from 35.12 percent to 33.33 percent and increases the Soviet share of the 1954 UN budget from 12.28 percent to 14.15 percent.

November 27 The General Assembly again urges South Africa to place South-West Africa, which it has administered as a League of Nations mandate, under the UN Trusteeship Council.

November 29 A Sudanese referendum endorses complete independence from Britain, the former colonial power.

December 2 In New Delhi, Prime Minister Nehru tells Vice President Nixon that he objects to U.S. "encirclement" of the Soviet Union and to French "aggression" in Indochina.

December 2 The Soviet Union and India sign a five-year bilateral trade agreement.

December 3 The UN General Assembly adopts, by a 42–5 vote, a resolution expressing grave concern over the reported atrocities against UN Command personnel by North Korean and Chinese Communist forces in Korea.

December 4–8 A Big Three meeting in Bermuda discusses the questions of Austria and Germany, as well as East–West relations.

December 5 Britain and Iran announce renewal of diplomatic relations and settlement of their financial dispute following Iran's nationalization of the Anglo–Iranian Oil Company by the former ultranationalist prime minister, Mohammed Mossadegh.

December 7 Premier Chou En-lai of the People's Republic of China warns the General Assembly that the United States is "fomenting consequences of a serious nature" in Korea.

December 7 The General Assembly urges states still holding World War II prisoners of war to repatriate them.

December 8 Addressing the General Assembly, President Eisenhower proposes his "atoms for peace" program by the establishment of an organization devoted exclusively to it. He invites the Soviet Union to contribute part of its atomic stockpile to an international pool to develop peaceful uses of atomic energy and create an International Atomic Energy Agency "to find the way by which the miraculous inventiveness of man shall not be dedicated to his death, but consecrated to his life."

December 8   The General Assembly approves efforts to evacuate foreign troops from Burma.

December 9   Despite Soviet bloc opposition, the General Assembly approves Hammarskjöld's UN secretariat reorganization plan to centralize more authority in his office. The Assembly also grants the secretary-general clearer power to dismiss secretariat personnel.

December 9   The General Assembly authorizes a UN operating budget of $47,827,110 for 1954.

December 9   Deputy Foreign Minister Vishinsky indicates that the Soviet Union will reject President Eisenhower's proposal on the peaceful uses of atomic energy. The USSR insists that the unconditional prohibition of nuclear weapons is a prerequisite for international arms control.

December 17   In a speech at the Albert Hall in London, Hammarskjöld lauds President Eisenhower's atoms for peace idea as a new and important field of activity for the world organization.

December 20   Italy and Yugoslavia complete the withdrawal of their troops from frontier positions in the Trieste area.

December 23   The post-Stalin regime executes Lavrenti Beria, former chief of the Soviet secret police, and six aides for treason and other state crimes.

December 29   Secretary of State Dulles announces that the United States will try to hold talks with the Soviet Union on Eisenhower's plan for pooling atomic energy resources.

1954

January 1   Hammarskjöld's New Year's message notes that peace depends not only on governments but also on a "positive development of the attitude of individual men and women toward life and their neighbors."

January 4 Czechoslovakia is suspended from the World Bank for failing to pay the balance of its capital subscription.

January 5 Lester B. Pearson, the Canadian secretary of external affairs, cautions the West not to expect a satisfactory solution to Cold War problems in talks with the Soviets.

January 6 The Soviets agree to discuss U.S. plans for an international atomic energy conference.

January 8 After an Asian tour, Vice President Richard Nixon still opposes U.S. recognition of the People's Republic of China.

January 18 John Foster Dulles suggests six changes in the UN Charter. He would transfer greater responsibility to the veto-proof General Assembly and eliminate the Security Council veto over admission of new members and the peaceful settlement of disputes.

January 19 Soviet Foreign Minister Molotov agrees to discuss cooperative peaceful uses of atomic energy with Secretary of State Dulles during the upcoming foreign ministers conference in Berlin.

January 21 The first U.S. atomic-powered submarine, the *Nautilus*, is launched.

January 22 The Security Council's call for Syria and Israel to cooperate in diverting the waters of the River Jordan is vetoed by the Soviet Union.

January 22 The U.S. Air Force shoots down a Soviet jet fighter off Korea.

January 23 The Neutral Nations Repatriation Commission (NNRC) releases all remaining anti-Communist Chinese and North Korean prisoners of war in Korea, a move endorsed by Hammarskjöld.

January 25 The Big Four foreign ministers meet in Berlin to discuss the Austrian and German problems. The conference ends in failure on February 18 after the Soviets insist on the "neutralization" of these World War II belligerents.

January 29 The leftist government of Guatemala accuses the United States and allied Central American governments of planning to invade the country.

February 1 Soviet Foreign Minister Vyacheslav Molotov proposes that the four occupying powers in Germany, and an "all-German government," draft a peace treaty.

February 5 Israel requests the UN Security Council to impose sanctions on Egypt unless the latter lifts its Suez Canal blockade of Israeli traffic.

February 8 Western leaders urge the Soviet Union to persuade the People's Republic of China to stop supplying the (Communist) Vietminh forces fighting the French in Indochina.

February 10 Molotov proposes to the Berlin Big Four conference a 50-year European security pact to replace NATO; the idea is rejected out of hand by Western diplomats.

February 12 Molotov suggests that the Big Four speedily negotiate an Austrian peace treaty but demands that occupation troops remain in the country "to prevent any attempts at a new Anschluss," that is, merger with Germany as Adolph Hitler had decreed in 1938.

February 18 At Berlin, the Big Four foreign ministers agree that a Far Eastern peace conference to be held in Geneva will include the People's Republic of China. But deadlock on European security arrangements continues.

February 24 The United States invites South Korea and 13 other countries that contributed forces to the United Nations Korean Command to attend the upcoming Geneva conference.

February 24 Guatemalan President Jacobo Arbenz Guzman rejects the appeal of the United Fruit Company for expropriation of an additional 174,000 acres of agricultural land by his government.

February 26 The USSR cedes the Crimea, previously part of the Russian Soviet Socialist Republic and with a population consisting predominantly of ethnic Russians, to the Ukrainian Soviet Socialist Republic.

March 1 Aggravated by U.S. weapons sales to Pakistan, Indian Prime Minister Jawaharlal Nehru refuses U.S. military aid and requests the withdrawal of Americans from the United Nations Military Observer Group in India and Pakistan (UNMOGIP); UNMOGIP monitors the Kashmir cease-fire of 1948.

March 3 The battle of Dien Bien Phu begins as France tries to orchestrate a decisive engagement against the Vietnamese rebels fighting French rule.

March 3 The U.S. government files suit in the International Court of Justice against the Soviet Union and Hungary for damages resulting from their forcing down a U.S. Air Force plane in Hungary in 1951.

March 10 Hammarskjöld says that he would not remove members of any UN working group as long as they did their jobs; these individuals are "without nationality" as far as their work is concerned. He thus rejects Nehru's request that American observers be removed from UNMOGIP because they could "no longer be treated by us [Indians] as neutrals."

March 13 The British plan to encourage East–West trade is offered to the UN Economic Commission for Europe (ECE) with full U.S. support.

March 17 The United States reports that a major shipment of Communist-made weapons has reached Guatemala, avoiding the U.S. embargo.

March 18 Former British UN delegate Sir Gladwyn Jebb advocates UN membership for the People's Republic of China when a General Assembly majority opines that Communist China has abandoned aggression in Korea. Hammarskjöld supports the idea.

March 18 Hammarskjöld succeeds his father, Knut Hjalmar Leonard Hammarskjöld, as a member of the Swedish Academy. For the first time in the academy's 166-year history, a son replaces his father.

March 22 Lester B. Pearson declares that Canada will consider diplomatic relations with the People's Republic of China if Peking is conciliatory at the upcoming Geneva conference and provides assurances that it will cease aggression in Korea.

March 22 The London Gold Market, closed since 1939, reopens with the precious metal priced at $35 an ounce.

March 25 The Soviet Union grants full sovereignty to the German Democratic Republic (Communist East Germany) and announces the end of its occupation.

March 25 Hammarskjöld reports that he has given up efforts to arrange direct high-level Jordanian–Israeli peace talks because Jordan insisted that the Armistice Commission is the only appropriate channel for negotiations.

March 29 Jawaharlal Nehru urges both superpowers to suspend hydrogen bomb tests.

March 29 The Security Council's call for Egypt to comply with its 1951 resolution that Israeli shipping not be barred from the Suez Canal is vetoed by the Soviet Union.

March 31 Rear Adm. Lewis L. Strauss, chairman of the U.S. Atomic Energy Commission, reveals that the United States can build a bomb capable of destroying any city in the world.

April 2 Prime Minister Nehru proposes that all states with atomic and hydrogen weapons agree to a "standstill" on further nuclear tests while the United Nations strives to outlaw such devices entirely.

April 3 The Western Big Three and the Soviet Union endorse an early meeting of the UN Disarmament Commission to work for international arms limitations.

April 5 President Eisenhower pledges that the United States will not be the first to use the hydrogen bomb.

April 7 Eisenhower publicly refers to the "falling domino principle" to justify U.S. containment of the Communist bloc, a slogan that Secretary of State Dulles soon applies to the whole of Southeast Asia.

April 13 Britain decides to join the European Defense Community (EDC).

April 18 Lt. Col. Gamal Abdel Nasser becomes the Egyptian premier for the second time in two months, replacing Maj. Gen. Mohammed Naguib.

April 22 The Convention Relating to the Status of Refugees, adopted by the General Assembly in 1951, comes into force. It guarantees minimum rights for individuals seeking asylum outside their homeland.

April 23 Cambodia formally notifies Hammarskjöld of Vietnamese

Vietminh "aggression" and reserves the right to seek specific UN action in the future.

April 26 Guatemala categorically rejects a U.S. claim for $15,854,849 for compensation to the United Fruit Company relating to property expropriated under Guatemalan agrarian reform laws.

April 27 After a 15-year absence, the Soviet Union rejoins the International Labor Organization, now part of the UN system.

April 29 India and Communist China conclude a pact for "peaceful coexistence" under which India recognizes Tibet as part of the PRC.

May 3 The Soviet Union ratifies the Convention on the Prevention and Punishment of the Crime of Genocide of 1948, which entered into force in 1951. The United States, imbued with a states' rights philosophy under the Republican Eisenhower administration, is still reluctant to sign.

May 7 The French stronghold of Dien Bien Phu falls to the Vietminh (Vietnamese) army under Gen. Vo Nguyen Giap after a 55-day siege. Of the 16,000-man garrison, 6,000 French Union troops are killed or wounded and 10,000 are captured. France will soon decide to withdraw from Indochina.

May 13 The United States and Canada agree to build the St. Lawrence Seaway to enable oceangoing vessels to reach inland Great Lakes ports from the Atlantic seaboard.

May 16 The United States announces a "worldwide offensive" to expose the "spurious intellectual and ideological appeals" of Communism.

May 17 Dulles suggests that the United States may intervene militarily in Indochina in light of France's disaster at Dien Bien Phu.

May 17 The U.S. State Department reports the arrival of a sizable shipment of arms from Poland at Puerto Barrios, Guatemala.

May 29 Thailand requests Security Council action (UN border observers) to prevent war in Indochina from spilling into its territory.

June 1 Supported by the United States, Guatemalan Col. Carlos Castillo Armas leads an invasion force from Honduras against the leftist government of Col. Jacobo Arbenz Guzman.

June 4   Prince Bau Loa and Premier Joseph Laniel sign treaties establishing Vietnam's complete independence from France.

June 14   Vietnam's governmental reorganization makes Ngo Dinh Diem premier.

June 15   At a meeting under way since April 26, the foreign ministers of the states involved fail to agree on terms for the peaceful reunification of North and South Korea.

June 15   The International Court of Justice decides it lacks jurisdiction to adjudicate conflicting claims by the United Kingdom, Italy, and Albania regarding the ownership of gold removed from Rome by Germany in 1943.

June 17   Prime Minister Winston S. Churchill announces that Britain and the People's Republic of China will negotiate the establishment of full diplomatic relations.

June 18   The Soviet Union vetoes Thailand's request to the Security Council for a peace observation commission.

June 20   The Security Council calls on all parties involved in the Guatemalan dispute to terminate any action likely to lead to bloodshed. The council resolution to transfer consideration of the dispute to the Organization of American States (OAS), as the United States requests, is vetoed by the Soviet Union.

June 22   UN-sponsored talks on disarmament again end without agreement.

June 28   After a secret White House conference, Eisenhower and Churchill agree to work for a collective defense system in Southeast Asia and to make the German Federal Republic (West Germany) "an equal partner in the community of Western nations."

June 28   In Guatemala, the U.S.-backed junta of Castillo Armas overthrows the leftist regime of Jacobo Arbenz Guzman, mooting the debate in the United Nations.

June 29   The Potomac Charter signed by Eisenhower and Churchill calls for "general and drastic reduction of world armaments" and the use of atomic energy "to enrich and not to destroy mankind."

July 7   The Convention on the Political Rights of Women, approved by the General Assembly in 1952, comes into force.

July 8 T. Clifton Webb, New Zealand's minister of external affairs, urges the UN to admit the People's Republic of China and also keep Nationalist China (Taiwan) as a member.

July 9 The new Guatemalan administration headed by Col. Castillo Armas informs the Security Council that peaceful conditions have been restored in the country.

July 13 In an advisory opinion, the International Court of Justice at The Hague decides that the UN General Assembly "has no rights on any ground" to cancel $179,420 in compensation approved by the UN Administrative Tribunal in favor of 11 American employees dismissed from UN service due to pressure from the U.S. government.

July 15 The UN Trusteeship Council upholds U.S. nuclear tests in the Pacific Trust Territories, rejecting Soviet and Indian resolutions calling for a halt.

July 21 The Geneva Conference signs three agreements ending the seven-and-a-half-year war in Indochina. Vietnam is temporarily divided along the 17th parallel (a Vietminh-controlled North Vietnam and a French-sponsored South Vietnam), but elections under international supervision are to be held within two years to reunite the country. Cambodia and Laos will remain under temporary French control. The agreements are signed by France, the Vietminh, Britain, the Soviet Union, the People's Republic of China, Cambodia, and Laos, but not the United States or South Vietnam, which object to the terms. Almost 77,000 square miles of territory and 12 million Indochinese come under Communist rule in North Vietnam while 15 million will live under anti-Communist governments in South Vietnam, Cambodia, and Laos making up the rest of Indochina.

July 28 Agitation by Greek Cypriots for Enosis (union with Greece) is opposed by Britain, which plans to make Cyprus its major Mediterranean base if it loses the one on the Suez Canal following an anticipated Anglo–Egyptian agreement.

July 29 Contingent upon France's withdrawal from the proceedings, the International Court of Justice removes the Electricité de Beyrouth (Lebanon) case from its list.

August 3 Hammarskjold appoints Maj. Gen. E. M. L. Burns of

Canada to replace Maj. Gen. Vagn Bennike as chief of the United Nations Truce Supervision Organization (UNTSO) in the Middle East.

August 8   Hammarskjöld urges UN members not to allow "improvised" regional arrangements to weaken the world body. His first annual report to the General Assembly implicitly criticizes the recent Berlin and Geneva parleys for bypassing the United Nations.

August 19   In a reshuffle of secretariat positions, Ralph Bunche (U.S.), a Nobel Peace Prize winner for his work in the Middle East, is named undersecretary without portfolio, the highest UN post ever held by an American, not to mention African-American.

August 24   In his first meeting with ranking Western statesmen since coming to power in 1949, Chinese Communist leader Mao Tse-tung confers in Peking with visiting British Labour Party officials.

August 24   The U.S. government outlaws the American Communist Party, "an instrumentality of a conspiracy to overthrow the government of the United States."

August 29   The Soviet Union supports PRC demands that Taiwan be brought under Communist rule; it charges that U.S. forces are training the Chinese Nationalist army to attack the Communist mainland.

August 30   The French National Assembly rejects the European Defense Community Treaty of 1952 and ends hopes for an integrated European army.

September 3   Chinese Communist guns begin the intermittent shelling of the Chinese Nationalist islands of Quemoy and Matsu in the Formosa Straits.

September 4   Soviet fighters down a U.S. Navy Neptune P2–V aircraft on patrol over the Sea of Japan off the Siberian coast.

September 6   The United States and its European allies announce plans for an international atomic resources development pool without Soviet participation. It is to develop "new atomic technology for peaceful use."

September 8   The United States and seven other governments create the Southeast Asia Treaty Organization (SEATO) for collective defense against Communist attacks. The pact (United States, Britain,

France, Australia, New Zealand, the Philippines, Pakistan, and Thailand) significantly fails to win the participation of many Southeast Asian countries.

September 10   A U.S. resolution for UN Security Council investigation of Soviet attacks on U.S. planes allegedly flying over international waters is vetoed by the Soviet delegate, Andrei Vichinsky.

September 17   The Soviet news agency TASS announces detonation of another Soviet hydrogen bomb.

September 19   Before the annual General Assembly debate on seating the People's Republic of China in the United Nations, the United States charges Communist China with 39 "warlike" acts against vessels and aircraft of seven countries since 1949.

September 21   The General Assembly again postpones (45–7–5) discussing China's UN representation.

September 21   Hammarskjöld protests the Israeli occupation of the strategic demilitarized zone of El Auja in the Negev Desert. Under the 1949 Egyptian–Israeli Armistice Agreement, El Auja is in a neutral zone.

September 23   John Foster Dulles tells the General Assembly that the United States will establish an international atomic energy program despite Soviet refusal to participate.

September 24   Meeting since September 13, the Convention Relating to the Status of Stateless Persons is approved by the General Assembly; stateless individuals lawfully in the territory of signatories are guaranteed the same treatment as nationals with respect to certain rights.

September 27   To protect the United States and Canada from surprise attack, the two countries agree on a distant early warning (DEW) line, the third string of radar stations north of their common border.

October 1   A UN staff committee headed by UN Undersecretary-General Ralph Bunche begins a study for establishing an international pool of atomic energy resources for peaceful purposes.

October 3   The United States, Canada, and seven Western European countries sign an agreement granting sovereignty to the German Federal Republic (West Germany).

October 4 The UN War Prisoners Commission reports that 1,365,851 German, Italian, and Japanese soldiers from World War II are still being held in the Soviet Union and the People's Republic of China, or are otherwise missing.

October 5 The Trieste dispute is settled. Under the terms of settlement, Italy is to receive the northwest section of the former Free Territory of Trieste (Zone A), including the city and seaport, while Yugoslavia is to retain the southern section of the Istrian Peninsula (Zone B). This Western-brokered compromise effectively partitions the Free Territory of Trieste created in 1947 and terminates UN Security Council protection.

October 11 The Soviets announce that their occupation of Port Arthur (Dairen) will end in June 1955 and that the People's Republic of China will regain sovereignty.

October 14 The U.S. delegation criticizes Hammarskjöld for circulating a PRC resolution to the Security Council denouncing American attempts to "encircle" Communist China.

October 14 The People's Republic of China and India sign a two-year trade agreement.

October 18 The General Assembly's Third (Social, Humanitarian, and Cultural) Committee approves a new fund to help 350,000 European refugees, under UN care, to become self-supporting by 1959.

October 19 A new Anglo–Egyptian Treaty obligates Britain, after 72 years of control, to evacuate its 80,000-man garrison from its Suez Canal base within 20 months. Egypt pledges to keep the base combat ready, to permit reentry of British forces if an outside power attacks any Arab state or Turkey, and to allow freedom of navigation in the 103-mile waterway.

October 22 Following the Geneva accords, President Eisenhower authorizes a crash program to train the South Vietnamese army.

October 23 The North Atlantic Treaty Organization ends its occupation of West Germany, recognizes its sovereignty, approves its admission into NATO, and endorses a Western European Union formed on October 11.

October 23 The Soviet Union formally proposes a Big Four conference to consider German reunification, withdrawal of occupation forces from Germany, and the convocation of an all-European security conference. President Eisenhower rejects the Soviet proposal.

October 29 The General Assembly approves the disarmament and internment of foreign troops in Burma.

October 31 In Algeria, the National Liberation Front (FLN) begins an insurrection against French rule.

October 31 Hammarskjöld receives an honorary doctorate from Columbia University in New York.

November 5 U.S. Ambassador to the United Nations Henry Cabot Lodge Jr. reports that eight states negotiating to establish a world atomic energy agency agree that each nuclear power will retain its own fissionable materials, earmarking part for international use. Lodge proposes that Hammarskjöld call an international conference to discuss all phases of the peaceful uses of atomic energy.

November 5 Burma and Japan sign a peace treaty terminating their state of belligerency since World War II.

November 6 In the first violent act in Algeria's war of independence, nationalist rebels kill nine and wound 10. France, the ruling power, will manage to retain control of its administrative "department" in a long and bloody war of national liberation until a settlement in July 1962 agreeing to Algerian independence.

November 6 The meeting of the General Agreement on Tariffs and Trade, a UN-affiliated agency, censures the United States for maintaining quantitative import restrictions on dairy products.

November 7 Soviet fighters shoot down an American RB–29 reconnaissance aircraft north of Hokkaido Island, Japan, killing one crewman.

November 10 The United States protests the downing of the RB–29 aircraft, claiming that the Kurile Islands, where the incident occurred, belong to Japan "in accordance with the San Francisco peace treaty." The Soviets reject that contention, insisting on Soviet sovereignty over the Kuriles.

November 18 In a dispute over jurisdiction with Hammarskjöld, Dr. Frank A. Calderone, medical director of UN Health Services, resigns effective December 31.

November 22   The Soviet representative at the United Nations, Deputy Foreign Minister Andrei I. Vichinsky, dies. Among others, Hammarskjöld delivers a eulogy in the General Assembly.

November 23   The General Assembly's First (Political and Security) Committee approves a Western resolution for a world scientific conference in 1955 to discuss the peaceful uses of atomic energy and to create an International Atomic Energy Agency.

November 24   Radio Peking reports that 11 U.S. airmen, whose aircraft was shot down in the Chinese–North Korean border area on January 12, 1953, will be tried as spies by the People's Republic of China.

November 26   At its fifth pledging conference, the General Assembly approves $27,965,550 for technical assistance to developing nations.

December 1   U.S. Secretary of State Dulles declares that a naval blockade of Communist China by the United States is "certainly a possibility" if peaceful efforts fail to free American fliers shot down by Communist China, during the Korean War, and held by the PRC as spies.

December 2   The U.S. Senate censures Senator Joseph R. McCarthy, Republican of Wisconsin, for irresponsible charges of Communist subversion in the U.S. government and the military, as well as at the UN secretariat. This Senate action effectively neutralizes the relentless anti-Communist fighter.

December 4   The General Assembly unanimously approves the general lines of Eisenhower's "atoms for peace" resolution.

December 7   The 16 members of the United Nations Command in Korea urge General Assembly condemnation of Communist China's jailing of 13 Americans (including 11 fliers) as spies.

December 8   Ambassador Lodge asks the General Assembly to use its "moral authority" to obtain freedom for U.S. prisoners held in China.

December 10   The General Assembly condemns the People's Republic of China for continuing to hold 11 American airmen as spies as a violation of the Korean armistice agreement of July 27, 1953. Hammarskjöld is directed to seek their immediate release.

December 10   Premier Pierre Mendès-France declares that France rejects complete independence for any of its North African territories.

December 11   Hammarskjöld asks Premier Chou En-lai to discuss the release of all UN Korean prisoners of war still being held in China. Chou agrees to meet the secretary-general in Peking.

December 14   The General Assembly asks the Food and Agriculture Organization (FAO) to study the feasibility of establishing a world food reserve.

December 17   The General Assembly authorizes a UN operating budget of $49,963,800 for 1955.

December 21   Dulles argues that potential use of nuclear weapons for European defense gives NATO's military chiefs an optional "forward strategy" to deter aggression.

December 23   Yugoslav President Tito and Indian Prime Minister Nehru issue a joint declaration that peaceful coexistence of rival ideologies is imperative. The two leaders reject proposals for a neutralist bloc of Third World nations because it would further complicate the Cold War.

1955

January 2   Hammarskjöld, en route to Peking to negotiate a prisoner release, receives a cool reception in India, which opposes his mission to the People's Republic of China.

January 5   Hammarskjöld arrives in Peking but makes clear that no UN recognition of Communist China is implicit in his trip. Rather he, as secretary-general, has the right to consult with both UN members and nonmembers independently of any resolution by any UN political organ.

January 9   Acting independently of Hammarskjöld, India urges the People's Republic of China to release the American airmen and earn international goodwill.

January 10   Hammarskjöld and Chou En-lai issue a communiqué stating only that four days of talks have been "useful" and that contacts will continue.

January 12 Secretary of State Dulles enunciates his policy of defense: "To depend primarily upon a great capacity to retaliate instantly by means and at places of our choosing." The U.S. policy is dubbed "massive retaliation."

January 14 Returning to New York, Hammarskjöld reports to the Security Council that "no deals of any kind" were made in Peking. He repeats, however, that it would be appropriate for the PRC to be a member of the United Nations.

January 15 The Soviet Union recognizes the independence and sovereignty of the German Federal Republic (West Germany).

January 18 Dulles asserts that the United States may have to act unilaterally to secure the release of its imprisoned personnel in China if UN efforts fail.

January 19 Eisenhower urges the use of UN good offices to bring about a cease-fire in the Formosa Straits (between mainland China and islands held by Nationalist China).

January 21 The People's Republic of China invites the families of 17 imprisoned Americans to visit, but the U.S. State Department does not "encourage" such visits because it could not provide the "normal protection" given to citizens. Hammarskjöld opines that he has "no doubt" that such families would be safe in China.

January 25 Eisenhower asks the Congress for authority to use U.S. armed forces to defend Taiwan, the Pescadores Islands, and adjacent Nationalist Chinese territories.

January 25 Spain receives permanent observer status at the United Nations, the eighth nonmember state to enjoy this privilege.

January 25 The United States and Panama sign a new treaty on the Canal Zone increasing yearly fee payments and returning to Panama certain adjoining land areas.

January 29 The Soviet Union vetoes a Security Council call for a cease-fire in the Formosa Straits offshore from Quemoy and Matsu, which the Chinese Communists had intermittently shelled since September 3, 1954. Moscow reiterates its demand for the ouster of Nationalist China from the United Nations and its replacement by Communist China.

January 31   The Security Council invites the PRC to participate in its discussion of the Taiwan issue. Hammarskjöld cables Peking to that effect, but the offer is declined.

February 8   Marshal Nikolai Bulganin becomes Soviet premier following the resignation of Georgi Malenkov for admitted incompetence.

February 9   South Africa begins the forced removal of blacks to "new towns" located outside cities as it implements its apartheid policy.

February 15   U.S. Secretary of Defense Charles Wilson disputes Molotov's claim that the Soviet Union leads the United States in nuclear weapons development.

February 17   Britain announces its plan to produce a hydrogen bomb.

February 18   A collective security alliance between Turkey and Iraq, known as the Baghdad Pact, is signed.

February 19   The Southeast Asia Treaty Organization (SEATO) goes into effect. Its members first meet at headquarters in Bangkok, Thailand, on February 23. SEATO nations agree to assist one another to fight Communist subversion.

March 29   The Security Council condemns an Israeli armed attack in Gaza, where Egyptian administration has been in effect since 1948.

April 5   After nearly half a century in the House of Commons, Sir Winston Churchill, 80, resigns and is succeeded as British prime minister by Sir Anthony Eden.

April 6   The International Court of Justice holds that Guatemala owes no compensation to Liechtenstein on behalf of Friedrich Nottebohm, a citizen of the latter living in Guatemala.

April 15   Austria and the Soviet Union agree that Soviet occupation forces will leave Austria by December 31, 1955.

April 18–24   The First Nonaligned Nations Conference (29 Asian and African countries) is held in Bandung. President Sukarno of Indonesia attacks racism and colonialism and calls for self-determination, independence, and UN membership for all. Indian Prime Minister Nehru condemns NATO as a protector of colonialism. Premier Chou En-lai of the People's Republic of China dominates the meetings.

April 19 Hammarskjöld declares that the United Nations cannot now be "usefully employed" to ease the Formosa Straits situation, even though the "elements of an explosion" are present.

April 28 Vietminh insurgents rebel against Premier Ngo Dinh Diem's regime in South Vietnam, the opening round of a new civil war.

May 2 The World Bank reports that it has loaned $2.2 billion for developmental projects since its creation in 1944.

May 5 The Federal Republic of (West) Germany becomes a sovereign state with the ratification of the Paris agreement. American and Allied occupation is ended formally, but American troops remain in West Germany on a contractual basis.

May 6 Britain asks the International Court of Justice to confirm its sovereignty over the Falkland Islands (Malvinas) in the South Atlantic, but Argentina refuses World Court adjudication.

May 7 Hammarskjöld reports intensified contacts with the People's Republic of China regarding the release of the American fliers.

May 9 The German Federal Republic is formally admitted into NATO, a development seen as a challenge by the Soviet Union.

May 14 The USSR organizes the Warsaw Pact, which includes eight European socialist states united in defense against the "remilitarization" of West Germany.

May 15 The Big Four foreign ministers sign an Austrian State Treaty recognizing that country's sovereignty and providing for the withdrawal of all occupation forces. The pact confirms Austria's pre-1938 borders, before its annexation by Hitler's Nazi Germany.

May 19 Hammarskjöld announces that UN-sponsored disarmament talks in London have produced "a few new points of great importance" but calls for greater patience in arms control.

May 26 Soviet Premier Bulganin and First Communist Party Secretary Khrushchev visit Yugoslavia to end seven years of estrangement. Soviet officials formally recognize the existence of different forms of socialist development and pledge noninterference in any nation's internal affairs.

May 30   The PRC Consul in Geneva notifies his American counterpart that four downed U.S. airmen were released from a Chinese mainland prison.

June 1   Jacob Malik, Soviet ambassador to Britain, and Japanese envoy Shumichi Matsumoto open talks on a Soviet–Japanese peace treaty.

June 2   Yugoslav President Tito and Soviet Premier Bulganin sign a cooperation agreement.

June 7   The International Court of Justice renders its advisory opinion on South-West Africa. The World Court confirms that the General Assembly may vote resolutions on the only remaining League of Nations mandated territory that South Africa has refused to place under UN trusteeship.

June 11   The Soviet daily *Pravda* accuses the United States of turning "economically backward countries into agrarian, raw-material supplying vassals."

June 14   In a speech at Johns Hopkins University in Baltimore, Hammarskjöld describes his philosophy of life: "maturity of mind . . . is reflected in an absence of fear, in recognition of the fact that fate is what we make it."

June 19   Speaking at Stanford University's commencement, Hammarskjöld admits that the time is "far from ripe for world government."

June 22   Indian Prime Minister Nehru ends a two-week visit to Moscow by joining Soviet Premier Bulganin in a declaration urging peaceful coexistence, disarmament, and UN membership for the People's Republic of China.

June 22   Hammarskjöld renews Maj. Gen. E. M. L. Burns' appointment as head of UNTSO.

June 25   As Hammarskjöld receives an honorary degree from the University of California, he recommends less "conference diplomacy" and more "quiet diplomacy" at the United Nations.

June 26 The 10th anniversary of the UN founding is commemorated in San Francisco.

July 8 The Soviet Union announces it will reenter the World Health Organization.

July 12 Nehru joins Egyptian President Gamal Abdel Nasser to warn underdeveloped countries against "involvement in military pacts or alignments with great powers."

July 13 French Premier Edgar Faure proposes that the Big Four reduce their arms expenditures by a fixed amount and pool the savings to assist less developed countries.

July 18 The Big Four heads of state and foreign ministers meet in Geneva. Hammarskjöld's opening address encourages efforts to settle world issues and fosters an atmosphere of accommodation and cooperation known as the "Geneva spirit."

July 23 The Big Four conference agrees to resume discussions on German reunification, European security, disarmament, and East–West relations in October.

July 27 Austria regains its sovereignty as occupation troops, present since 1945, conclude their withdrawal.

July 27 Bulgarian antiaircraft downs an Israeli El Al airline in its airspace.

July 29 Hammarskjöld celebrates his 50th birthday in Sweden. He is notified that the 11 captive U.S. airmen are about to be released from a Chinese prison.

July 30 Chou En-lai says that the PRC hopes its upcoming talks with the United States in Geneva will pave the way for further negotiations.

August 4 Communist China releases the 11 imprisoned U.S. airmen.

August 8 At Geneva, over 1,200 delegates from 72 countries and seven UN specialized agencies attend the first United Nations International Conference on the Peaceful Uses of Atomic Energy. The conference stems from President Eisenhower's atoms for peace proposal to the General Assembly (December 8, 1953), and Hammarksjold discloses that work is already beginning for a second conference.

August 11   Japan joins the General Agreement on Tariffs and Trade (GATT), loosely associated with the United Nations.

August 16   The UN operating budget for 1956 is the lowest since 1950: outlays of $46,278,000 are $685,800 less than in 1955, reflecting Hammarskjöld's cost-cutting measures.

August 29   A London conference among British, Turkish, and Greek representatives to discuss the future of the British Crown Colony of Cyprus becomes deadlocked by September 7.

September 8   The Security Council calls on Egypt and Israel to cooperate with the chief of the United Nations Truce Supervision Organization (UNTSO).

September 10   The United States and the People's Republic of China agree on a mutual exchange of private citizens.

September 19   Argentine President Juan Perón is deposed by an army revolt and goes into exile, first in Paraguay and later in Spain.

September 20   The 10th session of the General Assembly convenes. Again a U.S. resolution, which passes by 42–12–5, defers consideration of Communist China's representation in the world organization.

September 25   South Vietnam declares itself a republic after Ngo Dinh Diem wins a referendum over Emperor Bao Dai.

September 26   At its sixth pledging conference, the General Assembly authorizes $28,964,563 for technical assistance to developing countries.

September 27   Egyptian President Nasser signs an accord with Czechoslovakia exchanging Egyptian cotton for Soviet bloc weapons, the first such arms deal for any Middle Eastern country.

September 29   French Foreign Minister Antoine Pinay declares that France opposes easing Cold War tensions if that means dissolution of NATO and withdrawal of U.S. forces from Europe.

September 30   Contrary to the recommendations of its General Committee, the issue of Algeria's independence from French rule is placed on the UN General Assembly's agenda.

October 11   Iran joins the Middle East Treaty Organization (METO, or Baghdad Pact), which now includes Iraq, Turkey, Pakistan, and Britain.

November 3   The General Assembly approves creation of the International Finance Corporation (IFC) as a World Bank affiliate.

November 3   Hammarskjöld expresses "grave concern" after Israel attacks the strategic El Sabha outpost in the El Auja demilitarized zone in the Negev Desert.

November 13   Secretary of State Dulles endorses a Canadian compromise plan to admit some Eastern bloc states into the United Nations along with Western and nonaligned countries.

November 16   In Geneva, the Big Four foreign ministers fail to agree on German reunification, disarmament, or East–West relations.

November 25   Because of French opposition, the General Assembly drops Algerian self-determination from its agenda.

December 1   The Special Political Committee of the General Assembly recommends pending membership applications of 18 countries.

December 3   The General Assembly adopts resolutions reiterating that South-West Africa should be placed by South Africa under UN trusteeship.

December 9   The General Assembly creates a Special United Nations Fund for Economic Development (SUNFED) to assist developing countries.

December 11   Israel attacks Syrian positions along the Sea of Galilee.

December 14   The General Assembly approves a "package deal" admitting 16 new members to the UN, bringing total membership to 76. Albania, Austria, Bulgaria, Cambodia, Ceylon, Finland, Hungary, Ireland, Italy, Jordan, Laos, Libya, Nepal, Portugal, Romania, and Spain are accepted, but Japan and Outer Mongolia are vetoed in the Security Council by the Soviet Union and Nationalist China, respectively. These are the first admissions of new members on Hammarskjöld's watch because Cold War politics had frozen entrants since 1950.

December 15   The General Assembly establishes the UN Tax Equalization Fund. Revenues from staff assessments are credited to each member state while amounts paid to staff members as relief from double taxation are debited to the appropriate member state.

December 16   The General Assembly authorizes a UN operating budget of $48,566,350 for 1956.

1956

January 1   Sudan becomes independent and joins the League of Arab States (Arab League) on January 19.

January 11   Secretary of State Dulles declares that superpower rivalry to help underdeveloped countries is as vital as the arms race.

January 15   Hammarskjöld leaves on his first Middle Eastern tour. His extended trip, lasting till February 24, takes him to Israel, Jordan, Egypt, and Lebanon as well as Asia, Australia, and New Zealand.

January 19   The Security Council censures Israel for its December 11, 1955, attack on Syrian positions on the Sea of Galilee, a "flagrant violation" of the existing armistice agreement.

February 1   President Eisenhower and Prime Minister Eden issue the Declaration of Washington, warning the peoples of Asia and Africa not to look to the Soviet Union for political or economic aid.

February 6   Riots greet French Premier Guy Mollet in Algiers.

February 14   Premier Nikita Khrushchev attacks Joseph Stalin's "cult of personality" as he opens the 20th congress of the Communist Party of the Soviet Union. Khrushchev's "secret speech" causes turmoil in the Communist world.

February 27   Hammarskjöld notes that while he does not think that "complete settlements are within reach" in the Middle East, "I do believe in the possibility of an orderly progress toward solutions."

March 1   France recognizes the independence of Morocco, previously a French protectorate.

March 2   Lt. Gen. John Bagot Glubb, British commander of Jordan's Arab Legion since 1939, is dismissed by King Hussein after anti-British demonstrations.

March 9   British officials in Cyprus arrest Archbishop Makarios as a terrorist and deport him with several aides to the Seychelles Islands. The British vow to crush "Greek Cypriot terrorism" before reopening talks on self-government for the island.

March 14 Because Czechoslovakia refuses to accept the International Court of Justice's jurisdiction in a case brought by the United States on account of a U.S. Air Force plane downed by Czech MIG aircraft on March 10, 1953, the World Court removes the case from its list.

March 16 Chile and Argentina refuse to accept the jurisdiction of the International Court of Justice in the case instituted by Britain regarding its claims to certain lands and islands in the Antarctic. Consequently, the court removes the proceedings from its list.

March 20 Japan and the Soviet Union suspend peace treaty talks in London; fishing and trade issues prevent agreement.

March 20 France recognizes Tunisian independence, and Habib Bourguiba is elected president.

March 21 Harold Stassen, the U.S. delegate to the UN Disarmament Commission, proposes that the United States and the Soviet Union each set aside an area of 20,000 to 30,000 square miles in which to test the operation of an American disarmament plan providing for reciprocal inspection. Other American ideas are reduction of armed forces to 2.5 million men each and proportional cuts in military budgets.

March 23 Pakistan becomes the world's first Islamic republic.

March 27 The Soviets submit a counterplan to the UN Disarmament Commission. But disagreements and mistrust prevent any effective disarmament until late in the Cold War some 30 years later.

April 6 Following a Security Council directive of April 4, Hammarskjöld leaves for a month's tour of the Middle East aimed at reducing violations of the various Arab–Israeli armistice agreements of 1949.

April 17 The Cominform, short for Communist Information Bureau—the Soviet-led coalition of world Communist parties—is dissolved as a gesture of conciliation to Yugoslav President Tito's independent socialist policy. In 1948, the Cominform had expelled the Yugoslav Communist Party because of Tito's defiance of Soviet supremacy.

April 18 Agreement is reached among 12 states, including both superpowers, on a charter for an International Atomic Energy Agency (IAEA).

April 23 Deputy Foreign Minister Gromyko tells the UN Disarmament Commission that the Soviet Union will not permit aerial inspection of an "open skies" nature in place of ground control.

April 29 Hammarskjöld mediates a new cease-fire between Israel and Jordan. His tour also achieves cease-fires between Israel and Lebanon and between Israel and Syria, effective May 1.

May 4 Dulles urges NATO to study Soviet tactical shifts to economic warfare in the developing countries.

May 9 On returning from his Middle Eastern tour, Hammarskjöld reports on it to the General Assembly.

May 16 Egypt recognizes the People's Republic of China.

May 21 The United States detonates its first airborne hydrogen bomb over the Pacific.

May 30 In a speech at McGill University in Montreal, Hammarskjöld endorses Lester Pearson's suggestion for creating the UN Program for the Provision of Operational, Executive, and Administrative Personnel Services (OPEX) to fill top-level posts in developing countries.

May 31 The United Nations Command in Korea expels Czechoslovak and Polish inspection team members from South Korea for nonneutral conduct. It rejects a Communist proposal for talks by North and South Korea on peaceful reunification (June 1).

June 1 The United States endorses Vienna as host for the proposed International Atomic Energy Agency (IAEA).

June 1 The International Court of Justice issues an advisory opinion on South-West Africa, holding that the General Assembly is legally entitled to authorize its Committee on South-West Africa to grant hearings to petitioners.

June 4 The Voice of America radio network broadcasts a version of Premier Khrushchev's "secret speech" launching de-Stalinization.

June 13 Britain's Suez Canal base is turned over to Egypt in accordance with the 1954 Anglo–Egyptian Treaty.

June 22 Gamal Abdel Nasser is elected Egypt's president under its new constitution.

June 25 The International Labor Organization's Committee on Forced Labor concludes a draft treaty declaring any form of compulsory work a violation of the UN Charter.

June 26 Under pressure from France, the Security Council declines to discuss Algerian self-determination.

June 27 Hammarskjöld leaves New York for his first visit to the Eastern bloc.

June 28–30 Polish workers riot in Poznan to protest restrictions and living conditions. Over 100 die and hundreds are wounded in the biggest anti-Communist demonstration in Eastern Europe since the East German uprising of June 17, 1953.

June 29 President Eisenhower approves his National Security Council's proposal to end East–West censorship and broadcast jamming, encourage cultural exchanges, and establish direct U.S.–Soviet air service. A thaw in superpower relations is apparent.

July 15 Soviet Foreign Minister Dimitri Shepilov offers to open immediate negotiations with the United States and Britain on a tripartite ban on future nuclear tests.

July 16 The United States charges that the Soviet Union is holding at least 10 crew members from two downed American aircraft.

July 18 Yugoslav President Tito meets with Egypt's President Nasser and Indian Prime Minister Nehru to discuss neutralist policy. The three together represent the leadership of the nonaligned world.

July 19–20 The United States and Britain withdraw their offer of financial aid to the Aswan High Dam project in Egypt. The ostensible reason is that Egypt's economy has become excessively burdened by its arms purchases, but Nasser's "cozying up" to the Soviet bloc and friendship with the PRC are more plausible explanations. A World Bank loan premised on Anglo–American grants is also withdrawn.

July 23 Hammarskjöld reports that a "checking" visit to the Middle East convinced him that Arab–Israeli armistice agreements were still effective.

July 26 President Nasser nationalizes the Compagnie Universelle du Canal de Suez after the United States and Britain withdraw their

Aswan High Dam aid offer. He announces that Suez Canal transit revenues will finance the dam and promises that shareholders of the Universal Suez Canal Company shall be duly indemnified.

August 1   Britain, France, and the United States call for a conference to discuss Egypt's nationalization of the Suez Canal.

August 8   Prime Minister Nehru charges that any Anglo–French military moves will aggravate problems surrounding Egypt's nationalization of the Suez Canal Company and arouse great resentment in Asia "with its colonial memories."

August 16   In London, 22 members of the newly formed Suez Canal Users Association (SCUA) discuss an American plan to "internationalize" the waterway, easing the earlier war scare.

August 23   The SCUA conference ends, and 17 participants ask Egypt to negotiate a settlement on the basis of "internationalization."

September 3–9   President Nasser consults with an international commission headed by Australia's Prime Minister Robert Menzies over its plans for international control of the Suez Canal. Nasser's insistence that international law legitimizes Egypt's right to nationalize foreign assets on its territory ends the talks.

September 11   Britain and France agree on economic pressures to make Egypt accept multinational control of the Suez Canal. The United States voices opposition to any use of force to solve the dispute.

September 14   French pilots walk off the job and Egyptians take over operational control of the Suez Canal.

September 14   Hammarskjöld deplores new incidents along the Jordanian–Israeli border.

September 16   The Scandinavian countries recommend transferring the Suez Canal dispute to the United Nations.

September 19–21   A Second Suez Canal Users Association plan is proposed by Britain, but this second conference also concludes without agreement on the international operation of the Suez Canal.

September 23–26   The Security Council hears British and French charges as well as Egyptian countercharges in the Suez Canal dispute.

September 27 Hammarskjöld tells the Security Council that, despite all his efforts since April, he has failed to make the cease-fire agreements of the Middle East armistice more lasting.

September 27 The first Poznan riot trials begin, but the Polish government imposes only light sentences and frees many indicted.

October 1–4 As a Third Suez Canal Users Association conference opens in London, Hammarskjöld confers with Western, Soviet, and Egyptian diplomats on the upcoming Security Council debate.

October 5 The Security Council debates British and French complaints against Egypt's nationalization of the Suez Canal.

October 8 Soviet Foreign Minister Shepilov asks that an authoritative committee of the Security Council, including Egypt, Britain, France, the United States, India, and the Soviet Union, be set up for the Suez negotiations.

October 9–12 The foreign ministers of Britain, France, and Egypt meet privately with Hammarskjöld in an effort to reach a compromise on Suez. The secretary-general makes public six principles they formulated as the basis of a Suez settlement.

October 13 A revised British–French draft resolution is adopted by the Security Council urging that any Suez settlement satisfy the six principles agreed upon by Britain, France, and Egypt.

October 17 The three countries express willingness to continue negotiations on the Suez issue.

October 17 At its seventh pledging conference the General Assembly authorizes $30,874,133 for technical assistance to developing countries for 1957.

October 19 Polish Communist leaders defy the Kremlin and elect "Titoist" Wladyslaw Gomulka to head a government more independent of Moscow.

October 20 Tangiers becomes part of Morocco after a nine-power conference ends the city's previous international status.

October 23 An uprising, later known as the Hungarian Revolution, breaks out in Budapest as students and factory workers seek to rid the country of Communist and Soviet domination. Police fail to quash their demonstrations.

October 23   Eighty-two UN members unanimously approve a revised statute to establish an International Atomic Energy Agency; the IAEA will inspect atomic raw materials received by states and ensure their use for peaceful purposes.

October 24   Imre Nagy becomes Hungarian premier as anti-Soviet rioting surges across the nation.

October 25   János Kádár replaces Stalinist hardliner Ernö Gerö as head of the Hungarian Socialist Workers (Communist) Party, but rioters demand further concessions.

October 26   At a conference at UN headquarters, the statute of the IAEA is approved unanimously. Within three months it will be signed by 80 countries.

October 27   As the revolt spreads, Hungarian Communist Party leaders promise to work for the withdrawal of Soviet troops stationed in the country.

October 27   Eisenhower questions Israeli Prime Minister David Ben-Gurion about rumors concerning mobilization of the Israeli armed forces.

October 27   The Security Council places "the situation created by the action of foreign military forces in Hungary" on its agenda.

October 29   Israel invades Egypt's Sinai Peninsula.

October 30   Britain and France veto an American Security Council resolution calling for an immediate Israeli–Egyptian cease-fire and the withdrawal of Israeli forces from the Sinai. Britain and France issue a joint ultimatum giving Egypt and Israel 12 hours to "withdraw" no less than 10 miles from each side of the Suez Canal. By previous arrangement, Israel "accepts" the ultimatum that Egypt rejects.

October 30   As Soviet forces momentarily withdraw from Budapest, Hungary's Premier Nagy promises free elections and an end to one-party rule.

October 31   British and French aircraft bomb Cairo and the Suez Canal zone after Egypt rejects their cease-fire demands.

October 31   The Security Council, blocked by the Anglo–French veto of its Suez cease-fire call, approves an emergency session of the General Assembly under the "Uniting for Peace" resolution.

November 1   The General Assembly opens its first emergency special session on Suez.

November 2   The General Assembly approves a U.S. draft resolution for a cease-fire in Egypt. The resolution also urges the withdrawal of all forces and the rapid reopening of the Suez Canal, which was closed when the Egyptians sank obstructions in the waterway.

November 2   Hammarskjöld names a three-member committee to monitor the British–French–Israeli response to the cease-fire appeal.

November 2   In Budapest, Premier Nagy announces that Hungary has left the Warsaw Pact and requests UN monitoring of his nation's crisis.

November 2   An emergency session of the General Assembly condemns a new Soviet invasion of Hungary, which escalates on November 4.

November 3   Britain and France reject the UN cease-fire, and begin landing troops in the Suez Canal zone on November 4.

November 4   The General Assembly approves a Canadian resolution requesting the secretary-general to establish "an emergency international UN force" to supervise a Middle Eastern cease-fire.

November 4   The Security Council emergency meeting considers the massive Soviet attack on Hungary and calls on the USSR to desist from the use of force, a resolution vetoed by Moscow. Accordingly, the General Assembly opens its second emergency session dealing with the situation in Hungary. The Assembly condemns the Soviet government for depriving Hungary of its independence and urges it to withdraw its forces. The Assembly also condemns the Hungarian government for violating its citizens' human rights. The Assembly additionally requests member states and nongovernmental organizations to cooperate in supplying humanitarian relief to the Hungarian people.

November 5   The General Assembly unanimously approves establishment of the United Nations Emergency Force (UNEF) for the Middle East led by Canada's Maj. Gen. E. M. L. Burns. The peacekeeping force is widely viewed as the brainchild of the Canadian UN delegate Lester B. Pearson.

November 6   After the Soviet Union threatens unilateral action to halt the Suez fighting, Eisenhower orders a global alert of U.S. forces.

November 6   U.S. opposition to the Anglo–French attack against Egypt is decisive, and the four warring states accept the General Assembly's cease-fire resolution. Hammarskjöld completes his recommendations for creating UNEF.

November 6   President Eisenhower and Vice President Nixon win a landslide reelection to a second term, again defeating Democratic Party candidate Adlai Stevenson.

November 7   The General Assembly calls for the withdrawal of all attacking forces from Egypt.

November 8   Hammarskjöld appoints Dutch and Danish salvage firms to clear the Suez Canal from obstructions scuttled by the Egyptians after the start of the tripartite attack. They remove 48 impediments to navigation, and eventually, under Lt. Gen. Raymond A. Wheeler (Ret.) of the U.S. Army Corps of Engineers, West German, Belgian, Italian, Swedish, and Yugoslav craft join the salvage fleet.

November 9   A General Assembly resolution demands that the Soviets withdraw from Hungary "without further delay."

November 10   Eisenhower rejects a Swiss proposal for a Big Four summit, asserting that the real hope for global peace lies in UN action.

November 12   Egypt agrees to accept UNEF on its territory.

November 12   With the election of three Arab countries—Morocco, Tunisia, and Sudan—to UN membership, the Afro-Asian bloc of 26 states now represents a significant voting total of 79 in the General Assembly, especially when combining with the Soviet bloc of nine votes.

November 13   Hammarskjöld offers to distribute relief supplies in Hungary through UN agencies.

November 14   Soviet troops crush Hungary's last rebel holdouts. The death toll in the uprising is estimated at 25,000 Hungarians and 7,000 Soviet military personnel.

November 14   Hammarskjöld asks the Hungarian government to admit UN observers in the country, but Premier Imre Nagy has been ousted and replaced by hard-line Communist János Kádár, Moscow's protégé.

November 14   The first UNEF contingent arrives in Egypt.

November 15   The units of the United Nations Emergency Force are deployed along the Suez Canal. Eventually, 6,000 blue-helmeted "soldiers of peace" from 10 countries will be present in Egypt.

November 16   The General Assembly again postpones, by a vote of 47–24–9, the issue of Chinese representation in the United Nations.

November 16–17   In Cairo, Hammarskjöld and Nasser agree on the composition of UNEF and very ambiguously on terms for the force's withdrawal from Egyptian territory. The aide-mémoire concerning the terms of UNEF withdrawal from Egyptian territory is to become highly controversial when President Nasser exercises his option and the third Arab–Israeli War breaks out following UNEF evacuation in 1967.

November 17   Khrushchev tells Western ambassadors in Moscow, "History is on our side. We will bury you!" It is not a threat, but a prediction of future victory.

November 18   The Soviets sign an agreement with Premier Gomulka conceding to Poland greater independence, territorial integrity, nonintervention in domestic affairs, limitation on Soviet troop movements, and the forgiving of Polish debts to the USSR.

November 21   The General Assembly agrees to apportion the first $10 million of the cost of UNEF according to the regular assessment formula.

November 22   Hungarian Premier Nagy is arrested by Soviet military authorities as he leaves his refuge at the Yugoslav embassy in Budapest.

November 23–24   Third World countries introduce a General Assembly resolution demanding an immediate and unconditional withdrawal of all foreign troops from Egypt and it wins approval.

November 24   Hammarskjöld appoints Gen. Raymond A. Wheeler, John J. McCloy, and Col. Alfred Katzin to advise and assist on the clearance of obstructions from the Suez Canal.

November 28   Hammarskjöld announces that 4,500 officers and men from eight countries now make up UNEF in Egypt.

December 2   Hammarskjöld meets with British and Egyptian delegates to discuss a speedy reopening of the Suez Canal.

December 2   With an invading force of 82 Cuban exiles, Fidel Castro lands in Cuba. Although most of his band is captured or killed, Castro organizes a guerrilla campaign—the 26th of July Movement—operating from the Sierra Maestra against the government of Fulgencio Batista.

December 3   Responding to joint pressure from the United States and the United Nations, Britain and France agree to fully evacuate their forces from the Suez Canal area by December 22.

December 5   Israeli forces remain in the Sinai as Britain and France begin their withdrawal from Egypt.

December 5   The Hungarian regime rejects Hammarskjöld's request to visit Budapest to personally survey the situation.

December 12   The General Assembly approves a U.S. resolution condemning the Soviets' "violation of the Charter in depriving Hungary of its liberty and independence and the Hungarian people of their fundamental rights."

December 18   Japan is admitted as the UN's 80th member.

December 19   Hammarskjöld accepts British and French assistance in clearing the Suez Canal on condition that their salvage vessels are manned by "neutral" crews.

December 21   The General Assembly authorizes a UN operating budget of $48,807,650 for 1957 and $10 million for UNEF (and an additional $2 million on February 27, 1957).

December 21   Hammarskjöld informs the General Assembly that Israel has pledged gradual withdrawal of its forces in the Sinai to the 1949 armistice line.

December 22   The British and French forces complete their withdrawal from the Suez Canal area.

December 26   The Soviet Union ends its state of war with Japan, in force since 1945.

December 29   UN salvage crews begin clearing the Suez Canal in preparation for its reopening to maritime traffic.

1957

January 1 In agreement with France, West Germany makes the Saar its 10th state.

January 5 President Eisenhower requests U.S. congressional authority to use American forces against threatened or actual Communist "aggression" or "subversion" in the Middle East, a policy later known as the Eisenhower Doctrine.

January 5 Hammarskjöld reports to the General Assembly that his team investigating the Hungarian crisis has been denied entrance. He recommends alternative steps to survey the situation there.

January 6 The Soviet Union denounces U.S. aid to Middle Eastern countries as a plot to turn the area into a "permanent hotbed of military conflict."

January 6 Following a series of raids across the Northern Ireland border by the Irish Republican Army (IRA), Irish Prime Minister John A. Costello condemns all efforts to forcefully unite the six northern counties of Ulster, part of the United Kingdom, with the independent Republic of Ireland in the south.

January 9 Britain's discredited Prime Minister Anthony Eden resigns over the handling of the Suez crisis. Queen Elizabeth II appoints Harold Macmillan as Eden's successor.

January 10 The General Assembly establishes the UN Special Committee on the Problem of Hungary to maintain direct observation on Hungary, take testimony, collect evidence, and receive information before reporting its findings to the General Assembly.

January 14 Ambassador Henry Cabot Lodge Jr. presents a new American plan for world disarmament to the General Assembly's First (Political and Security) Committee.

January 14 Israel informs Hammarskjöld that its withdrawal from the Sinai will be completed by January 22 but makes no commitment regarding Sharm al-Sheikh and Gaza.

January 16 The U.S. State Department expresses support for the proposed European Common Market.

January 19 By a vote of 74–2–2, the General Assembly reaffirms that Israeli withdrawal from Egyptian territory must be complete and unconditional.

January 21   President Eisenhower is inaugurated for his second term; his inaugural address extends the 1947 Truman Doctrine to protect the Middle East from Communist aggression.

January 22   Israel completes its withdrawal from Egyptian territory except for Sharm al-Sheikh defending the entrance to the Gulf of Aqaba and the Gaza Strip. Any withdrawal from Sharm al-Sheikh is contingent on the UNEF remaining there to ensure freedom of navigation in the Straits of Tiran and access to the Israeli port of Eilat.

January 24   The Security Council reiterates its wish for a free plebiscite in Kashmir, contested by India and Pakistan.

January 30   The General Assembly deplores apartheid in South Africa and urges the parties to negotiate.

February 2   The General Assembly requests that Israel withdraw its forces from all Egyptian territory; UNEF responsibilities are expanded.

February 3   Israel refuses to withdraw from the Gaza Strip and Sharm al-Sheikh unless the United Nations provides stronger guarantees of its security.

February 9   The Soviet Union becomes the first state to ratify the charter of the International Atomic Energy Agency (IAEA).

February 15   The General Assembly calls for a peaceful settlement of the Algerian conflict.

February 15   Andrei A. Gromyko, regarded as a hard-liner, replaces Dimitri Shepilov as Soviet foreign minister.

February 20   The Security Council requests Gunnar Jarring to seek a solution to the Kashmir dispute involving India and Pakistan, but a possible UN peacekeeping force in the contested territory is vetoed by the Soviets.

February 22   Lebanese Foreign Minister Charles Malik calls on the General Assembly to impose sanctions against Israel for its continued refusal to withdraw from the Gaza Strip and Sharm al-Sheikh.

February 22 Hammarskjöld informs the General Assembly that Egypt has agreed to "special arrangements" for the use of the UNEF, UNRWA, and other UN agencies following Israeli withdrawal.

March 1 Israel withdraws from the Gaza Strip and Sharm al-Sheikh on the "assumption" that UNEF will administer the former and that navigation in the Gulf of Aqaba will remain unimpeded.

March 4 The Soviets assert that Israel's withdrawal conditions will force UNEF to remain in Egypt for the indefinite future.

March 5 The U.S. Senate approves the Eisenhower Doctrine to deal with Communist aggression or subversion in the Middle East.

March 6 Ghana, merging the former British colonies of the Gold Coast and Togoland, is proclaimed independent. UNEF takes control of Sharm al-Sheikh and the Gaza Strip after the Israeli withdrawal.

March 8 Hammarskjöld reports Israel's full compliance with UN resolutions regarding withdrawal from Egyptian territory.

March 8 Ghana is admitted as the UN's 81st member.

March 13 Britain terminates its 1948 treaty of alliance with Jordan; all British troops will leave that country within six months.

March 25 The Treaty of Rome establishing the European Economic Community (EEC) and the European Atomic Energy Community (EURATOM) is signed by Belgium, France, Italy, Luxembourg, the Netherlands, and the German Federal Republic.

March 28 Hungarian Premier János Kádár agrees to accept Soviet economic aid and the continued stationing of its troops in Hungary.

March 28 Archbishop Makarios is released from exile in the Seychelles Islands but is forbidden by the British authorities to return to his native Cyprus.

April 14 Pope Pius XII denounces the nuclear arms race and nuclear weapons testing.

April 26 Hungary issues its formal invitation urging the secretary-general to visit that country, but a spokesman says Hammarskjöld has no such plan.

April 28 UN-controlled operations clearing the Suez Canal are completed after four months and the waterway is reopened to international traffic, except that of Israel.

April 29   UN mediator Gunnar Jarring reports to the Security Council that he is unable to suggest concrete proposals likely to solve the Indian–Pakistani Kashmir dispute.

May 7   Premier Khrushchev launches a program to modernize the Soviet economy, which suffers from excessive central planning.

May 9   The Suez Canal Users Association announces that all its members except France will resume using the Suez Canal and pay transit tolls to the Egyptian Suez Canal Authority. Egypt's sovereign right to nationalize the canal is thus tacitly recognized.

May 10   Hammarskjöld visits Prime Minister David Ben-Gurion in Jerusalem, but no substantive agreements on pending issues result.

May 11   In Washington, South Vietnamese President Diem joins with Eisenhower to proclaim that Communists are "a continuing threat to the safety of all free nations in Asia."

May 15   Britain detonates another H-bomb in the Pacific.

June 3   The United States pledges to cooperate with the Baghdad Pact (Middle East Treaty Organization), and to assist members Iraq, Iran, Turkey, Pakistan, and Britain in countering Communist aggression.

June 5   Britain detonates another H-bomb in the Pacific.

June 13   France accepts Egypt's conditions for running the Suez Canal.

June 13   The Soviet Union rejects Eisenhower's proposal for a limited trial of nuclear test inspection plans.

June 25   U.S. disarmament negotiator Harold Stassen asserts that the success of troop reduction plans rests on improved political conditions, including a solution of the German reunification issue.

June 30   The International Geophysical Year (IGY) is announced for 1959. Scientists from 64 countries will join UN-sponsored study and research programs in oceanography, meteorology, the Antarctic, and space.

July 2   The United States formally proposes that the world's atomic powers suspend nuclear weapons testing for 10 months.

July 3   Premier Khrushchev deposes three former Stalinists in the Soviet hierarchy. Georgi Malenkov, Vyacheslav Molotov, and Lazar Kaganovich are transferred to remote positions.

July 9   Despite terrorist attacks in France, President René Coty reiterates his government's refusal to grant independence to Algeria.

July 26   In Guatemala, Col. Castillo Armas, who overthrew the leftist regime of Jacobo Arbenz Guzman in June 1954, is assassinated.

July 28   The United States, Britain, France, and the German Federal Republic sign the Berlin Declaration calling for a free and reunited Germany.

July 29   The IAEA legally comes into being and begins its operations in Vienna. Its goal is to control the proliferation of atomic devices.

August 2   At a press conference, Hammarskjöld says he might yet visit Hungary if directed to do so by the General Assembly. He denies any UN double standard in dealing with the Hungarian and Egyptian crises; he blames seeming differences on the "unequal measure of compliance" with UN directives by the Soviets in Hungary and by Britain, France, and Israel regarding Suez in Egypt.

August 26   The Soviet Union announces its first successful test-firing of an intercontinental ballistic missile (ICBM), ahead of the United States by about four months.

August 31   Malaya becomes independent of British rule but retains membership in the British Commonwealth of Nations.

September 4   Hammarskjöld rejects former Prime Minister Winston Churchill's criticism of UN ineffectiveness because of the equal vote enjoyed by the smaller and allegedly less responsible member states. He declares that limitations on the world body's effectiveness result from the "facts of international life" and are beyond the reach of "merely constitutional reform." Churchill had predicted possible collapse of the organization unless there was a major Charter revision.

September 5   The *Annual Report of the Secretary-General, 1956–1957* urges creation of a standby UN international force similar to UNEF.

September 5   Although some members of Cuba's armed forces join an uprising led by Fidel Castro, Batista easily crushes the revolt.

September 9   The Soviet Union vetoes UN membership for South Korea and South Vietnam.

September 10   The UN Special Committee on the Problem of Hungary submits its initial report. It finds that the events of October and November 1956 were a peaceful and spontaneous demonstration by Hungarian students, workers, soldiers, and intellectuals that was transformed into an armed uprising when the political police opened fire.

September 14   Hungary announces that Thailand's Foreign Minister Prince Wan Waithayakon, the UN special representative on the Problem of Hungary, will not be permitted to enter the country. Waithayakon and his successor, Sir Leslie Munro, will consistently report noncooperation by the Hungarian and Soviet authorities.

September 17   Malaya is admitted as the world organization's eighty-second member.

September 17   Hammarskjöld meets with the UNEF Advisory Committee and speculates on the crisis that would occur if Egypt requested UNEF withdrawal from its territory.

September 24   The General Assembly again postpones the issue of Chinese representation in the United Nations, by a vote of 47–27–7.

September 26   The Security Council unanimously recommends (11–0) and the General Assembly unanimously reelects (80–0) Dag Hammarskjöld secretary-general for a second five-year term, effective April 10, 1958.

September 30   The USSR rejects the comprehensive disarmament plan presented by the Western powers at the UN Disarmament Commission talks in London.

September 30   The relief program to Hungary involving food, medicine, clothing, and other supplies by the United Nations, its specialized agencies, and the International Committee of the Red Cross is formally concluded. But assistance to Hungarian refugees by the United Nations High Commissioner for Refugees (UNHCR) and others continues.

October 1   Switzerland brings the Interhandel case to the International Court of Justice seeking to retrieve the company's assets from the United States.

October 5　The Soviet Union orbits Sputnik I, the first artificial earth satellite.

October 10　The eighth pledging conference of the General Assembly authorizes $32,317,900 for technical assistance to developing countries.

October 10　A case involving the guardianship of a Dutch infant residing in Sweden and raised under the Swedish regime of protective upbringing is brought to the International Court of Justice by the Netherlands on behalf of the child's father and deputy guardian.

October 12　Hammarskjöld warns the General Assembly that the continued existence of the United Nations Emergency Force is in "grave risk" unless $12.8 million is provided to pay its debts.

October 13　The General Assembly postpones until 1959 its review of the UN Charter.

October 14　Lester B. Pearson of Canada, the major contributor to the concept of UNEF, the first UN peacekeeping force, wins the 1957 Nobel Peace Prize.

October 16　The aerial incident of July 27, 1955, involving the destruction of an El Al Israeli airliner by Bulgaria leads to proceedings at the International Court of Justice by Israel, Britain, and the United States seeking compensation. Citizens of all three countries were killed when the plane was shot down.

October 18　Pearson urges that UN troops be deployed along the Turkish–Syrian border to prevent violence between feuding neighbors.

October 25　The General Assembly establishes a Good Offices Committee to mediate the South-West Africa issue.

October 26　Soviet Marshal Georgi Zhukov is relieved of his duties as minister of defense; Khrushchev reportedly feared the popularity of Zhukov, a World War II hero.

October 28　Indonesia threatens to seize West New Guinea from Dutch control if the United Nations does not settle the conflict over the territory.

November 1   The General Assembly recesses indefinitely its debate on the Turkish–Syrian border dispute after Syrian delegates decide not to press for a commission to investigate tension between the two countries.

November 3   The Soviet Union launches Sputnik II into space.

November 5   Hammarskjöld urges that a 3 percent surcharge be added to all Suez Canal transit tolls to reimburse the United Nations for $8.3 million spent clearing the waterway.

November 6   On the 40th anniversary of the Communist Revolution, Party Secretary Khrushchev calls for "peaceful coexistence" between East and West.

November 13   A threatened Soviet boycott of the 11-member UN Disarmament Commission forces the United States, Britain, France, and Canada to expand the body.

November 15   Portugal extends its 1951 Azores Common Defense Pact with the United States.

November 15   Hammarskjöld announces that Lt. Gen. Raymond A. Wheeler (Ret.), who supervised the clearance of the Suez Canal, will head a UN study for development of Southeast Asia's Lower Mekong River Basin.

November 19   Membership of the UN Disarmament Commission is increased from 11 to 25 by the General Assembly.

November 22   The General Assembly approves an assessment on member states to meet the budget of UNEF through 1958.

November 24   Hammarskjöld expresses full "personal confidence" in Col. Byron V. Leary, U.S. Marine Corps, acting chief of UNTSO, after Jordan declares him persona non grata for allegedly tilting toward Israel.

November 26   The General Assembly continues the Office of the United Nations High Commissioner for Refugees for five years but approves the termination of the United Nations Korean Reconstruction Agency (UNKRA) by June 30, 1958.

November 26   The General Assembly deplores South Africa's failure to alter its racial policy of apartheid.

November 27   A border dispute between Belgium and the Netherlands is brought to the International Court of Justice.

November 29   Hammarskjöld leaves for Beirut, Amman, Jerusalem, and Damascus in hopes of easing tension in the Middle East.

December 4   Hammarskjöld reaches an agreement with Israel and Jordan on the resumption of Israeli convoys to Mount Scopus, an Israeli enclave inside Arab Jerusalem.

December 4   Povl Bang-Jensen, deputy head of the UN Special Committee on Hungary, is suspended by Hammarskjöld for refusing to surrender to the secretary-general lists of Hungarian refugees interviewed by the Special Committee. Bang-Jensen feared that the names might be used by Communist authorities to retaliate against the refugees' relatives still in Hungary.

December 14   The General Assembly approves Hammarskjöld's suggested surcharge on Suez Canal tolls to cover the cost of clearing the waterway totaling $8.3 million.

December 14   The General Assembly authorizes a UN operating budget of $55,062,850 for 1958, and $30 million additional for UNEF expenses.

December 16   Hammarskjöld appoints Francisco Urrutia Holguin as his personal representative in Jordan and Israel.

December 16–19   NATO holds its first heads of government conference in Paris. The 15 members agree to form a nuclear missile force but also to seek a disarmament pact with the Soviet Union.

December 17   The United States successfully tests its first ICBM.

December 21   After forbidding a UN observer group to visit Budapest, Hungary's UN delegate refuses to transmit to his government a letter from the UN Special Committee on the Problem of Hungary.

December 22   Hammarskjöld visits Cairo and Gaza, spending time with members of UNEF and UNRWA.

December 26   Delegates from 40 African and Asian states and colonies hold their first Afro-Asian Peoples Solidarity Conference in

Cairo, extending the nonaligned movement initiated by Tito, Nehru, Nasser, and Sukarno in Bandung in 1955. They adopt resolutions backing Soviet appeals for peaceful coexistence, condemning Western imperialist and colonialist policies, and attacking the Eisenhower Doctrine. A Soviet spokesman offers economic and technical aid.

1958

January 1 The European Economic Community (EEC) and the European Atomic Energy Community (EURATOM) are to go into effect with Belgium, France, Italy, Luxembourg, the Netherlands, and West Germany as members.

January 1 The Federation of the West Indies—comprising Antigua, Barbados, Dominica, Grenada, Jamaica, Montserrat, St. Kitts-Nevis-Anguilla, St. Lucia, St. Vincent, Tobago, and Trinidad—is established.

January 4 Sputnik I, the first Soviet earth satellite, disintegrates in space after orbiting since October 1957.

January 13 Hammarskjöld receives a petition from Nobel Prize winner Linus Pauling and 9,235 scientists from 43 countries calling for an immediate international agreement to ban nuclear weapons testing.

January 16 Lester B. Pearson becomes leader of Canada's Liberal Party.

January 18 Hammarskjöld accepts the recommendation from the UN Special Committee on the Problem of Hungary that lists of anti-Communist refugee witnesses should be destroyed.

January 18 Francisco Urrutia Holguin, Hammarskjöld's personal representative in the Middle East, reports that Israel and Jordan have agreed to demilitarize the strategic Mount Scopus area of Jerusalem.

January 21 Hammarskjöld asserts that the UN Disarmament Commission will remain in existence despite Soviet threats to boycott the group; he notes that disarmament talks outside the United Nations are an "optical illusion."

January 22 The Security Council unanimously adopts a resolution calling for tighter UN control of the Jerusalem demilitarized zone between Israel and Jordan.

January 23   U.S. Ambassador Lodge suggests a ban on Security Council vetoes on questions involving the peaceful settlement of disputes (Chapter 6 of the UN Charter).

January 27   Hammarskjöld urges the UN Scientific Committee on the Effects of Atomic Radiation to ignore political pressures and to speak out "with a single objective voice" on the medical and genetic hazards of radiation.

January 27   Secretary of State Dulles reassures Baghdad Pact members that the United States would use "great force" in the event of a Communist attack in the Middle East.

January 30   Israel complains to the Security Council of a "new wave of aggression" by Syria at its border.

January 31   Explorer I, the first successful U.S. earth satellite, is launched from Cape Canaveral, Florida, and discovers the Van Allen radiation belt 600 miles above the earth.

February 1   Egypt's President Gamal Abdel Nasser and Syria's President Shukri al-Kuwatly proclaim the merging of their two countries into the United Arab Republic (UAR), confirmed in a national plebiscite in both states on February 21.

February 1   Maj. Gen. Olaf H. Kyster, chief UN delegate to the Korean Military Armistice Commission, rejects Communist protests against the introduction of atomic weapons into South Korea.

February 8   French planes bomb a Tunisian–Algerian border village, Sakiet-Sidi-Youssef, for allegedly harboring Algerian FLN rebel fighters; 79 Tunisians die. Tunisia blockades French military bases in the country, demanding the withdrawal of all 15,000 French troops that remained in Tunisia under the 1956 independence agreement.

February 14   In response to the creation of the United Arab Republic, Jordan and Iraq merge to become the Arab Federation.

February 18   The Security Council considers the bombing of Sakiet-Sidi-Youssef but adjourns without debate after the United States and Britain offer their good offices.

February 22   The Security Council considers Sudan's boundary claims against Egypt.

February 24   In Geneva, the United Nations Conference on the Law of the Sea (UNCLOS) opens with representations from 86 countries to draft a universal definition of national territorial waters and to extend international law over world maritime issues.

March 3   Hammarskjöld appoints Maj. Gen. Carl Carlsson von Horn (Sweden) as the new chief of UNTSO.

March 6   The newly formed United Arab Republic merging Egypt and Syria replaces the two federation partners at the United Nations, reducing total membership from 82 to 81.

March 8   Yemen federates with the merged Egypt and Syria in a looser arrangement known as the United Arab States.

March 9   Japan opens to traffic its 11,245-foot underwater tunnel linking Honshu and Kyushu Islands.

March 13   The Saudi delegate to the UNCLOS announces that his country has formally extended its territorial waters to 12 miles from its coastline, thereby "legally" closing the Gulf of Aqaba to Israeli shipping.

March 13   Soviet Foreign Minister Gromyko announces his country's suspension of nuclear weapons tests, calling on the United States and Britain to do likewise.

March 14   Iran's Shah Mohammed Reza Pahlavi divorces Queen Soraya for failing to produce a male heir to the throne.

March 15   To break the deadlock at the UNCLOS regarding the definition of territorial waters, the United States abandons its traditional adherence to the three-mile limit.

March 17   Exiled Cuban student leader Fidel Castro urges an uprising against the government of President Fulgencio Batista.

March 17   With the admission of Japan as the 21st state, the Intergovernmental Maritime Consultative Organization (IMCO) becomes operative. Its purposes are to regulate the safety of life at sea and ensure efficient navigation.

March 27   Communist Party First Secretary Nikita Khrushchev replaces Nikolai Bulganin as chairman of the Council of Ministers (prime minister). The Soviet Union thus returns to virtually one-man rule for the first time since Stalin's death in March 1953.

March 30   Israeli and Syrian border troops clash in a renewed dispute over Israeli land reclamation work in the Lake Huleh area.

April 3   The Security Council is informed that India has rejected all proposals to settle its Kashmir dispute with Pakistan.

April 5   Fidel Castro proclaims "total war" against Cuba's Batista regime as his forces open a drive against it.

April 9   On the eve of beginning his second term as secretary-general, Hammarskjöld comments, "The future will be all right because there will always be enough people to fight for a decent future."

April 10   Dag Hammarskjöld begins a second five-year term, asserting that his "sense of duty" forced him to accept the position.

April 18   Hammarskjöld praises American author Archibald MacLeish for getting poet Ezra Pound released from a Washington mental hospital where he was confined because of "treasonable" World War II broadcasts from Rome.

April 19   Marshal Tito is unanimously reelected as Yugoslav president for a third four-year term.

April 23   It is announced that France has lost some 6,000 men and the rebels 62,000 since the Algerian war began in November 1954.

April 27   The UNCLOS in Geneva concludes after its failure to agree on a new definition of territorial sea limits. But some progress extending the scope of international law is achieved just the same.

April 29   Hammarskjöld urges the Security Council to work for the cessation of nuclear weapons tests, a halt in nuclear weapons production, and adequate inspection to ensure compliance.

April 29   A preliminary accord titled Heads of Agreement on compensation for the 1956 nationalization of the Suez Canal is signed by the UAR (Egypt) and the Universal Suez Canal Company.

April 30   The USSR confirms that it is discontinuing its nuclear weapons tests.

May 1   On a state visit to Moscow, Egyptian President Nasser pledges his support of Soviet foreign policy. In return, the Soviets promise to back the liberation of all Africans and Asians.

May 2   At the Security Council, the Soviet Union vetoes the U.S.-sponsored resolution establishing an international nuclear inspection zone in the Arctic region.

May 6   Communist China and North Korea demand the withdrawal of all UN troops from South Korea as a condition for a "peaceful settlement of the Korean question, including the question of holding free elections."

May 12   In Beirut, protests break out against the regime of Lebanese President Camille Chamoun. Foreign Minister Charles Malik accuses the UAR of formulating the uprising.

May 13   On a Latin American goodwill mission, Vice President Richard M. Nixon encounters a hostile mob in Caracas, Venezuela, and cuts short his seven-nation tour.

May 15   The Algiers Committee of Public Safety, headed by French Brig. Gen. Jacques Massu, temporarily assumes power in Algeria.

May 16   Hammarskjöld announces procedural revisions that give him personal direction of all UN disarmament efforts.

May 19   Hammarskjöld urges agreements on the use of outer space similar to those that guarantee freedom of the high seas.

May 19   The United States and Canada establish the North American Air Defense Command (NORAD) to guard against attack on either country.

May 20   The French National Assembly renews the government's special powers to combat the nationalist rebellion in Algeria.

May 22   Lebanon formally complains to the Security Council of cross border infiltrations and intervention in its domestic affairs by the Syrian region of the UAR.

May 25   A second French bombing incident in Tunisia causes a war-threatening crisis between the two countries as troops from both forces clash at French bases at Remada and Gabès.

May 26   Col. George A. Flint (Canada), chairman of the UN

Israeli–Jordanian Mixed Armistice Commission, is killed when Jordanian troops and Israeli policemen exchange fire on Mount Scopus in Jerusalem.

May 31 The French army, concerned about a possible "sellout" in Algeria, demands that Charles de Gaulle become premier. De Gaulle agrees on the condition that he is granted full powers to avert a civil war and change the constitution of the Fourth Republic.

June 1 The French National Assembly grants Premier Charles de Gaulle full decree powers for six months. His accession averts a threat of civil war, since two senior officers, Brig. Gen. Jacques Massu and Gen. Raoul Salan, have seized control in Algeria.

June 2 Premier de Gaulle appeals to Tunisian President Habib Bourguiba to help settle the difficulties between their two countries.

June 10 The UN Conference on International Commercial Arbitration closes after adopting a convention that enters into force on June 7, 1959.

June 11 The Security Council establishes the United Nations Observation Group in Lebanon (UNOGIL) to prevent infiltrations of fighters and weapons across the Syrian–Lebanese border. The vote is 10–0–0 as the USSR abstains.

June 17 A French–Tunisian agreement will withdraw French forces from all of Tunisia, except the Bizerte naval base.

June 17 The Hungarian government announces the execution of former Premier Imre Nagy, Maj. Gen. Pál Maleter, and two other leaders of the Hungarian Revolution of 1956. Angry anti-Communist demonstrations sweep across Western nations as the U.S. Congress unanimously condemns Soviet "barbarism and perfidy."

June 19–25 Hammarskjöld presides over UNOGIL's first meeting in Beirut. While in the Middle East, he also holds talks in Jordan, Israel, and Egypt. On his return to Beirut, he looks into Lebanon's alleged attempts to discredit UNOGIL.

June 21 The UN Special Committee on the Problem of Hungary officially deplores the executions of Imre Nagy and the other Hungarian revolutionary leaders.

June 26 To draw attention to his struggle against the regime of Fulgencio Batista, Fidel Castro's rebels kidnap 47 Americans and three Canadians from the Guantánamo Bay area. Following negotiations, all are released by July 18.

June 29   The United States demands the immediate return of nine U.S. airmen on an unarmed transport plane forced down by Soviet fighters in Soviet Armenia.

July 1   Honduras and Nicaragua bring their border dispute to the International Court of Justice.

July 3   Hammarskjöld dismisses Povl Bang-Jensen for insubordination to superiors and other misconduct while serving on the UN Special Committee on the Problem of Hungary.

July 4   UNOGIL's first report to the Security Council notes that it has not uncovered evidence of UAR support for Lebanese rebels.

July 11   The United States demands sanctions against Soviet airmen who shot down an unarmed U.S. transport plane over Soviet Armenia.

July 13   Through the good offices of the International Bank for Reconstruction and Development (World Bank), Egypt (UAR) and the stockholders of the Universal Suez Canal Company sign a final agreement, confirming that of April 29, on compensation following nationalization of the waterway. Under its terms, the United Arab Republic is to pay some $81 million to the shareholders as well as relinquish all of the Suez Canal Company's external assets to them.

July 14   Brig. Gen. Abdul Karim Kassem leads an army coup in Baghdad, Iraq, that assassinates pro-Western King Faisal, Crown Prince Abdul Illah, and Prime Minister Nouri al-Said. King Hussein of Jordan, feeling threatened, asks for Britain's protection.

July 14   The UN Special Committee on the Problem of Hungary issues a supplementary final report that strongly indicts Soviet and Communist actions in that country.

July 14   Hammarskjöld appoints Pier P. Spinelli as his special representative in Jordan.

July 16   Some 8,000 U.S. Marines land in Beirut despite Hammarskjöld's efforts to dissuade Washington. Eisenhower explains that the marines will protect American lives and defend Lebanese independence, allegedly threatened by rebels supported by the United Arab Republic and the Soviet Union.

July 17 British troops arrive in Jordan. King Hussein feared that, following the assassination of his cousin, King Faisal of Iraq, his monarchy was also threatened.

July 18 The Security Council defeats a Soviet motion calling on the United States and Britain to "remove their troops from the territories of Lebanon and Jordan immediately" while the Soviets veto an American proposal for the use of UN troops in Lebanon.

July 19 In Cairo, leaders of Algeria's independence movement declare a provisional government for Algeria with Ferhat Abbas as its president.

July 20–21 Hammarskjöld recommends the expansion of UNOGIL as a way to allow American troops to make a graceful exit from Lebanon. But Japan's motion to that effect in the Security Council is vetoed by the Soviets.

July 22 Hammarskjöld informs the Security Council that he will take immediate steps, which include beefing up UNOGIL, "to help prevent a further deterioration of the situation" in the Middle East.

July 25 Eisenhower advises Soviet Premier Khrushchev that he will attend a summit conference on the Middle East crisis, as the Soviet leader had suggested, held within the UN framework. But the U.S. president stipulates that the agenda should not be limited to a mere consideration of U.S. and British intervention in Lebanon and Jordan. On August 5, Khrushchev rejects the proposal.

July 31 General Fouad Chehab is elected Lebanon's president, replacing Camille Chamoun.

August 2 In the wake of the coup in Baghdad, King Hussein of Jordan dissolves the Arab Federation, which had merged his country with Iraq. The United States, following Britain, recognizes the new Iraqi regime of Brig. Gen. Abdul Karim Kassem.

August 4 The Greek Cypriot underground declares a truce with British security forces and Turkish Cypriots, the first move toward solving the Cyprus question.

August 7 The Security Council unanimously adopts a U.S. resolution calling for an immediate emergency session of the General Assembly on the Middle East.

August 8   Called by the Security Council the day before, the General Assembly opens its third special emergency session on the Middle East at which President Eisenhower presents a six-point peace plan.

August 8   The U.S. nuclear submarine *Nautilus* completes a 1,830-mile undersea voyage that took it under the North Pole.

August 9   The United States reaffirms its decision not to recognize Communist China.

August 21   As the emergency session on the Middle East ends, the General Assembly unanimously passes a compromise resolution calling for "practical arrangements" to uphold the "purpose and principles of the United Nations Charter in relation to Lebanon and Jordan." The Assembly also requests Hammarskjöld to facilitate the early withdrawal of American and British troops from Lebanon and Jordan, respectively, which the two Western powers pledged to do.

August 22   The U.S. claims compensation at the International Court of Justice for the destruction of a U.S. Navy plane by the Soviets off Vladivostok, over the Sea of Japan, on September 4, 1954.

August 23   The Communist Chinese resume shelling Nationalist China's offshore islands of Quemoy and Matsu.

August 24   In one of its first racial incidents, hundreds of whites and blacks clash in Nottingham, England.

August 30   The final report of the Geneva Conference of Nuclear Experts states that 180 control posts could identify virtually all nuclear explosions above 1,000-ton TNT equivalent.

September 1   The second UN International Conference on the Peaceful Uses of Atomic Energy opens in Geneva.

September 2   Hendrik F. Verwoerd becomes South African premier.

September 3   Hammarskjöld stops in Cairo and Jerusalem on his way to Baghdad to meet Brig. Gen. Abdul Karim Kassem, Iraq's new head of state.

September 4   Communist China announces the extension of its territorial waters to 12 miles.

September 8   The Soviet Union announces that it has put a 100,000-kilowatt atomic power station in Siberia into operation, the world's largest.

September 11   President Eisenhower proclaims on national television that the United States would fight to prevent the conquest of the islands of Quemoy and Matsu by Communist China.

September 11   In his annual report to the General Assembly, Hammarskjöld suggests that disarmament be promoted by talks among international scientific, military, and legal experts.

September 20   UNOGIL in Lebanon reports the presence of 214 military observers from 21 countries as the withdrawal of American marines has been under way since September 14.

September 23   The General Assembly supports (42–28–11) a U.S. resolution not to consider the question of Chinese representation during its current session. Similar action occurs at the second IAEA conference in Vienna.

September 23   Belgium brings the Barcelona Traction, Light, and Power Company case to the International Court of Justice, claiming compensation on behalf of Belgian shareholders.

September 28   The constitution of the French Fifth Republic is approved by popular referendum in metropolitan France and overseas France.

September 28   By voting no in a referendum, Guinea, a former colony, declines membership in the French Community. Guinea is the only French West African territory to do so, and France withdraws all financial and administrative aid as Ahmed Sékou Touré, a Marxist, becomes Guinea's first president.

September 30   The U.S. Atomic Energy Commission reports that the Soviet Union has resumed exploding nuclear energy devices, ending its unilateral test ban announced six months earlier.

October 1   Hammarskjöld urges that the United Nations control any atomic test monitoring system resulting from an East–West test ban agreement.

October 1 UNOGIL confirms that armed infiltration into Lebanon is virtually nil.

October 5 The French Fifth Republic comes into existence with the publication of its new constitution.

October 6 The International Bank for Reconstruction and Development (World Bank) reports that in fiscal 1958, it made 34 loans totaling $711 million.

October 6 The Chinese Communist government orders a one-week halt to the shelling of the Nationalist Chinese offshore islands of Quemoy and Matsu, provided the United States suspend its escort of Nationalist Chinese vessels, which Washington approves on October 8.

October 9 Hammarskjöld denies the General Assembly's Fifth (Administrative and Budgetary) Committee charge that he is concentrating too much power into his own hands.

October 9 Pope Pius XII dies.

October 13 Rebel leader Fidel Castro warns that any candidate in the general election of November 3 in Cuba faces execution for treason.

October 15 Hammarskjöld urges the General Assembly to create a standby force to swiftly meet specific conflict situations.

October 16 At its ninth pledging conference, the General Assembly approves $27 million for the Expanded Program of Technical Assistance (EPTA) and $21 million for the Special United Nations Fund (SUNFED) to assist developing countries.

October 16 The Soviet Union strongly protests alleged violations of Soviet Far Eastern airspace by U.S. aircraft.

October 20 The French UN delegate announces that France would not be bound by any nuclear test ban agreement.

October 20 The Chinese Communists break their self-imposed truce and resume shelling Quemoy Island.

October 20 After three months, the 2,000 British troops begin to pull out of Jordan.

October 20   Thailand's armed forces commander, Field Marshal Sarit Thanarat, seizes power and cracks down on Communists while abolishing other political parties.

October 22   Hungary rejects an American request that Cardinal Jozsef Mindszenthy, a refugee at the U.S. legation in Budapest since the 1956 revolution, be granted a safe-conduct to Rome to participate in the election of the new pope.

October 23   The Soviet Union agrees to loan Egypt $100 million for the construction of the first stage of the Aswan High Dam, a gigantic hydroelectric project on the River Nile. The funds will pay for technicians, materials, and equipment.

October 23   Chiang Kai-shek's Nationalist government in Taiwan announces that it will not use force to return to the Communist-controlled Chinese mainland.

October 25   The last U.S. Marines are withdrawn from Lebanon.

October 25   Communist China announces that it will not shell Nationalist China's offshore islands on even-numbered days of the month.

October 28   Angelo Giuseppe Cardinal Roncalli, patriarch of Venice, is elected pope and assumes the name of John XXIII. He later convenes the Second Vatican Council promoting ecumenicalism and will become the most popular pontiff of the century.

October 28   The United States requests the International Court of Justice to discontinue proceedings in its claim for damages from Bulgaria regarding the aerial incident of July 27, 1955. The World Court complies on May 30, 1960.

October 29   The Soviet bloc reiterates its refusal to share the costs of the United Nations Emergency Force, arguing that Britain, France, and Israel alone were responsible for the 1956 Suez attack.

October 30   The General Assembly again deplores the racial abuses of South Africa's apartheid policy.

October 31   The United States, Britain, and the Soviet Union meet in Geneva to discuss discontinuance of nuclear weapons tests.

November 2   The last British troops are withdrawn from Jordan.

November 4   Membership of the UN Disarmament Commission is increased from 25 to all 81 UN member states.

November 14   The General Assembly adopts a resolution (54–9) for the reunification of North and South Korea through UN-supervised elections.

November 19   Hammarskjöld disbands UNOGIL, established on June 11, after Lebanon withdraws its complaints against UAR infiltrations.

November 23   Kwame Nkrumah and Sékou Touré agree on the Ghanaian–Guinean union.

November 27   Soviet Premier Khrushchev threatens to give East Germany control of all communications lines to West Berlin unless the Western powers agree within six months to make West Berlin a demilitarized free city with its own government.

November 28   The Congo (Brazzaville), Mauritania, Upper Volta, Gabon, and Mali in West Africa become independent states within the French Community. The Central African Republic follows suit on December 1, and the Ivory Coast and Dahomey on December 4.

November 28   At the request of Cambodia and Thailand, Hammarskjöld appoints a special representative to mediate their dispute regarding ownership of the temple of Preah Vihear.

November 28   The International Court of Justice rules in favor of Sweden following a challenge by the Netherlands regarding the guardianship of a Dutch infant brought up in Sweden.

December 4   Paul G. Hoffman is appointed managing director of the Special United Nations Fund.

December 6   The UN Administrative Tribunal upholds Hammarskjöld's dismissal of Povl Bang-Jensen, previously deputy head of the UN Special Committee on the Problem of Hungary.

December 9   Because of Soviet objections, the International Court of Justice removes from its list a case brought by the United States seeking compensation for a U.S. Navy plane downed on September 4, 1954.

December 10   The General Assembly resolves to convene a Second

United Nations Conference on the Law of the Sea (UNCLOS II) in Geneva in 1960.

December 10 UNOGIL officially ends after submitting a final report of calm along the Syrian–Lebanese border.

December 11 In a press interview, Soviet Premier Khrushchev warns that any attempt by Western powers to force access to Berlin would mean war.

December 12 Guinea is admitted as the UN's 82d member.

December 12 The General Assembly approves (59–9) the establishment of an ad hoc committee to study international cooperation in the peaceful uses of outer space.

December 12 The General Assembly endorses the reports of the UN Special Committee on the Problem of Hungary and in turn denounces the execution of Imre Nagy and three of his associates. The Assembly appoints Sir Leslie Munro of New Zealand to succeed Prince Wan Waithayakon as special representative on the Problem of Hungary.

December 13 In a note to the 15 NATO members, the Soviet Union reiterates its demand for the creation of a free city in West Berlin.

December 13 The General Assembly authorizes a UN operating budget of $60,802,120 for 1959 and $25 million for UNEF. The Assembly adjourns after rejecting a resolution to recognize Algerian independence from France.

December 14 The United States, Britain, and France reject Soviet demands that they withdraw from West Berlin and that the four-power occupation of the entire city be ended.

December 15 The 1959 edition of *Jane's Fighting Ships* rates the Soviet Union as second only to the United States in naval power. *Jane's All the World's Aircraft* reports a new Soviet six-jet bomber operating at twice the speed of sound.

December 18 The conference on means to prevent surprise attacks adjourns in deadlock in Geneva, but the conference on prohibiting nuclear tests makes some progress on a draft treaty.

December 21 General Charles de Gaulle is overwhelmingly elected

French president for a seven-year term, the Fifth Republic's first head of state.

December 25 Hammarskjöld spends Christmas with members of the UNRWA and Palestinian refugees in Gaza.

December 29 In Addis Ababa, Hammarskjöld opens the first session of the UN Economic Commission for Africa (ECA).

1959

January 1 The European Economic Community, consisting of France, West Germany, Belgium, Luxembourg, the Netherlands, and Italy, becomes effective as it joins the European Coal and Steel Community (ECSC) and the European Atomic Energy Community (EURATOM) in a move toward continental integration.

January 1 Fidel Castro's rebel forces capture Havana after President Fulgencio Batista's dictatorial regime collapses. The next day, Castro proclaims Manuel Urrutia Ileo head of a provisional government.

January 1 President Nasser, accusing Communists of working against Arab unity, orders the arrest of several hundred across Egypt after a similar crackdown in Syria, the other component of the UAR.

January 3 Alaska becomes the 49th American state.

January 3 The Soviet Union announces a moon probe with a rocket, which shoots past the planet and orbits around the sun as the first artificial planet. But its radio transmitters become silent shortly after the launch.

January 4–6 Bloody riots in Leopoldville, Belgian Congo, against colonial rule help bring an end to the earlier drift and delay in Brussels. The cabinet soon issues a statement: "Belgium intends to organize in the Congo a democracy capable of exercising its prerogative of sovereignty, and of deciding on its independence."

January 7 Following in the wake of Britain and other countries, the United States recognizes the Castro government of Cuba.

January 8 Gen. Charles de Gaulle assumes power as president of the French Fifth Republic. France's colonies are given six months to decide on their future status regarding association with the mother country.

January 13   Belgium announces that it will grant its Congo colony independence. Patrice Lumumba, head of the Congolese National Movement, accepts the Belgian plan even though it does not set a date.

January 13   Fidel Castro establishes revolutionary courts that will function until all "criminals" of the Batista regime are tried.

January 16   Britain and Egypt reach an agreement on the settlement of financial problems flowing from Cairo's nationalization of the Suez Canal Company and the ensuing attack by Britain and two allies.

January 21   Fidel Castro denounces U.S. criticism of the execution of Batista supporters in Havana.

January 25   Pope John XXIII announces plans to call the first ecumenical conference since 1870 to reunite Christian communities.

February 6   After the settlement of their dispute concerning the temple of Preah Vihear, Cambodia and Thailand decide to restore diplomatic relations.

February 7   Plans are announced for large-scale Soviet aid to Iraq's economic development, to China's industrial expansion and, shortly, Mongolia's.

February 11   Laos renounces the 1954 Geneva Agreement terminating hostilities in Indochina.

February 13   France institutes proceedings against Lebanon at the International Court of Justice. The case arises out of certain measures adopted by Lebanon with regard to two French companies—the Compagnie du Port, des Quais et des Entrepôts de Beyrouth and the Société Radio-Orient.

February 14   A joint Soviet–Chinese communiqué proclaims the "unbreakable unity" of the two countries.

February 16   Fidel Castro, who insists that he is neither a socialist nor a Communist, becomes Cuba's prime minister. In the first three months of his regime, several hundred Batista supporters are tried and executed.

February 17   The United States orbits the first weather satellite, Tiros 1.

February 19   Britain, Greece, Turkey, and the leaders of the Greek and Turkish Cypriot communities agree on terms for establishment of an independent Cyprus by August 16, 1960. Britain will retain control over two military bases after relinquishing sovereignty, and the two ethnic communities will share political power, roughly in proportion to their sizes (80 percent Greek and 20 percent Turkish).

February 21   British Prime Minister Harold Macmillan begins an 11-day visit to the Soviet Union, the first such event since World War II. While there, he rejects Khrushchev's offer of a Soviet–British nonaggression pact.

March 1   Archbishop Makarios III, the Greek Cypriot leader, is allowed by the British to return to his country from exile.

March 2   Iran renounces the 1921 treaty, which stipulated that the Soviet Union could send its troops into that country.

March 4   Premier Khrushchev repeats that he will sign a separate peace treaty with the German Democratic Republic (East Germany) unless the West accepts Soviet demands on Berlin.

March 4   A U.S. lunar probe flies by the moon and orbits the sun.

March 14   President de Gaulle refuses to place a third of France's naval forces in the Mediterranean under NATO command. The French leader openly disagrees with the United States on nuclear policy.

March 17   The Soviet Union signs a technical assistance agreement with North Korea.

March 18   Hawaii becomes the 50th American state.

March 21   In the Interhandel case, the International Court of Justice rules that Switzerland had not exhausted all legal remedies available to it in the U.S. courts to press for the return of assets seized from the company in 1942.

March 21   The International Court of Justice rejects Switzerland's petition that the World Court order the United States to release $200 million in seized stock of General Aniline and Film Corporation or submit the case to arbitration.

March 23 President Eisenhower extends the peacetime draft in the United States to July 1, 1963.

March 24 Iraq withdraws from the U.S.-inspired Baghdad Pact (METO) of 1955 designed to check the spread of Communism in the Middle East.

March 28–31 The Chinese Communists crush a revolt in Tibet; the Tibetan leader, the Dalai Lama, flees from Lhasa to asylum in India.

March 30 Japan offers to submit its running dispute with the USSR over northern Pacific fishing rights to the International Court of Justice.

April 1 The Western Big Three foreign ministers reiterate their refusal to accept the Soviet Union's unilateral repudiation of its Berlin obligations. They reject the substitution of East German for Soviet authority in implementing those obligations.

April 2 Hammarskjöld tells newsmen that he has been "in touch" with Egyptian leaders regarding their seizures of Israeli cargoes transiting the Suez Canal in foreign vessels. The Egyptians impounded such cargoes on February 26 and again on March 13.

April 14 John Foster Dulles resigns as U.S. Secretary of State (health reasons) and is replaced by Christian A. Herter.

April 15 Fidel Castro begins an unofficial 11-day tour of the United States and Canada during which he confers with Hammarskjöld, Secretary of State-designate Christian Herter, Vice President Nixon, and congressional leaders. During the visit, Castro characterizes his Cuban revolution as humanistic and professes friendship for the United States.

April 18 The UN Conference on the Elimination or Reduction of Future Statelessness fails to reach agreement on how to limit the freedom of states to deprive citizens of their nationality.

April 25 The St. Lawrence Seaway, 400 miles long and taking five years to build, is opened for shipping, allowing maritime traffic between the Atlantic and mid-America.

May 1 A group of 87 invaders, mostly Cubans, seeking to overthrow the Panamanian government, surrenders.

May 2 Hammarskjöld offers the United Nations as a forum for discussing both Berlin and German reunification. He suggests that if the forthcoming foreign ministers' talks in Geneva are inconclusive, the Berlin problem should pass directly to the Security Council.

May 11 The Big Four foreign ministers meet in Geneva on the problems of Berlin, German reunification, an all-German peace treaty, and European security. By August 5, when the conference ends, they make little progress.

May 15 Premier Fidel Castro orders an end to military trials of war "criminals."

May 17 Chinese Communist mainland artillery bombards Nationalist China's Matsu Island.

May 18 The Cuban cabinet approves an agrarian reform law setting strict limits on sugar plantation ownership by individuals or companies.

May 18 Burmese forces attack Nationalist Chinese guerrillas operating in Burma.

May 21 Hammarskjöld opposes proposals to create a UN "garrison" in Berlin, telling a news conference that assumption of a military role by the world organization in Berlin would be "of a very serious political nature."

May 26 Transkei is inaugurated at Umtata as the first all-African Bantustan homeland in a segregated South Africa.

May 26 The International Court of Justice finds that it lacks jurisdiction in the case of an Israeli airliner downed by Bulgaria on July 27, 1955.

May 28 The International Olympic Committee (IOC) under its American president, Avery Brundage, withdraws recognition of Nationalist China (Taiwan) and promises to admit Communist China upon its application.

May 30 Khrushchev rejects the Big Three's seven-point proposal for the future of Berlin.

June 1 Iraq declines U.S. military aid, seen as conflicting with its policy of positive neutrality.

June 4 Hammarskjöld tells a press conference that he hopes Israel and Egypt would agree to bring the Suez Canal blockade issue before the International Court of Justice. The secretary-general refuses to confirm reports that he has urged Egypt to halt its interference with Israeli cargoes trying to transit the waterway.

June 4 The Castro regime expropriates large landholdings and foreign-owned property in Cuba.

June 4 President de Gaulle's government requests Allied support for its Algerian policy in return for France's full participation in NATO.

June 15 Hammarskjöld proposes that the General Assembly create an Arab Development Bank to finance economic growth in the Middle East and assist Palestinian refugees. He urges that the United Nations Relief and Works Agency for Palestine Refugees in the Near East (UNRWA) be continued until all Palestinian refugees have been absorbed into the region's economic life.

June 20 The International Court of Justice confirms Belgian sovereignty over two disputed enclaves within Dutch territory near the border.

June 26 The 400-mile St. Lawrence Seaway, linking the Great Lakes to the Atlantic Ocean, is formally dedicated by President Eisenhower and Britain's Queen Elizabeth II, acting as Canada's head of state.

June 30 In Cairo, Hammarskjöld strives to persuade Egypt's leaders to end their ban on Israeli-owned or chartered vessels and on Israeli cargoes in foreign bottoms trying to transit the Suez Canal.

July 1 The United States resumes economic and technical aid to the UAR.

July 13 In Paris, Hammarskjöld warns President de Gaulle that still another resolution on Algeria's hostility to France may pass the General Assembly, which has been happening since 1956.

July 14 Twenty-five Afro-Asian states request Hammarskjöld to place "the question of Algeria" on the agenda of the 14th General Assembly session opening in September.

July 17 In a dispute with Premier Fidel Castro over "moral differences," Cuba's President Manuel Urrutia resigns and is replaced by Osvaldo Dorticós Torrado.

July 21   Mamie Eisenhower, wife of President Dwight Eisenhower, christens the *Savannah*, the first U.S. nuclear merchant vessel.

July 23   At the U.S. National Exhibition in Moscow, Vice President Nixon and Premier Khrushchev argue the respective merits of capitalism versus Communism in their celebrated "Kitchen Debate."

July 23   French forces begin a large-scale offensive against Algerian rebels in the Kabylia region.

July 30–31   Laos reports that Communist-led Pathet Lao guerrillas, armed by North Vietnam, have attacked its army posts in the north.

August 3   Upon the request of the United Kingdom, the International Court of Justice removes from its list Britain's claim for damages from Bulgaria relating to an aerial incident on July 27, 1955.

August 4   Hammarskjöld tells a press conference that he approves of renewed Big Four disarmament discussions that "prepare the ground" but that the United Nations "retained the ultimate responsibility" for disarmament negotiations.

August 5   The Big Four foreign ministers' conference in Geneva recesses indefinitely after failing to reach agreement on Berlin or Germany. However, the Big Four agree to establish a new Ten-Nation Disarmament Committee (TNDC) outside the UN framework to assume the functions of the 82-member UN Disarmament Commission.

August 8   In Monrovia, Liberia, nine African and Middle Eastern countries agree to support the rebel Algerian provisional government (GPRA).

August 11   The U.S. State Department accuses North Vietnam of direct aid to Laotian rebels.

August 12   The Organization of American States (OAS) denounces the existence of "antidemocratic regimes" after complaints by six Caribbean members.

August 13   Hammarskjöld appoints Adrian Pelt, former UN commissioner in Libya, to be the secretary-general's special representative in Guinea.

August 13   Israel rejects an Egyptian-inspired Hammarskjöld proposal to solve the Suez Canal blockade question by allowing Israeli cargoes which are transiting the canal in foreign vessels, to be purchased by their consignees before leaving Israeli ports. Under the scheme, non-Israelis would hold title to the freight in question as it traveled across the Egyptian waterway.

August 13   Fidel Castro announces that a revolt against his regime has been crushed.

August 15   Tunisia charges that Algerian-based French planes have attacked Bhiret Zitouna on its territory. Soon President Bourguiba terminates Tunisia's customs union with France.

August 18   Hammarskjöld's plan to integrate Palestinian refugees within their Arab host countries is rejected by nine Arab states who fear permanent resettlement of the refugees outside of their homeland. Hammarskjöld had proposed a five-year outlay of up to some $2 billion to provide productive employment for 950,000 Palestinian refugees living in Arab countries.

August 19   The Baghdad Pact is reconstituted, without Iraq, as the Central Treaty Organization (CENTO).

August 20   Laos requests Hammarskjöld to provide UN assistance to end its civil war; both superpowers blame intervention on each other.

August 21   Hawaii is officially proclaimed the 50th American state.

August 26   The U.S. government promises Laos additional funds and equipment to fight the Communist "threat" as there are reports of further penetration by Communist-led rebels endangering Luang Prabang, the royal capital, and Vientiane, the administrative capital.

August 29   Prime Minister Nehru charges that Chinese Communists have twice crossed India's northern border, but he rejects calls for immediate military retaliation as he reinforces the Indian–Tibetan border.

September 2   In his annual report to the General Assembly, Hammarskjöld endorses the increased use of "quiet diplomacy" to reach agreements without public debate. He defends the UN's "primary responsibility" to maintain world peace, lest the globe "lapse into bilateralism."

September 2   With the alleged help of North Vietnam, Laotian rebels launch a military drive that seizes control of 80 villages.

September 4   The Laotian government asks the Security Council to dispatch an emergency force, charging that the rebels are assisted by North Vietnam's "flagrant aggression."

September 7   The Security Council creates the Subcommittee of Inquiry on the Situation in Laos to investigate the Laotian charge of North Vietnamese "aggression."

September 7   The United States, Britain, France, and the Soviet Union announce the formation of the Ten-Nation Disarmament Committee (TNDC) outside the United Nations and composed of an equal number of states from the Eastern and Western blocs. The UN Disarmament Commission encourages it to negotiate.

September 14   A Soviet space rocket hits the moon.

September 15   Soviet Premier Nikita Khrushchev begins an unprecedented 12-day visit to the United States during which he confers with President Eisenhower and Eleanor Roosevelt. Visits to an Iowa farm and Hollywood highlight the trip.

September 18   In the General Assembly, Soviet Premier Khrushchev calls for general and complete disarmament within four years, after the British present a plan for a three-stage disarmament.

September 22   The question of China's representation in the General Assembly is postponed by a vote of 44–29–9 for the ninth successive year.

September 22   The first telephone cable linking Newfoundland, Canada, and Brittany, France, enters service.

September 28   President Eisenhower announces his agreement with Soviet Premier Khrushchev that the latter withdraw his ultimatum regarding Berlin.

October 6   The Cambodian–Thai dispute regarding the temple of Preah Vihear is referred to the International Court of Justice.

October 7   The International Court of Justice removes from its list a claim for compensation regarding a U.S. Air Force B–29 plane downed by the Soviets over Japanese airspace on November 7, 1954, because of Moscow's challenge to the World Court's jurisdiction.

October 7   Iraq's Premier Kassem is wounded in an assassination attempt in Baghdad.

October 8 Winning a nearly unprecedented third consecutive election, British Prime Minister Harold Macmillan's Conservative Party almost doubles its majority in the House of Commons.

October 10 Turkey and the United States announce an agreement to station American missiles in that country.

October 30 Rioting mobs clash with police and troops in Stanleyville, Belgian Congo, after Brussels announces a revised plan for its colony's independence.

November 1 Indian Prime Minister Nehru declares that the army was making "adequate military preparations" to meet Communist China's attacks against India's border regions.

November 3 President de Gaulle proclaims France's intention to withdraw from integrated NATO military forces.

November 4 The Subcommittee on Laos informs the Security Council that there is no clear evidence of North Vietnamese involvement in the fighting in that country or of flagrant aggression by Hanoi. Crown Prince Savang Vathana succeeds his father as the Laotian monarch.

November 5 The Nobel Peace Prize is awarded to Philip Noel-Baker, a British statesman, for his efforts in the cause of disarmament.

November 5 President Sékou Touré of Guinea declares in the General Assembly that the newly independent African states need foreign aid but would reject "paternalism."

November 8 The Sudan and Egypt (UAR) agree on the distribution of Nile waters in anticipation of the completion of the Aswan High Dam. Egypt will pay Sudan $43 million in compensation for territory flooded by the High Dam reservoir.

November 10 Hammarskjöld visits Laos despite a strong Soviet protest. Moscow opposes a UN presence in that country.

November 15–16 Hammarskjöld appoints Sakari S. Tuomioja of Finland as his personal representative in Laos. The Soviets charge the secretary-general's action is "designed to cover by the name of the [UN] . . . further interference of the Western powers in Laos."

November 17 The General Assembly again denounces (62–3)

South Africa's racial policies and apartheid with "deep regret and concern."

November 20   A joint U.S.–Soviet resolution calling for steps to achieve "general and complete disarmament" is unanimously adopted by the General Assembly. Proposals are transmitted to the UN Disarmament Commission as well as the new TNDC.

November 20   The General Assembly adopts an Afro-Asian resolution (51–16) to request France to cancel its projected nuclear test in the Algerian Sahara.

November 25   The General Assembly votes 51–10 to debate the "question of Hungary" as an important and urgent issue.

November 30   Premier János Kádár declares that Soviet forces will remain in Hungary until international tensions are eased.

December 1   Culminating the International Geophysical Year, 12 states (including the U.S. and the USSR) with territorial or scientific interests in the south polar region conclude the Antarctic Treaty. The agreement opens the continent for scientific research but forbids all military activities, including nuclear weapons testing and the dumping of radioactive wastes. The treaty becomes a model for setting aside global areas as the "common heritage of mankind."

December 4   Lt. Gen. E. M. L. Burns resigns his command of the UN Emergency Force in the Middle East to become disarmament adviser to the Canadian government.

December 5   The General Assembly authorizes a UN operating budget of $63,149,700 and $20 million for UNEF.

December 7   The General Assembly directs Hammarskjöld to convene a conference on "diplomatic intercourse and immunities."

December 9   The General Assembly deplores Soviet and Hungarian disregard of earlier UN resolutions on the situation in Hungary.

December 10   The General Assembly asks South Africa to negotiate with India and Pakistan on the treatment of South Africa's ethnic residents.

December 12   The General Assembly establishes the permanent

Commission on the Peaceful Uses of Outer Space but rejects a compromise resolution on the Algerian issue.

December 13   Archbishop Makarios III, formerly the leader of the Enosis (union with Greece) movement, is elected president of Cyprus.

December 17   Hammarskjöld directs UN technical assistance groups to discuss the implementation of proposals for Laotian economic development made by Sakari Tuomioja.

December 18   Hammarskjöld protests to President Nasser the halting of the Greek freighter *Astypalea*, bound from Haifa to Djibouti via the Suez Canal and carrying 400 tons of Israeli cement.

December 21   Hammarskjöld leaves New York for an extended trip to 24 African and two European countries.

December 22   President Eisenhower and King Mohammed V of Morocco agree the United States will relinquish its military bases in that country by the end of 1963.

December 25   At a nationalist congress in the Belgian Congo, five Congolese parties demand immediate and unconditional independence.

December 29   President Eisenhower announces that the United States is reserving the right to resume nuclear tests on January 1, 1960.

December 30   Premier Khrushchev accepts a Big Three invitation to a summit meeting in Paris in May 1960.

1960

January 1   The treaty establishing the European Free Trade Association (EFTA), or Outer Seven, is signed by countries outside the Common Market. Austria, Britain, Denmark, Norway, Portugal, Sweden, and Switzerland are members.

January 8   The U.S. Navy bathyscaphe *Trieste* descends to a record depth of 24,000 feet in the Pacific and shortly to 35,800 feet.

January 9   Egyptian President Nasser breaks ground for the construction of the Aswan High Dam on the River Nile.

January 11   The United States protests the expropriation of American-owned property in Cuba.

January 14   After a seven-year interruption, talks between the United States and the Soviet Union resume on the latter's World War II lend-lease debts.

January 18   Egypt announces that the Soviet Union will finance the second stage of the Aswan High Dam.

January 19   The United States and Japan sign the Mutual Security and Cooperation Treaty, which grants Washington base and anchoring privileges. The Soviets soon issue a protest.

January 20   A conference on the Belgian Congo's political future is convened in Brussels. This roundtable conference is attended by the three major Belgian parliamentary parties (including the governing party) and representatives of the Congolese nationalist movement.

January 22   Brig. Gen. Jacques Massu, French commander of the Algerian region, is removed for his public criticism of President de Gaulle's liberal self-determination policy toward Algeria. French rightists violently oppose Massu's demotion.

January 25   Tunisian President Habib Bourguiba calls on France to leave its naval and air bases at Bizerte by February 8.

January 25   Belgian Congo colonial officials release nationalist spokesman Patrice Lumumba to attend the Brussels conference on the future of the Belgian Congo.

January 27   The Brussels conference sets June 30, 1960, as the date for the Belgian Congo's unconditional independence. This suddenness will prove to have dire consequences in the establishment of a sovereign Congolese republic.

January 29   President de Gaulle calls on the French army to put down the insurrection of French colons (settlers) fearful of Algerian independence.

February 1   The insurrection of "ultra" French right-wing extremists against de Gaulle's liberal Algerian policies collapses and its leader is imprisoned. The president is given power to rule by decree for a year.

February 1 The first black American sit-in protest begins in the South.

February 8 President Bourguiba postpones Tunisia's deadline for France's withdrawal from Bizerte.

February 11 Soviet Premier Khrushchev hails India's neutrality in a speech in New Delhi.

February 13 France detonates its first plutonium bomb in the Algerian Sahara and becomes the world's fourth nuclear power.

February 13 Fidel Castro and Soviet First Deputy Premier Anastas Mikoyan sign a trade agreement under which the USSR will provide Cuba with $100 million in credits and purchase one million tons of Cuban sugar a year for five years. The U.S. fears Cuba is becoming a new Soviet "satellite."

February 20 The Brussels conference on the Belgian Congo's political future issues a 16-point program for independence slated for June 30, 1960.

February 25 Israel complains to the Security Council about "extensive military preparations" by the UAR.

February 27 The French Ministry of Defense reports that 13,000 French troops have died in the five years of the Algerian uprising.

February 28 The Soviet Union pledges credit of $250 million to Indonesia.

March 1 Guinea accepts Soviet credits and socialist planning after its withdrawal from the French franc zone. Within days, Guinea becomes the first country outside the Communist bloc to recognize East Germany.

March 7 Returning from Algiers, President de Gaulle reiterates his hopes for an "Algerian Algeria," not the rightists' desired "French Algeria."

March 14 Israeli Prime Minister David Ben-Gurion meets with Hammarskjöld in New York to discuss Israeli–Egyptian border clashes and Israel's thwarted use of the Suez Canal.

March 15 The Ten-Nation Disarmament Committee (TNDC) opens its first session.

March 17   The second UN Law of the Sea Conference (UNCLOS II) discusses the limits of territorial waters.

March 21   Black protests against South Africa's pass laws culminate in killings by the police: 56 die and 156 are wounded in the Sharpeville "massacre." Shortly, Pretoria temporarily suspends the pass laws but restores them on April 6.

March 29   The Soviet Union and the People's Republic of China (Communist China) extend their trade pact.

March 30   At the request of 29 Afro-Asian states, the UN Security Council meets to consider the situation in South Africa.

March 30   South Africa declares a state of national emergency to deal with widespread strikes and mass protests against its racial pass laws and apartheid. Prime Minister Hendrik Verwoerd denounces Security Council discussion of racial strife in South Africa as unwarranted interference in his country's internal affairs.

April 1   By a vote of 9–0–2, the Security Council urges South Africa to end apartheid and the political repression of the black community and requests Hammarskjöld to consult with its government to that end. Britain and France abstain, agreeing that South Africa's racial policies are a domestic matter.

April 2   The U.S. State Department rejects assertions by Premier Khrushchev in Paris that the Soviet Union could unilaterally invalidate the right of the Western allies in Berlin by signing a separate treaty with East Germany.

April 8   In South Africa, the African National Congress (ANC) and the Pan-African Congress (PAC), two leading black political organizations, are banned by the government for a year. The next day, South Africa's Prime Minister Hendrik Verwoerd is seriously wounded by a white farmer opposing racial separateness following antiapartheid demonstrations in which 89 blacks are shot by the police.

April 8   Hammarskjöld declares that Egypt's confiscation of Israeli cement cargo on a Greek freighter transiting the Suez Canal violates the UN Charter.

April 12   The International Court of Justice rules in the case involving Portugal's right of access to its enclaves of Dadra and Nagar-

Aveli in India. The World Court finds that India has not acted contrary to the obligations imposed on it by the right of passage belonging to Portugal.

April 13 The Western Big Three informally agree to propose the reunification of divided East and West Berlin as a first step toward a reunified Germany. Many believe the issue can be finally settled at the Paris summit in May.

April 21 Brasilia becomes the new capital of Brazil.

April 22 Premier Castro charges that the United States is plotting to overthrow his Cuban regime.

April 24 Eisenhower and de Gaulle agree that discussions on nuclear and conventional disarmament should take priority over the problems of Berlin and Germany at the upcoming summit in Paris.

April 25 Khrushchev declares that any Western attempt to maintain its rights in Berlin by force would be matched by Soviet power. He argues that a separate peace treaty between the Soviet Union and East Germany would terminate Western entry rights into West Berlin.

April 26 The UNCLOS II adjourns in Geneva after failing to resolve national differences on the width of territorial waters and coastal fishing rights.

May 1 An American U–2 high-altitude reconnaissance aircraft is shot down over Sverdlovsk in the Soviet Union. Its captured pilot, Francis Gary Powers, soon confesses to flying an "intelligence mission."

May 3 France complains to the Security Council that Tunisia has made attack bases available to Algerian rebels, a countercharge to Tunisia's protest against French assaults on rebel positions inside Tunisia.

May 7 Cuba and the Soviet Union resume diplomatic relations severed in 1952.

May 9 Congolese soldiers and Leopoldville police clash as tribal tensions between Baluba and Lubia tribesmen spread in the soon to be independent Belgian colony.

May 13–14   Hammarskjöld meets South Africa's foreign minister in London; they agree the secretary-general will visit Pretoria.

May 17   The East–West summit meeting in Paris adjourns abruptly after Premier Khrushchev demands a public apology from President Eisenhower for America's U–2 spy mission. The Soviet leader cancels his invitation for Eisenhower to visit the USSR as the Security Council is seized with the Soviet complaint concerning violation of its airspace.

May 22   De facto authority in Stanleyville, Orientale Province, has passed from Belgian officials to the nationalist followers of Patrice Lumumba. In Leopoldville, Lumumba's Congolese National Movement emerges as the strongest political group in elections to the Chamber of Deputies.

May 24   The Soviets release nine U.S. airmen forced down over East Germany.

May 26   By a vote of 7–2–2, the Security Council rejects a Soviet resolution condemning the United States for its "acts of aggression" involving U–2 overflights of the USSR.

May 27   President Eisenhower terminates U.S. economic aid to Cuba.

May 29   Ex-President Syngman Rhee of South Korea, who resigned following student prodemocracy demonstrations on April 27, flees to Hawaii.

May 31   In his first public appearance since being wounded by a disgruntled white farmer, South Africa's Prime Minister Verwoerd says that whites must remain "the guardians of the black man."

June 8   The International Court of Justice renders an advisory opinion on the constitutionality of the Maritime Safety Committee—specifically, whether it is constituted in accordance with the statute of the Intergovernmental Maritime Consultative Organization (IMCO) operative since March 17, 1958. The World Court answers the General Assembly's question in the negative.

June 12   Leftist riots in Tokyo force President Eisenhower to cancel his planned visit to Japan after touring the Philippines, Taiwan, Okinawa, and South Korea.

June 13   Belgian officials ask Patrice Lumumba to explore the possibility of forming the Congo's first cabinet.

June 20   The rebel provisional government of the Algerian Republic (GPRA) accepts President de Gaulle's offer to settle the war on the basis of his self-determination plan.

June 21   In a major address in Romania, Premier Khrushchev declares that war with capitalist countries is not inevitable and urges a flexible interpretation of Marxist–Leninist theory. The speech indicates a growing ideological rift between his "peaceful coexistence" beliefs and the more rigidly Marxist Chinese Communist leadership.

June 21   Patrice Lumumba becomes premier designate when his Congolese National Movement receives a majority vote in the newly elected parliament. But his foe, Joseph Kasavubu, is elected president on June 24, an arrangement that bodes ill for the Congo's future.

June 23   By a vote of 8–0–3, the Security Council calls on Israel to make "appropriate" reparations for violating Argentine sovereignty. Israel abducted former Nazi official Adolf Eichmann from Argentina to stand trial in Jerusalem for World War II crimes against Jews.

June 23   Castro threatens to seize all American-owned property in Cuba in retaliation for the U.S. economic boycott and "aggression."

June 24   Hammarskjöld apprises the Committee of Eight studying the administrative problems of the UN secretariat.

June 25   French officials and Algerian liberation representatives begin secret, as yet inconclusive talks, on independence.

June 27   The five Soviet bloc countries withdraw from the Ten-Nation Disarmament Committee established to discuss disarmament issues outside the UN framework; the committee's existence is terminated.

June 27   The leaders of twelve Communist parties support Khrushchev's "peaceful coexistence" thesis regarding the capitalist West.

June 29   Chinese Communist leaders publicly reject Khrushchev's line on the noninevitability of war with capitalist states; they deride "modern revisionism" based on undue fear of nuclear war.

June 29   The Cuban government seizes a U.S.-owned oil refinery in Santiago de Cuba when plant officials refuse to process Soviet crude oil. On July 1, Cuba appropriates the two remaining foreign-owned oil refineries.

June 30   The former Belgian Congo is proclaimed the independent Republic of the Congo by Belgium's King Baudouin I. At independence ceremonies in Leopoldville, Kasavubu expresses goodwill toward Belgium but Lumumba militantly denounces colonialism.

July 4   Israel announces the completion of its first nuclear reactor.

July 5   Native elements of the Force Publique, the Belgian-officered Congolese army, mutiny in Leopoldville and Thysville and engage in violence against white civilians. Tribal warfare and civil strife add to the turmoil in the Congo.

July 6   Citing Fidel Castro's hostility toward Washington, Eisenhower cuts Cuba's sugar import quota in the United States by 95 percent.

July 8   European civilians begin to flee the Congo in the face of increasing violence by mutinous soldiers.

July 9   Khrushchev threatens to use Soviet rockets to protect Cuba from possible U.S. military intervention after Eisenhower declares that the United States will never permit a regime "dominated by international Communism" to exist in the Western hemisphere.

July 10   With Congolese troops in revolt against their Belgian officers and a separatist movement emerging in Katanga Province, Premier Lumumba appeals to Washington for military assistance. Eight hundred Belgian troops arrive to restore calm as Washington spurns Lumumba.

July 11   Moise Tshombe proclaims the independence of Katanga Province from the Republic of the Congo and requests Belgian military aid. Albert Kalonji declares the independence of Kasai Province.

July 11   Belgian troops intervene at Matadi to prevent looting and ensure access to the Congolese port. Over a dozen Congolese are killed and 13 Belgians are wounded.

July 12   President Joseph Kasavubu and Premier Patrice Lumumba request the urgent dispatch of UN military assistance to the Congo in their first telegram to Hammarskjöld.

July 13 At the Congo's request in a second telegram to the secretary-general, Hammarskjöld calls a special session of the Security Council to consider action regarding Belgian troops deployed to protect white residents from attacks. Hammarskjöld suggests the dispatch of a UN emergency force to keep order.

July 14 By a vote of 8–0–3, the Security Council calls on Belgium to withdraw its troops from the Congo and authorizes Hammarskjöld to send UN troops to end the fighting and restore order in the country. Hammarskjöld appoints Maj. Gen. Carl Carlsson von Horn (Sweden) from the United Nations Truce Supervision Organization to head the new United Nations Operation in the Congo (ONUC) on its peacekeeping mission.

July 14 Refuting Khrushchev's earlier declaration that the Monroe Doctrine had died a "natural death" and that the USSR would support Cuba in its efforts to eliminate the U.S. naval base at Guantánamo Bay, President Eisenhower reaffirms American opposition to possible Soviet extension of Communism to the Western hemisphere.

July 15 Lumumba demands the immediate end of Belgian intervention in the Congo as the first Tunisian ONUC troops arrive.

July 15 Khrushchev announces that the Soviet Union will send Lumumba military support if Belgian troops are not withdrawn.

July 17 The Congolese government issues an ultimatum to the Security Council to clear all Belgian troops from the Congo within 72 hours.

July 19 The Security Council votes 9–0–2 to refer Cuba's charges against the United States to the Organization of American States (OAS).

July 20 The United States launches its first Polaris missile from a submerged submarine, a significant advance in the arms race.

July 21 Mrs. Sirimavo Bandaranaike becomes prime minister of Ceylon (later Sri Lanka), the first female head of government in modern times.

July 22 The Security Council reiterates its July 14 resolution that Belgium "speedily" withdraw its forces from the Congo.

July 23   Iran becomes the first Muslim non-Arab country to recognize Israel.

July 23   Cuba signs a trade agreement with Communist China similar to the one it enjoys with the Soviet Union. China is to buy 500,000 tons of Cuban sugar annually for five years.

July 24   Premier Patrice Lumumba visits New York to seek greater UN support; he lobbies for American economic aid for his strife-torn Congo.

July 26   The Soviet Union vetoes a Security Council resolution calling for an impartial investigation of the destruction of a U.S. reconnaissance plane in the Arctic.

July 26   Hammarskjöld appoints Sture Linner, a Swede, to head the UN Civilian Operation in the Congo, after Hammarskjöld and Premier Lumumba agree in New York on the dispatch of administrative and technical experts to the Congo to replace senior Belgian civil servants.

July 27   Disarmament talks in Geneva end inconclusively.

July 28   The League of Arab States (Arab League) imposes an economic boycott on Iran for its recognition of the state of Israel.

July 29   Hammarskjöld initials the Basic Agreement between the Secretary-General and the Congo Government (UN Document S/4389/Add.5) detailing the respective responsibilities of the Congolese government in Leopoldville and the United Nations Operation in the Congo. This contract will be superseded by the Status Agreement of November 27, 1961, between the United Nations and the Republic of the Congo.

July 30   The Congolese government demands that ONUC troops be sent into Katanga Province immediately to end its secession from the central authority in Leopoldville (later Kinshasa).

August 2   Hammarskjöld announces that ONUC forces in the field total 11,155 officers and men from eight countries (Ethiopia, Ghana, Guinea, Ireland, Liberia, Morocco, Sweden, Tunisia) and that they have replaced Belgian forces in all Congolese provinces except Katanga.

August 3   Argentina and Israel end their dispute concerning the abduction of former Nazi leader Adolf Eichmann from Buenos Aires to Jerusalem.

August 4   A piloted U.S. X–15 plane reaches a record 2,196 m.p.h. at an altitude of 136,500 feet, also unprecedented.

August 5   Hammarskjöld cancels his plans to send ONUC troops into Katanga and announces that he will seek specific Security Council authorization to do so after officials there prevent UN civilians from landing in Elisabethville, its capital.

August 9   Ignoring Soviet opposition, the General Assembly votes to reconvene the United Nations Disarmament Commission on August 16.

August 9   By a vote of 9–0–2, the Security Council requests Belgian troops and officials to withdraw from Katanga Province and orders ONUC to replace them.

August 9   Pathet Lao rebels capture the Laotian administrative capital of Vientiane.

August 10   Katanga's Tshombe cables Hammarskjöld that ONUC will be accepted provided it makes no effort to restore Lumumba's authority.

August 12   On his second visit to the Congo, lasting until August 15, Hammarskjöld arrives in Elisabethville, Katanga, with four plane loads of Swedish ONUC troops. He pledges both peacekeeping and noninterference in the Congo's internal disputes.

August 13   The International Law Commission (ILC), a UN agency created to formalize the reach of international law, asserts that no state enjoys sovereignty claims in space.

August 13   Lumumba criticizes Hammarskjöld for using white troops in ONUC's entry into Katanga.

August 14   Belgium announces the formal end of its military presence in Katanga, yielding Elisabethville to ONUC.

August 16   After 82 years of British rule, Cyprus becomes independent with Greek Cypriot Archbishop Makarios as president and Turkish Cypriot Fazil Kutchuk as vice president.

August 16   Premier Lumumba decrees martial law throughout the Congo for a six-month period.

August 17   Francis Gary Powers, the American pilot of the U–2 spy plane, pleads guilty in a Moscow court to having flown an intelligence mission. Sentenced to a 10-year prison term, he is later exchanged for a Soviet spy in February 1962.

August 18   Canadian ONUC signal corpsmen are manhandled by Congolese soldiers in Leopoldville.

August 19   James J. Wadsworth succeeds Henry Cabot Lodge Jr. as U.S. ambassador to the United Nations.

August 20   Hammarskjöld appoints Rajeshwar Dayal of India as his personal representative in the Congo succeeding Ralph Bunche (U.S.). Lumumba charges that ONUC troops are trying to substitute UN colonialism for Belgian control.

August 22   The Security Council endorses Hammarskjöld's refusal to use ONUC troops to suppress the secessionist movement in Katanga Province.

August 24–27   Lumumba sends Congolese central government troops into Kasai Province and crushes the secessionist movement under Albert Kalonji. Congolese soldiers beat up ONUC personnel in Stanleyville.

August 31   As an aftermath of the Korean War, the United Nations Korean Reconstruction Agency (UNKRA), begun in 1951, ends operations, having awarded nearly $150 million in aid.

August 31   The Dominican Republic complains of "aggression" by Venezuela, but the Security Council defers to the OAS to settle the dispute.

August 31   South Africa lifts the state of emergency imposed following the March riots.

August 31   Hammarskjöld formally protests Belgium's failure to withdraw all its troops from the Congo.

September 2   The Soviet Union delivers several aircraft to the Lumumba regime for the transportation of its troops.

September 2   Cuba recognizes Communist China and severs diplomatic relations with Nationalist China.

September 5   Congo President Joseph Kasavubu dismisses Premier

Patrice Lumumba and replaces him with Joseph Ileo as Lumumba issues a counterorder ousting Kasavubu. Leopoldville police and soldiers demonstrate their continued support for Lumumba, and the Congo unravels further.

September 5 President de Gaulle rejects Algerian rebel proposals for a UN-sponsored referendum on Algeria's political future, claiming that the matter is outside "the competence of the United Nations."

September 6 ONUC troops close the Congo's major airports to prevent the use of Soviet planes by the Leopoldville central government against secessionists.

September 7 ONUC suspends Leopoldville radio broadcasts in an effort to forestall open conflict between Lumumba and Kasavubu supporters.

September 7 The Congo's National Assembly declares the mutual ousters of Premier Lumumba and President Kasavubu "null and nonexistent."

September 8 The German Democratic Republic (East Germany) announces that West Germans must henceforth obtain police authorization to travel to East Berlin. The West characterizes this action as the most serious infringement of the four-power agreement regulating the divided city.

September 9 Hammarskjöld declares that attacks by Congolese central government troops on Baluba tribesmen in Kasai Province were tantamount to genocide.

September 10 Premier Khrushchev, like Cuban Premier Fidel Castro, is mandated to remain in the borough of Manhattan in New York City while attending the UN General Assembly session.

September 11 Lumumba is turned back by ONUC troops when he tries to use the Leopoldville radio station to rouse support while the Soviets ask Hammarskjöld to return the Congo's airports and radio facilities to Congolese control.

September 12 Hammarskjöld's introduction to the *Annual Report of the Secretary-General, 1959–1960* opposes a standing UN military force as "unnecessary and impractical."

September 13   ONUC reopens Congo's airfields to "peaceful traffic."

September 14   Colonel Joseph-Désiré Mobutu, commander of the Congolese National Army, establishes a caretaker Council of Commissioners of 15 members and retains Joseph Kasavubu as president, but in fact assumes effective control of the central government and places Lumumba under house arrest.

September 14   Khrushchev attacks Hammarskjöld, charging that the secretary-general's Congo policy benefits only Western "colonialists."

September 16   On behalf of the ruling army regime, President Kasavubu orders the withdrawal of all Soviet and Czechoslovak diplomats from the Congo.

September 17   The Soviet Union vetoes a Security Council resolution generally endorsing Hammarskjöld's actions in the Congo. The General Assembly, which takes over the issue from the stalemated Security Council, approves the secretary-general's policies at its fourth special emergency session on the Congo. The following day Hammarskjöld denies the Soviet charges that he has mismanaged the UN mission in the Congo.

September 18   Colonel Mobutu orders the withdrawal of all Congolese forces from secessionist Katanga and Kasai Provinces.

September 19   Jamaica withdraws from the Federation of the West Indies.

September 20   Khrushchev leads many heads of state and government in attending the 15th session of the General Assembly. The latter urges members to refrain from granting military assistance to the Congo outside the UN framework.

September 20   Cameroon, the Central African Republic, Chad, Congo-Brazzaville, Congo-Leopoldville, Cyprus, Dahomey, Gabon, Ivory Coast, Madagascar, Niger, Somalia, Togo, and Upper Volta are admitted as new UN members, bringing the total to 96.

September 21   Austrian Foreign Minister Bruno Kreisky requests a General Assembly discussion on the status of the German-speaking minority in Alto Adige (South Tyrol), formerly Austrian land now under Italian control.

September 21 Hammarskjöld warns Moise Tshombe that ONUC will use force if necessary to prevent attacks by Katangan troops on Baluba tribesmen living in Katanga. This is the first mention of the use of force by UN troops in the Congo.

September 23 In a militant speech to the General Assembly, Khrushchev demands Hammarskjöld's resignation and his replacement by a three-man executive directorate—a troika—representing the West, East, and nonaligned blocs.

September 23 The United States denounces Khrushchev's proposals for reorganizing the secretariat as "a real declaration of war against the structure, the personnel and the location" of the world organization.

September 25 Valerian Zorin succeeds Anatoly Sobolev as the permanent Soviet delegate to the United Nations.

September 26 Rajeshwar Dayal, Hammarskjöld's special representative in the Congo, reports that the republic faces disease and disintegration unless factional strife ends; there are now 16,382 ONUC troops in the country.

September 28 Mali and Senegal are admitted as the 97th and 98th UN members.

September 29 President Kasavubu approves the assumption of interim executive and administrative power by the high commissioners under Colonel Mobutu.

September 29 The State Department advises American dependents in Cuba to return to the United States and citizens to travel to Cuba only if they have "compelling reasons."

September 30 The German Federal Republic (West Germany) decides to break off trade relations with the German Democratic Republic (East Germany) unless travel restrictions imposed on its citizens are ended.

October 3 Premier Khrushchev declares in the General Assembly: "I want to reaffirm that we do not trust Mr. Hammarskjöld and cannot trust him." Hammarskjöld rejects the Soviet leader's demand for his resignation unless the organization's membership as a whole wishes his ouster.

October 5   An all-white referendum approves making South Africa a republic and severing its ties to the British Commonwealth. The nonwhite majority of some 11 million is barred from voting.

October 7   The Soviet Union gives de facto recognition to the rebel provisional government of the Algerian Republic (GPRA).

October 7   Nigeria is admitted as the 99th member of the United Nations.

October 8   The General Assembly votes 42–34–22 not to discuss the question of Communist Chinese representation in the United Nations. It is the closest vote since the issue was first raised in 1950 and an indication of failing American policy to bar the People's Republic of China from the world body.

October 11   The ONUC command refuses to permit the arrest of Premier Lumumba by the Congolese National Army.

October 12   At a General Assembly meeting, Soviet Premier Khrushchev engages in some unceremonious behavior after the Assembly rejects his demand that it debate the disarmament question. The Assembly's president cuts short the day's session to end Communist heckling of Western delegates. Khrushchev leaves New York the following day.

October 13   A U.S. citizen and seven Cubans are executed in Santiago for participating in an invasion of Cuba.

October 14   Cuba nationalizes all the remaining large industrial and commercial enterprises, including banks.

October 16   Mobutu and Tshombe reportedly agree that Katanga will be an autonomous unit within the Republic of Congo.

October 18   In the General Assembly, Cuba accuses the United States of violating its airspace.

October 19   The United States imposes an embargo on all exports to Cuba except for certain foodstuffs and medical supplies, a policy that is still in effect, except for minor modifications, in the early twenty-first century.

October 21   The Soviet bloc countries refuse to contribute to the cost of ONUC.

October 24   On United Nations Day, Hammarskjöld attends a concert by the Philadelphia Symphony Orchestra. The secretary-general initiated the tradition of the orchestra's playing Beethoven's Ninth Symphony, which Hammarskjöld described as an "enormous confession of faith in the victorious human spirit and its human brotherhood."

October 25   Cuban Foreign Minister Raul Roa tells the General Assembly that the United States is preparing a "massive invasion" of his country.

October 26   Belgium rejects Hammarskjöld's protest of the return of Belgian colonial officials to Katanga, which the secretary-general called a cause of continuing tension.

October 26   East Germany demands that U.S. civilians present identity papers to border guards before entering East Berlin.

October 26   Alexis Saint-Léger, writing as St. John Perse, is awarded the 1960 Nobel Prize in literature. The work of this former French diplomat is greatly admired by Hammarskjöld.

October 27   Hammarskjöld reiterates his demand that Belgium withdraw all its military and civilian personnel from the Congo.

October 28   The United States tells the Organization of American States that Cuba is receiving substantial weapons shipments from the Communist bloc and increasing its ability to spread revolution in the Americas.

October 29   Hammarskjöld appoints a 15-nation African–Asian Conciliation Commission to visit the Congo under UN auspices and seek a political agreement among its feuding leaders.

October 31   The General Assembly urges Italy and Austria to negotiate the status of the German-speaking minority in Italian-ruled Alto Adige (South Tyrol).

November 3   Hammarskjöld's special representative in the Congo, Rajeshwar Dayal, warns the General Assembly of deteriorating conditions under the Mobutu regime and the usurpation of governmental power by the high commissioners. Dayal concludes that restoration of authority to President Kasavubu and the Lumumba-controlled parliament may offer the only hope of a return to order.

November 4   President de Gaulle pledges to honor the formation of an independent Algeria if an election shows this to be the preference of a majority of Algerian Muslims. This statement favoring Algerian self-government is denounced by French rightists in both metropolitan France and Algeria.

November 4   Ethiopia and Liberia file a complaint with the International Court of Justice charging South Africa with violating its obligations in South-West Africa, a League of Nations mandated territory. (Eventually, on July 18, 1966, the World Court rules that the two complainants have no standing in the case.)

November 7   President Kasavubu asks the General Assembly to seat the anti-Lumumba delegation, which he heads. Shortly, the General Assembly's Credentials Committee votes 6–1 to recommend seating the Kasavubu delegation.

November 8   John F. Kennedy is elected president of the United States, defeating Richard M. Nixon. Senator Lyndon B. Johnson is voted vice president.

November 8   Ten Irish ONUC soldiers are killed by Baluba tribesmen in an ambush at Niemba in northern Katanga.

November 9   The General Assembly postpones indefinitely its debate on the Congo.

November 11   President Ngo Dinh Diem of South Vietnam is overthrown by a paratroop brigade in Saigon but is restored to power in a day.

November 12   Congolese troops loyal to pro-Lumumba leader Antoine Gizenga gain control of Stanleyville in Orientale Province.

November 13   Guatemalan troops revolt against their government, and there are allegations that Fidel Castro is behind the failed coup.

November 14   Belgian Foreign Minister Pierre Wigny denounces ONUC as a failure. He warns that Belgium may quit the United Nations if Hammarskjöld persists in his "stupid" demand that Belgian officials withdraw from the former colony.

November 16   Hammarskjöld temporarily postpones sending the 15-member Afro-Asian Conciliation Commission to the Congo because of Kasavubu's public opposition.

November 18   The International Court of Justice confirms an arbitral decision awarding to Honduras a disputed border area also claimed by Nicaragua.

November 19   Twenty Western countries approve a charter for an Organization for Economic Cooperation and Development (OECD), replacing the previous, more narrow focused Organization for European Economic Cooperation (OEEC). The new body intends to expand trade and aid to less developed countries.

November 20   Hammarskjöld reports that the world organization's treasury is virtually empty and that the United Nations Operation in the Congo may have to be withdrawn if $20 million in new funds are not raised by December.

November 20   Laotian Premier Souvanna Phouma announces his agreement with the rebel Pathet Lao to form a coalition government.

November 21   Two Tunisian soldiers are killed in the first clash between ONUC troops and Congolese National Army regulars.

November 22   By a vote of 53–24, the General Assembly seats Congo's Kasavubu–Mobutu delegation rather than a rival slate of Lumumba supporters.

November 24   Kasavubu leaves New York without agreeing to Hammarskjöld's plan to send the Afro-Asian Conciliation Commission to the Congo.

November 27   Kasavubu, Mobutu, Tshombe, and other leaders meet ostensibly to try and restore political integration in the Congo.

November 28   A U.S. district court in New York rules that Igor Melekh, a Soviet UN employee accused of spying, is not protected by diplomatic immunity.

November 28   After settling a territorial dispute with Morocco, Mauritania achieves its independence.

November 28   Lumumba narrowly escapes capture by a contingent of Mobutu's Congolese troops seeking his arrest and flees Leopoldville.

December 1   Patrice Lumumba is arrested by the troops of Colonel Mobutu in Kasai Province and returned to Leopoldville, where he is charged with inciting the army to rebellion.

December 5   The French delegate boycotts the General Assembly when it begins to discuss the Algerian issue.

December 5   The leaders of 81 Communist parties across the world sign a manifesto pledging to achieve the victory of Communism by peaceful means, if possible, and by war if necessary. They reaffirm the primacy of the Communist Party of the Soviet Union (CPSU) against China's claim for world Communist leadership.

December 5   Rajeshwar Dayal reports that Lumumba was severely beaten by Congolese soldiers after his arrest. The Soviet Union calls for Lumumba's immediate release and the restoration of the pro-Lumumba Congolese parliament. Hammarskjöld merely appeals for Patrice Lumumba's humane treatment and for "due process," but Colonel Mobutu refuses to allow UN or International Red Cross representatives to visit the Congolese premier to investigate reports of his mistreatment.

December 7   Yugoslavia, Ceylon, and the United Arab Republic announce that they are withdrawing their troops from ONUC to protest the "anti-Lumumba" policies of the world body.

December 8   Soviet representative Valerian Zorin accuses Hammarskjöld of helping "hired assassins" bring down Lumumba's "legitimate" regime in the Congo.

December 9   ONUC forces try to protect Europeans in Stanleyville from a threatened massacre by Lumumba supporters.

December 9   In Laos, the neutralist government of Premier Souvanna Phouma collapses.

December 11   Sixty-five are killed and 300 wounded as French paratroopers and rioting "ultras" clash in Algiers. The latter want to keep Algeria French.

December 11   The United States fails to obtain Canada's cooperation in its economic squeeze of Cuba.

December 12   Morocco and Guinea withdraw their troops from ONUC.

December 12   A new Congolese government is declared by pro-Lumumba Antoine Gizenga in Stanleyville, rivaling the Kasavubu-

Mobutu regime in Leopoldville. Gizenga declares that Stanleyville would henceforth be the Congo's capital.

December 13 The Soviet Union vetoes a Security Council resolution granting Hammarskjöld increased power in the new Congolese crisis resulting from the arrest of Lumumba.

December 13 Five states establish a Central American Common Market to increase trade and eliminate tariffs among the members.

December 14 By a vote of 89–0–9 (the United States and Western colonial powers abstaining), the General Assembly approves the Declaration on the Granting of Independence to Colonial Countries and Peoples. Viewed as the Third World's Magna Carta, "almost an amendment of the Charter," this document demands freedom for all subject peoples in trust and nonself-governing territories.

December 16 Ferhat Abbas, head of the rebel Algerian provisional government, urges his countrymen to boycott the upcoming French referendum on Algeria's future.

December 18 In Laos, a pro-Western rightist regime is installed under Prince Boun Oum, and the United States resumes arms shipments to the country following the recapture of Vientiane from leftist forces.

December 19 The General Assembly recognizes Algeria's right to self-determination and the UN's responsibility in promoting its independence.

December 20 The General Assembly debate on the Congo ends without any agreement on appropriate UN action. Hammarskjöld declares that unless the Assembly provides him with specific instructions, he will continue current policies.

December 20 The Vietcong, composed of several Communist dissident groups, organizes the National Front for the Liberation of South Vietnam (NFLSV).

December 20 The General Assembly authorizes a UN operating budget of $72,969,300 and $19 million for UNEF for 1961. For ONUC it approves $24 million for the first quarter of 1961.

December 21 Hammarksjold appoints Maj. Gen. Sean McKeown of

Ireland to replace Maj. Gen. Carl von Horn of Sweden as new commander of ONUC.

December 24 Meeting in Conakry, President Sékou Touré (Guinea), Kwame Nkrumah (Ghana), and Modibo Keita (Mali) agree to form a union of these three West African states.

December 30 Laos requests UN support against a reported invasion by North Vietnamese and possibly Chinese Communist troops, eliciting a U.S. warning.

December 31 ONUC closes Stanleyville airport to prevent Soviet transport aircraft from flying supplies to the city's pro-Lumumba forces under Antoine Gizenga.

December 31 Cuba requests a Security Council investigation of an alleged imminent military aggression by the United States.

1961

January 1 Communist forces capture the central plain and the city of Phong Saly in Laos.

January 2 Hammarskjöld formally criticizes Belgium for permitting Ruanda–Urundi, its UN Trusteeship territory, to be used as a base for military operations against the Congo.

January 3 After Cuba requests that U.S. embassy personnel in Havana be reduced to a total of 11 within 48 hours, Washington severs diplomatic and consular relations with that country.

January 3 The UN Conciliation Commission for the Congo begins an extended visit through February 20 in an effort to bring the feuding sides together.

January 4 Pro-Lumumba demonstrators demand his release when Hammarskjöld arrives in Leopoldville for talks with Mobutu.

January 5 The Security Council fails to act on Cuban charges of a planned U.S. military invasion of the island.

January 6–12 In Pretoria, Hammarskjöld discusses apartheid, race relations, and human rights with South African government leaders.

January 7   Meeting in Casablanca, several African leaders criticize the UN's "one-sided" Congo operation.

January 7   Some 400 to 600 troops loyal to Gizenga advance from Stanleyville through Kivu Province into northern Katanga.

January 8   In a national referendum, 72 percent of all voters in France, Algeria, and French overseas territories approve President de Gaulle's plan to grant Algeria self-determination.

January 9   The Security Council is called into special session to hear Soviet charges of continuing Belgian intervention in the Congo's internal affairs.

January 11   ONUC dispatches a 600-man force to prevent fighting between pro-Lumumba forces and Katangan troops in northern Katanga.

January 14   The Security Council refuses to adopt a Soviet resolution condemning Belgian "aggression" in the Congo.

January 16   The U.S. State Department announces restrictions on travel by Americans to Cuba.

January 17   In a farewell television address, President Dwight D. Eisenhower warns the United States to "guard against the acquisition of unwarranted influence by the military–industrial complex."

January 17   Congolese President Kasavubu and Moise Tshombe of secessionist Katanga Province agree to hold a conference on constitutional reform in February.

January 18   The Congolese government and that of Katanga announce that ex-Premier Patrice Lumumba has been transferred from the Thysville military prison in Leopoldville to a facility in Jadotville, Katanga.

January 19   ONUC announces that Lumumba's transfer to Katanga is an "internal affair" beyond its jurisdiction.

January 20   John F. Kennedy is inaugurated president of the United States.

January 23   ONUC warns the pro-Lumumba Gizenga regime in Stanleyville, Orientale Province, that attacks on Europeans in retaliation for Lumumba's transfer to Katanga will not be tolerated.

January 23   Following his meeting with South African Prime Minister Hendrik Verwoerd from January 6 to January 12 in Pretoria about its racial policies and apartheid, Hammarskjöld reports to the Security Council that "so far no mutually acceptable arrangement has been found." But he adds that this is not necessarily conclusive.

January 24   Hammarskjöld discloses that he has unsuccessfully urged President Kasavubu to return Lumumba to Leopoldville and to permit his participation in talks on the Congo's future.

January 25   At his first news conference, President Kennedy announces that he has ordered an emergency airlift of food and medical supplies to famine-stricken areas of the Congo. Also, the Soviet Union has released the two surviving crewmen of the U.S. Air Force RB–47 reconnaissance jet shot down over the Barents Sea in 1960.

January 27   Katanga publicly denies that it is creating Belgian-led legions of mercenaries.

January 28   Kasavubu informs Hammarskjöld that the Leopoldville government will seek foreign military aid if ONUC does not suppress the pro-Lumumba revolt by "rebels."

January 30   Hammarskjöld advises Kasavubu that the current ONUC mandate prevents it from intervening in the Congo's internal political struggles, but he will transmit Kasavubu's request to the Security Council.

February 1   Hammarskjöld urges the Security Council to grant him increased powers to meet the Congolese crisis situation. He advises the council to turn down Kasavubu's request for UN intervention against pro-Lumumba forces.

February 1   The League of Arab States (Arab League) decides to arm Algerian resistance fighters battling the French army.

February 9   President Kasavubu names a provisional government with Joseph Ileo as premier.

February 10   Katangan officials report that Lumumba has escaped from the farm where he was being held a prisoner; Hammarskjöld orders an investigation of the alleged escape.

February 12   Katangan officials declare that they will not cooperate with the UN investigation of Lumumba's alleged escape because it was an "internal affair."

February 13 Katangan officials announce that Patrice Lumumba was killed on February 12 by unidentified tribesmen at an unidentified location.

February 14 The Soviet Union withdraws its recognition of UN Secretary-General Hammarskjöld and demands his immediate dismissal for "complicity" with Belgium in Lumumba's assassination. It also demands withdrawal of ONUC from the Congo "within a month." The Soviet delegate in the Security Council notes that his country will recognize the pro-Lumumba regime of Antoine Gizenga in Orientale Province, as does the UAR.

February 15 The Soviet draft resolution is defeated 8–1–2 in the Security Council. Hammarskjöld declines to resign, claiming that he has done all that his mandate allowed him to do to protect Lumumba and that resignation at this time would only weaken the United Nations.

February 15 President Kennedy warns the Soviet Union that the United States must oppose Moscow's attempt to intervene unilaterally in the Congo. Meanwhile, following the lead of the Soviet Union and the United Arab Republic, East Germany, Yugoslavia, and Ghana recognize the Gizenga regime as the legitimate government of the Congo.

February 17 *Antiphon*, written by the American playwright Djuna Barnes and translated into Swedish by Hammarskjöld, is performed at the Swedish Royal Dramatic Theater in Stockholm.

February 18 Ghana's President Kwame Nkrumah proposes that an all-African UN force be sent to the Congo with full powers to restore law and order.

February 19 King Savang Vathana of Laos requests the formation of a committee of representatives from Burma, Cambodia, and Malaya to help end the civil war in his country. The king declares that Laos intends to remain a neutral state.

February 21 In a 9–0–2 vote, with France and the Soviet Union abstaining, the Security Council authorizes ONUC to use force to prevent full-scale civil war in the Congo. The resolution calls for (1) the depoliticization of the Congolese National Army, (2) removal of all Belgian military and political personnel, (3) reconvening the Congolese parliament, and (4) an inquiry into the circumstances of Patrice Lumumba's death. Congolese Premier Joseph Ileo characterizes the council's resolution as a violation of his country's sovereignty.

February 23　Khrushchev endorses Ghana's call for an all-African force to replace ONUC and restore order under the "legitimate" Gizenga government. The Soviet leader also repeats his proposal to replace Hammarskjöld with a three-man troika.

February 23　ONUC reports that 14 political prisoners held by the Gizenga regime in Stanleyville have been executed in apparent retaliation for the killing of six pro-Lumumba prisoners held by the South Kasai regime of Albert Kalonji.

February 24　Congolese troops loyal to Antoine Gizenga gain control of Luluabourg in Kasai Province. Gizenga's regime has won recognition from over 20 Communist-bloc and neutralist governments.

February 25　Leopoldville demands that ONUC halt Gizenga's advance into new regions of the Congo.

February 27　Hammarskjöld tells President Kasavubu that he is prepared to enforce the Security Council's mandate to halt disturbances in the Congo as ONUC accuses Congolese troops in Leopoldville of brutal assaults against UN personnel.

February 28　Secretary-General Hammarskjöld reports that he has requested 22 African states to contribute 6,000 fresh troops to ONUC. Meanwhile, Premier Ileo of the Congo, "President" Tshombe of Katanga, and "President" Kalonji of South Kasai agree to resolve the Congolese crisis without further outside intervention; they warn against the "danger of UN trusteeship, Communist tyranny, and a Korean-style war."

March 1　President Kennedy creates the Peace Corps to improve educational, agricultural, and living standards in the Third World.

March 1　Following the reoccupation of Luluabourg by the Kasavubu government, 44 pro-Gizenga civilians are killed in random retaliation.

March 2 In a report to the General Assembly, Hammarskjöld requests $135 million to cover ONUC expenses in 1961.

March 2 The Algerian rebel regime agrees to the resumption of direct peace talks with France.

March 3–6 Incidents between Congolese National Army (ANC) troops and ONUC forces at Banana, Matadi, and Kitona result in two Sudanese ONUC fatalities and an unknown number of ANC casualties.

March 4 Congolese troops force the withdrawal of Sudanese ONUC units from Banana on the Atlantic coast. The following day, other ONUC troops evacuate the key Congo River port of Matadi.

March 8 Kasavubu, Tshombe, and Kalonji (but not Gizenga) begin to meet in Tananarive, Malagasy Republic, to discuss the Congo's future.

March 10 As pro-Communist forces launch a major offensive in central Laos, the Laotian government announces its acceptance of "a policy of strict neutrality" to end the civil war.

March 10 The Security Council fails to take action on Liberia's complaint against Portugal's policy in its colony of Angola.

March 12 In Tananarive, the anti-leftist Congolese leaders announce agreement on a loose, confederal arrangement for the Congo with Kasavubu as its president. They urge that ONUC activities must end, "since unity has been achieved."

March 13 President Kennedy proposes the Alliance for Progress to assist Latin American countries in order to raise living standards, provide basic education, end hunger, and become self-sustaining.

March 14 In a note to Hammarskjöld, Belgium charges that ONUC has failed to provide protection to white residents of the Congo.

March 16 The General Assembly censures South Africa for its refusal to accept UN Trusteeship status for South-West Africa. The Assembly appeals to members with "particularly close and continuous relations" with South Africa to try to influence Pretoria to get it to follow its UN obligations.

March 18 Leopoldville reports that the Gizenga government has rejected the new Congolese confederation led by Kasavubu.

March 19 Hammarskjöld extends the term of Rajeshwar Dayal as his personal representative in the Congo, despite Congolese government requests for Dayal's replacement.

March 20 Kasavubu calls for the immediate withdrawal of ONUC because it has allegedly failed in its mission.

March 21 The Geneva talks on the possible banning of nuclear weapons are resumed.

March 21 The UN Congo Conciliation Commission reports that the nation "is on the verge of catastrophe" from civil war, famine, and the threat of foreign intervention. It stresses the need for an end to foreign meddling and a federal constitutional arrangement.

March 23 President Kennedy warns the Soviet Union that the United States will not tolerate the loss of Laos to pro-Communist forces as they continue their advance.

March 28 The Soviet bloc, France, and 19 Latin American states refuse to pay their assessed share of the costs of ONUC for 1960 and 1961.

March 30 The United States informs the General Assembly that it will provide a voluntary contribution above its assessed share to defray ONUC expenses.

March 31 The Katanga regime reports that a joint force of native troops and white mercenaries has retaken much of northern Katanga.

April 3 Katangan mobs attack Swedish ONUC troops guarding Elisabethville airport.

April 5 Hammarskjöld presents the General Assembly with a "standing offer of resignation" that it may accept whenever it believes that the Soviet Union is justified in demanding his dismissal.

April 7 Hammarskjöld tells the General Assembly that only $17 million of a projected $100 million for UN economic assistance to the Congo has been collected.

April 9 Ngo Dinh Diem is reelected president of South Vietnam.

April 9 Albert Kalonji, leader of South Kasai, proclaims himself "King of the Baluba Peoples."

April 10 Belgium is granted discontinuance of its case against the Barcelona Traction, Light, and Power Company, which the International Court of Justice drops from its list.

April 11 President de Gaulle announces that France does not wish "to participate either with her men or her money in any present or possible enterprises" of the United Nations, especially in the Congo.

April 12 Major Yuri A. Gagarin of the Soviet Union becomes the first cosmonaut to successfully orbit the earth, which he circles in the spaceship *Vostok I.*

April 12 President Kennedy pledges that the armed forces of the United States would not intervene in Cuba under any circumstances to bring about the overthrow of Fidel Castro's regime.

April 13 The General Assembly again condemns South Africa's racial policies. A vote of 95–1 (with Portugal in opposition) declares apartheid "repugnant to human dignity" and urges all members to work within the Charter to bring about its end. In fact, apartheid laws were only to be terminated in 1991.

April 13 Portugal sends reinforcements to Angola to quell an antigovernment uprising.

April 15 At the Security Council, Foreign Minister Raul Roa again accuses the United States of preparing an invasion of Cuba.

April 15 The General Assembly adopts a resolution (61–5–33) renewing its demand for an immediate withdrawal of all "Belgian and other foreign military and paramilitary personnel and advisers" not under UN command. For the first time the United States abstains on a Congo vote, joining Britain and France.

April 17–20 Some 1,600 Cuban rebels, trained and supported by the United States, land in the Bay of Pigs (Cochinos) in southern Cuba. The ill-prepared invasion ends in disaster without U.S. air support as Castro's forces repel the attackers with heavy loss of life and political embarrassment for the United States. On October 10, 1962, the United States will pay $60 million to ransom 1,113 prisoners.

April 17 Kasavubu signs an agreement to cooperate in the implementation of the Security Council's Congo resolution of February 21.

April 18 The United States informs the United Nations that Washington is prepared to pay one-half of ONUC's costs until the General Assembly reconvenes in September.

April 18 The UN Conference on Diplomatic Intercourse and Immunities is concluded. (Its convention and two optional protocols enter into force on April 24, 1964.)

April 21 A General Assembly vote of 37–17–38 continues UNRWA assistance to Palestinian refugees.

April 21 Right-wing French army units under Gen. Maurice Challe stage an insurrection in Algeria and take control of Algiers. French troops loyal to President de Gaulle reoccupy Algiers on April 26 as the movement for Algeria's independence continues.

April 22 The General Assembly approves a $100 million budget for ONUC military operations from January to October 1961.

April 23 De Gaulle assumes full powers to deal with a possible coup attempt by right-wing military insurgents led by Gen. Maurice Challe in Algeria.

April 24 A Congolese constitutional conference gets under way in Coquilhatville, Equateur Province. The conference is disrupted when Tshombe attacks Kasavubu's willingness to implement the Security Council resolution of February 21. When the conference ends in May, the participants agree to organize a federal republic of 20 states. Antoine Gizenga, head of the dissident leftist pro-Lumumba regime in Stanleyville, is now isolated.

April 24 Britain and the Soviet Union jointly appeal for a Laotian cease-fire, the reconvening of the International Control Commission, and a conference to discuss the country's future.

April 26 Premier Moise Tshombe of Katanga Province is seized by Congolese troops at Coquilhatville after walking out of the Congolese constitutional conference.

April 28 The International Control Commission for Laos consisting of Canada, India, and Poland is reconvened in New Delhi.

April 28 In an incident at Port Francqui, Kasai Province, 48 Ghanaian ONUC soldiers are killed and three wounded while two ANC troops are fatalities. A much larger number of Ghanaians and their British officers (some 120) are rumored to have been murdered.

April 30   The Soviet Union awards the 1960 Lenin Peace Prize to Cuban Premier Fidel Castro.

May 1   In a May Day speech, Fidel Castro claims Cuba is a socialist state, heralding Castro's later announcement on December 2 that he plans to make the country a Communist society.

May 2   Katanga demands Moise Tshombe's release by the Leopold-ville government and declares its readiness to cooperate with ONUC.

May 2   Canada announces its agreement with Communist China to sell it a record volume of grain, worth $362 million.

May 2   India accuses the People's Republic of China of violating its border and of creating tension among Asian countries.

May 5   Navy Commander Alan B. Shepard Jr. makes the first U.S. manned space suborbital flight in a Mercury capsule.

May 15   UN personnel are ordered to leave South Kasai Province after more than 50 ONUC troops are killed in tribal-related attacks at Port Francqui.

May 16   The conference on Laos meets in Geneva, following a British- and Soviet-sponsored cease-fire between the Laotian government and pro-Communist rebels. The United States approves the British–Soviet compromise to seat all three rival Laotian delegations.

May 17   Premier Castro announces that he is prepared to trade 1,217 Cuban rebel prisoners captured at the Bay of Pigs invasion for 500 American bulldozers.

May 20   Peace talks between Algerian rebels, led by Belkacem Krim and French minister Louis Joxe, begin in Evian-les-Bains, France.

May 22   The Committee of Eight formed to study reorganization of the UN secretariat deadlocks on conflicting proposals to curtail the powers of the secretary-general. The proposals aim at finding a compromise between the existing structure and the Soviet demands for a three-man executive, or troika.

May 25   Hammarskjöld's personal representative in the Congo, Rajeshwar Dayal, resigns in the face of growing opposition from the central Congolese government, which believes him partial to the dissident forces of Antoine Gizenga. Dayal is replaced by Sture Linner of Sweden.

May 26 The International Court of Justice rejects Thailand's procedural challenge to its jurisdiction in the controversy relating to the temple of Preah Vihear, eventually determined to be in Cambodian territory by the World Court on June 15, 1962.

May 28 The Coquilhatville constitutional conference closes with the Congolese leaders agreeing on a federal system.

May 30 Dominican President Generalissimo Rafael Leonidas Trujillo Molina, in power since 1930, is assassinated by army officers.

May 30 In an often celebrated speech at Oxford University, Hammarskjöld defines his concept of the international civil service led by a secretary-general with exclusively international responsibilities. Hammarskjöld stresses the need for neutrality in the face of challenges to politicize the UN secretariat.

May 30 Cameroon institutes proceedings against Britain at the International Court of Justice, charging the United Kingdom with failure to respect its UN Trusteeship obligations.

May 30 South Africa becomes a republic and ends its ties to the British Commonwealth of Nations.

June 2 The Soviets respond to Hammarskjöld's Oxford University speech by attacking his allegedly constant usurpations of power.

June 3 Generalissimo Francisco Franco, the Spanish head of state, denounces Western policy, capitalism, and democracy in a speech opening the new Cortes (parliament).

June 3–4 President Kennedy and Premier Khrushchev meet in Vienna to discuss German reunification, a nuclear test ban and disarmament, and Laotian neutrality. The president later reports to the nation that his talks with Khrushchev lessened chances of a "dangerous misjudgment on either side."

June 6 Antoine Gizenga informs Hammarskjöld that he will support the reconvening of the Congolese parliament if ONUC provides protection for attending delegates.

June 9 The Security Council adopts a resolution (9–0–2) calling on Portugal to "desist forthwith from repressive measures" in Angola as Lisbon beefs up its armed forces to put down the insurrection in its African colony.

June 12   Hammarskjöld declares that the Congolese political crisis appears to be over and announces a $10 million UN loan to the Congo.

June 13   The peace talks between Algerian rebel leaders and France are suspended because of an impasse over the possible partition and control of the Sahara.

June 14   Premier Castro agrees to accept tractors instead of the 500 bulldozers he had requested in exchange for the captured Bay of Pigs invasion prisoners, provided the tractors are also worth $28 million. But the U.S. Tractors for Freedom Committee abandons the exchange plan.

June 16   In Washington, U.S. officials promise to provide South Vietnam with more American military advisers, weapons, and financial support.

June 19   Kuwait becomes independent, ending its British protectorate status, but keeps a defense arrangement with the former colonial power.

June 19   Gizenga (Stanleyville) and Kasavubu (Leopoldville) agree to call a Congolese parliamentary conference under ONUC protection.

June 21   The Committee of Eight reports that it cannot agree on restructuring the UN secretariat.

June 22   Moise Tshombe, imprisoned on April 26, is released and publicly pledges to cooperate with the reconvening of the Congolese parliament.

June 22   Three Laotian princes—rightist Boun Oum, neutralist Souvanna Phouma, and leftist Souphanouvong—agree to form a coalition government at a meeting in Zurich. Ultimately, their negotiations end in deadlock.

June 23   Major Robert M. White of the U.S. Air Force beats his previous record by piloting an X–15 rocket plane at 3,690 m.p.h.

June 25   Citing historic ties dating back to the Ottoman era, Iraqi

Premier Abdul Karim Kassem claims sovereignty over Kuwait and threatens to annex it.

June 28 Tshombe repudiates his June 22 promise to participate in the reconvening of the Congolese parliament and pledges to defend an "independent Katanga," reversing his earlier decision to end the secession of his province.

June 30 The United Nations reports that Portugal has refused to allow a five-man UN delegation to investigate conditions and bloody clashes in its colony of Angola.

June 30 Hammarskjöld reiterates his call to reorganize the upper echelons of the UN secretariat. He recommends creating assistant secretaries-general for "political" work and undersecretaries-general for "administrative" duties.

July 1 At the request of the Kuwaiti ruler, Sheikh Abdullah al-Salem al-Sabah, British forces land in Kuwait City to protect the country against Iraqi claims of sovereignty. Arab League troops replace British units by October, and no Iraqi invasion occurs until August 1990 under President Saddam Hussein.

July 3 Hammarskjöld proposes that the UN secretariat's professional staff be reorganized to reflect more accurately the new geographic composition of the world body, but he rejects Soviet demands for a political distribution of all positions.

July 4 Moise Tshombe of Katanga refuses to send representatives to the Congolese national parliament's meeting in Leopoldville.

July 7 After considering Kuwait's complaint against Iraq, because of a Soviet veto the Security Council fails to adopt a resolution calling on all states to respect the independence of Kuwait. Such sovereignty is upheld by the arrival of British forces.

July 8 The Communist Chinese foreign minister denies reports of a growing rift between his country and the Soviet Union.

July 11 Premier Khrushchev denounces UN opposition to Soviet proposals for a "troika" UN executive. He warns that the Soviet Union would resist UN decisions if they were detrimental to Soviet security.

July 14 In his encyclical *Mater et Magistra*, Pope John XXIII appeals for aid to underdeveloped areas that would not create a new form of colonialism or spread materialism.

July 15   The United States and Britain ask Hammarskjöld to raise the deadlocked test ban issue before the 16th session of the General Assembly.

July 19   Tunisia, a former French protectorate that became independent in 1956, severs diplomatic relations with France after its forces fail to occupy the French naval base near Bizerte, Tunisia, around which it establishes a blockade. Tunisia charges France with aggression in the Security Council.

July 20   Iraq walks out of a meeting of the League of Arab States (Arab League) in Cairo when the latter votes to admit Kuwait into the organization. Baghdad denounces the Arab League for siding with "British imperialism."

July 20   Peace talks between the French government and the Algerian rebels resume at Lugrin, France.

July 21   Ignoring Tunisia's complaint of French "acts of aggression" and leaving some 700 Tunisians dead, the reinforced French garrison breaks the siege of the Bizerte naval base and occupies parts of the city of Bizerte itself.

July 22   By a vote of 10–0–0 (with France absent), the Security Council approves an "interim" resolution calling for a cease-fire in Tunisia and for all forces to return to their original positions.

July 24   Hammarskjöld meets President Habib Bourguiba in Tunis to discuss the Bizerte crisis, returning to New York on July 27.

July 25   As access to Berlin is again threatened, President Kennedy recommends a 217,000-man increase in the size of U.S. armed forces and $3.5 billion in higher defense spending to meet the "worldwide Soviet threat."

July 27   The Congolese parliament opens its meeting. By August 2, it agrees to end the crisis by electing Cyrille Adoula as premier.

July 28   "President" Tshombe declares that he will defend Katanga's independence by force.

July 28   Peace talks between the French government and Algerian rebels are again suspended after Paris rejects Algerian claims to the Sahara region.

July 28 Hammarskjöld reports to the Security Council on his visit to Tunisia and his inability to solve the Bizerte crisis.

July 30 The Laotian National Assembly approves a constitutional amendment giving the king of Laos the power to name a government without parliamentary consent.

August 1 President Kasavubu appoints and parliament confirms Cyrille Adoula as Congolese premier, replacing Joseph Ileo.

August 2 President Kennedy reaffirms the U.S. opposition to the seating of Communist China in the United Nations.

August 5 The Soviet-backed regime of Antoine Gizenga in Stanleyville dissolves itself to support the new government of Cyrille Adoula in Leopoldville. It is not until December 21, under the terms of the Kitona Accord, that Moise Tshombe recognizes the Adoula government.

August 9 A renewed threat by Premier Khrushchev to sign a separate peace treaty with East Germany precipitates an influx of refugees into West Berlin.

August 10 Hammarskjöld announces receipt of a letter from Congolese Premier Adoula, which reports that "the Congolese Parliament . . . has ended the Congolese constitutional crisis by unanimously placing its confidence in a Government of national unity and political reconciliation."

August 13 East Germany closes the border between East and West Berlin to halt the exodus of its citizens to the West.

August 13 The UN Statistical Office estimates the world population to be 3 billion and growing by 1.7 percent a year.

August 14 Dag Hammarskjöld extends UN recognition to the Adoula government in Leopoldville.

August 15–17 East Germany builds a wall dividing East from West Berlin, a brutal means to prevent the mass exodus of East Berliners to the West as the Big Three protest East German prohibitions on traffic between the two sectors of Berlin.

August 17   The United States and all Latin American governments, except Cuba, sign the Alliance for Progress charter. The Alliance will provide $20 billion in investments for Latin America over a 10-year period.

August 18   President Kennedy orders the reinforcement of the 5,000-man U.S. garrison in West Berlin.

August 21   The General Assembly convenes in special session to consider the French–Tunisian dispute over the Bizerte naval base.

August 23   Hammarskjöld cables Mahmoud Khiary, chief of UN Civilian Operations in the Congo. The secretary-general recommends that the Adoula government "immediately issue an order" strengthening ONUC's hand in arresting prohibited foreigners in the Congo.

August 24   In the General Assembly, Cuba challenges the right of the United States to retain its Guantánamo Bay naval base in that country leased to Washington by agreements signed in 1903 and 1934.

August 24   Joseph E. Johnson (United States) is appointed by Hammarskjöld to be his special UN envoy to seek a solution to the Palestine refugee problem.

August 25   A General Assembly resolution (66–0–30) reaffirms the Security Council resolution of July 22 calling for a cease-fire in Tunisia (still unimplemented by France), recognizes the sovereign right of Tunisia to call for the withdrawal of French forces from the country, and urges peaceful negotiation with France to that end. The resolution concludes the Assembly's special session, which opened on August 21.

August 27   Ben Yussef Ben Khedda replaces Ferhat Abbas as head of the Algerian provisional government.

August 31   The Soviet Union announces that it has resumed nuclear testing.

September 1   Following its announcement about resumed nuclear tests, the Soviet Union detonates a "substantial" atmospheric nuclear device in Central Asia.

September 1   The Nonaligned Nations Conference opens in Belgrade. The conference appeals to President Kennedy and Premier Khrushchev for immediate negotiations to establish world peace.

September 5   President de Gaulle announces that France will relinquish sovereignty over the Algerian Sahara.

September 5   The United States resumes nuclear weapons testing.

September 6   In a 27-point declaration at the conclusion of its meeting, the Belgrade Conference of Nonaligned Nations appeals for "peaceful coexistence" and strongly denounces colonialism. Especially attacked is U.S. intervention in Cuba.

September 8   Hammarskjöld greets UN headquarters secretariat members on the occasion of Staff Day.

September 9   The first of several assassination attempts by right-wingers leaves French President de Gaulle unharmed.

September 13   Fighting breaks out between ONUC forces and Katangan army units and hired foreign mercenaries. "Round one" ends inconclusively on September 21. (Two other armed clashes between ONUC and Katangan forces, dubbed "round two" and "round three," take place subsequently.)

September 15   President Kennedy explains that the United States has ended its three-year nuclear moratorium because of the resumption of tests by the Soviets. He says the Soviets have conducted 10 tests since August 31, 1961.

September 17–18   Hammarskjöld and the other 15 crew and passengers aboard his plane are killed in a crash near Ndola, Northern Rhodesia, where he intended to meet Tshombe and negotiate an end to the fighting between Katangan and UN forces. The exact cause of the accident remains unknown. Hammarskjöld's death spurs the Soviets to intensify their campaign to abolish the secretary-general's office and replace it with a three-member executive, or troika.

September 18   Tunisian and French officials agree on the withdrawal of French troops from the European quarter of the city of Bizerte.

September 21   A cease-fire to end the fighting in Katanga Province is signed by Mahmoud Khiary, chief of UN Civilian Operations in the Congo, and Moise Tshombe after 63 ONUC soldiers are killed and 186 are captured.

September 22   The United States establishes diplomatic relations with Kuwait, where Arab League troops from Jordan, Saudi Arabia, Sudan, Tunisia, and the UAR have replaced British units to prevent an Iraqi invasion.

September 26   Indian Prime Minister Jawaharlal Nehru, recommended by some Westerners to succeed Hammarskjöld, refuses to consider the secretary-generalship.

September 27   Sierra Leone is admitted as the 100th UN member.

September 28   Dag Hammarskjöld is buried in Uppsala, Sweden, in the first state funeral given to a commoner since 1900.

September 29   Syria peacefully secedes from the United Arab Republic after a revolt by Syrian army officers against Egyptian dominance. The following day, the new Syrian government expels 27,000 Egyptians from the country.

October 1   President Robert F. Chiari of Panama announces that he has asked the United States to revise the Panama Canal Zone Treaty to give his country rights over the waterway. Complete U.S. control will be relinquished in 1999.

October 2   In a joint communiqué issued in Peking, Communist China and Cuba declare unbreakable friendship.

October 2   A revised Soviet proposal to replace Hammarskjöld with an acting secretary-general and three deputies is turned down by the United States.

October 10   The United States detonates its third underground nuclear device since suspending its voluntary test moratorium.

October 11   President Kennedy reassures South Vietnam that the United States will support its resistance to the intensified Communist campaign.

October 11   Major Robert M. White flies the X–15 rocket plane to a height of 217,000 feet (about 41 miles), setting another record for a winged, pilot-controlled aircraft.

October 11   The General Assembly censures South Africa 67–1 for its racial apartheid policies.

October 13   Following its withdrawal from the UAR, Syria reassumes its separate UN membership as the 101st state in the world organization.

October 13   After two weeks of negotiations, Valerian Zorin declares that the Soviet Union is willing to accept a single acting secretary-general to replace Hammarskjöld, quietly dropping Moscow's "troika" plan for the secretary-generalship.

October 15   It is reported that U Thant, Burma's ambassador to the United Nations, will be elected as the new acting secretary-general.

October 23   The Nobel Peace Prize for 1961 is awarded posthumously to former Secretary-General Dag Hammarskjöld.

October 26   The General Assembly orders an investigation into the causes of the air crash that killed Dag Hammarskjöld and 15 UN aides and crew members.

November 3   The General Assembly unanimously elects U Thant as acting secretary-general to complete Hammarskjöld's term to April 1963, ending the East–West dispute that had left the United Nations without a chief executive officer since Hammarskjöld's death on September 18.

Appendix A

Members of the United Nations

1945 Argentina, Australia, Belarus (Byelorussia), Belgium, Bolivia, Brazil, Canada, Chile, China, Colombia, Costa Rica, Cuba, Czechoslovakia,* Denmark, Dominican Republic, Ecuador, Egypt,[†] El Salvador, Ethiopia, France, Greece, Guatemala, Haiti, Honduras, India, Iran, Iraq, Lebanon, Liberia, Luxembourg, Mexico, Netherlands, New Zealand, Nicaragua, Norway, Panama, Paraguay, Peru, Philippines, Poland, Russian Federation,[‡] Saudi Arabia, South Africa, Syrian Arab Republic,[†] Turkey, Ukraine, United Kingdom of Great Britain and Northern Ireland, United States of America, Uruguay, Venezuela, Socialist Federal Republic of Yugoslavia[§]

1946 Afghanistan, Iceland, Sweden, Thailand

1947 Pakistan, Yemen"

1948 Myanmar

1949 Israel

1950 Indonesia

1955 Albania, Austria, Bulgaria, Cambodia, Finland, Hungary, Ireland, Italy, Jordan, Lao People's Democratic Republic, Libyan Arab Jamahiriya, Nepal, Portugal, Romania, Spain, Sri Lanka

1956 Japan, Morocco, Sudan, Tunisia

1957 Ghana, Federation of Malaya (Malaysia)[#]

1958 Guinea

1960 Benin, Burkina Faso, Cameroon, Central African Republic, Chad, Congo, Côte d'Ivoire, Cyprus, Democratic Republic of the Congo, Gabon, Madagascar, Mali, Niger, Nigeria, Senegal, Somalia, Togo

1961 Mauritania, Mongolia, Sierra Leone, Tanganyika (United Republic of Tanzania)**

1962 Algeria, Burundi, Jamaica, Rwanda, Trinidad and Tobago, Uganda

1963 Kenya, Kuwait, Zanzibar (United Republic of Tanzania)**

1964 Malawi, Malta, Zambia

1965   Gambia, Maldives, Singapore[#]
1966   Barbados, Guyana, Lesotho
1967   Democratic Yemen["]
1968   Equatorial Guinea, Mauritius, Swaziland
1970   Fiji
1971   Bahrain, Bhutan, Oman, Qatar, United Arab Emirates
1973   Bahamas, German Democratic Republic and Federal Republic of Germany (Germany)
1974   Bangladesh, Grenada, Guinea-Bissau
1975   Cape Verde, Comoros, Mozambique, Papua New Guinea, Sao Tome and Principe, Suriname
1976   Angola, Samoa, Seychelles
1977   Djibouti, Vietnam
1978   Dominica, Solomon Islands
1979   Saint Lucia
1980   Saint Vincent and the Grenadines, Zimbabwe
1981   Antigua and Barbuda, Belize, Vanuatu
1983   Saint Kitts and Nevis
1984   Brunei Darussalam
1990   Liechtenstein, Namibia
1991   Democratic People's Republic of Korea, Estonia, Federated States of Micronesia, Latvia, Lithuania, Marshall Islands, Republic of Korea
1992   Armenia, Azerbaijan, Bosnia and Herzegovina,[§] Croatia,[§] Georgia, Kazakhstan, Kyrgyzstan, Republic of Moldova, San Marino, Slovenia,[§] Tajikistan, Turkmenistan, Uzbekistan
1993   Andorra, Czech Republic,[*] Eritrea, Monaco, Slovak Republic,[*] The former Yugoslav Republic of Macedonia[§]
1994   Palau
1999   Kiribati, Nauru, Tonga
2000   Tuvalu, Federal Republic of Yugoslavia[§]

[*]Czechoslovakia dissolved (1992) to create two independent member states: Czech Republic and Slovak Republic.
[†]Egypt and Syria were original members under the union, United Arab Republic. Syria assumed its independent status in 1961. In 1971 the United Arab Republic changed its name to the Arab Republic of Egypt.
[‡] Union of Soviet Socialist Republics dissolved to into eleven member countries, most of which became UN member states.
[§]The Socialist Federal Republic of Yugoslavia dissolved to create independent member states, Bosnia and Herzegovina, Croatia, Slovenia, former Yugoslav Republic of Macedonia, and Federal Republic of Yugoslavia.
["]Yemen and Democratic Yemen merged in 1990 and represent a unified state in the UN under the name "Yemen."
[#]Formerly part of the Federation of Malaya, Singapore became an independent state as well as a member of the UN.
[**]Tanganyika and Zanzibar united to create the United Republic of Tanganyika and Zanzibar and became UN member under the new name (1964); now United Republic of Tanzania.

Appendix B

Excerpt from Chapter XV of the Charter of the United Nations

ARTICLE 97

The Secretariat shall comprise a Secretary-General and such staff as the Organization may require. The Secretary-General shall be appointed by the General Assembly upon the recommendation of the Security Council. He shall be the chief administrative officer of the Organization.

ARTICLE 98

The Secretary-General shall act in that capacity in all meetings of the General Assembly, of the Security Council, of the Economic and Social Council, and of the Trusteeship Council, and shall perform such other functions as are entrusted to him by these organs. The Secretary-General shall make an annual report to the General Assembly on the work of the Organization.

ARTICLE 99

The Secretary-General may bring to the attention of the Security Council any matter which in his opinion may threaten the maintenance of international peace and security.

ARTICLE 100

1. In the performance of their duties the Secretary-General and the staff shall not seek or receive instructions from any government or from any other authority external to the Organization. They shall refrain from any action which might reflect on their position as international officials responsible only to the Organization.
2. Each member of the United Nations undertakes to respect the exclusively international character of the responsibilities of the Secretary-General and the staff and not to seek to influence them in the discharge of their responsibilities.

ARTICLE 101

1. The staff shall be appointed by the Secretary-General under regulations established by the General Assembly.
2. Appropriate staffs shall be permanently assigned to the Economic and Social Council, the Trusteeship Council, and, as required, to other organs of the United Nations. These staffs shall form a part of the Secretariat.
3. The paramount consideration in the employment of the staff and in the determination of the conditions of service shall be the necessity of securing the highest standards of efficiency, competence, and integrity. Due regard shall be paid to the importance of recruiting the staff on as wide a geographical basis as possible.

Source: Charter of the United Nations and Statute of the International Court of Justice (New York: Department of Public Information, United Nations, 2000).

Appendix C

Hammarskjöld's Press Statement before Assuming Secretary-General Position

Dag Hammarskjöld made this statement to the press at Idlewild International Airport in New York on April 9, 1953, when he arrived to assume his position as the new secretary-general.

On this occasion, when I am landing in New York to take up my new responsibilities, you may well expect me to have something to say to you. I should, myself, like to do more at this first meeting on American soil than just to introduce myself. But yet, there are only a few very general remarks which I feel that I could—and should—make here and now.

I will tell you why.

First a personal reason. I want to do a job, not to talk about it—not even afterwards, so much the less in advance. But further. Of course, I—like all of you, like all engaged in diplomatic or political activity—have my views and ideas on the great international issues facing us. But those personal views of mine are not—or should not be—of any greater interest to you today than they were just a couple of weeks ago. Those views are mine as a private man. In my new official capacity the private man should disappear and the international public servant take his place. The public servant is there in order to assist, so to say from the inside, those who take the decisions which frame history. He should—as I see it—listen, analyze, and learn to understand fully the forces at work and the interests at stake, so that he will be able to give the right advice when the situation calls for it. Don't think that he—in following this line of personal policy—takes but a passive part in the development. It is a most active one. But he is active as an instrument, a catalyst, perhaps an inspirer—he serves.

Irrespective of the political responsibilities of the secretary-general to which I have just referred, he has an important, indeed an overwhelming job as chief administrator of the UN Secretariat. To me it seems a challenging task to try and develop the UN administrative organization into the most efficient instrument possible. My experience from other administrations tells me that even in the best one there is always much to improve. On the other hand, I feel that an administration inspired by sound self-criticism, never blunted by conceit or false loyalties, and self-improving in that spirit, has a just claim to the respect and confidence of the governments and the public.

In articles recently published it has been said that I am interested in mountaineering. But I have never climbed over famous peaks. My experience is limited to Scandinavia where mountaineering calls more for endurance than for equilibristics, and where mountains are harmonious rather than dramatic, matter of fact (if you permit me such a term in this context) rather than eloquent. However, that much I know of this sport that the qualities it requires are just those which I feel we all need today: perseverance and patience, a firm grip on realities, careful but imaginative planning, a clear awareness of the dangers but also of the fact that fate is what we make it and that the safest climber is he who never questions his ability to overcome all difficulties.

Source: UN Press Release SG/287, April 9, 1953, quoted in Andrew W. Cordier and Wilder Foote, eds., *Public Papers of the Secretaries-General of the United Nations: Dag Hammarskjöld, 1953–1956* (New York: Columbia University Press, 1972), 2:29–30.

Appendix D

National Clearance Procedures

This document specifies the national clearance procedures for U.S. citizens applying for or holding positions in the United Nations Secretariat when Dag Hammarskjöld assumed office in April 1953.

The preliminary investigation conducted by the U.S. Civil Service Commission shall be a full background investigation conforming to the investigative standards of the Civil Service Commission, and shall include reference to the following:

a. U.S. Federal Bureau of Investigation (FBI) files.
b. U.S. Civil Service Commission files.
c. U.S. military and naval intelligence files as appropriate.
d. The files of any other appropriate Government investigative or intelligence agency.
e. The files of appropriate committees of the U.S. Congress.
f. Local law-enforcement files at the place of residence and employment of the person, including municipal, county, and state law-enforcement files.
g. Schools and colleges attended by the applicant.
h. Former employers of the applicant.
i. References given by the applicant.
j. Any other appropriate source.

However, in the case of short-term employees whose employment does not exceed ninety days, such investigation need not include reference to sub-paragraphs (f) through (j) of this paragraph.

Whenever information disclosed with respect to any person being investigated is derogatory, within the standard set forth in Part II of this order, the United States Civil Service Commission shall forward such information to the Federal Bureau of Investigation, and the Bureau shall conduct a full field investigation of such person: Provided, that in all cases involving a United States citizen employed or being considered for employment on the internationally recruited staff of the United Nations for a period exceeding ninety days, the investigation required by this Part shall be a full field investigation conducted by the Federal Bureau of Investigation.

Source: Extract from United States Executive Order 10422 of January 9, 1953, as amended by Executive Order 10459 of June 2, 1953 (paragraphs 3.7 and 4). The full text of Executive Order 10459 appears as the Appendix to Annex I of UN document A/2533 of November 2, 1953.

Appendix E

"Old Creeds in a New World"

Titled "Old Creeds in a New World," this is Dag Hammarskjöld's contribution to Edward R. Murrow's radio program, *This I Believe* (November 1953).

The world in which I grew up was dominated by principles and ideals of a time far from ours and, as it may seem, far removed from the problems facing a man of the middle of the twentieth century. However, my way has not meant a departure from those ideals. On the contrary, I have been led to an understanding of their validity also for our world of today. Thus, a never abandoned effort frankly and squarely to build up a personal belief in the light of experience and honest thinking has led me in a circle: I now recognize and endorse, unreservedly, those very beliefs which once were handed down to me.

From generations of soldiers and government officials on my father's side I inherited a belief that no life was more satisfactory than one of selfless service to your country—or humanity. This service required a sacrifice of all personal interests, but likewise the courage to stand up unflinchingly for your convictions concerning what was right and good for the community, whatever were the views in fashion.

From scholars and clergymen on my mother's side I inherited a belief that, in the very radical sense of the Gospels, all men were created equals as children of God, and should be met and treated by us as our masters in God.

Faith is a state of the mind and the soul. In this sense we can understand the words of the Spanish mystic, St. John of the Cross: "Faith is the union of God with the soul." The language of religion is a set of formulas which register a basic spiritual experience. It must not be regarded as describing, in terms to be defined by philosophy, the reality which is accessible to our senses and which we can analyze with the tools of logic. I was late in understanding what this meant. When I finally reached that point, the beliefs in which I was once brought up and which, in fact, had given my life direction even while my intellect still challenged their validity, were recognized by me as mine in their own right and by my free choice. I feel that I can endorse those convictions without any compromise with the demands of that intellectual honesty which is the very key to maturity of mind.

The two ideals which dominated my childhood world met me fully harmonized and adjusted to the demands of our world of today in the ethics of Albert Schweitzer, where the ideal of service is supported by and supports the basic attitude to man set forth in the Gospels. In his work I also found a key for modern man to the world of the Gospels.

But the explanation of how man should live a life of active social service in full harmony with himself, as a member of the community of the spirit, I found in the writings of those great medieval mystics for whom "self-surrender" had been the way to self-realization, and who in "singleness of mind" and "inwardness" had found strength to say yes to every demand, which the needs of their neighbors made them face, and to say yes also to every fate life had in store for them when they followed the call of duty, as they understood it. "Love"— that much misused and misinterpreted word—for them meant simply an overflowing of the strength with which they themselves filled when living in true self-oblivion. And this love found natural expressions in an unhesitant fulfillment of duty and in an unreserved acceptance of life, whatever it brought them personally of toil, suffering— or happiness.

I know that their discoveries about the laws of inner life and of action have not lost their significance.

Source: Andrew W. Cordier and Wilder Foote, eds., *Public Papers of the Secretaries-General of the United Nations: Dag Hammarskjöld 1953– 1956* (New York: Columbia University Press, 1972), 2: 194–196.

Appendix F

Tenth Annual Report

This is an excerpt from Dag Hammarskjöld's introduction to the 10th *Annual Report of the Secretary-General to the General Assembly on the Work of the Organization, 1954–1955,* July 8, 1955.

THE TENTH YEAR

I submit herewith the tenth annual report of the Secretary-General to the Member States on the work of the United Nations.

The role of the Organization in world affairs is subject every year to reflection and judgment in the light of the ever-changing flow of developments. This year, the cumulative experience of ten years provides a basis for a longer view of which we should make use.

Article 109 of the Charter requires the General Assembly at its coming tenth session to consider the proposal to hold a conference to review the present Charter. Since the question is posed in this form—leaving it open as to both whether and when to hold such a conference—the forthcoming discussion seems clearly to have been intended to afford an opportunity to the Governments of Member States for consideration on a wider basis than on purely constitutional grounds.

The lessons to be drawn from the whole course of history since 1945, the past development of the international institutions based on the Charter, the desirable and attainable course for the future so far as this can be foreseen in the light of all the factors involved—these must necessarily be weighed before a sound judgment can be reached. Such a review, if it is to contribute in future years to strengthening the influence of the United Nations for peace and for other purposes set forth in the Charter, will require time of discussion and analysis. As pointed out in the preface to the *Repertory of Practice of United Nations Organs,* which has been circulated to Members, there may thus be valid arguments for a decision at the coming Assembly session in favor of holding a Charter review conference, while leaving until later the question of when it should be convened. The coming discussion will, I hope, maintain and carry further the spirit of re-dedication and the broad approach that characterized the tenth anniversary meetings of Members in San Francisco in June.

In this, the tenth year of the United Nations, there seems to be a trend toward lesser tension in world affairs. During its first nine years the United Nations has had to operate in an atmosphere poisoned by the failure to reach agreed settlements of problems arising out of the Second World War and its aftermaths in Europe and in Asia. Now the Treaty for Austria has at last been concluded. The first meeting since 1945 of Heads of Governments of four of the Great Powers will have taken place by the time this report is circulated to the Member States. In the Far East, the Bandung Conference of Asian and African nations reflected an attitude and approach that may bear increasing fruit in the future and affirmed the strong support of all the peoples represented there for the Purposes and Principles of the United Nations. These developments give reason for hope that they may be followed by others in the same direction.

One measure of the direction in which we are moving will be the manner in which the institutions of the United Nations are used by the Member Governments. In recent years, the main attention has been concentrated on arrangements designed to give a measure of security on a regional basis, in the absence of a more universal system of security. If there is now to be serious and sustained exploration of the possibilities for co-operation on a wider basis, the role of world organization must necessarily gain a new dimension.

THE ROLE OF THE ORGANIZATION
IN DIPLOMACY

The value of the United Nations as a common meeting ground has often been affirmed. In the past, however, the United Nations in this respect has been regarded more as a symbol of hope for the future than as a source of present progress towards reducing the danger of a new major war, though much else of general benefit has resulted from its activities. Now, in the situation that seems to be developing, this role of the United Nations should acquire a new diplomatic and political significance.

There are strong reasons for using the institutions of the United Nations for questions appropriate to world organization, unless special circumstances make it necessary to go outside those institutions. One reason is the interest of the Member Governments in strengthening the institutions which they have endowed with a primary responsibility for world peace, by using them when they should be used. Another reason derives from the great upheaval in the relationship of nations and peoples that is under way. We are still in the early stages of this development, but its direction, in one respect at least, is clear enough. The peoples of Asia today, of Africa tomorrow, are moving towards a new relationship with what history calls the West. The world organization is the place where this emerging new relationship in world affairs can most creatively be forged.

We have only begun to make use of the real possibilities of the United Nations as the most representative instrument for the relaxation of tensions, for the lessening of distrust and misunderstanding, and for the discovery and delineation of new areas of common ground and interest. The Organization should be more than an instrument of what may be described as conference diplomacy. This new diplomacy, with its public debates, serves and will continue to serve many essential needs in the international life of our times. It is not, however, sufficient for the efforts towards understanding and reconciliation which are of such importance now. The United Nations can and should support these efforts in other ways. Conference diplomacy may usefully be supplemented by more quiet diplomacy within the United Nations, whether directly between representatives of Member Governments or in contacts between the Secretary-General and Member Governments. The obligations of the Charter, the environment of institutions dedicated to seeking out the common ground among the national interests of Member States, the wide representation from all continents and cultures, the presence of the Secretariat established as a principal organ of the United Nations for the purpose of upholding and serving the international interest—all these can provide help not to be found elsewhere, if they are rightly applied and used.

Within the framework of the Charter there are many possibilities, as yet largely unexplored, for variation of practices. The United Nations is at a very early stage in that development of constitutional life based on the written word which is familiar and normal in the life of nations. It is my hope that solid progress can be made in the coming years in developing new forms of contact, new methods of deliberation and new techniques of reconciliation. With only slight adjustments, discussions on major issues of a kind that have occurred outside the United Nations could often be fitted into its framework, thus at the same time adding to the strength of the world organization and drawing strength from it. There is, for example, the provision of the Charter, so far unused, for special periodic meetings of the Security Council. Might not this provision be invoked and procedures developed in the Council which would give increased continuity and intensified contact in the treatment of certain questions of world concern? Let us hope that possibilities of this and similar kinds will be explored in an imaginative spirit and in full recognition of the need to give to the United Nations a chance to develop its full potentialities as an institution and to bring to bear, with greater effect, the influence of the Charter upon the peaceful resolution of the issues of our time.

Source: United Nations General Assembly, Official Records, Tenth Session, *Report of the Secretary-General to the General Assembly on the Work of the Organization, 1954–1955,* Supplement no. 1, A/2911 (New York: UN General Assembly, July 8, 1955), pp. xi–xii.

Appendix G

Principal Members of the United Nations Secretariat as of December 31, 1960

This is an intraorganizational chart of the top echelons of the UN secretariat in Dag Hammarskjold's last full year in office, 1960.[1]

Secretary-General: Dag Hammarskjöld

EXECUTIVE OFFICE OF THE SECRETARY-GENERAL

Executive Assistant to the Secretary-General: Andrew W. Cordier
Director of Special Unit: Alfred G. Katzin

OFFICE OF LEGAL AFFAIRS

Legal Counsel: Constantin A. Stavropoulos

OFFICE OF THE CONTROLLER

Controller: Bruce R. Turner

OFFICE OF PERSONNEL

Director of Personnel: W. A. B. Hamilton

OFFICE OF UNDER-SECRETARIES FOR SPECIAL POLITICAL AFFAIRS

Under-Secretaries: Ralph J. Bunche, C. V. Narasimhan

DEPARTMENT OF POLITICAL AND SECURITY COUNCIL AFFAIRS

Under-Secretary: Georgi P. Arkadev

DEPARTMENT OF ECONOMIC AND SOCIAL AFFAIRS

Under-Secretary: Philippe de Seynes
Commissioner for Technical Assistance: Roberto M. Huertematte
Executive Secretary, Economic Commission for Europe: Vladimir Velebit
Executive Secretary, Economic Commission for Asia and the Far East:
  U Nyun
Executive Secretary, Economic Commission for Latin America: Raúl
  Prebisch
Executive Secretary, Economic Commission for Africa: Mekki Abbas

DEPARTMENT OF TRUSTEESHIP AND INFORMATION FROM NON-SELF-GOVERNING TERRITORIES

Under-Secretary: Dragoslav Protitch

OFFICE OF PUBLIC INFORMATION

Under-Secretary: Hernane Tavares de Sá

OFFICE OF CONFERENCE SERVICES

Under-Secretary: Victor Hoo

OFFICE OF GENERAL SERVICES

Director: David B. Vaughan

TECHNICAL ASSISTANCE BOARD

Executive Chairman: David K. Owen

UNITED NATIONS SPECIAL FUND

Managing Director: Paul G. Hoffman

EUROPEAN OFFICE OF THE
UNITED NATIONS, GENEVA

Under-Secretary, Director of the European Office: Pier P. Spinelli

UNITED NATIONS CHILDREN'S FUND
(UNICEF)

Executive Director: Maurice Pate

UNITED NATIONS RELIEF AND WORKS
AGENCY FOR PALESTINE REFUGEES
IN THE NEAR EAST (UNRWA)

Director: John H. Davis

OFFICE OF UNITED NATIONS
HIGH COMMISSIONER FOR REFUGEES

High Commissioner: Auguste R. Lindt (until December 31, 1960)[2]

UNITED NATIONS OPERATIONS
IN THE CONGO

Special Representative of the Secretary-General in the Congo: Ralph J.
Bunche; Andrew W. Cordier; and Rajeshwar Dayal
*Chief of United Nations Civilian Operations and Technical Assistance
Board Resident Representative:* Sture Linner
Supreme Commander, United Nations Force in the Congo: Major General
Carl C. von Horn (July 14–December 31, 1960)[3]

UNITED NATIONS EMERGENCY FORCE (UNEF)

Commander: Lieutenant General Prem Singh Gyani

UNITED NATIONS REPRESENTATIVE
IN INDIA AND PAKISTAN

Representative: Frank P. Graham

UNITED NATIONS TRUCE SUPERVISION
ORGANIZATION IN PALESTINE

Chief of Staff: Major General Carl C. von Horn

UNITED NATIONS MISSION
IN AMMAN, JORDAN

Special Representative of the Secretary-General: Pier P. Spinelli

UNITED NATIONS MISSION
IN VIENTIANE, LAOS

Special Consultant to the Secretary-General: Edouard Zellweger

NOTES

1. Source: *Yearbook of the United Nations, 1960,* appendix 3, p. 732.
2. Félix M. Schnyder (from February 1, 1961)
3. Major General Sean McKeown (as of January 1, 1961)

Appendix H

ONUC Civilian and Military Representatives in the Congo, 1960–1961

Special representatives of the secretary-general (title changed to officer in charge from May 26, 1961):
1. Ralph J. Bunche (U.S.), July 13, 1960–August 27, 1960
2. Andrew W. Cordier (U.S.), August 27, 1960–September 6, 1960
3. Rajeshwar Dayal (India), September 8, 1960–May 25, 1961
4. Indar Jit Rikhye (acting in Dayal's absence) (India), November 3, 1960–November 23, 1960
5. Mekki Abbas (acting in Dayal's absence) (Sudan), March 10, 1961–May 25, 1961
6. Sture Linner (Sweden), May 25, 1961–February 10, 1962

ONUC force commanders:
1. Major General Carl Carlsson von Horn (Sweden), August 1960–December 1960
2. Lieutenant General Sean McKeown (Ireland), January 1961–March 1962

Representatives in Elisabethville, Katanga Province:
1. Ian E. Berendsen (New Zealand), August 1960–March 1961
2. Georges Dumontet (France), March 1961–May 1961
3. Conor Cruise O'Brien (Ireland), June 1961–November 1961
ONUC force commanders in Katanga Province:

1. Colonel H. W. Byone (Ireland), August 1960–December 1960
2. Brigadier K. A. S. Raja (India), March 1961–April 1962

Appendix I

Victims of
DC–6 Aircraft Crash

This is a list of the victims of the crash of the DC–6 aircraft belonging to the Swedish Transair Company during the night of September 17–18, 1961, near Ndola Airport, Northern Rhodesia (now Zambia).

Dag Hammarskjöld   Secretary-general of the United Nations

Heinz A. Wieschhoff   Deputy to the undersecretary, Department of Political and Security Council Affairs, and the secretary-general's chief adviser on Africa

Vladimir Fabry   Legal adviser of the United Nations Operation in the Congo (ONUC)

William J. Ranallo   Chauffeur, bodyguard, and personal aide of Dag Hammarskjöld

Alice Lalande   Secretary to Dr. Sture Linner, head of ONUC civilian branch, "on loan" to Dag Hammarskjöld and the only woman on board

Harold M. Julian   UN security guard and only victim to survive the crash for a few hours

Serge L. Barrau   UN security guard

Francis Eivers   UN aide

Captain Per Hallonquist   Commander

Nils-Eric Aahreus   Copilot

Lars Litton   First officer

Nils Goran Wilhelmsson   Flight engineer

A. P. Harald Noork   Radio operator

Karl Erik Rosen   Radio operator

Warrant Officer S. O. Hjelte   ONUC infantryman and guard

Private P. E. Persson   ONUC infantryman and guard

Appendix J

The New York Times Editorial on Hammarskjöld's Death

This is an editorial that appeared in *The New York Times* on September 19, 1961, the day after Dag Hammarskjöld's death.

DAG HAMMARSKJÖLD

But for the patient, indefatigable leadership of Dag Hammarskjöld, the United Nations might not exist today. Quietly, shrewdly, persistently he labored to maintain it against heavy odds and to enhance its effectiveness in a world that teeters on the brink of catastrophe.

Mr. Hammarskjöld established his office and the United Nations as instruments of a code of moral law. If humanity survives the menace of a nuclear holocaust that he strove so valiantly to avert, history will surely mark his career as one of the great forces for a better world.

He began his tenure at the United Nations modestly, the epitome of a devoted international civil servant. By displaying absolute neutrality and fairness, by showing absolute discretion in keeping confidences he gained the trust of all parties and built up his role as peaceful arbiter.

Such successes as his quiet negotiation of the Arab–Israeli withdrawal from the Gaza strip, the establishment of the United Nations Emergency Force to keep the peace there and his handling of the confused Congo situation are outstanding examples of his diplomatic and organizing abilities. In these and other moves he based his authority on the spirit of the Charter and a liberal interpretation of United Nations instructions which he often inspired. This enabled him to act with independence in the pattern of the responsible leader of a world parliament.

Mr. Hammarskjöld's death is an incalculable loss. He had built himself and his office into one of the great hopes for world peace. He came to represent what was honorable and rational in a chaotic world full of hate and suspicion. There could be no better tribute to him than to bring his body back in state and bury it in United Nations ground under a fitting monument to remind all men of the values for which he lived and died.

Source: "Dag Hammarskjöld," *The New York Times,* September 19, 1961, sec. 1, p. 34.

Appendix K

Biographical Profiles

RALPH J. BUNCHE

Ralph J. Bunche was born in Detroit, Michigan, on August 7, 1904. He graduated from the University of California (1927) and Harvard University (1928 and 1934), and did additional work at Northwestern University in Chicago and the London School of Economics. As the first African-American Ph.D. in political science, Bunche specialized in colonial administration and race relations, and he had a lifelong interest in decolonization issues. He taught political science at Howard University in Washington, D.C., from 1928 to 1940. He was chief research analyst for the U.S. Office of Strategic Services (OSS) from 1941 to 1944, after which he joined the U.S. Department of State, where he was a division head through October 1945.

Bunche went to the United Nations in 1946 as director of the Division of Trusteeship Affairs in the Secretariat. He was the principal secretary of the UN Palestine Commission in 1947 and then acting UN mediator for Palestine in 1948. After Count Folke Bernadotte was assassinated, Bunche, as UN mediator, was largely responsible for engineering the various Arab–Israeli "proximity talks" because the delegations refused to meet face-to-face. Bunche carried negotiating points back and forth between the adversaries, skillfully interweaving his own suggestions in the process and leading to the armistice agreements of 1949. For this he received the Nobel Peace Prize in 1950. As UN undersecretary-general for political affairs (1958–1970), Bunche also played an important role as Secretary-

General Dag Hammarskjöld's first special representative in the Congo from July to August 1960 and as Secretary-General U Thant's special representative in Yemen in 1963. Bunche died in 1971.

LESTER B. PEARSON

Lester Pearson was born in Newtonbrook, Ontario, Canada, on April 23, 1897, the son of an itinerant Methodist minister. He attended collegiate institutes in Peterborough and Hamilton and then the University of Toronto, from which he graduated with honours in history in 1919. After service with the British and Canadian forces in World War I, he attended Oxford University, earning another B.A. in 1923 and an M.A. in 1925. After being on the faculty of the University of Toronto from 1923 to 1928, he was appointed first secretary in Canada's Department of External Affairs in that year. In this capacity, he attended the most important international conferences, including the United Nations Conference on International Organization from April to June 1945, where he helped formulate the United Nations Charter. He became Canada's undersecretary of state for external affairs in 1946 and then secretary of state in 1948. In these capacities, he was a member of the Canadian delegation to the UN General Assembly in 1946–1947, president of the General Assembly's seventh session in 1952–1953, and chairman of the Canadian delegation, 1948–1956.

Pearson was considered for the position of UN secretary-general in 1946 and then in 1953. His candidacy was vetoed by the Soviets in the first instance because they wished to have a European and in the second because of Canada's membership in the North Atlantic Treaty Organization of which Pearson was a staunch promoter. He became head of Canada's Liberal Party in 1958 and prime minister in 1963, serving until 1968. As prime minister, he allowed American nuclear warheads to be stationed on Canadian bases. During his long career in public service, Pearson earned over 20 honorary degrees from universities in Canada, the United States, Britain, and elsewhere. He was awarded the Nobel Peace Prize in 1957 for his role in the creation of the United Nations Emergency Force (UNEF) during the Suez crisis the previous year. He died in 1972.

PATRICE LUMUMBA

Patrice Emergy Lumumba (1925–1961) was born in Katako Kombe, Kasai Province, in what was then Belgian Congo. Educated at Belgian mission schools, he then trained as a postal employee and worked at the post office in Stanleyville, studying law and literature through correspondence courses. Later he was convicted of embezzlement—to finance his nationalist cause, he explained—and served time in prison. On his release, he became a successful beer company executive. He continued to be active in nationalist groups, particularly the Mouvement National Congolais (MNC), rivaling Joseph Kasavubu, president of the Association of the Lower Congo (Abako). The May 1960 elections just prior to independence found Lumumba's party ahead, but he was unable to form a government and consequently Belgium picked Kasavubu as premier. However, Lumumba later won enough support in the National Assembly to form a government and became the first premier of the independent Republic of the Congo, with Kasavubu named president, a mostly ceremonial post. The leaders inherited a country of tribal dissension, political inexperience, and economic crisis. Almost immediately Katanga, the richest province, seceded. Southern Kasai Province followed suit.

In July 1960, Lumumba and Kasavubu asked the United Nations for political, military, and economic support, which were granted, including the dispatch of nearly 20,000 peacekeeping troops. Later, however, Lumumba became very critical of UN Secretary-General Dag Hammarskjöld for refusing to use his ONUC forces to reintegrate the secessionists into the Congo. Essentially, the Security Council stood by Hammarskjöld.

Kasavubu dismissed Lumumba for relying too heavily on Soviet backing and aid. His detractors had even accused him of Communism. But in one of his speeches Lumumba said, "We are not Communists, Catholics, Socialists. We are African nationalists." He tried to resist but was finally removed by the Congolese army under Colonel Joseph-Désiré Mobutu. Lumumba was arrested but escaped. He was rearrested and transferred to his political enemies in Katanga Province, where he was assassinated in January or February 1961, reportedly by angry tribesmen and foreign mercenaries. He left a wife and four children. His death precipitated the climax of the Soviet attacks against Hammarskjöld, whom the Soviets accused of complicity in it. The event also cooled the relationship between some other African leaders and the UN secretary-general. Decades later, Patrice Lumumba is still commemorated in some circles as the epitome of African nationalism and a martyr to that cause.

JOSEPH KASAVUBU

Joseph Kasavubu (1910?–1969) was born in Tshela, a village near Leopoldville, in what was then Belgian Congo. He was educated by Catholic missionaries and studied for the priesthood. But in his last year at the seminary at Kabwe, Kasai Province, he turned to lay teaching. Later he was a clerk in government offices in the capital, Leopoldville, as well as an agronomist for the colonial administration. He became president of the Ethnocultural Association of the Lower Congo (Abako), which developed into a powerful political force. Elected burgomaster of a commune in Leopoldville, he urged the Congo's independence. Joseph Kasavubu and Patrice Lumumba were rival nationalist leaders who became the first president and premier, respectively, of the independent Republic of the Congo in June 1960.

In the political and economic turmoil that followed, the United Nations peacekeeping force under the overall direction of Secretary-General Dag Hammarskjöld sent troops to the Congo. Kasavubu ousted Lumumba from the premiership but he tried to fight back, only to lose out to the newly appointed commander in chief of the Congolese army, Colonel Joseph-Désiré Mobutu. The latter established a military regime while retaining Kasavubu as a figurehead president. One of Kasavubu's first actions after forcing Lumumba out was to eject from the Congo Communist diplomats and technicians, whom the premier had invited to the Congo against Kasavubu's wishes. In November 1960, the UN General Assembly voted to assign Kasavubu's government the Congo's seat in that body in preference to a rival Lumumba delegation. Mobutu replaced Kasavubu in a bloodless coup in 1965. Kasavubu retired to his farm at Boma with his wife and six children and died in 1969.

MOISE TSHOMBE

Moise Kapenda Tshombe (1919–1969) was born in Musumba, Katanga Province, in the then Belgian Congo. The son of a businessman, he studied at an American Methodist mission school and then in Europe. On his return, he joined his father's stores in and around Elisabethville, plantations, and a European hotel. Tshombe had become active in politics and retained close relationships with Belgian colonial interests. Eventually, he became premier of copper-rich Katanga, which produced some two-thirds of the Congo's national income. And indeed, Tshombe's detractors came to describe him as a Belgian puppet and a front man for the mining interests. In the tumult and violence that followed hard on the Congo's independence in June 1960, Katanga seceded and Tshombe was elected its president by the Katangan Assembly. Meanwhile, the central Congolese Government had requested UN Secretary-General Dag Hammarskjöld to help restore order and its authority throughout the territory as it refused to recognize Katanga's secession. A peacekeeping force, the United Nations Operation in the Congo (ONUC), was deployed to prevent the country's political and economic disintegration. But there was constant friction between Tshombe and the United Nations, at times leading to armed clashes between Katangan (and mercenary) troops and ONUC. In the summer of 1961, ONUC troops moved into Katanga in large numbers. The province eventually ended its secession and made its peace with the central government in Leopoldville.

Tshombe, summoned by President Joseph Kasavubu to return from his exile in Europe, became premier of the reunited Congo from 1964 to 1965, when Tshombe was dismissed by President Kasavubu and military leader Joseph-Désiré Mobutu for inviting white mercenaries again to fight rebels. Tshombe returned to Europe. In 1967, he was kidnapped while flying with some "business partners" from Ibiza to Palma, Majorca, Spain. The plane was ordered to Algiers, where Tshombe was arrested. He died there, still a prisoner, two years later after the Algerian head of state refused to extradite him back to Leopoldville where President Mobutu wished to have him tried for treason. Tshombe left a wife and eight children.

JOSEPH-DÉSIRÉ MOBUTU

Joseph-Désiré Mobutu (1930–1997) was born in Lisala, Equateur Province, in what was then Belgian Congo. After completing secondary school, he was selected by the Belgians to attend the Institut des Etudes Sociales de l'Etat (Public Institute of Social Studies) in Brussels, an honor for a Congolese at that time. Upon his return, he enlisted in the Force Publique, the Belgian-officered colonial army, and reached the rank of sergeant-major, the highest possible for a Congolese. Mobutu then became a newsman and acquired an interest in politics. Like Patrice Lumumba, he joined the Mouvement National Congolais (MNC), which advocated the end of Belgian rule. In June 1960, Mobutu was named secretary of state for national defense in the first independent government of the Republic of the Congo headed by Premier Patrice Lumumba. Mobutu fell out with Lumumba and eventually with the country's first president, Joseph Kasavubu. In November 1965 he seized power, which he had in effect wielded behind the scenes for a long time as commander in chief of the Congolese National Army. He eventually amended the constitution to give the president greater authority. For years, while the Cold War continued and the United States looked askance at the Congo's Soviet-backed neighbor, Angola, Mobutu enjoyed American support and the Congo's economy improved. But Mobutu's importance to the West declined as the Cold War subsided, and the country's economy languished in the midst of persistent charges of corruption and continued tribal strife.

In the 1990s, Mobutu's autocratic rule was increasingly attacked amid demands for democracy, the liberalization of party life, and elections. The Congolese president made a few grudging concessions. In the meantime, in his program of "authenticity" to rid the country of the final vestiges of its colonial legacy, Mobutu changed many of the former Belgian designations. In the early 1970s, his country became Zaire, its capital Kinshasa, and he himself, Mobutu Sese Seko. He has had admirers as well as detractors. According to one Belgian newspaper, "The Congo needs not one but one thousand Mobutus to pull through." In May 1997, Mobutu was ousted by rebel General Laurent Kabila. Mobutu went into exile in Rabat, Morocco, where he died from prostate cancer on September 7, 1997. Mobutu left behind a wife and five children and was reputedly one of the wealthiest men in the world.

Bibliography

The public and, to a lesser extent, the private life of Dag Hammarskjöld are well documented. Of notable importance in the voluminous literature are the records of his numerous utterances on all occasions edited by Andrew W. Cordier and Wilder Foote, close aides at the United Nations. There are also Hammarskjöld's *Annual Reports*—nine of them—in which he combined philosophical conceptual views of the world in his introduction with the factual events mirrored in the text proper. Last but not least is the secretary-general's own autobiographical *Castle Hill* about his early life in Sweden and especially his autobiographical *Markings*. The latter is by no means a diary, as it fails to identify or even mention particular events or individuals that may have been vaguely alluded to in the various entries, most of which coincide with Hammarskjöld's tenure at the United Nations. Published posthumously first in Sweden and then in its English translation, *Markings* is more of an inspirational journal describing the spiritual journey of its author. Hammarskjöld also wrote for such publications as the *United Nations Bulletin*.

To the extent that one can get to know this very private individual, the two books by another close UN aide, Brian Urquhart, written at a 15-year interval, especially the first semiofficial biography *Hammarskjöld*, are also extremely useful. The author had access to Hammarskjöld's unpublished private papers. Noteworthy also is Larry Trachtenberg, "A Bibliographic Essay on Dag Hammarskjöld," in Robert S. Jordan, ed., *Dag Hammarskjöld Revisited: The UN Secretary-General as a Force in World Politics*. Trachtenberg lists a few of the major collections of documents that deal with the secretary-general.

They include the Dag Hammarskjöld papers in Stockholm and the Gunnar and Alva Myrdal papers, also in Stockholm. In the United States, the Ralph Bunche papers, the Andrew Cordier papers, the UN archives, and the official UN records are also very important. The Jordan book itself, published in 1983, includes an excellent compilation of secondary sources in its bibliography.

The remaining secondary sources may be dichotomized as follows: the vast majority—who admired, even adulated, Hammarskjöld— explained most of his deeds and even misdeeds (when they are mentioned at all) in the best possible light. On the other hand a small minority take a contrarian view, both with reference to Hammarskjöld's character (one-sided) and professional acts, especially on the administrative side.

The fact remains that even in the contemporary literature, Hammarskjöld's era in the world organization is often used as a benchmark by which other secretaries-general and indeed the United Nations itself are evaluated.

Alker, Hayward R., and Bruce M. Russett. *World Politics in the General Assembly.* New Haven, Conn.: Yale University Press, 1965.

The American Assembly. *Arms Control: Issues for the Public.* Englewood Cliffs, N.J.: Prentice-Hall, 1961.

Armstrong, Hamilton Fish. "U.N. Experience in Gaza." *Foreign Affairs* 35, no. 4 (1957): 600–619.

———. "U.N. on Trial." *Foreign Affairs* 39, no. 3 (1961): 388–415.

Ascoli, Max. "On Reading Hammarskjöld." *The Reporter,* May 20, 1965, pp. 37–40.

Asher, Robert E., et al. *The United Nations and the Promotion of the General Welfare.* Washington, D.C.: Brookings Institution, 1957.

Aulen, Gustaf. *Dag Hammarskjöld's White Book: An Analysis of "Markings."* Philadelphia: Fortress, 1969. A profile by a Swedish cleric and friend of Hammarskjöld's faith and religiosity as evidenced in his autobiographical *Markings.* Refutes the charge made by some, especially in Sweden, that Hammarskjöld nearly blasphemously considered himself to be a latter-day messiah destined to save the world.

Bailey, Sydney D. *The Secretariat of the United Nations.* Rev. ed. New York: Praeger/Carnegie Endowment for International Peace, 1964.

Beskow, Bo. *Dag Hammarskjöld: Strictly Personal—A Portrait.* Garden City, N.Y.: Doubleday, 1969. A profile by a Swedish portrait-painter friend of Hammarskjöld highlighting him as the private man rather than the international civil servant. Beskow tries to refute what he claims to be "rumors and lies so often repeated that they take on a false air of historical fact." The work includes relatively intimate photographs of Hammarskjöld in his Swedish and New York environment.

Boudreau, Thomas E. *Sheathing the Sword: The U.N. Secretary-General and the Prevention of International Conflict.* Westport, Conn.: Greenwood, 1991, chap. 3, "The Struggle Continues: Dag Hammarskjöld." Breaks up the secretary-general's UN career in terms of the crises that he had to meet from China to the Congo.

Boyd, Andrew. *United Nations: Piety, Myth, and Truth.* London: Pelican, 1962.

Boyd, James M. *United Nations Peace-Keeping Operations: A Military and Political Appraisal.* New York: Praeger, 1971.

Burns, Arthur Lee, and Nina Heathcoate. *Peacekeeping by UN Forces: From Suez to the Congo.* New York: Praeger, 1963.

Burns, Lt. Gen. E. M. L. *Between Arab and Israeli.* New York: Obolensky, 1963. The Canadian commander of UNEF assays the Middle East problem.

Castaneda, Jorge. *Legal Effects of United Nations Resolutions.* New York: Columbia University Press, 1969.

Chamberlin, Waldo, Thomas Hovet, and Richard N. Swift, eds. *Annual Review of United Nations Affairs, 1957–1958.* Dobbs Ferry, N.Y.: Oceana, 1959.

Claude, Inis L. *The Changing United Nations.* New York: Random House, 1967.

Clifford, J. M. *The Thirty-Eighth Floor.* New York: McGraw-Hill, 1965. Some detailed accounts of the inner workings in the secretary-general's executive office.

Cohen, Benjamin V. *The United Nations: Constitutional Development, Growth, and Possibilities.* Cambridge: Harvard University Press, 1961.

Commission to Study the Organization of Peace. "The UN Secretary-General: His Role in World Politics." 14th Report. New York: Commission to Study the Organization of Peace, 1962.

Copp, DeWitt, and Marshall Peck. *Betrayal at the UN: The Story of Paul Bang-Jensen.* New York: Devin-Adair, 1961. A highly critical, well-documented work by rightist supporters of the Danish UN Secretariat staff member dismissed by Hammarskjöld for insubordination and unbecoming conduct.

Cordier, Andrew W. "Motivations and Methods of Dag Hammarkskjöld." In Andrew W. Cordier and Kenneth L. Maxwell, eds., *Paths to World Order,* pp. 1–21. New York: Columbia University Press, 1967. Interesting insights by Hammarskjöld's executive assistant about the secretary-general's attitude toward the organization and some aspects of his life. Also, Henry P. van Dusen, "Dag Hammarskjöld: The Inner Person," pp. 22–44.

Cordier, Andrew W., and Wilder Foote, eds. *Public Papers of the Secretaries-General of the United Nations: Dag Hammarskjöld, 1953–1961.* Vols. 2–5. New York: Columbia University Press, 1972–1975. A more comprehensive and up-to-date version of Wilder Foote's *Dag Hammarskjöld: Servant of Peace* (q.v.). *Public Papers* is the best documented work on the subject. In addition to masterly prefatory comments by the coeditors, the four volumes include speeches, statements, verbatim press conferences, and other statements and writings by the secretary-general.

———. *The Quest for Peace: The Dag Hammarskjöld Memorial Lectures.* New York: Columbia University Press, 1965. Includes an essay by Undersecretary-General Ralph J. Bunche on the Congo operation.

Curtis, Gerald L. "Dag Hammarskjöld." *The New Yorker,* September 30, 1961, pp. 35–37. A spur-of-the-moment tribute.

Dallin, Alexander. *The Soviet Union and the United Nations: An Inquiry into Soviet Motives and Objectives.* New York: Praeger, 1962. Includes a chapter on the Congo operation.

Dayal, Rajeshwar. *Mission for Hammarskjöld: The Congo Crisis.* Princeton: Princeton University Press, 1976. A highly informative work, especially on the inner complexities of Congolese politics, by Hammarskjöld's controversial special representative in the Congo from September 1960 to May 1961.

Eagleton, Clyde, Waldo Chamberlin, and Richard N. Swift, eds. *Annual Review of United Nations Affairs, 1954.* New York: New York University Press, 1955.

Eagleton, Clyde, and Richard N. Swift, eds. *Annual Review of United Nations Affairs, 1953.* New York: New York University Press, 1954.

———. *Annual Review of United Nations Affairs, 1955–1956.* New York: New York University Press, 1957.

Eichelberger, Clark M. *The United Nations: The First Fifteen Years.* New York: Harper & Row, 1960. An authoritative description of the United Nations from 1946 to 1960 in the light of the human and scientific revolutions occurring mostly during the Hammarskjöld years. Dwells perceptively on what the members wanted the United Nations to be.

Eisenhower, Dwight D. *The White House Years: Waging Peace, 1956–1961.* Garden City, N.Y.: Doubleday, 1965.

Emerson, Rupert. "Colonialism, Political Development, and the UN." *International Organization* 19, no. 3. (1965): 484–503.

Epstein, Howard M., ed. *Revolt in the Congo, 1960–1964.* New York: Facts on File, 1965. A chronological record of events in the Congo from newspaper dispatches.

Epstein, William. *Disarmament: Twenty-Five Years of Effort.* Toronto: Canadian Institute of International Affairs, 1971.

Fabian, Larry L. *Soldiers without Enemies: Preparing the United Nations for Peacekeeping.* Washington, D.C.: Brookings Institution, 1971.

Falk, Richard A. "The South-West Africa Case: An Appraisal." *International Organization* 21, no. 1 (1967): 1–23.

Fall, Bernard B. *Anatomy of a Crisis: The Laotian Crisis of 1960–1961.* Garden City, N.Y.: Doubleday, 1969.

Federation of Rhodesia and Nyasaland. Commission on the Accident involving SE-BDY. *A Report of the Commission on the Accident involving SE-BDY (Carrying Dag Hammarskjöld, Secretary-General of the UN)*. Salisbury: Assembly Papers C. Fed. 202, 1962.

Finger, Seymour M., and John Mugno. *The Politics of Staffing the United Nations Secretariat*. New York: Ralph Bunche Institute, City University of New York, 1974.

Foote, Wilder, ed. *Dag Hammarskjöld: Servant of Peace*. New York: Harper & Row, 1962. An invaluable source by the UN public affairs officer reproducing Hammarskjöld's important speeches and statements as well as comments about him by his contemporaries.

Forsythe, David P. "The United Nations and Human Rights: 1945–1985." *Political Science Quarterly* 100 (Summer 1985): 249–270.

Fosdick, Raymond B. *The League and the United Nations after Fifty Years: The Six Secretaries-General*. Newtown, Conn.: Fosdick, 1972.

Franck, Thomas M. *Nation against Nation: What Happened to the U.N. Dream and What the U.S. Can Do about It*. New York: Oxford University Press, 1985. The author, a professor at the School of Law, New York University, and former director of research at UNITAR, dwells extensively on the Hammarskjöld years in tracing the evolution of U.S. policy toward the world organization.

Gavshon, Arthur L. *The Mysterious Death of Dag Hammarskjöld*. New York: Walker, 1962. Claims that there may be more than meets the eye regarding the crash of the secretary-general's plane in September 1961.

Gillet, Nicholas. *Dag Hammarskjöld*. London: Heron, 1970.

Goodrich, Leland M. "Geographical Distribution of the Staff of the UN Secretariat." *International Organization* 16, no. 3 (1962): 465–482.

———. "The Political Role of the Secretary-General." *International Organization* 16, no. 4 (1962): 720–735.

———. *The United Nations in a Changing World*. New York: Columbia University Press, 1974. Still one of the classics in the field. Chapter 5, "The Secretary-General and His Staff," is especially relevant to the Hammarskjöld era.

Goodrich, Leland M., Edvard Hambro, and Anne P. Simmons. *Charter of the United Nations: Commentary and Documents*. 3d ed. New York: Columbia University Press, 1969.

Goodrich, Leland M., and Anne P. Simmons. *The United Nations and the Maintenance of International Peace and Security*. Washington, D.C.: Brookings Institution, 1955.

Gordenker, Leon. *The UN Secretary-General and the Maintenance of Peace*. New York: Columbia University Press, 1967. Deals extensively with Hammarskjöld's Peking mission in 1955 and explains how the success of his endeavor tended to increase the use of his office in subsequent crises.

Gross, Leo. "The United Nations and the Rule of Law." *International Organi-zation* 19, no. 3 (1965): 537–561.

Halpern, Manfred. "The U.N. in the Congo." *Worldview* 6, no. 10 (1963): 4–8. A positive appraisal of the UN operation.

Hammarskjöld, Dag. *Annual Report of the Secretary-General to the General Assembly on the Work of the Organization, 1952–1961.* New York: General Assembly Official Records, United Nations, 1953–1961. Dag Hammarskjöld continued the tradition begun by Secretary-General Trygve Lie of making his introduction to the secretary-general's annual report his major annual policy statement and review. Accordingly, in analogy with *Markings,* his spiritual diary, the introduction to the *Annual Reports* (q.v.) for the years of his tenure is very instructive about his professional views and purposes.

———. *Castle Hill.* Uppsala: The Dag Hammarskjöld Foundation, 1971. A brief memoir about Hammarskjöld's early life in Uppsala, throwing light not only on the boy's physical surroundings but also on some of his more evident personality traits such as his moodiness, remoteness, even frigidity.

———. *The Dag Hammarskjöld Papers.* Stockholm: Manuscript Department, the Royal Library.

———. "The International Civil Servant in Law and Fact." In Wilder Foote, ed., *Servant of Peace: A Selection of the Speeches and Statements of Dag Ham-marskjöld,* pp. 329–349. New York: Harper & Row, 1962. In this celebrated lecture at Oxford University on May 30, 1961, Hammarskjöld spells out the need for the secretary-general's independence from political pressures in the performance of his duties whose primary purpose should always be the promotion of internationalism via the United Nations.

———. Introduction to *Annual Report of the Secretary-General to the General Assembly on the Work of the Organization, 1952–1953.* General Assembly Official Records, Eighth Session, Supplement no. 1 (A/2404), July 15, 1953. This report was almost entirely devoted to Trygve Lie's final year in office.

———. Introduction to *Annual Report of the Secretary-General to the General Assembly on the Work of the Organization, 1953–1954.* General Assembly Official Records, Ninth Session, Supplement no. 1 (A/2663), July 21, 1954.

———. Introduction to *Annual Report of the Secretary-General to the General Assembly on the Work of the Organization, 1954–1955.* General Assembly Official Records, Tenth Session, Supplement no. 1 (A/2911), July 8, 1955.

———. Introduction to *Annual Report of the Secretary-General to the General Assembly on the Work of the Organization, 1955–1956.* General Assembly Official Records, Eleventh Session, Supplement no. 1A (A/3137/Add. 1), October 4, 1956. This was the first introduction appearing as a separate document to give the General Assembly members the opportunity to com-ment on it during the plenary if they desired.

———. Introduction to *Annual Report of the Secretary-General to the General Assembly on the Work of the Organization, 1956–1957.* General Assembly

Official Records, Twelfth Session, Supplement no. 1A (A/3594, Add. 1), September 4, 1957. Drafted on August 22, 1957.

————. Introduction to *Annual Report of the Secretary-General to the General Assembly on the Work of the Organization, 1957–1958*. General Assembly Official Records, Thirteenth Session, Supplement no. 1A (A/3844/Add. 1), August 25, 1958.

————. Introduction to *Annual Report of the Secretary-General to the General Assembly on the Work of the Organization, 1958–1959*. General Assembly Official Records, Fourteenth Session, Supplement no. 1A (A/4132/Add. 1), August 20, 1959.

————. Introduction to *Annual Report of the Secretary-General to the General Assembly on the Work of the Organization, 1959–1960*. General Assembly Official Records, Fifteenth Session, Supplement no. 1A (A/4390/Add. 1), August 31, 1960.

————. Introduction to *Annual Report of the Secretary-General to the General Assembly on the Work of the Organization, 1960–1961*. General Assembly Official Records, Sixteenth Session, Supplement no. 1A (A/4800/Add. 1), August 17, 1961.

————. *Markings*. Translated from the Swedish version by Leif Sjöberg and W. H. Auden. New York: Knopf, 1964. According to Hammarskjöld himself, the road or trail or benchmarks to which the title refers "is a sort of white book concerning my negotiations with myself—and with God." It is a kind of diary, often in verse, which seems to allude to major aspects of the secretary-general's professional and especially emotional and spiritual life, possibly shedding light on a very private individual.

————. "The Promise of the U.N.: Hammarskjöld Answers Ten Questions." *The New York Times Magazine*, September 15, 1957, sec. 6, pt. 1, pp. 21, 84. In answering questions about the UN's effectiveness, its role, and its prospects, Hammarskjöld opined that the world body existed to help governments and peoples use it to maximize their opportunities for progress.

————. "Two Differing Concepts of the United Nations Assayed." *International Organization* 15, no. 4 (1961): 549–563. This is Hammarskjöld's last introduction to the *Annual Report* of 1960–1961 in which he analyzes more clearly than ever the state of the organization following the turbulent events of that year.

Hazzard, Shirley. *Countenance of Truth: The United Nations and the Waldheim Case*. New York: Viking Penguin, 1990. While obviously focusing on the fourth secretary-general, the writer, who worked in the secretariat for a decade, strikes interesting analogies between Kurt Waldheim and Dag Hammarskjöld.

————. *Defeat of an Ideal: A Study of the Self–Destruction of the United Nations*. Boston: Little, Brown, 1973. A challenging critique by a well–known Australian–born writer who held a modest position in the UN secretariat during the Hammarskjöld years. Hazzard writes appreciatively of the internationalist creativity of the secretary–general but charges him with being remote and lacking concern for staff members.

Heilprin, Marilyn. "The Evolution of the United Nations Presence under Dag Hammarskjöld." M.A. thesis, American University, 1963.

Heinz, G., and H. Donnay. *Lumumba: The Last Fifty Days.* Translated from the French by Jane Clark Seitz. New York: Grove, 1970. The events that preceded the assassination of the Congolese leader.

Hempstone, Smith. *Rebels, Mercenaries, and Dividends: The Katanga Story.* New York: Praeger, 1962. A highly critical account of UN efforts to end the secession in the dissident Congolese province.

Henderson, James L. *Hammarskjöld: Servant of a World Unborn.* London: Methuen Educational, 1969.

Henkin, Louis. "The United Nations and Human Rights." *International Organization* 19, no. 3 (1965): 504–517.

Hershey, Burnet. "Dag Hammarskjöld: A Personal Portrait." *Look,* October 24, 1961, p. 140.

———. *Soldier of Peace: Dag Hammarskjöld.* Chicago: Britannica Books, 1961.

Higgins, Rosalyn. *The Development of International Law through the Political Organs of the United Nations.* New York: Oxford University Press, 1963.

———. "The Place of International Law in the Settlement of Disputes by the Security Council." *American Journal of International Law* 64, no. 1 (1970): 1–18.

———. *United Nations Peacekeeping, 1946–1967: Documents and Commentary.* Vols. 1–2. New York: Oxford University Press, 1980. An authoritative collection that emphasizes the UNEF and ONUC in Hammarskjöld's time as prototypes of "preventive diplomacy."

Hoffmann, Stanley. "In Search of a Thread: The UN in the Congo Labyrinth." *International Organization* 16, no. 2 (1962): 331–361. Contrasts Hammarskjöld's sweeping efforts with the limitations imposed on ONUC.

———. "Sisyphus and the Avalanche: The United Nations, Egypt, and Hungary." *International Organization* 11, no. 3 (1957): 446–469.

Horn, Maj. Gen. Carl Von. *Soldiering for Peace.* New York: McKay, 1967. Mostly a personal account by the controversial Swedish commander of ONUC in the Congo from July to December 1960.

Hoskyns, Catherine. *The Congo Since Independence, January 1960–December 1961.* London: Royal Institute of International Affairs, 1965. A detailed political analysis of the Congo's internal affairs and UN activities.

Hovet, Thomas. *Bloc Politics in the United Nations.* Cambridge: Harvard University Press, 1960.

Hovet, Thomas, and Erica Hovet, eds. *A Chronology and Fact Book of the United Nations, 1941–1979: Annual Review of United Nations Affairs.* 6th ed. Dobbs Ferry, N.Y.: Oceana, 1979. An invaluable compendium making it possible to trace by date important events in all the UN principal organs, specialized agencies, and subsidiary agencies.

International Court of Justice, *Yearbook.* The Hague: International Court of Justice, 1954–1961.

Jacobson, Harold K. "ONUC's Civilian Operations: State-Preserving and State-Building." *World Politics* 17, no. 1 (1964): 75–107. An analysis of UN civilian operations in the Congo in their political setting.

———. "The United Nations and Colonialism: A Tentative Appraisal." *International Organization* 16, no. 1 (1962): 37–56.

James, Alan. *The Politics of Peace-Keeping.* New York: Praeger, 1969.

James, Robert Rhodes. *Staffing the United Nations Secretariat.* Institute for the Study of International Organization, University of Sussex, Brighton, U.K., 1st ser., no. 2, pp. 19–23.

Jarring, Gunnar. "Dag Hammarskjöld: In Memoriam." *Swedish Pioneer Historical Quarterly* (Stockholm), January 1962.

Jessup, Philip C., and Howard J. Taubenfeld. *Controls for Outer Space and the Antarctic Analogy.* New York: Columbia University Press, 1959.

Jordan, Robert S., ed. *Hammarskjöld Revisited: The UN Secretary-General as a Force in World Politics.* Durham, N.C.: Carolina Academic Press, 1983. Simple accounts of the major milestones in Hammarskjöld's political life written by academics and senior UN officials, including Secretary-General Kurt Waldheim.

Kay, David A. *The New Nations in the United Nations, 1960–1967.* New York: Columbia University Press, 1970. Citing the 15th General Assembly session in September 1960—Hammarskjöld's last—as an important turning point in UN history, this very scholarly work highlights the impact of the new member states from Africa and other developing regions on the world organization.

———. "The United Nations and Decolonization." In James Barros, ed., *The United Nations: Past, Present, and Future.* New York: Free Press, 1972.

Kelen, Emery. *Hammarskjöld.* New York: Putnam's, 1966. A colorful but adulatory insight into Hammarskjöld's family and personal circumstances by a former staff member of the UN secretariat.

Kelen, Emery, ed. *Hammarskjöld: The Political Man.* New York: Funk & Wagnalls, 1968. Quotations from some of Hammarskjöld's statements and writings arranged by subject matter, with introductory comments by the editor. A useful compendium for readers unable to access Wilder Foote, ed., *Dag Hammarskjöld: Servant of Peace* or especially Andrew W. Cordier and Wilder Foote, eds., *Public Papers of the Secretaries-General of the United Nations* (q.v.).

King, Gordon. *United Nations in the Congo: A Quest for Peace.* New York: Carnegie Endowment for International Peace, 1962.

Kraft, Joseph. "The Untold Story of the UN's Congo Army." *Harper's Magazine,* November 1960, pp. 75–84.

Lall, Arthur. *The UN and the Middle East Crisis.* New York: Columbia University Press, 1968.

Langrod, Georges. *The International Civil Service: Its Origins, Its Nature, Its Evolution.* Translated from the French by F. G. Berthoud. Dobbs Ferry, N.Y.: Oceana, 1963.

Lash, Joseph P. *Dag Hammarskjöld: Custodian of the Brush-Fire Peace.* Garden City, N.Y.: Doubleday, 1961.

———. "Dag Hammarskjöld's Conception of His Office." *International Organization* 16, no. 3 (1962): 542–566.

———. "The Man on the 38th Floor." *Harper's Magazine,* October 1959, pp. 47–52.

———. "The UN's Hammarskjöld." *The Progressive* 21, no. 1 (1957): 17–20.

Lefever, Ernest W. *Crisis in the Congo: A United Nations Force in Action.* Washington, D.C.: Brookings Institution, 1965. A study of the four-year operation, with emphasis on the U.S. role.

———. *Uncertain Mandate: Politics of the UN Congo Operation.* Baltimore: Johns Hopkins University Press, 1967. A very readable and factual account with a good annotated bibliography drawn almost exclusively from primary sources.

Legum, Colin. *Congo Disaster.* Baltimore: Penguin, 1961.

Levine, Israel. *Dag Hammarskjöld: Champion of World Peace.* New York: Messner, 1962.

Lie, Trygve. *In the Cause of Peace.* New York: Macmillan, 1954.

Lippmann, Walter. "Dag Hammarskjöld, United Nations Pioneer." *International Organization* 15, no. 4 (1961): 547–548. A tribute to the deceased Hammarskjöld by one of the most eminent American newsmen of the time.

Lodge, Henry Cabot, Jr. "A Colleague's Salute . . ." *Life,* September 29, 1961, p. 50. A tribute to Hammarskjöld by the former U.S. ambassador to the United Nations, his occasional adversary.

Loveday, A. *Reflections on International Administration.* London: Oxford University Press, 1956.

Luard, Evan. *A History of the United Nations.* Vol. 1, *The Years of Western Domination, 1945–1955.* New York: St. Martin's, 1982.

Mangone, Gerard J. *A Short History of International Organization.* New York: McGraw-Hill, 1954.

Mangone, Gerard J., ed. *UN Administration of Economic and Social Programs.* New York: Columbia University Press, 1966.

Mayer, Ann M. *Dag Hammarskjöld: The Peacemaker.* Mankato, Minn.: Creative Education, 1974.

Meigs, Cornelia. *The Great Design: Men and Events in the United Nations from 1945 to 1963.* Boston: Little, Brown, 1964.

Meron, Theodor. *The United Nations Secretariat: The Rules and the Practice.* Lexington, Mass.: Heath, 1977.

Miller, Linda B. *World Order and Local Disorder: The United Nations and Internal Conflicts.* Princeton: Princeton University Press, 1967. A well-researched book covering succinctly but proficiently several of the major issues with which the United Nations was seized in the Hammarskjöld years, including Guatemala, Hungary, Lebanon, Vietnam, Cambodia, and especially the Congo.

Miller, Richard I. *Dag Hammarskjöld and Crisis Diplomacy*. Dobbs Ferry, N.Y.: Oceana, 1962. An informative but slightly boring work by an American newsman tracing the evolution of the United Nations during Hammarskjöld's time, primarily through Security Council and General Assembly resolutions.

Montgomery, Elizabeth. *Dag Hammarskjöld: Peacemaker for the United Nations*. Champaign, Ill.: Garrard, 1973.

Moore, Raymond A., Jr. *The United Nations Reconsidered*. Studies in International Affairs, no. 2. Columbia: University of South Carolina Press, 1963. Essays by important American, British, and French public figures on different aspects of the United Nations, especially applicable to the Hammarskjöld era but also looking into the world organization's future.

Morgenthau, Hans J. "The U.N. of Dag Hammarskjöld Is Dead." *The New York Times*, March 14, 1965, sec. 6, p. 32. An evaluation by one of the most famous advocates of political realism.

Murray, James N. *The United Nations Trusteeship System*. Urbana: University of Illinois Press, 1957.

Nicholas, Herbert G. *The United Nations as a Political Institution*. 4th ed. New York: Oxford University Press, 1971.

———. "U.N. Peace Forces and the Changing Globe: The Lessons of Suez and the Congo." *International Organization* 17, no. 2 (1963): 321–337.

"Obituary Notices: Mr. Dag Hammarskjöld," *The* (London) *Times*, September 19, 1961, p. 13.

O'Brien, Conor Cruise. *To Katanga and Back: A UN Case History*. New York: Grosset & Dunlap, 1962. An account by Hammarskjöld's controversial representative in Katanga from May to December 1961 that gives the reasons for his resignation.

———. *Murderous Angels: A Political Tragedy and Comedy in Black and White*. Boston: Little, Brown, 1968. An imaginative, perceptive account of the circumstances surrounding Hammarskjöld's mysterious death in the air crash of September 17–18, 1961.

O'Brien, Conor Cruise, and Feliks Topolski. *The United Nations: Sacred Drama*. Illustrated by Felix Topolski. New York: Simon & Schuster, 1968. A running commentary by Hammarskjöld's representative in Katanga, an Irish writer and statesman, generously illustrated with sketches and other graphics.

Orwa, D. Katete. *The Congo Betrayal: The UN–US and Lumumba*. Nairobi: Kenya Literature Bureau, 1985. An African's view of the Congo crisis.

Paffrath, Leslie. "The Legacy of Dag Hammarskjöld." *Saturday Review*, July 24, 1965, pp. 33, 49.

Pearson, Lester B. "Force for the UN." *Foreign Affairs* 35, no. 3 (1957): 395–404.

The Canadian diplomat generally credited with the concept of a peace-keeping force explains UNEF.

Pechota, Vratislav. *The Quiet Approach: A Study of the Good Offices Exercised by the United Nations Secretary-General in the Cause of Peace.* New York: UNI-TAR, 1972.

Rivlin, Benjamin, and Leon Gordenker, eds. *The Challenging Role of the UN Secretary-General.* Westport, Conn.: Praeger, 1993. An essay in Chapter 7 by Nitza Nachmias entitled "The Role of the Secretary-General in the Israeli–Arab and the Cyprus Disputes" includes a section entitled "Hammarskjöld: Peacekeeping Architect" that highlights his role at Suez and the fact that President Nasser's view prevailed over Hammarskjöld's when it came to conditions for UNEF's withdrawal from Egypt in 1967.

Qubain, Fahim Issa. *Crisis in Lebanon.* Washington, D.C.: Middle East Institute, 1961.

Robertson, Terrence. *Crisis: The Inside Story of the Suez Conspiracy.* New York: Atheneum, 1965. How Britain, France, and Israel colluded to topple Egypt's President Gamal Abdel Nasser and reverse his decision to nationalize the Suez Canal Company in 1956.

Rosenthal, A. M. "Dag Hammarskjöld Sizes Up His UN Job." *The New York Times Magazine,* August 16, 1953, sec. 6, pp. 10ff.

Rosner, Gabriella. *The United Nations Emergency Force.* New York: Columbia University Press, 1963. A historical, legal, political, and operational study of the Suez episode in 1956–1957.

Rovine, Arthur W. *The First Fifty Years: The Secretary-General in World Politics, 1920–1970,* chap. 5. Leiden: Sijthoff, 1970. Outlines how Hammarskjöld extended the powers of the secretary-general's office far beyond the limits dreamed possible by UN founders.

Russell, Ruth B. *The General Assembly: Patterns/Problems/Prospects.* New York: Carnegie Endowment for International Peace, 1970.

Russell, Ruth B., and Jeannette F. Mather. *A History of the United Nations Charter.* Washington, D.C.: Brookings Institution, 1958.

Sady, Emil J. *The United Nations and Dependent Peoples.* Washington, D.C.: Brookings Institution, 1956.

Schwebel, Stephen N. *The Secretary-General of the United Nations: His Political Powers and Practice.* Cambridge: Harvard University Press, 1952.

Settel, T. S., ed. *The Light and the Rock: The Vision of Dag Hammarksjold.* New York: Dutton, 1966.

Sharp, Walter R. "Trends in United Nations Administration." *International Organization* 15, no. 3 (1961): 393–407.

———. *The United Nations Economic and Social Council.* New York: Columbia University Press, 1969.

Sheldon, Richard N. *Dag Hammarskjöld.* New York: Chelsea House, 1987. A profile of the secretary-general, including vignettes and photographs.

Simon, Charlie M. *Dag Hammarskjöld.* New York: Dutton, 1967.

Smith, Bradford. "Dag Hammarskjöld: Peace by Juridical Sanction." In Bradford Smith, ed., *Man of Peace*, pp. 310–345. Philadelphia: Lippincott, 1964.

Snow, C. P. "Dag Hammarskjöld." In *Variety of Men*, pp. 201–223. New York: Scribner's, 1967.

Söderberg, Sten. *Hammarskjöld: A Pictorial Biography*. New York: Viking, 1962. A Swedish painter and friend of Hammarskjöld describes the paradox in the secretary-general's life as being that of a boy who grew up as the stay-at-home daughter of a fawning mother but also a brilliant career official. He could be a bachelor workaholic but had very broad literary, philosophical, religious, and outdoor interests as well.

Stanton, Edwin F. "A 'Presence' in Laos." *Current History* 38, no. 226 (1960): 337–341, 346.

Stein, Eric. "Mr. Hammarskjöld, the Charter Law, and the Future Role of the United Nations Secretary-General." *American Journal of International Law* 56, no. 1 (1962): 9–32.

Stevenson, Adlai E. *Looking Outward: Years of Crisis at the United Nations*. New York: Harper & Row, 1963. An account, briefly coinciding with Hammarskjöld's tenure, by President John F. Kennedy's chief delegate to the United Nations. Stevenson was also a U.S. presidential candidate in 1952 and 1956.

Stoessinger, John G., et al. *Financing the United Nations System*. Washington, D.C.: Brookings Institution, 1964. Discusses ONUC and other peacekeeping operations.

Stolpe, Sven. *Dag Hammarskjöld: A Spiritual Portrait*. Translated from the Swedish by Naomi Walford. New York: Scribner's, 1966. A Swedish writer and childhood friend of Hammarskjöld's describes him as an almost unique example of a Christian mystic who was strong enough to stand up for his principles in the face of acute hostility.

Swift, Richard N., ed. *Annual Review of United Nations Affairs, 1959, 1960–61, 1961–62*. Dobbs Ferry, N.Y.: Oceana, 1960, 1962, 1963. A topical analysis by a panel of academics and UN specialists.

Systauw, J. J. G. *Decisions of the International Court of Justice: A Digest*. 2d ed. Leiden: Sijthoff, 1969.

Taubenfeld, Howard J. "A Treaty for Antarctica." *International Conciliation* 531 (January 1961): 245–317.

Teltsh, Kathleen. *Crosscurrents at Turtle Bay: A Quarter Century of the United Nations*. Chicago: Quadrangle, 1970.

Teng, Catherine G., and Kay L. Hancock, eds. *Synopses of United Nations Cases in the Field of Peace and Security, 1946–1965*. New York: Carnegie Endowment for International Peace, 1966. Each case, several of them decided during the Hammarskjöld years, is summarized in terms of its duration, substance, parties involved, and other particulars.

Thorpe, Deryck. *Hammarskjöld: Man of Peace*. Ilfracombe, U.K.: Stockwell,

1969. A detailed account of the fateful flight of the Transair SE-BDY DC–6B aircraft from Leopoldville airport to an area some nine and a half miles from Ndola airport, Northern Rhodesia, on the night of September 17–18, 1961. A compelling narrative (although flawed by some factual errors) that examines several possible causes of the tragedy, including the fantastic allegation that Hammarskjöld, depressed by his Congo failure, had himself taken a bomb on board to commit a presumably well-concealed suicide.

UNA–USA. *Leadership of the United Nations: The Roles of the Secretary-General and the Member-States.* New York: United Nations Association of the USA, 1986.

United Nations. *The Blue Helmets: A Review of United Nations Peacekeeping.* 3d ed. New York: United Nations, 1996. Includes UNEF and ONUC with maps of deployment.

————. *United Nations Archives.* New York: Archives Section, United Nations.

————. *United Nations Bulletin.* April 1953 to June 1954. New York: Office of Public Information, United Nations, 1953–1954.

————. *United Nations Review.* July 1954 to September 1961. New York: United Nations, 1954–1961.

————. *United Nations Speeches by Heads of State, 1945–1971.* Sound recordings. Westport, Conn.: Mass Communications, 1973.

Urquhart, Brian. *Hammarskjöld.* New York: Knopf, 1972. One of the most authoritative, detailed, and informed biographies of Hammarskjöld. It is based on the author's personal experience and on the secretary-general's unpublished papers made available to him. Urquhart, a British-born undersecretary-general, served for over four decades.

————. *A Life in Peace and War.* New York: Harper & Row, 1987. This second major work by one of Hammarskjöld's undersecretaries-general at the close of his own UN career sheds additional, slightly more nuanced, light on his much admired superior.

Van Dusen, Henry P. *Dag Hammarskjöld: The Statesman and His Faith.* New York: Harper & Row, 1964. An American clergyman's profile of Hammarskjöld's spiritual life, which the author sees as evolving from uncritical credence to honest doubt to firmly rooted faith, with frequent references to Hammarskjöld's own *Markings.* A shorter version may be found in Henry van Dusen, "Dag Hammarskjöld: The Inner Person." In Cordier and Maxwell, *Paths to World Order,* pp. 22–44.

Virally, Michel. "Vers une Réforme du Secrétariat des Nations Unies?" (Toward a reform of the United Nations Secretariat?). *International Organization* 15, no. 2 (1961): 236–255.

Wadsworth, James J. *The Glass House: The United Nations in Action.* New York: Praeger, 1966. An account by another U.S. ambassador to the United Nations.

Wainhouse, David W. *Remnants of Empire: The United Nations and the End of Colonialism.* New York: Harper & Row/Council on Foreign Relations, 1964.

West, Robert L. "The United Nations and the Congo Financial Crisis: Lessons of the First Year." *International Organization* 15, no. 4 (1961): 603–617.

Wightman, David. *Economic Cooperation in Europe: A Study of the United Nations Economic Commission for Europe.* New York: Stevens, 1956.

Wigny, Pierre. "Belgium and the Congo." *International Affairs* 37. no. 3 (1961): 273–284. The former Belgian minister of foreign affairs defends his country's policies toward the Congo before and after its independence.

Wilcox, Francis O., and Carl M. Marcy. *Proposals for Changes in the United Nations.* Washington, D.C.: Brookings Institution, 1955.

Winchmore, Charles. "The Secretariat: Retrospect and Prospect." *International Organization* 19, no. 3 (1965): 622–639. Appropriately highlights the fact that it is the secretariat as a whole, not the secretary-general alone, that is designated as one of the six principal UN organs, as evidenced in Article 7 and parts of Articles 97 to 101 of the Charter.

www.nobel.se/peace/laureates/1961/hammarskjold-bio.html.

www.nobel.se/peace/laureates/1961/press.html.

Young, Crawford. *Politics in the Congo: Decolonization and Independence.* Princeton: Princeton University Press, 1965. A political analysis of decolonization and colonial policies.

Zacher, Mark W. *Dag Hammarskjöld's United Nations.* New York: Columbia University Press, 1970. A scholarly, well-researched, and annotated (but excessively detailed and complex) analysis of the world body from a functional perspective.

Index

Acheson, Dean, and "Uniting for Peace" resolution, xiii
admission of new members to the United Nations, 34, 275–276
Adoula, Cyrille, 136, 137, 139
Algeria, 76–78; de Gaulle and, 77
Algerian National Liberation Front (FLN), 77
ANC. *See* Congolese National Army
Anglo-French-Israeli attack on Egypt. *See* Suez War
Annual Report of the Secretary–General to the General Assembly on the Work of the Organization, 20 passim
Antarctic Treaty (1959), 107
apartheid: and the Sharpeville massacre, 98; and South Africa, xiii, 96–100; and South-West Africa, xiii, 99–100
Arab-Israeli problem, x: and armistice agreements of 1949, xiv, 42–43, 61, 66; and Palestinian refugees, 65–67; and United Nations General Assembly partition plan (1947), xiv
Armas, Carlos Castillo, 66–72

arms control/disarmament, xiv, 105–110
atomic energy, peaceful uses of, 107, 110–112

Bang-Jensen, Povl (Paul), 27, 84–89. *See also* United Nations Special Committee on the Problem of Hungary
Beck-Friis, Baron, Johan, mission to Cambodia and Thailand, 57
Belaunde, Victor A., and Group of Three, 26
Belgian Congo. *See* Republic of the Congo
Belgium: expulsion of personnel from the Congo, 136–137; interference in the Congo by, 116, 119–121, 123–125, 128, 134
Ben-Gurion, David, 62
Bernadotte, Count Folke, xiv
Beskow, Bo, 6, 10–11
Bizerte crisis, 78–81
Bomboko, Justin, 127, 130, 131, 133
Bourguiba, Habib, and Bizerte crisis, 78–79
Boutros-Ghali, Boutros, on Egypt's nationalization of the Suez Canal (1956), 62

Budgets, of the United Nations
    system, xv, *114*
Bunche, Ralph J., xiv, 2, 147: bio-
    graphy of, 297–298; in the
    Congo, 123, 292; replaced by
    Rajeshwar Dayal in the Congo,
    130; in the United Nations Sec-
    retariat, 290
Burns, Maj. Gen. E.M.L., 46

Cambodia, 39, 56–58, 150; and
    World Court case involving the
    temple of Preah Vihear, 58
Chamoun, Camille, 52
Churchill, Winston S., "iron cur-
    tain" speech of, xii
Cold War, x, xii: and the United
    Nations, xiii; and Ham-
    marskjöld's diplomacy, 38
College of High Commissioners
    (Congo), 127, 133
Colonialism, x; and the Cold War,
    xiv. *See also* decolonization
Committee on the Peaceful Uses of
    Outer Space, 113
Committee of Twenty Four. *See*
    Special Committee on the Situa-
    tion with regard to the Imple-
    mentation of the Declaration on
    the Granting of Independence
    to Colonial Countries and Peo-
    ples
Communist (Mainland) China. *See*
    People's Republic of China
Conference on the Discontinuance
    of Nuclear Weapons Tests, 108,
    112
Congo crisis, 117–140
Congolese colonial army. *See* Force
    Publique
Congolese constitution. *See* Loi
    Fondamentale
Congolese National Army (ANC),
    119, 125, 126

Constantinople Convention of
    1888. *See* Suez Canal
Cordier, Andrew W., 1, 80, 85, 152:
    in the Congo, 292; in the United
    Nations Secretariat, 289

Dayal, Rajeshwar: Hammarskjöld
    reluctant to replace, 136; as
    Hammarskjöld's special repre-
    sentative in the Congo, 130, 292;
    and Patrice Lumumba, 127;
    opposition to, by the Congolese
    central government, 143–144;
    and the United Nations Obser-
    vation Group in Lebanon
    (UNOGIL), 53
Declaration on the Granting of
    Independence to Colonial
    Countries and Peoples (General
    Assembly Resolution 1514), 92,
    93, *95,* 115
decolonization, xiii; and the United
    Nations, xiv, 91–96, *95. See also*
    Third World
Disarmament Commission, 108,
    109
Drummond, Sir Eric, 38
Dulles, John Foster, 62

Economic and Social Council
    (ECOSOC), 23
ECOSOC. *See* Economic and Social
    Council
Eisenhower, Dwight D., xii: and
    General Assembly Resolution
    1514, 94; memoirs of, on
    Guatemala crisis, 68; and peace-
    ful uses of atomic energy, 111
Elisabethville (Lubumbashi), land-
    ing of ONUC troops at airport,
    124–125. *See also* Katanga
    Province
Emoluments in the United
    Nations: of Hammarskjöld, 14,

28; of senior UN Secretariat staff, 28

EPTA. *See* Expanded Program of Technical Assistance

Expanded Program of Techincal Assistance (EPTA), 104–105, *105*

FAO. *See* Food and Agriculture Organization

Fawzi, Mahmoud, and "effective stand" policy on Israeli use of Suez Canal, 63, 64

FLN. *See* Algerian National Liberation Front

Food and Agriculture Organization (FAO), 103

Force Publique, 118

Funding of ONUC, 140–142; compared to UNEF, 140, 151. *See also* United Nations Operation in the Congo

de Gaulle, Charles: and Algeria, 77; and Bizerte, 79–81; and funding of ONUC, 141; and Guinea, 102

"Geneva spirit, " 111

Georges-Picot, Guillaume, and Group (Committee) of Eight Experts, 26; and administrative policy disagreements with Hammarskjöld, 27

Gizenga, Antoine, 123, 131–132, 136; Soviet support of, 134

GPRA. *See* Provisional Government of the Algerian Republic

Gross, Ernest A., 86–87

Group (Committee) of Eight Experts, 24, 26

Group of Three Experts, 24, 26–27

Guatemala, 22, 67–72, 149; invasion of, 68–69

Guzman, Jacobo Arbenz, 68–72

Hammarskjöld, Agnes Almquist: death of, 11, 153; relationship with son Dag, 4, 11

Hammarskjöld, Dag: activism defended by, 21–22, 37, 52; and administrative reform, 23–28, 35; admission of mistakes on Congo by, 143–144; and Africa, 115; and Algeria, 60, 76–78; and apartheid, 98–100; and appointment as UN secretary–general, 15; and arms control, 106–107; and atomic energy, 100–112; and Povl Bang-Jensen, 27, 60, 84–89; and Bizerte, 60, 78–81; boycotted by Soviets, 129–130, 132, 135; and the Cambodian-Thai dispute, 56–58; career of 13–14; censures tripartite attack on Egypt, 63; and Charter Chapter VII, 18; and Charter article, 98, 20; and Charter article 99, 18–20, 37, 44, 52, 80, 120; chronology of, 153–154; and the Congo, 115–152; cultural tastes of, 2–4; death of, 8–9, 10, 138, 294; early life of, 11; and economic and social development, 101–105; editorial on death of, ix, 295–296; education of, 12–13; and "effective stand" on Suez Canal use by Israeli shipping, 63; and Egypt's prohibition of Suez Canal use by Israel, 60, 63, 64; emoluments of, 14, 28; and filling of constitutional space by, x, 18–19, 21, 22, 54, 74, 83, 115; and final visit to the Congo, 137; and friends of, 6; and Guatemala, 60, 67–72; and honorary degrees conferred on, 9; and Hungary, 72–76, 89nl; and inherent powers, 39; and the "inner man" in, 4–6, 7, 10; intro-

Hammerskjöld, Dag (*continued*)
duction to the tenth *Annual
Report of the Secretary-General
to the General Assembly on the
Work of the Organization,
1954–1955* by, 285–288; and Jordan, 55–56; and Nikita
Khrushchev's demand for
ouster of, 129; and Laos, 54, 60,
81–83; and Lebanon, 52–55; and
love of the outdoors, 4; and
Patrice Lumumba's death,
132–133; and Lumumba's
safety, 131; Lutheran upbringing of, 8; and membership of the
United Nations in 1961, 275;
and mission to Peking, 22,
39–42; and Nobel Peace Prize, 9,
154; oath of office of, x; obituary
of, 35; opposition to circumventing of the United Nations
by, 70, 102, 107–108, 110; and
Palestinian refugees, 59, 64–67;
and peaceful uses of atomic
energy, 110–112; and peaceful
uses of outer space, 113; persona of, 1–11; political role of, x,
19–22; and public relations, 1,
33–34; reelection of, as UN secretary-general, 21, 52; speech on
radio program by, 283–284;
statement before assuming position as UN secretary-general,
279–280; and the Suez Canal, 59,
60–64; and the Suez War (1956),
43–48; supported by Security
Council on Congo policy, 134;
and supremacy of the Security
Council over regional organizations, 68–72; and technical assistance, 100–105, *105;* and techniques used by, 37–39; and the
United Nations Charter, 17–35;

"valedictory" speech of, 1, 21,
39; and visits to Africa, 102; and
women, 4–6
Hammarskjöld, Hjalmar Leonard,
11: death of, 12, 153; influence
on son Dag, 12; as Swedish
prime minister, 12
Heurtematte, Roberto M., 83, 290
Horn, Maj. Gen. Carl Carlsson von:
as commander of ONUC, 144,
292; as commander of UNTSO,
292; controversy regarding, 144;
replaced by Lt. Gen. Sean McKeown, 144
Hungarian Revolution; and
refugees, 74–75; and the Soviet
Union, 72–76
Hungary, 22, 149; and Hammarskjöld, 75–76, 89nl. *See also*
United Nations Special Committee on the Problem of Hungary

IAEA. *See* International Atomic
Energy Agency
IBRD. *See* International Bank for
Reconstruction and Development (World Bank)
ICJ. *See* International Court of Justice (World Court)
Ileo, Joseph, 126, 127, 133
International Atomic Energy
Agency (IAEA), 107, 111
International Bank for Reconstruction and Development (IBRD),
103
International Conference on the
Peaceful Uses of Atomic
Energy, 111
International Court of Justice (ICJ):
adjudicates Cambodia-Thailand
dispute on the temple of Preah
Vihear, 58; gives advisory opinion on funding of ONUC,

141–142; invalidates
Ethiopian–Liberian complaint
on apartheid in South–West
Africa, 100; upholds United
Nations Admisistrative Tribunal's awards to dismissed
American UN Secretariat
employees, 32; upholds UNEF
funding under Charter article
17 (2), 51
Iraq. *See* Kassem, Abdel Karim

Jordan, United Nations mission in
Amman, 55–56, 292

Kádár, János, 74, 76, 84. *See also*
Hungary
Kalonji, Albert. *See* Kasai Province
Kamina (Katanga Province) treaty
base, 124, 137
Kanza, Thomas, 130
Kasai Province: attack on, by Congolese National Army, 126;
declares independence, 118,
126, 130
Kasavubu, Joseph, 117–119, 125,
126–127, 130–133: agreement
with the United Nations,
135–136; biography of, 300;
issues amnesty, 139; Soviets
demand the arrest of, 134
Kassem, Abdel Karim, 53
Katanga (Shaba) Province: arrival
of ONUC in, 123–125; Belgians
in, 119–139 passim; declares
independence, 118, 130; Soviet
involvement in, 125
Kennedy, John F., and support of
ONUC, 134
Khiari, Mahmoud. *See* United
Nations civilian operations in
the Congo
Khrushchev, Nikita: and the

Congo, 128; and decolonizaiton,
93;
Khrushchev, Nikita (cont.) and
Hammarskjöld, 21, 125–134 passim; and replacement of the
secretary-general's position
with a troika executive, 128–129;
and the secretary-general's
political neutrality, 24
Kitona Declaration, 139
Kitona (Leopoldville Province)
treaty base, 124
Korean War: armistice at Panmunjom, xiv; and downed American
airmen in United Nations Command (Korea), 39–42; and the
United Nations, xii

Labouisse, Henri, 65
Laos, 81–83; United Nations mis-
sion in Vientiane, 292
Lebanon, 22, 52–55; landing of U.S.
Marines in Beirut, 53. *See also*
United Nations Observation
Group in Lebanon (UNOGIL)
Leopoldville (Kinshasa), central
government crisis in, 117–127
passim
Lie, Trygve: character as contrasted
with Hammarskjöld's, 2,
150–151; comments by and rela-
tionship with Hammarskjöld,
xi, 14; recommends administra-
tive reform, 25; tenure as UN
secretary-general, x–xi
Linner, Sture, replaces Rajeshwar
Dayal in the Congo, 144, 292
Lodge, Henry Cabot Jr., 33; and
Guatemala crisis, 69–72
Loi Fondamentale, 117; affirmed
by Moise Tshombe, 139
Loyalty of American employees at
the UN Secretariat, 34, 149: and

Loyalty of American employees
(*continued*)
Hammarskjöld, 31; and President
Gerald Ford's Executive Order
11890, 32–33; and Trygve Lie,
30, 31, 32; and President Harry
Truman's Executive Order
10422, 31, 34
Luluabourg. *See* Kasai Province
Lumumba, Patrice, 117–127 passim, 129, 130: biography of,
299–300; death of, 131–132
Lundula, Sgt. Victor, 119

McCarthyism: and national clear-
ance procedures for American
UN Secretariat personnel,
281–282; and UN Secretariat,
30–31, 34, 88. *See also* loyalty of
American employees at the UN
Secretariat
McKeown, Lt. Gen. Sean, replaces
Maj. Gen. Carl C. von Horn in
the Congo, 144, 292
Malenkov, Georgi M., xii
Markings, ix–x, 5, 7–8, 10. *See also*
Hammarskjöld and the "inner
man"
Military Staff Committee (of the
Security Council), xiv–xv
Mobutu, Joseph-Désiré, 117–119,
130: appoints Moise Tshombe as
Congolese president, 140; bio-
graphy of, 301–302; coup in
Leopoldville by, 127; death of,
145; installs new Leopoldville
government, 133; and Partice
Lumumba, 119, 126, 127; and
role in death of Lumumba,
131–132; Soviet disapproval of,
134
Mpolo, Maurice, 132
Myrdal, Mrs. Alva, 33

Nagy, Imre, 73, 76. *See also* Hun-
gary
Narasimhan, C.V., 2, 290
Nasser, Gamal Abdel, 43, 55: stand
on Israeli navigation in the Suez
Canal, 62–64; and withdrawal of
UNEF from Egyptian territory,
48–50, 60–64
Nationalist China. *See* Taiwan
NATO. *See* North Atlantic Treaty
Organization
Nehru, Jawaharlal, 15
Nkrumah, Kwame, relationship
with Hammarskjöld, 133
North Atlantic Treaty Organiza-
tion (NATO), xiii

OAS. *See* Organization of American States
O'Brien, Connor Cruise: criticizes
Hammarskjöld's authoritarian
administrative style, 26; deal-
ings with Moise Tshombe,
136–137; on Hammarskjöld's
handling of the UN Secretariat
loyalty issue, 31; and use of
ONUC in Katanga, 137–138, 293
OECD. *See* Organization for Eco-
nomic Cooperation and Devel-
opment
Okito, Joseph, 132
ONUC. *See* United Nations Opera-
tion in the Congo
Operational Executive and Admin-
istrative Personnel Services
(OPEX), 103–104
Operation Rumpunch in Katanga,
Rounds One, Two, and Three,
137, 139
OPEX. *See* Operational Executive
and Administrative Personnel
Services
Organization of American States

(OAS), and the Guatemala crisis, 69–72

Organization for Economic Cooperation and Development (OECD), Hammarskjöld's views on, 102

Orientale Province, declares independence, 118, 130

outer space, peaceful uses of, 112–113

Palestinian refugees: General Assembly recommends compensation to or repatriation for, 67; origins of problem, 64–65. *See also* Arab-Israeli problem

Partial Nuclear Test Ban Treaty (1963), 108

Pathet Lao (in Laos), 81–83

peacekeeping, xi; and peacemaking, 149. *See also* United Nations Emergency Force (UNEF) and United Nations Operation in the Congo (ONUC)

Pearson, Lester B., 15: biography of, 298; and Group of Three, 26; and UNEF, 45–46

"Peking formula" and Hammarskjöld, 39, 98

People's Republic of China, xii, xiii, 39–42. *See also* Hammarskjöld, mission to Peking

personnel problems, alleged unconcern of Hammarskjöld for, 30; Charter article 101 (3), 28

preventive diplomacy, xi, 37–39, 41–42: in the Cambodian-Thai dispute, 57; in the Congo, 116–117, 128, 144; in Jordan, 55–56; in Lebanon, 52–55; in the Middle East, 117; at Suez, 43–44. *See also* peacekeeping, quiet

diplomacy, United Nations presence

Price, Byron, administrative policy disagreements with Hammarskjöld, 27

Provisional Government of the Algerian Republic (GPRA), 78

quiet diplomacy, xi, 38–39. *See also* preventive diplomacy

Ranallo, William J., 6, 294

Republic of the Congo, 115–152

Salaries Survey Committee, 24

Scientific Committee on the Effects of Atomic Radiation, 112

Secretariat. *See* United Nations Secretariat

Security Council, xiv. *See also* Military Staff Committee

de Seynes, Philippe, 2, 290

Smith, George Ivan, 6

South-West Africa. *See* apartheid

Soviet–Chinese Treaty of Friendship and Mutual Aid, xiii

Special Committee on the Situation with regard to the Implementation of the Declaration on the Granting of Independence to Colonial Countries and Peoples (Committee of Twenty-Four) (1960), 115. *See also* decolonization

Special United Nations Fund for Economic Development (SUNFED), or Special Fund, 103–105, *105*

Spinelli, Pier P.: at Bizerte, 79; at the European Office of the United Nations, 291; in Jordan, 56, 292; in Togo, 56

Stalin, Joseph V., xii

Stanleyville (Kisangani). *See* Orientale Province
Stevenson, Adlai E., 51, 80, 143
Suez Canal: *Bat Galim* and other Israeli transit incidents, 61–64; clearing of, from obstructions in 1957, 60; diplomatic negotiations following nationalization of, 43–44; and Egyptian Suez Canal Authority, 61; Egypt's denial of navigation rights to Israel in, 42, 60–64; right of free and innocent passage in, 62; and Universal Suez Canal Company, 61. *See also* Suez War
Suez War, 42–52
SUNFED. *See* Special United Nations Fund for Economic Development

Taiwan, xii, xiii; abstains in Hammarskjöld's election vote, 15
technical assistance, 100–105
Ten-Nation Disarmament Committee (TNDC), 108–110
Thailand, 39, 56–58, 150; and World Court ruling involving the temple of Preah Vihear, 58
Thant, U: and the Congo crisis, 138–139; and criticism of Hammarskjöld's interpretation of terms for UNEF's withdrawal, 50; and UNEF's withdrawal in 1967, 50–51
Third World, x: and geographic representation in the UN Secretariat, 28, 34; growth of membership at the United Nations, 94; as voting bloc, 94–96, *95,* 115, 145nl. *See also* Declaration on the Granting of Independence to Colonial Countries and Peoples

TNDC. *See* Ten-Nation Disarmament Committee
Touré, Ahmed Sékou, relationship with Hammarskjöld, 133
Treaty on Principles Governing the Activities of States in the Exploration and Use of Outer Space (1967), 113
Tshombe, Moise, 118–119, 123–126; 129: biography of, 300–301; dismissal of, by Joseph–Désiré Mobutu, 145; as president of the Congo, 140, 145
Tuomioja, Sakari, 83

UMHK. *See* Union Minière du Haut Katanga
UNEF. *See* United Nations Emergency Force
UNESCO. *See* United Nations Educational, Scientific, and Cultural Organization
UNICEF. *See* United Nations Children's (Emergency) Fund
Union Minière du Haut Katanga (UMHK), 119, 124
Union of South Africa. *See* apartheid
United Fruit Company, holdings in Guatemala of, 68–69
United Nations Charter: Chapter VII viewed by Hammarskjöld, 18; Chapter XV, 277–278; Chapter XV, article 99, 18–20, 37, 44, 52, 80, 120
United Nations Children's Fund (UNICEF) (United Nations Children's Emergency Fund prior to 1953), 103
United Nations civilian operations in the Congo, 121, 125, 138, 144–145
United Nations Command (Congo), 139

United Nations Command (Korea), xii, 40, 46, 67–68

United Nations Conference on International Organization (1945), 19, 34; and Soviet demands for a collegiate UN administrative executive, 128–129

United Nations Congo Conciliation Commission, 125–126, 132; failure of, 130

United Nations Educational, Scientific, and Cultural Organization (UNESCO), 103

United Nations Emergency Force (UNEF), 38, 45–51: deployment of, in August 1957, *47;* funding of, 49–50; withdrawal of, in May 1967, 49–50. *See also* Suez War

UNHCR. *See* United Nations High Commissioner for Refugees

United Nations High Commissioner for Refugees (UNHCR), 103. *See also* Palestinian refugees

United Nations International Conference on the Peaceful Uses of Atomic Energy, 111, 112

United Nations Observation Group in Lebanon (UNOGIL), 52–55. *See also* Lebanon

United Nations Operation in the Congo (ONUC), 38, 123–125: civilian and military representatives in the Congo, 1961, 293; compared with UNEF, 46, 142–143; deployment of, in June 1961, *122;* evaluation of, 143; funding of, 140–142, 145; neutrality of, criticized, 133; transformed from peacekeeping to combatant force, 134

United Nations presence, xi, 38–39, 150. *See also* preventive diplomacy

United Nations Relief for Palestine Refugees (UNRPR). *See* Palestinian refugees

United Nations Relief and Works Agency for Palestine Refugees (UNRWA). *See also* Palestinian refugees

United Nations Scientific Committee on the Effects of Atomic Radiation, 111, 112

United Nations Secretariat: appointments in, xv; fixed term contracts in, 29; geographic distribution in, 28–29, 34; and McCarthyism in, x, 30–31; "merit" distribution in, 29; organizational problems in, xv; permanent career as against fixed-term appointments in, 29; personnel morale at, 30, 34; senior staff of, in 1961, 289–292. *See also* loyalty of American employees at the UN Secretariat

United Nations Special Committee on the Problem of Hungary, 75: and Povl Bang-Jensen, 84–89; barred from visiting Hungary, 84

United Nations Truce Supervision Organization (UNTSO), xiv, 46; and Lebanon, 53

United Nations Trusteeship Council, continues League of Nations mandate, 92–93. *See also* South-West Africa

United Nations–United States Headquarters Agreement (1947), 33, 34. *See also* Myrdal, Mrs. Alva

"Uniting for Peace" resolution (1950), xiii–xiv, 43, 128

UNOGIL. *See* United Nations
    Observation Group in Lebanon
UNRPR. *See* United Nations Relief
    for Palestine Refugees
UNRWA. *See* United Nations
    Relief and Works Agency for
    Palestine Refugees
UNTSO. *See* United Nations Truce
    Supervision Organization
Uppsala (Sweden), 9, 12; burial of
    Hammarskjöld in, 9, 154
Urquhart, Brian, 9, 10, 30, 34,
    144

Vietnam, Socialist Republic of
    (North Vietnam), and Laos,
    81–83

Waithayakon, Prince Wan, and
    Group of Three, 26
WHO. *See* World Health Organiza-
    tion
Wieschhoff, Heinz (Heinrich) A., 2,
    294
World Health Organization
    (WHO), 103
world map, *xvi*

About the Author

Born in Paris, France, and the product of French, British, and American education, the author majored in English (Phi Beta Kappa) at New York University before engaging in various aspects of international studies with emphasis on the Third World. His first employment was with the British Council (on Education) in Cairo, Egypt. Since then, he has held a position as an associate textbook editor for a New York publisher and is currently professor of government at Manhattan College in New York City.

In this work Dr. Heller has tried to answer the rhetorical question that he had set for himself, namely, whether a historical figure on the proverbial white horse can single-handedly change the flow of international events. He found that the answer to such a question depends on the framing of other and more fundamental inquiries, such as, From what perspective? Judged by what criteria? In the context of what time frame?